Teaching History for the Common Good

Teaching History
for the Common Good

Keith C. Barton
Linda S. Levstik

Routledge
Taylor & Francis Group
New York   London

Routledge is an imprint of the
Taylor & Francis Group, an informa business

Reprinted 2009 by Routledge

Cover design by Sean Trane Sciarrone

Cover art by Johann Baptist Homann. "Planiglobii terrestris cum utroq hemisphaerio caelesti generalis repraesentatio, 1716. Library of Congress Geography and Map Division, Washington, DC. Benton Map Collection. [Online] Available http://hdl.loc.gov/loc.gmd/g3200.ct000 123, accessed December 14, 2003.

Library of Congress Cataloging-in-Publication Data

Barton, Keith C.
    Teaching history for the common good / Keith C. Barton, Linda S. Levstik.
        p. cm.
    Includes bibliographical references and index.
    ISBN 0-8058-3930-5 (cloth : alk. Paper)
    ISBN 0-8058-3931-3 (pbk. : alk. Paper)
        1. History—Study and teaching (Elementary)—United States. 2. History—Study and teaching (Middle school)— United States. 3. Civics—Study and teaching (Elementary school)—United States. 4. Civics—Study and teaching (Middle school)—United States. Levstik, Linda S. II. Title.

LB1582.U6B37 2004
372.89—dc22   2003059643
                                                                                                              CIP

10 9 8 7 6 5 4

"Cultra Manor: The Ulster Folk Museum" from *The Collected Poems of John Hewitt,* ed. Frank Ormsby (Belfast, Northern Ireland: Blackstaff Press, 1991), reprinted with permission of Blackstaff Press on behalf of the Estate of John Hewitt.

Excerpts from "Choruses from 'The Rock'" from *COLLECTED POEMS 1909–1962* by T. S. Eliot, copyright 1936 by Harcourt, Inc., copyright © 1964, 1963 by T. S. Eliot, reprinted by permission of Harcourt Inc., and Faber and Faber, Ltd.

Excerpt from "Voices from Lemnos," from *OPENED GROUND: SELECTED POEMS 1966–1996* by Seamus Heaney. Copyright © 1988 by Seamus Heaney. Reprinted by permission of Farrar, Straus and Giroux, LLC and Faber and Faber, Ltd.

Contents

Preface

This book represents our attempt to make sense of both the growing body of research on students' historical thinking and enduring debates over the nature of the subject. History education is beset by continual controversy, as historians, politicians, educators, and the public at large argue about what should be taught to the nation's children and how it should be presented. Some argue for a unified national story, whereas others support multiple perspectives; some favor broad coverage of factual information, whereas others advocate the interpretation of evidence; some would extol the country's heroes, whereas others would emphasize its shortcomings and mistakes. In many cases, these disagreements reflect fundamental differences about the nature and purpose of the subject, and they will not be easily resolved.

Systematic theory and research, however, should be able to play a role in such debates. Research can never tell us what to teach or how to teach it, because such decisions reflect value judgments—and in history, these often reflect very deeply held values indeed. However, research can provide evidence of what students think and how their ideas interact with the information they encounter both in school and out, and it can show how these ideas differ across contexts. Such evidence can provide a corrective to the untested assumptions that plague so many discussions of history education. When we actually ask students what they think, we often find that our premises are in serious need of revision; when we compare teaching and learning across cultures, we discover that patterns we have taken for granted are nothing more than the products of our own limited experience. Theory, meanwhile, can help clarify terms of debate and provide a means of systematically comparing conflicting claims. Without theory, we argue past one another, and we have little shared ground to help us make sense of the evidence provided by research. In fact, research findings become "evidence" only in relation to specific questions or claims, and these must derive from some theory.

In this book, we review research on students' historical thinking, and we set it in the theoretical context of *mediated action*. Mediated action calls attention to the concrete actions that people undertake, the human agents responsible for such actions, the cultural tools that aid and constrain them, their purposes, and their social contexts. We believe this theory provides an important corrective to much of the recent scholarship on history education, which assumes that the academic discipline of history provides both the means and end for teaching the subject. Scholarship cannot contribute to public debate by setting up a rarified ideal of "real" history and dismissing the many popular uses of the past. People use history in a variety of ways and for a variety of purposes, and these will continue to be reflected in schools and other public contexts. Also, because children and adolescents are active agents of historical learning, their participation in multiple historical settings ensures that they will be influenced by the range of purposes and tools found there. This is why we find mediated action a particularly useful theory: It allows us to address the breadth of practices, settings, purposes, and tools that influence students' developing understanding of the past.

However, we aim to do more than simply describe the factors that influence students' thinking; we aim to evaluate them and to suggest which aspects educators should embrace, tolerate, or reject. We are as concerned as anyone with reforming history education so that it more closely matches our vision of proper educational goals. Our judgments, however, will not derive from standards based on the academic discipline; we think the quest to identify such standards is not only chimerical but ultimately irrelevant. Instead, we will ground our evaluation of history education in its potential to prepare students for participation in a pluralist democracy. Ultimately, we are concerned with how history can help citizens engage in collaboration toward a common good.

In chapter 1, we discuss the contribution of theory and research in greater detail, explain the theory of mediated action and how it guides our analysis, and describe research on children's (and adults') knowledge of and interest in history. In chapter 2, we lay out a vision of pluralist, participatory democracy and its relationship to the humanistic study of history; the principles in this chapter provide the basis for our evaluation of the approaches discussed in the remainder of the work. In chapters 3 through 6, we explore what we refer to as the four principal "stances" toward history: the *identification stance* (chap. 3) in which people assert similarities between history and some aspect of life in the present; the *analytic stance* (chap. 4), which involves examination of causes and consequences of historical events and the way evidence is used to construct accounts; the *moral response stance* (chap. 5), which is present when people make judgments about the triumphs and tragedies of the past or when they engage in simple remembrance; and the *exhibition stance* (chap. 6), which includes public displays, as well as issues of accountability and testing. In each of these four chapters, we review research on the extent to which children and adolescents understand and accept them, and we examine the ways in which they might contribute to—or detract from—participation in a pluralist democracy.

The next six chapters address six of the principal "tools" of history. In chapters 7 through 9, we deal with different aspects of narrative. In chapter 7, we describe narrative structure in general and how it affects the representation and understanding of historical information; in chapter 8, we examine a particular set of historical narratives, those that focus on individual achievement and motivation; and in chapter 9, we look at the story of freedom and progress, a narrative that dominates historical representation in the United States. In each of these chapters, we describe research on how these tools affect students' understanding, for both good and ill, and we compare the thinking of U.S. students to that of students in other countries.

In chapter 10, we deal with inquiry, one of the most advocated and least implemented tools for historical study; in this chapter, we devote particular emphasis to the ways in which inquiry may fail to achieve its full potential by degenerating into simple analysis of sources. In chapters 11 and 12, we examine the two faces of empathy—in chapter 11, we focus on the "rational" tool of perspective recognition, whereas in chapter 12, we address the role of caring in historical study. We argue that neither of these tools can fully contribute to democratic citizenship without the other, and that the attempt to include either of them in isolation is counterproductive. Finally, in chapter 13, we turn our attention to teachers rather than students, and we review research demonstrating that conventional wisdom on teachers' knowledge and practice is misguided. We argue that for teachers to embrace investigative, multiperspectival approaches to history, they need more than knowledge of history and teaching; they need a purpose that can only be served by these approaches. Preparation for participatory democracy provides such purpose.

It would be difficult to identify all the people who have contributed to our understanding of history education and its relationship to democracy; after they read the book, some of them might prefer that we not identify them. However, among those who have provided advice and suggestions, and who have deepened our thinking through their insights and reflections, are Richard Angelo, Rosalyn Ashby, Isabel Barca, Sandra Cimbricz, Margaret Crocco, O. L. Davis, Jr., Alaric Dickinson, Todd Dinkelman, Matthew Downey, Graeme Easdown, Terrie Epstein, Karen Ferguson, Stuart Foster, S. G. Grant, Carole Hahn, A. Gwynn Henderson, Diana Hess, Kathi Kern, Leslie King, Alison Kitson, Alan McCully, Peter Lee, Stéphane Lévesque, Tarry Lindquist, David Naylor, Walter Parker, Linda Przybyszewski, Marília Gago Quintal, Ruth Sandwell, Avner Segall, Peter Seixas, Laura Sparks, Stephen Thornton, Bruce VanSledright, James Voss, Angene Wilson, and Elizabeth Yeager. We are also indebted to the many students and teachers—in the United States, Ghana, New Zealand, and Northern Ireland—who have given so graciously of their time as we pressed them to explain what they thought about history. We also appreciate the participation and insights of teachers in the Region Five Academy on Historical Perspective, organized and led by Kate McAnally, and those in the American Legacies Fellows Program in Eastern Kentucky. We are also grateful for the willingness of our families to put up with us as we devoted as much attention to the past as the present; Shaunna, Hannah, Jeremy, and Jennifer should welcome our return, or at least we hope so.

Chapter 1

A Sociocultural Perspective
on History Education

Everyone knows what history is until he begins to think about it. After that, nobody knows.

—Alan Griffin[1]

No one likes the way history is taught. Conservatives think it's too multicultural, and multiculturalists think it's too conservative. Politicians say it doesn't promote patriotism, and social reformers say it doesn't promote critical reflection. Advocates of social studies fret that history receives too much emphasis, and history specialists fret that it doesn't receive enough. Lawmakers argue schools should teach to the test, and schools argue they should teach the way they think best. Researchers criticize teachers for not using primary sources, teachers criticize students for not wanting to learn, and students criticize textbooks for being deadly boring. What a mess.

There's nothing new about this madness. Debates over the content and method of history education in the United States go back at least 100 years. Sometimes these arguments have been limited to the professional communities of educators, and other times they have spilled over—often loudly—into the public sphere.[2] Nor are such controversies limited to the United States: Educators, politicians, and everyday citizens throughout the world worry about how history supports or subverts national and ethnic identity, how it increases hatred or promotes reconciliation, and how it props up repressive regimes or mobilizes reform. Teachers in the midst of such debates worry primarily about how to get their hands on better materials.

What's striking about the current state of history education in the United States, though, is how little it has benefited from the attention devoted to it over the last 20 years. In the 1980s, several books criticized the level of historical knowledge in the country, and these resulted in a variety of efforts to restore, reform, or revitalize history in schools.[3] Although the crisis was almost certainly overstated, and although some of the proposed reforms represented a step backward, renewed interest in the subject led to a number of promising developments. In the 1990s, for example, teachers and other ed-

1

ucators published several books describing exciting classroom practices—Tom Holt's *Thinking Historically*, James Percocco's *A Passion for the Past*, David Kobrin's *Beyond the Textbook*, and Monica Edinger's *Seeking History*, to name just a few. At the same time, new technologies and media dramatically increased the availability of historical materials. These days, teachers can access primary sources, simulations, and lesson plans with an ease the two of us never dreamt of when we began teaching.[4]

Over the same period, educational researchers have conducted numerous studies of how history is taught and how children make sense of the subject, both in the United States and internationally. As we will discuss throughout this book, these researchers have investigated teachers' classroom practices and their disciplinary understanding, as well as children's ideas about time, change, perspective, significance, and evidence.[5] Outside the field of education, historians, sociologists, anthropologists, and psychologists have examined "public memory," "vernacular history," "social memory," "commemoration," and other uses of history among adults.[6] Still other scholars have contributed thoughtful and penetrating works on the value of history and on continuing conflicts over how the past is represented—Jonathan Zimmerman's *Whose America?*, Peter Stearns' *Meaning over Memory*, and James Loewen's *Lies My Teacher Told Me*, for example, along with *History Wars* by Edward Linenthal and Tom Engelhardt, and *History on Trial* by Gary Nash, Charlotte Crabtree, and Ross Dunn.[7]

However, history is not simply the private obsession of history educators and other scholars, for debates about the past often find their way into media headlines and become the subject of public discussion. The national history standards produced a firestorm of controversy in their day, and smaller, more local battles have resulted in unending arguments about public historical representations.[8] Displays of the Confederate flag and pictures of Malcolm X, commemoration of Civil War figures, the use of derogatory terms and images of Native Americans as school mascots, and disagreements about whose stories should be told at the Alamo or Little Bighorn—all of these provoke strong feelings about the past among people who have little professional connection to history education.

Debate, discussion, scholarship, research, new technologies, and vivid descriptions of practice—one could be forgiven for thinking that the ferment of the last 2 decades might have led to shared understandings of the nature and purpose of history teaching, or at least a clear picture of where the fault lines lay. Yet although people argue at each other on the topic of history, few have engaged in the kind of collaborative deliberation that might lead to either synthesis or compromise. One could also be forgiven for thinking that classroom practice these days would make use of the range of materials and procedures that are so visible and available, but no. Too few children experience the sort of classrooms we read about in Percocco or Kobrin, Holt or Edinger. One of us, in fact, has a daughter currently enrolled in eighth grade U.S. history, and she analyzes exactly as many primary sources, reads exactly as many works of historical literature, takes part in exactly as many inquiry projects and simulations, and considers exactly as many alternative historical perspectives as her father did nearly 30 years ago: zero. We wish this were an isolated example, but we know that it isn't.

There are many reasons for the gap between promise and practice, but we believe one of the key factors, as Alan Griffin suggested, is that "everyone knows what history is until he thinks about it." Despite differing political perspectives or varied disciplinary backgrounds, many people consider the nature and purpose of history—or more to the point, of history teaching— to be entirely self-evident. When those who are interested in the subject begin with simplistic or unquestioned assumptions, discussion with others (who may have their own simplistic or unquestioned ideas) becomes exceedingly difficult. In the pages that follow, we try to provide more productive ways of thinking about history education. The result may be, as Griffin predicted, a situation in which "nobody knows" what history is, but we hope a combination of theory and research will clarify rather than obscure the range of possibilities for teaching and learning history.

USING THEORY AND RESEARCH TO MAKE SENSE OF HISTORY EDUCATION

Much of this book is based on research into students' and teachers' ideas about history. We are fortunate to be part of a group of educators in North America and Europe who have been conducting empirical studies on the teaching and learning of history for over a decade (and some for much longer than that). At one time, many of us began our papers and presentations by pointing out that "little is known about students' understanding of history," but those days are long gone, for today we know a great deal about the topic. However, most of these studies have been individually conceived and implemented, and the findings have been published in a variety of outlets across Europe and North America; as a result, we still lack a comprehensive synthesis and overview of research in this field. Although we cannot review every study on the topic, we'll describe many of those we consider most revealing and try to show how they provide insight into key characteristics of history education.

We believe research can play a critical role in improving practice. This is not because research tells us what we should do; educational policy and practice will always be bound up with underlying societal values (not to mention issues of power), and empirical studies cannot resolve such questions. However, they can force us to think about the unquestioned assumptions that impede discussion. Arguments about the proper form of history instruction often rely on empirical premises, and although these may seem self-evident, they sometimes have little foundation in reality. To take just one example, a few years ago, in a preservice methods class for teachers, one of us described the "expanding horizons" curriculum that involves the study of state history in fourth grade, U.S. history in fifth, and world history (or cultures) in sixth. A student in the class asked whether this curriculum was followed in other parts of the world, and she was told that in other countries, elementary children learn about their own history, of course, not ours.

That "of course" turned out to be misguided. Although assertions like this are common, it is not true that children invariably study the history of their own countries, at least not in the ways we take for granted in the United States. After 6 months of research on teaching and learning history in Northern Ireland, for example, it became clear that elementary students there do not study the history of "their own" country, because there is no consensus over which country is theirs, and studying the history of either Ireland or Great Britain—or Northern Ireland's position within them—would be too controversial. As a result, elementary students analyze the structure of historical societies that have little connection to modern-day Northern Ireland, and this influences how they make sense of historical change and causation, as well as how they think about the purpose of learning history—topics to be dealt with in greater detail in chapters 7 and 8. Research such as this cannot provide direct guidance for educators in the United States, but it can alert us to a range of possibilities and their potential consequences. In the following chapters, we will describe a number of studies—both our own and those of our colleagues—that reveal aspects of historical teaching and learning that are not immediately apparent, and that may help us think more deeply about history education.[9]

However, our goal is not just to lay out the results of this work and hope someone finds it useful. Indeed, one of our primary concerns is that research in the field has not been as helpful as it might have been, in part because those who are interested in history education—parents, teachers, researchers, policymakers, public historians, and others—have no shared understanding of the meaning or goals of instruction in the subject. Without some consensus on these broad issues—or at least a shared vocabulary for comparing different perspectives—research on students' thinking will have little impact on classroom practice, and debates about the content of the curriculum will continue to take the form of unproductive tirades in which proponents of one perspective or another scold their opponents (often imaginary ones) for their ignorance or treachery. Such "history wars" are unlikely to improve educational practice, because they provide no common ground for engagement among those with differing perspectives.

Most scholars who have written about history education recognize that there are different ways of approaching the past, but they often collapse these into simple dichotomies. These include distinctions between *history* and *heritage, history* and *the past, professional history* and *amateur history, analytic history* and *collective memory*, and that pair of old favorites, the *use of history* and the *abuse of history*. There are two problems with these distinctions. First, those who propose them often identify one approach as "real" history (usually synonymous with their image of the academic discipline) and dismiss the other as inadequate, inauthentic, or merely "popular."[10] Having rejected any history that differs from that which they prefer, they proceed to trash schools, the media, and the public for failing to live up to their ideal of authenticity. This makes for jolly good haranguing, but it provides little basis for public discourse. In fact, it undermines such discussion, because it fails to recognize the legitimacy of differing perspectives. Those who believe history should promote patriotism or group pride, for example, characterize arguments for disciplinary history as irrelevant prattle from academic "experts"; they do not accept the authority of such scholars, and they do not take their ideas seriously—except as a convenient target of ridicule. Teachers and other educational practitioners might be more likely to acknowledge this kind of academic expertise, but they will not be motivated by arguments that dismiss the majority of their practices as not constituting real history. Rather than promoting discussion of the nature and purpose of history education, then, invidious distinctions between academic and popular uses of the past shut down debate and leave us with little to talk about.

A second problem with these dichotomies is that they are too simplistic. Our world would be an uncomplicated one indeed if there were only two perspectives on history. As we discuss later in this chapter and throughout the book, we can easily identify at least four different historical practices that are important in schools; each of these can be oriented toward any of three distinct purposes and make use of six different cultural "tools." Four practices, multiplied by three purposes, compounded by six tools—this results in 72 different ways of making sense of the past, and we've limited ourselves to those found in schools and with an adequate research base! If we were to include all the uses of history found within popular culture, political discourse, local communities, and the academic discipline (no unified undertaking itself), we would find even more. Collapsing this diversity into simple oppositions like "history versus heritage" obscures more than it reveals.[11]

What is needed, then, is some way of talking about history education that does not oversimplify the range of approaches found in schools and society, and that does not set up an untenable and unproductive distinction between real history and everything else. That is what we aim to do in this book, by linking theory, research, and practice in a way that clarifies distinctions among differing perspectives without dismissing some as inherently illegitimate or inferior. In doing so, we hope to provide a way of thinking about history education that promotes dialogue rather than forestalling it. This is not to say we consider all approaches to history education equally valuable, but as will become clear in the next chapter, our judgments are grounded in assumptions about the contribution of history to democratic society rather than in mimicry of academic discourse. Rather than claiming that this perspective is a timeless and universal one, or that it inheres in the very nature of historical thought, we acknowledge that it derives from a particular vision of what history education might become in our own society and in our own time. We recognize that others may disagree with this vision, and our conceptual scheme should help clarify such disagreements rather than obscure them.

Throughout this book, we use sociocultural analysis as a way of organizing our discussion. Sociocultural viewpoints dominate current theorizing about human thought and action, and we consider them among the most productive ways of making sense of educational practice. A few years ago, we might have stopped with that observation, but the proliferation of perspectives within sociocultural analysis—including situated learning, legitimate peripheral participation, distributed cognition, activity theory, cultural psychology, and other approaches—requires that we elaborate more clearly the principles we consider salient. Our view of sociocultural theory is closest to that of James Wertsch's analysis of "mediated action," particularly in his use of Kenneth Burke's framework for understanding human action and motivation. Burke argued that any such analysis must take into account five interrelated elements. These are the following:

1. Act—the thoughts or deeds in which humans engage.
2. Scene—the setting or background in which acts take place.
3. Agent—the person who engages in the act being examined.
4. Agency—the means by which acts are carried out (more often referred to among sociocultural theorists as cultural tools or "artifacts").
5. Purpose—the motivation for engaging in action.[12]

Wertsch argues that this "pentad" contributes to our understanding of human action by emphasizing the interrelatedness of the five components. That is, an analysis that focused primarily on the environment (the scene) or the individual (the agent) would omit—or at least downplay—other elements necessary for a full understanding of people's actions. To achieve such understanding, we need to coordinate each of these five components within a single analysis. Although this is an admittedly difficult task, Wertsch suggests that it can be achieved, in part, by a focus on mediated action. This brings the "act" of Burke's pentad to the fore, but it conceptualizes acts as being performed by agents who use tools (or "mediational means") as a way of engaging in practices that differ by setting and that may serve different purposes.[13]

This approach can be characterized as sociocultural because it situates each of the five elements within a larger societal context: Tools have developed over time and are used in socially sanctioned ways, the actions people engage in are those considered useful in their societies, the purposes that guide their actions derive from cultural values, and so on. We believe that for history education, the most important implication of this approach is that it calls attention to the socially situated nature and purpose of students' actions—what they do with history—rather than focusing on the knowledge assumed to exist inside their heads or the skills they are believed to possess as individuals. In the remainder of this chapter, we provide an overview of how these elements guide our analysis of history education. Most of our discussion throughout the book will focus on students' learning; in the final chapter, though, we turn our attention to teachers, as we examine how sociocultural theory might clarify the influences that guide their practice.

THE FOUR STANCES: PURPOSE AND PRACTICE
IN LEARNING HISTORY

Sociocultural analysis, particularly from the standpoint of mediated action, focuses less on individual cognition than on social practice—what people do in concrete settings rather than the conceptual or procedural knowledge assumed to exist inside their heads. As a way of clarifying what it means to "do history," we have identified four specific actions students are expected to perform when they learn history; these are the "verbs" of history education, so to speak.

First, students are expected to *identify*: They are asked to embrace connections between themselves and the people and events of the past. This is one of the most common uses of history, and it is found, for example, when students learn about the exploration, settlement, and development of "our country." Second, students are expected to *analyze*: They are asked to establish causal linkages in history. This is the practice most often favored by reformers, and it is found whenever students examine the connections among elements of the past—such as the causes of the Civil War or the effects of the Industrial Revolution. Third, students are expected to *respond morally*: They are asked to remember, admire, and condemn people and events in the past. Although it may not be an explicit objective, this is a prevalent component of history education; few of us could study slavery or the Holocaust without condemnation, or the Civil Rights Movement or the end of apartheid without celebration. Finally, students are expected to *display*: They are asked to exhibit information about the past. Although each of the other three activities may incorporate display as well, we have included this as a separate category because sometimes students' displays are not an incidental element of history but the very endpoint of their experiences—such as when they are quizzed on their retention of textbook information or given standardized achievement tests.

It would be too simplistic to lump all experiences with history into four broad categories, though. Four distinctions may be better than the two found in dichotomies like history versus heritage, but they still fail to capture the range of students' experiences, even if we limit our attention to schools. On closer examination, each of the four activities contains variations deriving from the differing purposes they can serve. Analysis, for example, can be directed toward any of three principal ends—it can be used to determine the causes and consequences of historical events, it can be used to establish historical generalizations, or it can be used to reach conclusions from primary source material. Students engaged in each of these would be taking part in analysis—looking at how different elements of the past (or of representations of the past) fit together—but depending on the purposes that guided their participation, their activities might look very different. If the purpose were to understand the consequences of broad historical trends such as the Industrial Revolution, students need not ever examine a primary source; if, on the other hand, the purpose were to see connections between evidence and accounts, they would work with a great many primary sources and perhaps never read broad narratives describing political, social, or economic development across decades or centuries.

For each of the four principal activities of history education, we have identified three distinct purposes. Although we hesitate to introduce new terminology into the field, we refer to these combinations of purpose and practice as *stances*. Thus the *analytic stance* refers to instances in which students are asked to analyze some element of the past, but it includes three distinct purposes for doing so (understanding causes and consequences, developing generalizations, or learning how accounts are created). Similarly, the *identification stance* includes all those times when students are asked to identify with some element of the past, but such identification can be guided by three different purposes—creating a sense of individual or familial roots, becoming part of an "imagined community," or accepting the past as a "warrant" or "charter" for contemporary society. The moral response and exhibition stances also include a variety of purposes. In chapters 3 through 6, we examine each of these stances in more detail.

These stances—these combinations of purpose and practice—are not necessarily mutually exclusive. Students can analyze the causes of the American Revolution at the same time they identify with the origin of their country, and they can make moral judgments about the information they display in a classroom recitation. In fact, many history lessons will involve components from two, three, or even all four of the stances. However, it is useful to make conceptual distinctions among and within them for two principal reasons. First, educators may benefit from considering more carefully just what students are being asked to do when they study history, as well as from thinking more deeply about the purposes that guide those activities. If we want students to understand historical causation, asking them to display information will be ineffective, because display is best accomplished by memorization or copying, as we all remember from our own school experiences. Similarly, if we want students to understand the course of the Industrial Revolution, exclusive use of primary sources will be insufficient, because they need some sense of the "big picture" to make sense of those sources. Thinking more carefully about the connections between activities and purposes should help educators make more effective decisions about classroom practice.

Just as important, however, consideration of differences among stances may help us better understand why history is so contentious. Sometimes stances are mutually exclusive, and when the same topic can be situated in more than one stance, troubles arise. For many people, learning about Christopher Columbus involves identification: They feel connected to him either because they are a member of the same ethnic group or because he represents the "origin" of European settlement in North America. For others, learning about Christopher Columbus involves moral response: They condemn him (and his contemporaries) for their conquest and pillage of the western hemisphere. Conflict arises not just from different "perspectives" on or "interpretations" of Columbus; conflict arises from the fact that Columbus is the subject of two differing activities, and it is difficult for the two to coexist: Few people could identify with Columbus, or other European explorers and settlers, while at the same time condemning their actions.

Similarly, many arguments about including women or minorities in the curriculum derive from differing stances taken by those engaged in the debate. We've often heard that some figures have little historical significance—after all, who cares that Guion Bluford was the first African American astronaut or that Garrett Morgan invented the traffic light? For those working within the analytic stance, such information is trivial; learning about Bluford or Morgan does little to help students understand the causes and consequences of historical events. However, their inclusion isn't meant to help students understand such things, for students aren't expected to engage in analysis when learning about them. What students are expected to do is identify with them—for African American students, so they can see members of their own ethnic group as active participants in the nation's history, and for other students, so that they can see the United States as a multicultural society in which everyone can contribute to the nation's progress.

Greater clarity about the range of historical activities students are asked to engage in, as well as the purposes of those activities, might lead to more productive discussions about curriculum content. However, this requires acceptance of multiple purposes and practices. Some people recognize that their differences arise from disagreements over history's purpose, but they refuse to accept the legitimacy of any perspective other than their own. That is, they may admit that there are four stances on the learning of history, but dismiss any but their favorite. That gets us nowhere. These four stances are widespread in history education in the United States, and they are likely to continue to be prevalent for many years to come. We suspect most teachers in this country, and most members of the public, would argue that students should take part in all four. As we discuss each of these stances in later chapters, then, we will not try to establish which is the best or most authentic use of history, but to examine how each could best contribute to the ultimate goal of history education—participation in democratic life.

TOOLS FOR MAKING SENSE OF THE PAST

A basic assumption of sociocultural theory is that people make use of cultural tools as they engage in any activity; it is these tools that mediate their actions, for they represent the means by which people pursue their aims. Physical instruments such as a hammer, a teakettle, or a needle and thread are the kinds of traditional tools that first come to mind, but electronic technology in the form of hardware, software, and telecommunications devices also provides an obvious means by which we achieve our goals at work or in the home. Tools also include more abstract instruments: A mnemonic device allows us to remember the sequence of streets in downtown Cincinnati, a pie chart makes statistical data more comprehensible, and parliamentary procedure facilitates the organization of impersonal meetings. Concepts are the least tangible tools, but they are indispensable for making sense of the world: The concept of culture allows us to compare the behavior of different groups of people, and the concept of human rights helps us make decisions about foreign policy. Tools, then, exist at varied levels of generality; language itself is a tool, for example, and so too are linguistic devices such as sarcasm or hyperbole—as are specific instances of sarcasm, as well as the individual phrases, words, and phonemes that constitute those instances.[14]

Cultural tools amount to anything and everything that people use, and that level of generality might imply that the concept has limited utility for helping us understand human thought and action. However, its importance arises not because it motivates us to catalog all the possible tools people employ in a given activity but because it directs our attention to how tools shape thought and action—how they mediate our activity. No tool is infinitely flexible; all tools have, as Wertsch puts it, "affordances" and "constraints"—they allow us to carry out tasks in some ways and not others. In history education, then, we need to know not just what tools are available for students but how those tools simultaneously enable and limit their activity.

Depending on how narrowly we wanted to direct our gaze, we might identify any number of tools for learning history; in a sense, every concept used to discuss the past—feudalism, Ancient Egypt, abolitionists—functions as a tool for understanding history, as do all material resources, such as textbooks, videotapes, and chalkboards. Because the concept of mediated action has not been widely used in history education, there is no consensus over how to apply it most effectively in thinking about the subject. In our previous work, we have looked at the tools students use in making decisions about how to sequence and date historical images, and Wertsch has examined the use of narrative templates for talking about the history of both the United States and the former Soviet Union.[15] For our purposes here, we have limited our attention to six broad tools for learning history;

each of these is a procedure, device, concept, or attitude that applies to a range of topics and that has a profound impact on students' interpretation of historical information. Each also has a sufficient theoretical and research base to permit examination of its influence on students' engagement in the subject. These six tools are the subjects of chapters 7 through 12.

The first tool we consider is narrative structure; although narrative may not be as universal as some claim, it is clearly the principal format for structuring historical information and one that students are expected to employ when they learn history. The second tool is a specific class of narratives, those that focus on individual motivation and achievement; although historians also tell narratives about nations, economic systems, and social structures, students in the United States are most often exposed to those that focus on the thoughts and actions of individuals. From there we move on to a more specific narrative template, the story of American progress; this is an overarching narrative structure that influences how students interpret both the direction of historical change and the meaning of individual events within the broader sweep of the past.

The first three tools we consider, then, focus primarily on narrative—narrative structure itself, a class of narratives, and a specific narrative template. The next three are less directly tied to narratives, although they often overlap with their construction and interpretation. The first is the process of inquiry, in which students develop questions, evaluate evidence, and develop conclusions; this is a tool widely advocated but seldom used effectively, for reasons we discuss in chapter 10. The final tools represent two sides of the same coin—empathy. History educators have used this term in a variety of ways over the last quarter century, with those favoring one usage often denouncing those who employ it in another sense. It seems clear to us that *empathy* is one word that refers to two conceptually distinct tools—one involving rational examination of the perspectives of people in the past, the other revolving around caring and commitment. Although conceptually distinct, in practice neither of these tools is effective in isolation, and in chapters 11 and 12 we examine how the two depend on each other.

In each of our six chapters on cultural tools for learning history, we emphasize the affordances and constraints they provide. To make such judgments, though, we need an explicit basis for evaluation. The ways in which tools shape our thoughts and actions are, in themselves, neither advantageous nor disadvantageous—they just *are*. They become affordances or constraints only with reference to some external criteria. For example, the automated help feature in some software programs—in which a puppy dog or paper clip pops up periodically to provide advice—is neither an affordance or constraint in itself; it helps novices accomplish their work, but it slows down more experienced users. Evaluating its usefulness depends on whether we value assistance or speed. Similarly, tools for learning history affect the way students understand the past, but evaluating those effects depends on our values as educators; we have to decide what we want to accomplish before we can judge how best to get there. As we have noted previously, we believe the ultimate justification for history in schools is its contribution to democratic life, and this goal will guide our evaluation of each of these cultural tools.

CHILDREN AND ADULTS AS ACTIVE AGENTS OF HISTORICAL LEARNING

A sociocultural perspective on historical learning rests on the assumption that people actively engage in the historical practices of their society. Yet is that the case? We often hear that people in the United States know little about history and care even less. Politicians, academics, newspaper columnists, and other pundits are fond of pointing to the historical ignorance and apathy of the populace, sometimes going so far as to assert that Americans are uniquely ahistorical. Residents of other countries, they suggest, are more knowledgeable about and more connected to their pasts. Although comparative claims like these are difficult to investigate empirically, the assertion that people in the United States have little involvement in their history is demonstrable nonsense.

In the mid-1990s, for example, Roy Rosenzweig and David Thelen conducted a telephone survey of 1,500 U.S. residents. In extended interviews, they encouraged participants to discuss the role of the past in their lives by asking questions such as, "How often do you visit history museums?" "Have you done any research—formal or informal—into your family's history?" "What do you think of when you hear the word history/past/heritage/tradition?" "Do you use a knowledge of the past in your everyday life?" Respondents were eager to talk, and the interviews resulted in overwhelming evidence that people regularly take part in a wide range of historical activities, including visiting museums and historic sites, talking with grandparents and other relatives about the past, watching movies and reading books about history, looking at old photographs, researching their family's history, and working on historical hobbies or collections. Such pursuits cut across income, education, race, and gender. Rosenzweig and Thelen argue that the past is "clearly part of the rhythm of everyday life."[16]

For many people, such activities are more than casual pursuits; these "amateur historians" devote considerable time, money, and energy to their interests:

> They volunteer at local historical organizations, lead tours of historic houses, don uniforms for battle reenactments, repair old locomotives for the railway history society, subscribe to *American Heritage* and *American History Illustrated*, maintain the archives for their trade union or church, assemble libraries from the History Book Club, construct family genealogies, restore old houses, de-

vise and play World War II board games, collect early twentieth-century circus memorabilia, and lobby to preserve art deco movie houses.

Based on these interviews, Rosenzweig and Thelen conclude that "millions of Americans regularly document, preserve, research, narrate, discuss, and study the past."[17]

If history is so important to so many, why are they perceived as ignorant and apathetic? Perhaps because the history they are drawn to is the "wrong kind." Participants in this survey were most interested in personal experiences of people in the past, rather than public events or national narratives, and they felt most connected to history when they were directly engaged in activities like visiting museums, working on hobbies, or talking to grandparents. When asked to describe the history they had studied at school, their feelings were clear: They considered it "irrelevant," "incomplete," "dry," or most commonly, "boring."[18] When we hear someone say, "People aren't interested in history," it may actually mean, "They aren't interested in the history I want them to be interested in." That's obviously a different matter.

The disparity between perception and reality is just as pronounced when discussion turns to children. Over the years, we have encountered a strikingly consistent response from our colleagues—particularly those outside teacher education—when we tell them we do research on how children understand history. Almost without exception, they quickly retort, "Children *don't* understand history!," or "They don't know *anything* about it!" Children are dismissed, even more cavalierly than adults, as lacking in any historical knowledge, understanding, or appreciation. Yet this, too, is nonsense.

At about the same time Rosenzweig and Thelen were conducting their survey, we were asking students from kindergarten through sixth grade about history. Until the 1980s, most research had painted a dismal picture of children's ability to make sense of the subject; several studies pointed to the underdeveloped nature of their understanding of time, whereas others suggested that historical thought required levels of abstraction that eluded students until later adolescence.[19] Yet we knew that research in Great Britain, beginning in the 1970s, had suggested students were capable of more complex ideas about history (and at a younger age) than they had been given credit for.[20] In addition, one of us had conducted several studies of elementary children's responses to historical narratives, and in each study, it was clear that students were interested in history, drew on their background knowledge of the past, and engaged in complex reasoning about the subject, sometimes when they were as young as 7 years old.[21] We suspected the extent of children's historical thinking remained untapped by academic research, and we were particularly interested in how children made sense of historical time—one of the areas most often assumed to be beyond their reach.

We knew from the outset that we would have to develop a creative way of eliciting students' ideas. Open-ended interviews, in which researchers asked for clarification and students elaborated on their answers, had revealed a greater depth and range of ideas than the paper-and-pencil instruments used in older studies. However, we thought verbal questioning by itself might still be an inadequate way of getting at children's understanding of time, because our interviews might simply become oral versions of unproductive written measures. After all, questions like, "Which came first, the Civil War or the American Revolution?," were likely to result in similar (and uninteresting) answers whether presented orally or in writing. We also knew that students responded positively to history set within a narrative framework, but rich narratives would have been difficult to use during relatively brief interviews, and they would also have limited the expanse of time we could have talked about with students.[22]

We finally settled on the idea of using visual images to investigate children's understanding of time. We developed a set of nine pictures from different periods of the U.S. past (the Colonial Era, the Antebellum period, the late 1800s, the Depression Era, the 1950s, and so on), each of which included depictions of people going about their daily lives, and each of which contained multiple clues that might indicate when it was located in time.[23] We interviewed 58 students, and in each interview, we showed students the pictures (one at a time) and asked them to put them in order from "longest ago" to "closest to now." For each of their placements, we asked them to explain how they knew which pictures were older and which were newer. We then asked them when they thought each one was, and we also asked more general questions about history, such as "What can you tell me about how things have changed over time?," "What can you tell me about how things were different a long time ago?," and "Have you ever learned about history or the past or long ago outside of school?"[24]

This procedure turned out to be an effective way of eliciting thoughtful responses. Students were interested in the pictures and enjoyed arranging them; they also liked talking about history in more general terms. The pictures seem to have "warmed them up" to answer more verbal and abstract questions, and the images also provided concrete reference points they could refer to throughout the interviews. Perhaps more important, students appeared to appreciate our interest in their ideas; for many, it was as though they had been waiting to tell someone what they thought about history, and we had finally given them the opportunity. These interviews led to a great deal of information not only on students' understanding of historical time but also on the role of history in their lives.

Two elements of these interviews are particularly relevant for understanding children as agents of historical learning. First, it was clear they knew a great deal about the past. Even the youngest placed most pictures in the correct order, although they usually did not separate each into a distinct time period. In explaining their placements, they drew on an impressive amount of background knowledge about how life had changed over time, including changes in the appearance of clothes, furniture, and architecture, as well as the effect of technology on work and daily life. To take just one example, every student, even those in kindergarten, knew that covered wagons came before cars; the vast majority could also correctly sequence cars from the 1920s, the 1950s, and the 1990s. One indication of their familiarity with history was the readiness with which they engaged in our picture-arrangement task: Except for a few kindergarteners whose responses were ambiguous, all students knew just what we meant when we asked them to put pictures in order from oldest to newest. This was an activity that made sense to them, presumably because they had previous experience with discussions of the location of events (or images) in time. When 6-year-olds can sequence a set of pictures ranging over 200 years with this much ease, it suggests the perception of them as lacking in historical knowledge is in need of revision.

Our interviews also provided glimpses into the extent to which children were active participants in learning about the past. Rosenzweig and Thelen emphasized that adults were most interested in history that allowed for direct involvement, such as discussions with relatives, visits to museums with family members, historical hobbies, and genealogical research. They were least interested in the past when they were simply expected to absorb information—hence their consistent condemnation of school history. Yet what about children? Do they simply "accumulate" information from their elders, in school or out, who have been actively engaged in these pursuits? Our interviews provided tempting but inconclusive answers. A few students noted that they enjoyed learning about the past from relatives even when they found school history boring, and several described how their grandparents had discussed historic documents and artifacts with them. One explained that after her grandmother passed away, she and her family explored the contents of her desk; she observed, "When somebody is trying to teach it to me it sort of seems boring, but when you're looking through something and you find something it doesn't seem like you're learning history."[25] Although our interviews produced limited information on students' participation in such settings, comments like these suggested that children might be more than passive learners.

More information on students' participation in history came in another of our studies, in which 33 fourth and fifth graders were also asked to arrange images in chronological order. Some of these students, however, took part in multiple interviews over the course of a school year, and these were combined with classroom observations and informal discussions. The more intensive and extended nature of this study promoted greater rapport with students and allowed for more detailed discussion of the role of history in their lives. Also, because these students' teachers engaged them in a variety of stimulating and hands-on activities, students had numerous opportunities to reflect on the nature of history and their own understanding of the subject.[26]

Like participants in our previous research, these students displayed a great deal of background knowledge that enabled them to sequence pictures in time, and they pointed to a variety of influences on their understanding. However, it was clear they had not simply absorbed information about the past, and they were neither passive nor unwilling observers in the process of learning history. All of them said they were interested in history, and all said they enjoyed talking with relatives about the past. Moreover, many continually and actively sought out historical information. One girl, for instance, noted that she and her father "used to study history with cowboys and stuff 'cause he likes cowboys and he has kinds of hats and he used to draw, and I used to ask him a lot of stuff about it, because I thought it was interesting." Others reported asking their parents to tell them more about what they had learned in school; one boy explained, "We've talked about something in school, and then I'd go home and ask my parents something … and then we get started on a talk about how history happened." Some were even disappointed they hadn't had greater opportunities for learning about history—complaining, for example, that their previous classes at school did not include history, or that an uncle who fought in Vietnam refused to talk about his experiences.[27]

Just as important, these students held specific images of themselves and others as historically knowledgeable and aware individuals. They could describe, for example, their own interests in history—existing prior to and independent of formal study at school—as well as those of peers and relatives. One student explained that she, her mother, and her grandfather knew "some stuff about Indians because we're part Cheyenne, part Blackfoot," and another noted, "I'm interested in armies and war and stuff like that, and old presidents." When asked why history was something people study, one girl suggested, "Just to find out about what's happened in the past … that's something that everybody wants to know," whereas a boy explained

> Well, because they just want to find out about the Civil War and stuff; take Cecil [a classmate who had recently moved away] for instance, he was always reading books about the Civil War and everything, but then when you'd study something like how coins were made a long time ago, he wouldn't be really interested, he would be sitting there reading Civil War stuff or something.

Students also anticipated that they would one day pass on this knowledge to their own children and grandchildren; "It's like a tradition," as one pointed out. Not only had these students developed their own historical knowledge and interests before studying the subject at school, but they consciously perceived such interests as a basic feature of humanity—history is "something that everybody wants to know."[28]

Our research, as well as studies by a number of our colleagues, convinces us that even young children's ideas about the past are sufficiently complex and reflective to warrant a central role in theory and research on history education.[29] Not everyone will agree. At a university reception near the winter holidays a few years ago, one of us was introduced to a history professor who responded predictably when hearing about the focus of our research: "Children know *nothing! Nothing!*" After an explanation of just how much they do know—about fashion, technology, architecture, and so on—he curtly dismissed such findings. "That's not history," he said with a sneer, "that's culture." The holiday spirit, along with the restraining influence of several levelheaded colleagues, spared him interrogation over what was left of history when culture was removed, or just who put him in charge of categorizing knowledge of the past as historical or not. However, the difference between his perspective and ours highlights a key element of our interpretation of sociocultural theory. We are not interested in whether students conform to an abstract standard of "correct" historical thinking or understanding. We start on the other side of the equation, with students themselves; we want to know what they think about the past and how their ideas are related to the social contexts of which they are part.[30]

CONTEXTS OF HISTORICAL LEARNING

Another assumption of sociocultural theory is that human thought and action are embedded in social contexts that extend beyond the individual. People do not simply construct historical knowledge on their own; they do so as part of one or more social groups. In our interviews with children, it became clear that they were involved in multiple communities of historical learning. Although most had not studied a significant amount of history at school before fourth or fifth grade, they had begun constructing their ideas about history long before that. They told us, for example, that they had learned about history from electronic media, particularly television programs like *Happy Days* and *Little House on the Prairie*; from tradebooks and comic books they had read on their own; from objects like baseball trading cards and the *American Girls* dolls; from family trips to museums or historic sites; and most often, from relatives who told stories about their own childhoods, their family's history, or their participation in wars and other historical events. Often, these family discussions took place around the examination of documents, photographs, or other artifacts.[31] These settings obviously are similar to those Rosenzweig and Thelen found in their interviews, and they confirm that children begin to take part in the same historical pursuits as adults from an early age.

This has a number of implications for analysis of students' historical thinking. First, it means we need to pay attention to the kinds of history they encounter not only at school but in other settings that contribute to their ideas about the past. We need to know how history is represented in the museums and historic sites they visit, in the television programs and movies they watch, and in the historical literature they read outside school; we also need to know what kinds of historical information relatives pass along. Even within schools, we need to know about more than course requirements or curriculum objectives: We need to know how teachers convey information to students and how textbooks and other materials represent content. This means paying attention to more than discrete items of information; we also need to understand the overall purposes that guide history in these settings and how those affect the selection and structure of content. Because knowledge results from interactions between people and their environment, we will be able to make sense of how students have developed their ideas only if we understand the settings in which they have encountered the past. Fortunately, some of these topics have generated a fair amount of attention. Museums and textbooks, for example, have been the subject of several studies, and historical films and works of children's literature often receive critical analysis.[32] Throughout this book, then, we will call attention to the varied contexts in which students have learned about history, and we will take into account what we know about how history is represented in those settings.

Part of this consideration of social context will involve international comparisons, as well as comparisons of different ethnic groups within the same country. If we assume that settings for learning history influence how children make sense of the past, then we would expect to find different ideas among those who have encountered history in differing settings. There might be a number of ways of pursuing this question, but national citizenship and ethnic group membership are two of the most likely ways in which historical representations may differ. Students in different countries obviously are exposed to differing formal curricula, and museums and media often differ across national boundaries as well. Ethnicity, meanwhile, is such a profound determinant of social experience that representations of the past are likely to differ substantially among groups within the same country. Attention to these differences will help us better understand how students' ideas arise in interaction with their environments, and it may also alert us to previously unexamined assumptions about the nature of historical learning—as, for instance, when our own experience with international research demonstrated the fallacy of believing that children always study their national past.

There is another way in which a sociocultural perspective emphasizes the importance of settings, and this lies in the recognition that different contexts call for different practices. Not only does the content of historical information or its interpretation vary, but the way in which history is used may differ from one setting to another. As Wertsch points out, history is not an isolated endeavor but is "part of a more complex set of ongoing activities," and an examination of how people use history must take into account how their activities are embedded within a larger context, because "people often say and think one think in one context and quite another in another context." In his research on uses of history in the former Soviet Union, for example, Wertsch found that in public, individuals carefully controlled their display of historical knowledge so as not to contradict official narratives and interpretations; because public behavior was closely monitored by the state, failure to do so could have had significant negative consequences. However, in private—among close friends and family—individuals displayed greater interpretive freedom and sometimes sought out alternative historical perspectives that could not have been broached in public.[33]

In our own work, Northern Ireland provides the best example of the impact of setting on historical activity. In research conducted with Alan McCully, it became clear that secondary students there were aware school history differed from that used in the streets; the purpose of the former, many of them assumed, was to give a balanced account of the origins of the present-day world, whereas the former aimed to establish identity, justify political positions, or "annoy" people. Moreover, they recognized that their own use of history differed in the two settings, and that they could never voice perspectives on the streets that were perfectly acceptable, and even encouraged, at school. In their coursework, for example, they could criticize the actions of historical leaders of their own political and religious communities, but doing so outside school would be tantamount to treason. In Northern Ireland, then, distinctions in historical practice arise not from differences between public and private settings, as in the former Soviet Union, but from differences between two public realms—those of the school and the street.[34]

In both countries, analysis of historical thinking benefits from considering it not as a property of individual cognition that remains constant across settings, but as a social practice that individuals engage in differently depending on context. Unfortunately, there has been little research on how student's historical practices vary across settings. We know they engage in historical pursuits with relatives, in museums and at historic sites, and through television and books, but we know this primarily because of interviews conducted at school; even our information on "street history" in Northern Ireland derives from interviews with students who were pulled out of history classes to talk with educational researchers during structured interviews. For the most part, we haven't watched students use history outside formal educational contexts or talked with them naturally as they engage in such activities, nor, as far as we know, have other researchers.[35] As a result, we are not as well positioned to examine students' participation in a variety of specific social settings as we are to analyze the impact of societal contexts on school history. Most of this book, then, will be limited to students' encounter with history in schools, but our analysis will emphasize how the purposes and practices of school history reflect those of the wider society.

CONCLUSIONS

In this chapter, we have argued that children and adolescents have ideas about the past that merit serious consideration, and that they construct those ideas not just from what they learn at school but from the historical information they encounter in their families, their local and national communities, and the media. Research on these ideas and their social contexts can help us better understand how students make sense of the nature and purpose of history, and this can aid in developing meaningful programs of history education. In trying to bring order to the growing body of research on this subject, we will use Wertsch's concept of mediated action. A key tenet of this approach is that purpose plays a central role in human though and action. Throughout the book, we will address the varied purposes that guide historical activities, but our evaluation of those activities (and the tools that support them) will be grounded in a single, overarching purpose—preparation for a participatory, pluralist democracy. In the next chapter, we discuss what this kind of preparation might involve.

ENDNOTES

1. Alan Griffin, "History," in *World Book Encyclopedia*, 1962 ed. (Chicago: Field Educational Enterprises Corporation, 1962). Griffin begins his entry on *history* with this observation, attributing it to "a great authority," presumably himself. Nancy F. Palmer's entry in the 2002 edition of the same encyclopedia, on the other hand, begins with a less problematic assessment: "History is a branch of knowledge concerned with the study of past events." She goes on to characterize the subject's purpose in fundamentally conservative terms: "The study and writing of history make the past meaningful by preserving structure, values, and continuity for the present society." Nancy F. Palmer, "History," in *World Book Encyclopedia*, 2002 ed. (Chicago: World Book, 2002).

2. Peter Novick, *That Noble Dream: The "Objectivity Question" and the American Historical Profession* (New York: Cambridge University Press, 1988), 70–72, 185–93; Robert E. Keohane, "The Great Debate Over the Source Method," *Social Education* 13 (May 1949): 212-18; Jonathan Zimmerman, *Whose America? Culture Wars in the Public Schools* (Cambridge, Mass.: Harvard University Press), 9–133.

3. For example, Paul Gagnon and the Bradley Commission on History in Schools, Eds., *Historical Literacy: The Case for History in American Education* (New York: Macmillan, 1989); E. D. Hirsch, *Cultural Literacy: What Every American Needs to Know* (Boston: Houghton Mifflin, 1987); and Diane Ra vitch and Chester E. Finn, *What Do our 17-year-olds Know? A Report on the First National Assessment of History and Literature* (New York: Harper & Row, 1987).

4. Tom C. Holt, *Thinking Historically: Narrative, Imagination, and Understanding* (New York: College Entrance Examination Board, 1990); James A. Percoco, *A Passion for the Past: Creative Teaching of U.S. History* (Portsmouth, N.H.: Heinemann, 1998); David Kobrin, *Beyond the Textbook: Teaching History Using Documents and Primary Sources* (Portsmouth, N.H.: Heinemann, 1996); Monica Edinger, *Seeking History: Teaching with Primary Sources in Grades 4–6* (Portsmouth, N.H.: Heinemann, 2000).

5. For recent reviews of this body of research, see Peter Seixas, "Review of Research on Social Studies," in *Handbook of Research on Teaching*, 4th. ed., Ed. Virginia Rich-

ardson (Washington, D.C.: American Educational Research Association, 2001), 545–565; James F. Voss, "Issues in the Learning of History," *Issues in Education* (1998): 163–210; Suzanne M. Wilson, "Research on History Teaching," in *Handbook of Research on Teaching,* 4th. ed., Ed. Virginia Richardson (Washington, D.C.: American Educational Research Association, 2001), 527–544.

6. For example, John E. Bodnar, *Remaking America: Public Memory, Commemoration, and Patriotism in the Twentieth Century* (Princeton, N.J.: Princeton University Press, 1992); John R. Gillis, Ed., *Commemorations: The Politics of National Identity* (Princeton, N.J.: Princeton University Press, 1994); Pierre Nora, "Between Memory and History: *Les lieux de Mémoire,*" *Representations* 26 (special issue: "Memory and Counter-Memory," Spring 1989): 7–25; Michael Schudson, *Watergate in American Memory: How We Remember, Forget, and Reconstruct the Past* (New York: Basic Books, 1992); Barry Schwartz, *Abraham Lincoln and the Force of National Memory* (Chicago: University of Chicago Press, 2000); Marita Sturken, *Tangled Memories: The Vietnam War, the AIDS Epidemic, and the Politics of Remembering* (Berkeley: University of California Press, 1997); reviews include Alon Confino, "Collective Memory and Cultural History: Problems of Method," *American Historical Review* 102 (December 1997): 1386–1403; Kerwin Lee Klein, "On the Emergence of *Memory* in Historical Discourse," *Representations* 69 (Winter, 2000): 127–150; Jeffrey K. Olick and Joyce Robbins, "Social Memory Studies: From 'Collective Memory' to the Historical Sociology of Mnemonic Practices," *Annual Review of Sociology* 22 (1998): 105–40.

7. Jonathan Zimmerman, *Whose America? Culture Wars in the Public Schools* (Cambridge, Mass.: Harvard University Press, 2002); Peter N. Stearns, *Meaning over Memory: Recasting the Teaching of Culture and History* (Chapel Hill: University of North Carolina Press, 1993); James W. Loewen, *Lies My teacher Told Me: Everything Your American History Textbook Got Wrong* (New York: New Press, 1995); Edward T. Linenthal and Tom Engelhardt, Eds., *History Wars: The Enola Gay and Other Battles for the American Past* (New York: Metropolitan Books, 1996); Gary B. Nash, *History on Trial: Culture Wars and the Teaching of the Past* (New York: Knopf, 1997).

8. Linda Symcox, *Whose History? The Struggle for National Standards in American Classrooms* (New York: Teachers College Press, 2002); Gary B. Nash, Charlotte Crabtree, and Ross E. Dunn, *History on Trial: Culture Wars and the Teaching of the Past* (New York: Knopf, 1997).

9. Keith C. Barton, "History Education and National Identity in Northern Ireland and the United States: Differing Priorities," *Theory into Practice* 40 (Winter 2001): 48–54; students in Northern Ireland study the history of British/Irish relations in the first 3 years of secondary school. Stephen Thornton observes that research into student's thinking, by itself, cannot be an adequate guide to the design of instructional methods in "Subject Specific Teaching Methods: History," in *Subject-Specific Instructional Methods and Activities,* Vol. 8, *Advances in Research on Teaching,* Ed. Jere Brophy (New York: Elsevier Science, 2001), 295, 309. Carole Hahn discusses the value of comparative research in *Becoming Political: Comparative Perspectives on Citizenship Education* (Albany: State University of New York Press, 1998), 237.

10. David Lowenthal, *Possessed by the Past: The Heritage Crusade and the Spoils of History* (New York: Cambridge, 1998) 105–47; J. H. Plumb, *The Death of the Past* (Boston: Houghton Mifflin, 1969), 11–17; G. R. Elton, *The Practice of History* (New York:

Crowell, 1967), 29-36; James V. Wertsch, *Voices of Collective Remembering* (New York: Cambridge University Press, 2002), 40–43; Pieter Geyl, *Use and Abuse of History* (New Haven, Conn.: Yale University Press, 1955); Howard Zinn, "The Use and Abuse of History," in *Declarations of Independence: Cross-examining American Ideology* (New York: HarperPerennial, 1990), 48–66. Even scholars more interested in popular uses of the past tend to collapse the variety of possibilities into diametric opposites; see Klein, "Emergence of *Memory*," 128–129. A more complex typology, however, can be found in the work of Jörn Rüsen, most notably in "The Development of Narrative Competence in Historical Learning: An Ontogenetic Hypothesis Concerning Moral Consciousness," *History and Memory: Studies in Representation of the Past* 1 (December 1989): 35–59.

11. It is because we believe that these dichotomies obscure more than they clarify, and that the distinctions themselves usually reflect a purported hierarchy, that we do not distinguish between "history" and "the past" in this book.

12. James V. Wertsch, *Mind as Action* (New York: Oxford University Press, 1998), 13. Some of the most influential variations on sociocultural analysis can be found in John S. Brown, Allan Collins, and Paul Duguid, "Situated Cognition and the Culture of Learning," *Educational Researcher* 18 (January/February 1989): 32–42; Jean Lave and Etienne Wenger, *Situated Learning: Legitimate Peripheral Participation* (New York: Cambridge University Press, 1998); Edward Hutchins, "The Social Organization of Distributed Cognition," in *Perspectives on Socially Shared Cognition*, Eds. Lauren B. Resnick, John M. Levine, and Stephanie D. Teasley (Washington, D.C.: American Psychological Association, 1997), 283–307; Yrjö Engeström, Reijo Miettinen, and Raija-Leena Punamäki, Eds., *Perspectives on Activity Theory* (New York: Cambridge University Press, 1999); Michael Cole, *Cultural Psychology: A Once and Future Discipline* (Cambridge, Mass.: Harvard University Press, 1996).

13. Wertsch, *Mind as Action*, 11–21.

14. Among the most useful discussions of tool use from a sociocultural perspective are Wertsch, *Mind as Action*, 23–72; Cole, *Cultural Psychology*, 117–145; and Gordon Wells, *Dialogic Inquiry: Toward a Sociocultural Practice and Theory of Education* (New York: Cambridge University Press, 1999), 231–266.

15. Keith C. Barton, "'Oh, That's a Tricky Piece!': Children, Mediated Action, and the Tools of Historical Time," *Elementary School Journal* 103 (November 2002): 161–185; Wertsch, *Voices of Collective Remembering*, 87–116.

16. Roy Rosenzweig and David Thelen, *The Presence of the Past: Popular Uses of History in American Life* (New York: Columbia University Press, 1998), 5–9, 27.

17. Rosenzweig and Thelen, *Presence of the Past*, 24, 35.

18. Rosenzweig and Thelen, *Presence of the Past*, 12, 31, 109–113.

19. For reviews of research on children's understanding of historical time, see Barton, "'Oh, That's a Tricky Piece!'"; Keith C. Barton and Linda S. Levstik, "'Back When God Was Around and Everything': Elementary Children's Understanding of Historical Time," *American Educational Research Journal* 33 (Summer 1996): 419–454; and Stephen J. Thornton and Ronald Vukelich, "Effects of Children's Understanding of Time Concepts on Historical Understanding," *Theory and Research in Social Education*, 16 (Winter 1988): 69–82. On research suggesting developmental limitations in children's historical thinking, see reviews in Matthew T. Downey and Linda S. Levstik, "Teaching and Learning History," in *Handbook of Research on Social Studies Teaching and*

Learning, Ed. James Shaver (New York: Macmillan, 1991), 400–410; Christian Laville and Linda W. Rosenzweig, "Teaching and Learning History: Developmental Perspectives," in *Developmental Perspectives on the Social Studies*, Bulletin No. 66 of the National Council for the Social Studies, Ed. Linda W. Rosenzweig (Washington, D.C.: National Council for the Social Studies, 1982), 54–66; and Linda S. Levstik, "Teaching History: A Definitional and Developmental Dilemma," in *Elementary Social Studies: Research as a Guide to Practice*, Ed. Virginia Atwood (Washington, D.C.: National Council for the Social Studies, 1986), 68–84.

20. Key British studies from the 1970s and early 1980s include Martin Booth, "Skills, Concepts, and Attitudes: The Development of Adolescent Children's Historical Thinking," *History and Theory* 22 Beiheft (December 1983): 101–117; Denis Shemilt, *Evaluation Study: Schools Council History 13–16 Project* (Edinburgh: Holmes McDougall, 1980); and the essays in *Historical Teaching and Historical Understanding*, Eds. Alaric K. Dickinson and Peter J. Lee (London: Heinemann, 1978), and *Learning History*, Eds. Alaric K. Dickinson, Peter J. Lee, and Peter J. Rogers (London: Heinemann, 1984).

21. Linda S. Levstik, "The Relationship Between Historical Response and Narrative in a Sixth-Grade Classroom," *Theory and Research in Social Education* 28 (Winter 1986): 1–19; Linda S. Levstik, "Historical Narrative and the Young Reader," *Theory into Practice* 28 (Spring 1989): 114–119; and Linda S. Levstik and Christine C. Pappas, "Exploring the Development of Historical Understanding," *Journal of Research and Development in Education* 21 (Fall 1987): 1–15.

22. Recently, Pat Hoodless has investigated some aspects of children's understanding of chronology through narrative; see "An Investigation Into Children's Developing Awareness of Time and Chronology in Story," *Journal of Curriculum Studies* 34 (March 2002): 173–201, and "Children's Awareness of Time in Story and Historical Fiction," in *History and English in the Primary Schools: Exploring the Links*, Ed. Pat Hoodless (New York: Routledge, 1998), 103–115.

23. Similar procedures have been used in several studies in Great Britain, including Penelope Harnett, "Identifying Progression in Children's Understanding: The Use of Visual Materials to Assess Primary School Children's Learning in History," *Cambridge Journal of Education* 23 (June 1993): 137–154; John West, "Young Children's Awareness of the Past," *Trends in Education* 1 (Spring 1978): 9–14; "Children's Perception of Authenticity and Time in Historical Narrative Pictures," *Teaching History* 29 (February 1981): 8–10; "Time Charts," *Education 3–13* 10 (Spring 1982): 48–50.

24. Barton and Levstik, "'Back When God was Around'"; Linda S. Levstik and Keith C. Barton, "'They Still Use Some of Their Past': Historical Salience in Elementary Children's Chronological Thinking," *Journal of Curriculum Studies* 28 (September/October 1996): 531–576.

25. Levstik and Barton, "Historical Salience," 556.

26. Keith C. Barton, "'You'd Be Wanting to Know About the Past': Social Contexts of Children's Historical Understanding in Northern Ireland and the USA," *Comparative Education* 37 (February 2001): 89–106; "'My Mom Taught Me': The Situated Nature of Historical Understanding," paper presented at the annual meeting of the American Educational Research Association, 8–12 April, 1995, Eric Document Reproduction Service ED 387404; "Historical

Understanding Among Elementary Children" (Ed.D. diss., Lexington: University of Kentucky, 1994).

27. Barton, "Historical Understanding among Elementary Children," 77, 84–87.
28. Barton, "Historical Understanding among Elementary Children," 76–78.
29. Other studies of young children's historical understanding include Jere Brophy and Bruce VanSledright, *Teaching and Learning History in Elementary Schools* (New York: Teachers College Press, 1997), 72–194; Joan E. Blyth, *Place and Time With Children Five to Nine* (London: Croom Helm, 1984); and Hilary Cooper, *History in the Early Years* (London: Routledge Farmer, 2002).
30. This is also one reason we decline to define terms like *historical thinking* and *historical understanding*. Rather than defining these terms and then trying to ascertain whether or how students engage in them, we're interested in what research has to say about students' participation in activities related to the past; images of the nature of historical thinking or understanding should arise from research, not precede it. The other reason we find definitions of these terms unhelpful is that they imply the appropriate locus of research is individual skills, knowledge, or cognition; a major purpose of this book, on the other hand, is to problematize such individualistic approaches and focus on what students do with history.
31. Levstik and Barton, "Historical Salience," 555–563.
32. On textbooks, see Frances FitzGerald, *America Revised: History Schoolbooks in the Twentieth Century* (New York: Vintage Books, 1979); James W. Loewen, *Lies My Teacher Told Me: Everything Your American History Textbook Got Wrong* (New York: New Press, 1995); and Richard J. Paxton, "A Deafening Silence: History Textbooks and the Students Who Read Them," *Review of Educational Research* 69 (Fall 1999): 315–339. On museums and historic sites in the United States, see James W. Loewen, *Lies Across America: What Our Historic Sites Get Wrong* (New York: Touchstone, 1999); Mike Wallace, *Mickey Mouse History and Other Essays on American Memory* (Philadelphia: Temple University Press, 1996). Studies of classroom practice in history include John I. Goodlad, *A Place Called School* (New York: McGraw-Hill, 1984); S. G. Grant, *History Lessons: Teaching, Learning, and Testing in U.S. High School Classrooms* (Mahwah, N.J.: Lawrence Erlbaum Associates Inc., 2003); and Bruce A. VanSledright and Jere E. Brophy, *Teaching and Learning History in Elementary School* (New York: Teachers College Press, 1997). On students' response to film, see Peter Seixas, "Confronting the Moral Frames of Popular Film: Young People Respond to Historical Revisionism," *American Journal of Education* 102 (May 1994): 261–285.
33. Wertsch, *Voices of Collective Remembering*, 117–148; quotes from pp. 134 and 148.
34. These findings are part of unpublished research still under analysis at the time of this writing.
35. Two exceptions are Levstik, "Historical Narrative and the Young Reader," which examined one child's reading of historical fiction outside the classroom, and Greg Dimitriadis, "'Making History Go' at a Local Community Center: Popular Culture and the Construction of Historical Knowledge Among African American Youth," *Theory and Research in Social Education* 28 (Winter 2000): 40–64, which followed children's engagement with historical knowledge in films at a local community center.

Chapter **2**

Participatory Democracy
and Democratic Humanism

Thus the identification with the common lot which is the essential idea of Democracy becomes the source and expression of social ethics. It is as though we thirsted to drink at the great wells of human experience, because we knew that a daintier or less potent draught would not carry us to the end of the journey, going forward as we must in the heat and jostle of the crowd.

—Jane Addams[1]

Genealogists, university historians, mural painters, archivists, documentary filmmakers, museum curators, grandparents—all these people (and more) use information about the past to make sense of the world, but they are guided by a variety of purposes. Some of these aims are complementary, some are contradictory, and some are merely unrelated to each other. As we suggested in the last chapter, for example, examination of the Columbian encounter may take place as part of a dispassionate explanation of how human societies interact, a judgmental indictment of European conquest, or a modern creation myth that establishes a sense of identity. Similarly, the Irish Famine can serve as a scholarly explanation for immigration to the United States, a politically motivated example of British indifference to Irish suffering, or memorized fodder for an exam question. All of the most familiar historical topics—slavery, civil rights, World War II, suffrage, the American Revolution, and so on—can serve varied ends, for different people, in diverse contexts.

If we had enough time, we might expose students to all these purposes and apprentice them into many ways of knowing about the past. Then they could choose from a variety of forms of historical knowledge and develop their own rationales for why the subject is worth pursuing. And if we had unlimited resources, motivation, and interest, we could cover every topic in the history of the world, from the first humans through last week's headlines. The history standards developed in the 1990s took just such an approach: They recommended so much historical content that if they were taken seriously, students would have no time to study anything except history, all day every day, for 12 years. Even those of us who are passionately

25

devoted to teaching and learning history might consider that excessive. When we reflect on the real world of schooling—with all its demands and limitations—we see that choices must be made. We can't teach everything that happened in the past, nor can we treat every purpose equally. In this chapter, we lay out a rationale for making these choices, and we ground this rationale in a vision of humanistic education geared toward preparing students for participatory democracy. Ultimately, they must go forward "in the heat and jostle of the crowd," as Jane Addams put it, and history should help them identify "with the common lot which is the essential idea of Democracy."

THE NEED FOR A RATIONALE FOR HISTORY EDUCATION

Some readers may recoil at the suggestion that history education needs a rationale, for many people believe that the study of the past is self-justifying and requires no defense. In fact, some seem to think that developing an explicit justification somehow betrays history, as though the subject is "above" having a guiding purpose. In that view, elaborating a specific reason for studying history is simply a transparent attempt to introduce ideology or "social engineering" into the curriculum. In Britain, for example, some educators have told us matter-of-factly that history is an "academic subject" and that the purpose of teaching it is to enable students to pass examinations. They assume that history's place in the curriculum is justified by the fact that it is in the curriculum, and they neither expect nor desire any greater reason for teaching or learning the subject. To suggest that learning history needs a broader rationale is anathema.[2]

In the United States, some might give similar reasons for studying history, particularly with the increasing importance of high-stakes testing. In most states, though, students have not traditionally been tested on history, nor have the consequences of passing a single test been as high for individuals as they have been in Britain. However, a variation of this argument comes from those who claim history should be studied "for its own sake." We've never been sure what this phrase means. It's not clear what the sake of history is nor how it can have some kind of agency that demands our attention. Moreover, we're not sure how history could be studied for its own sake when there are many different kinds of history—which variety could claim precedence in such a contest? When people refer to studying history for its own sake, they may not be putting forth a reasoned argument so much as trying to associate the subject with other deities with whose sakes we should be concerned—Christ's sake, heaven's sake, Pete's sake, and so on. Like the argument that history should be studied so students can pass exams, this assertion is self-justifying: History simply *is*, and there's no point bothering to flesh out its function.[3]

However, history's place in the curriculum requires a clearer rationale than this. History needs justification, in part, because in an overcrowded curriculum, there is no obvious reason why schools should include the topic at all, rather than drop it in favor of more economics or geography—or for that matter, more mathematics or chemistry. Indeed, when history's position in the curriculum seems threatened, its supporters often begin to attend to such questions. This happened in the late 1980s, when a variety of works appeared in defense of the subject. Although some of these arguments were passionate and thoughtful, others were vague at best, contradictory at worst. As a result, although this flurry of attention generated a great deal of heat, it shed little light on why history should be a required topic of study. In the wake of these efforts, history education in the United States continued to occupy the same privileged position it had always enjoyed, but neither educators nor the general public shared any systematic conception of why students were repeatedly exposed to the topic, year after year after year. Without such shared understanding, schools were left with no meaningful basis on which to make decisions about which topics to study or how to study them, and the dead hand of tradition continued to control history education.[4]

Our aim in this chapter is not to respond to some manufactured crisis in history education but to establish a clear rationale for studying the subject, so that curricular and instructional choices can be made on a meaningful basis. In developing or implementing any curriculum, we have to make choices about what to teach and how to teach it, and these choices will be based on our assumptions about the goals of education. Should students learn about the Pilgrims or about Mother Jones? Should they study more U.S. or world history? Should they use a textbook or examine primary sources? Everyone makes these choices—historians, textbook publishers, school boards, and teachers—because no one can cover everything that happened in the past or use all possible teaching methods. Moreover, there is no "neutral" or "objective" approach to history that can guide such choices; they can be guided only by the goals we develop for the subject.

As we mentioned in chapter 1, some educators argue that history in schools should be modeled on the academic discipline, and we have to admit we've used similar arguments in the past. Today, however, this perspective does little to inspire or motivate us, because all human activity is historically and culturally situated, and disciplinary procedures are just one set of practices among many. As Stephen Thornton has argued, educators need to acknowledge that the demands and purposes of history as a school subject are not always the same as those of academic history, and that the discipline cannot provide criteria for what are, after all, educational judgments.[5] Thus, we prefer to begin not by defining history but by considering the subject's goals and the practices—from the wide array of "real" historical activities—that might support those. We hope to develop a consistent but culturally situated rationale for teaching and learning history in one specific time, place, and context—the public schools of the United States in the 21st century. Our discussion may have relevance for other settings, but history education elsewhere may depend on different rationales. We leave those arguments for others, so that we can focus on the settings we know best and to which we are most committed.

PUBLIC EDUCATION AND DEMOCRATIC CITIZENSHIP

We assume that the overarching goal of public education in the United States is to prepare students for participation in democratic life. We cannot justify an assertion like this by reference to a single, authoritative source, because we do not have a national system of education, and therefore, the purpose of schooling is not established by federal legislation, judicial mandate, or executive order. However, public schools in the United States share an origin in the common school movement of the 19th century, and the ideology of that movement revolved around the need to prepare citizens for a democratic, republican form of government; schools were meant to be, as Carl Kaestle puts it, "pillars of the republic." State and local curriculum guides still pay homage to citizenship education as a fundamental purpose of schooling, and the United States has a long tradition of philosophical reflection on the relationship between education and democracy. Democracy has never been the only goal of education in the United States; economic productivity and individual development have provided rival conceptions of the purpose of schooling. Yet throughout our history, the need to prepare students for citizenship in a democracy has furnished one of the most frequent and persuasive arguments in support of public education, and a recent Gallup poll found that this remains one of the most popular reasons for supporting a system of public schooling.[6]

However, saying that schools should prepare students for democratic citizenship may say so much that it says nothing at all. Sometimes it seems little more than a mantra, chanted without reflection on its deeper meaning or implications for practice. Walter Parker argues that citizenship education has suffered from "too much lip service" and that democracy has never been seriously undertaken as a curriculum project in the United States. "The democratic aim of public schooling," he maintains, "has been tucked safely away in the rationale and mission statements of school-district curriculum guidelines. Beyond the establishment of free public schooling, surprisingly little has been done to educate children for democracy."[7] We would argue that schools do devote a fair amount of attention to citizenship education, but that most of this attention is limited to narrow and unproductive visions of the task.

We know from experience that when many teachers hear the term *citizenship*, they think of patriotic rituals and indoctrination. The U.S. flag is a ubiquitous feature of classrooms, hallways, and auditoriums in schools throughout the country, and most children begin their days by reciting the Pledge of Allegiance, a practice often mandated by state law or local policy. In many schools, students also sing patriotic songs, either on a daily basis or as part of special programs or assemblies, and the national anthem is played at major sporting events at U.S. schools. Furthermore, much of the social studies curriculum, particularly at the elementary level, is geared toward developing reverence for American heroes, symbols, and political procedures. In some instances—we hope rare ones—teachers may even try to coerce students to support specific government policies, such as military interventions or other aspects of foreign relations.[8]

Yet although these images may come to mind as examples of citizenship education, they cannot be considered preparation for democratic citizenship, because they are no different than the practices that take place in nondemocratic political systems. In dictatorships, students also are taught to venerate the flag, sing patriotic songs, revere national leaders and symbols, and support government policies. Except for this last practice—automatic support of government policy—there's nothing inherently wrong with any of these, but it makes more sense to refer to such practices as education for "patriotism" or "nationalism" than for citizenship. The concept of citizenship education logically should be reserved for practices specific to the political system of which students are part—a democratic one in the case of the United States and many other countries.

The most common way U.S. students are taught about democratic political practices and institutions is through some version of civics. This subject focuses on how governmental institutions operate, including the rights and responsibilities of citizens. Curriculum guides may identify a wide range of objectives in this area, but in practice, the content of civics instruction usually is more limited. At the primary level, students become acquainted with basic procedures of voting and elections. Older students learn about the three branches of government, and those in junior and senior high study political parties, constitutional guarantees, taxation, and that venerable standard, "how a bill becomes law." Educators like R. Freeman Butts have called for schools to address this kind of political knowledge more extensively and systematically (to engage in a "revival of civic learning," to use Butts' phrase), and the curriculum standards for civic education, *Civitas*, provide extensive recommendations for increasing students' understanding of how government institutions function. Based on our experiences, students would benefit greatly from this kind of program, because they often have only a superficial understanding of government and politics. Such civic education certainly qualifies as education for democratic citizenship, because it focuses on how the institutions unique to U.S. democracy function, as well as how individuals interact with those institutions. Without such knowledge, citizens would have no idea what their rights were, and they would have no basis for making the choices entrusted to them as members of a democratic polity. It seems logical to assume that democratic governments will be more democratic if citizens understand how they work.[9]

However, many educators have argued that this is not enough. Simply knowing how the government works—how officials are elected or laws are made—does not guarantee participation. For many years, it has been easy to point to statistics illustrating not only a low turnout in elections but a general apathy toward political affairs, accompanied by feelings of mistrust toward politicians. To counter this political alienation, social studies educators have suggested students should learn more than how their government works; they should learn how to be citizens—to engage in the behaviors that characterize active participation in democratic societies. Shirley Engle and Anna Ochoa, for example, note that democratic citizenship involves the "willingness to be responsible for the state and to engage at all levels in the decisions that chart its course." They argue, therefore, that a central concern of social education should be equipping students with the knowledge, skills, and attitudes necessary to make intelligent decisions. This would include learning not just factual content related to society, culture, the environment, and so on, but also what they refer to as "basic intellectual skills" such as selecting information relevant to the solution of problems, identifying the underlying values involved in decisions and the likely consequences of chosen actions, and understanding the perspective of those whose views differ from one's own. Similarly, the "jurisprudential framework" developed by Donald Oliver and James Shaver provides a systematic method for teaching students how to analyze political controversies and issues of public policy.[10]

Teaching students to reach decisions about social, political, and economic issues—and giving them the chance to do so—is part of a long tradition in social education. However, some educators have taken this effort a step further and emphasized the importance not just of reaching decisions but of exercising political influence based on those decisions. This focus on political action has been the central concern of proposals such as that by Fred Newmann, Thomas Bertocci, and Ruthanne Landsness. They argue that "the primary educational mission" related to citizenship "is to teach citizens to exert influence in public affairs." This would include not only learning to reach and justify decisions but also developing more overtly political skills such as canvassing, fund-raising, bargaining and negotiating, preparing public testimony, using the media, and so on. Newmann and his colleagues have aptly titled their proposal "Skills in Citizen Action" because of their emphasis not just on teaching students to reach private decisions but on guiding them to take public action based on those decisions.[11]

We wholeheartedly agree with proposals for developing more active and reflective citizens. We want students to know how the government works, and we also want them to grow into citizens who have the skills necessary to reach intelligent decisions on matters of public policy and who know how to carry out their decisions. We expect that our society will be more democratic—and therefore more equitable and just—if students learn to do these things. Still, this is not enough. Even proposals that emphasize students' ability to participate in democratic government share two important limitations. First, they focus almost exclusively on interactions between individuals and the state. Newmann and his colleagues begin with the assumption that the purpose of civic education "is to teach students to function in a particular relationship with the state," and their skills for citizen action explicitly revolve around "competence to influence the state." Indeed, they define public affairs as those issues to which "institutions of government should respond—through legislation, administrative action, judicial opinion, selection officeholders, and other activities." The proposals by Butts, Engels and Ochoa, and Oliver and Shaver also emphasize governmental institutions: Students are expected to learn how to make decisions about the actions undertaken by government, and their political participation is assumed to relate directly to those institutions—whether through voting, lobbying, writing letters to representatives, or engaging in public protests. Citizenship, in this view, is defined and limited by the ways in which individuals interact with the state.[12]

That is part of democratic citizenship, but not all of it. We believe a wider set of social interactions characterizes the life of citizens *as* citizens in a democracy, and that there are more ways of being a citizen than through influencing government policy. A number of scholars have argued that the health of a democratic society is influenced by the quality of its civic life or the level of its "social capital," to use Robert Putnam's phrase. In this view, citizenship also consists of participation in the organizations of civil society—charitable organizations, parent–teacher groups, labor unions, churches, recreational clubs, neighborhood associations, faculties, cooperatives, professional organizations, and "societies for promoting or preventing this and that." Most of us are involved more deeply in groups like these than in the affairs of state, and through them, we may have our greatest exposure to democratic action. Indeed, the institutions of civil society often are more democratic than those of government, because they rely almost exclusively on voluntary participation and shared decision making by members. Historically, charities, religious bodies, self-help groups, unions, and similar organizations have provided means by which those who are politically marginalized—women, minorities, immigrants, workers—have organized to improve their own lives and those of others. As Nancy Fraser points out, when other formal public arenas exclude such groups, the multiple institutions of civil society can provide "discursive space" that allows for the "formulation of oppositional interpretations of identities, interests, and needs."[13]

In our view, preparing students to take part in civil society is just as central to citizenship education as engaging them in the analysis of government policy or teaching them how to contact a legislator. This is not an either/or proposition, because both elements are crucial to preparing students for a democracy. Civil society not only provides a location for the practice of democracy, but it also develops the skills necessary for citizens to take part in the arena of formal politics. Moreover, participation in civil society is one of the ways in which we develop our dreams and aspirations for society—the very goals to which democratic governments are meant to respond.

This brings us to a second drawback of many proposals for citizenship education: They typically assume that the perspectives brought to bear on policy issues develop prior to, and independently of, the political process, and they conceptualize the public sphere as the forum in which these private views compete for influence. Based on their own values, goals, and decisions, people develop positions related to issues such as education, health care, foreign relations, and so on, and then they engage in a process of persuasion and negotiation to win acceptance for their favored positions. Cooperation arises primarily when people work together with those whose ideas are similar to their own; of necessity, they work against those whose ideas are different. This is the characteristic mode of political participation in modern liberal democracies such as the United States: Policy positions compete for support in the political arena the way commodities compete for consumers in the economic one. It is a process that inevitably leads to winners and losers (or pragmatic compromises that may not fully satisfy anyone). Newmann, Bertocci, and Landsness are explicit about this element of education for citizen action: "Genuine controversy over public affairs inevitably spawns 'winners,' 'losers,' and people who see themselves as somewhere in between; it is impossible to have only winners."[14] In this conception, the public sphere provides a forum for the contest among private interests, and so public deliberation amounts to little more than an argument—and those who are the best at arguing (often because they have the most resources at their disposal) usually win.

We think democracy can do better than this. We think the public space of democratic society can be more than a location for adjudicating private interests. Democratic institutions should provide a means by which citizens develop shared interests and engage in joint decision making about the issues that affect their future. This is part of what Benjamin Barber refers to as "strong democracy." In this view, public deliberation provides a means by which citizens can "contrive to live together" to their mutual advantage, through the discovery of common ground. As Barber explains, such citizenship involves "a kind of 'we' thinking that compels individuals to reformulate their interests, purposes, norms, and plans in a mutualistic language of public goods. 'I want X' must be reconceived as 'X would be good for the community to which I belong.'"[15] We believe this joint planning for a common future can more fully bring about the freedom and equality toward which democratic societies aspire. Although it may never be possible for everyone to be a winner, surely democratic societies can have far more winners than they do currently. Not all issues will be amenable to widespread consensus, but a focus on the common good should result in much greater consensus than a zero-sum battle among competing interests.

This kind of democracy must also be pluralist. That is, it must acknowledge that individuals and groups will hold radically different, even contradictory, values and that they will have different conceptions of what constitutes a desirable future. Participatory democracy must allow people to bring their differences into the open, discuss them, and move forward with mutually acceptable actions whenever possible. This contrasts with the view of democracy advocated by communitarians and some conservative proponents of "civic virtue," who assume that a vision of the common good exists prior to the political process and that political decisions should be based on what "we" all believe. We find that alternative unacceptable—and essentially undemocratic—both because we don't believe a preexisting consensus on the common good exists, and also because the assumption that there is one would probably lead to stifling conformity. In the 21st century United States, consensus is something we must seek, and not something we can impose on each other as a condition of citizenship. We cannot exclude our fellow citizens from public discourse simply because they hold opinions contrary to our own; the only litmus test for democratic participation must be the willingness to engage in that participation in the first place.[16]

Yet pluralism also contrasts with conceptions of liberal democracy that assume preexisting differences, although acceptable, must remain "off the table" in public discourse. From that perspective, individuals enter the public realm and take part in a purely rational discourse unrelated to gender, ethnicity, religious belief, or other "nonpolitical" characteristics. This may not seem like much of a burden for those whose background, status, or style of discourse is already highly prized in society. Yet for many people, taking on this kind of universalist position is tantamount to denying their identity; they can gain access to public discourse only by shedding membership in groups that help them define who they are. Not surprisingly, this denigration of specific cultural identities (or those based on gender, class, language, sexuality, etc.) has led many people to adopt a directly contrary position, in which group identity becomes the defining characteristic of political participation. Supporters and opponents of "identity politics" have debated the legitimacy of inserting group interests into public discourse, but the dichotomous terms in which this issue is pursued (particularly by opponents of group interest) provide little inspiration for a democratic future. Rather than declaring group membership irrelevant to public discourse, or glorifying it to such an extent that competing group interests simply replace competing individual interests, a pluralist, participatory democracy must include such interests as part of deliberation toward a common future. As Walter Parker puts it, the central question of citizenship is, "How can we live together justly, in ways that are mutually satisfying, and which leave our differences, both individual and group, intact and our multiple identities recognized?" Although this question will not be an easy one to answer, we agree with Parker that the quest is at the core of modern democracy.[17]

Deliberation is a key component of this kind of participatory democracy. Without independent or preexisting grounds for making political judgments, citizens have to talk their way through issues confronting them.

They must jointly arrive at public decisions and agree to political actions, and they have to justify these decisions and actions to each other. Common ground is not discovered through this process so much as created. As David Mathews puts it, public deliberation is "the process by which the public defines the public's interest." This is not the same as the competitive debate, point scoring, or quest for domination that characterizes most public talk. Discourse in a participatory democracy is not about putting forth positions and pointing out flaws in those of opponents; rather, as in Jürgen Habermas' view, communication is "a process of potential transformation in which reason is advanced by debate itself." To achieve this, Mathews calls for a more "open, exploratory dialogue" that involves weighing, reflecting, and evaluating options; in this kind of deliberation, "we do publicly what we do personally when we are genuinely uncertain about what we should do—we try to keep our minds open to all alternatives so that we are not locked in by past positions." This open-mindedness is an essential component of participatory democracy. For our preexisting positions and commitments to be transformed into mutually satisfying courses of action, we have to be able to listen to others. As Barber notes, "talk as communication involves receiving as well as expressing, hearing as well as speaking, and empathizing as well as uttering."[18]

To sum up, when we talk about education for democracy, we have a very specific vision in mind, one that incorporates traditional elements of liberal, representative democracy but that expands this conception in important ways. Our view of democracy is essentially that of John Dewey, who argued that "a Democracy is more than a form of government; it is primarily a mode of associated living, of conjoint communicated experience."[19] In this view, democratic politics extends beyond the relations between individuals and the state to encompass the relations among citizens as they participate in collective action for the common good. This includes a wide range of interactions, relationships, and institutions other than those involving the formal mechanisms of representative government. Because we live in such a diverse society, this kind of participatory democracy must also be pluralist. We cannot assume consensus around a preexisting ideal of the common good, but neither can we expect people to discard their prior ideas (or their group identities) to take part in supposedly neutral and universal discourse. Instead, we must recognize that citizens enter the public sphere with deeply felt, and potentially conflicting, conceptions of the collective future, and that the purpose of democratic politics is to develop shared interests and visions. Democracy becomes a means by which we jointly create a vision of the common good from our diverse starting points, rather than an arena in which competing perspectives battle it out until one reigns supreme. Both participation and pluralism, meanwhile, depend on deliberation—the open-ended (and open-minded) discussion and reflection necessary for understanding our fellow citizens and for taking action toward a mutually satisfying future. This view of democracy—as participatory, pluralist, and deliberative—is the one we will have in mind as we evaluate history's potential contribution to citizenship. It is an optimistic and idealistic view, but we see no reason to aim for anything less.

EDUCATION FOR DEMOCRATIC PARTICIPATION

We cannot answer the question, "What kind of education prepares students for participatory democracy?" because, quite frankly, no one knows. There are no societies that currently exhibit the levels of participation, pluralism, and deliberation that we advocate, and as a result, there is no way to determine, empirically, which educational procedures most effectively develop the qualities needed for such citizenship. Participatory democracy is an ideal toward which we believe our society should strive, and in the absence of empirical evidence, we can only suggest the sorts of experiences that seem consistent with this ideal—the education we think could prepare students for participatory democracy. Also, because our suggestions must necessarily be tentative and speculative, we will offer no tightly defined objectives, no required curriculum, no 10-point list of "skills for participatory democracy." Rather, we recommend an overarching perspective on social education, one that will guide us throughout the book as we evaluate the potential contributions of history education.

We believe students will be best prepared for democratic citizenship if they receive a broadly humanistic education. Although concepts like humanism, humanistic education, and the humanities have a great deal of intuitive appeal, there is little consensus as to their meaning or implications. Nimrod Aloni, for example, identifies four distinct and competing educational theories that appeal to humanism as a foundational principle. These include classical humanistic education, which "implies the existence of an ideal of human perfection that should serve as a universal and objective model for regulating the education of all human beings *qua* human beings." In its modern form, this is the "great books" approach to education, with its emphasis on exposing students to "the best that has been thought and said in the world" (as defined, of course, by members of the Western cultural elite). Romantic humanistic education, on the other hand, is rooted in the work of Rousseau and, later, the humanistic psychologists of the 20th century. This approach focuses on the inner world and unique self of each individual; educationally, it emphasizes self-regulated development, natural unfolding of inner talent, and supportive human relations, leading to self-respect, love, and acceptance. These two approaches lie at opposite ends of the educational spectrum, and yet the concept of humanism is associated with each.[20]

These are perhaps the two most widely accepted perspectives on humanistic education, but our conception does not derive directly from either (although it shares some elements with each). Closer to our view is the "democratic humanism" identified by Amy Gutmann. This is a humanism that "supports an education that encourages citizens to deliberate about justice as part of their political culture."[21] Amy Gutmann is a prominent theorist of deliberative democracy, so it is hardly surprising that her view accords well with our vision of democratic society, but her formulation is also consistent with a long line of thinking about humanistic education; moreover, we believe this view has the potential to clarify history's contribution to democracy without making the subject an instrument of simple-minded indoctrination or a handmaiden to purely pragmatic concerns. Such an achievement requires that history be guided by three key elements of humanistic education.

First, it must promote reasoned judgment. Humanistic education has long been associated with developing powers of critical appraisal. As Elliot Eisner notes, "Humanists place premium on the human's ability to be critically rational, that is, to reason deeply and sensitively about important human matters." This approach is antithetical to the instrumental rationality that dominates most curriculum planning. Humanistic study involves neither accumulating discrete pieces of information nor "producing pre-specified competencies for discrete tasks," as William Stanley and James Whitson put it. Memorizing presidential terms, locating the "three causes of the Civil War" in a textbook, looking up the definition of feudalism—these may be part of some kinds of historical study, but they do not reflect a humanistic approach to the subject, because they involve no reasoning, no room for judgment. For the study of history to be humanistic, students must be involved in weighing alternatives, determining significance, and reaching conclusions. Eisner notes that because no precise yardstick exists for measuring intellectual or artistic value, such judgments require "attention and sensitivity to nuance, they require appreciation for context, they require the ability to deliberate and judge." The development of such abilities is fundamental to participatory democracy. Because there is no independent ground for political knowledge—no certain truths on which decisions can be made—action depends on careful reasoning and consideration of evidence. As Benjamin Barber suggests, the responsibility of citizens "is not merely to choose but to judge options and possibilities."[22]

The study of history clearly can promote reasoned judgment about human affairs. Reflection on the causes of historical events and processes, their relative significance, the potential outcomes of alternative courses of action, the impact of the past on the present—all these require the deep and sensitive reasoning characteristic of humanistic study. However, for such reasoning to take place, students must have something to reason about—they must be engaged in evaluating the causes and consequences of historical actions. This does not always happen, and there seem to be two notable obstacles to involving students in this process. The first is an approach that treats history as the inevitable unfolding of a preordained sequence of events; if history happened the way it had to happen, then there is nothing to judge. Causes and consequences become almost irrelevant, and the past is reduced to little more than a chronological sequence.

A more common barrier to engaging students in critical appraisal is the belief that historical study means repeating the arguments developed by others—that "learning history" involves reproducing agreed-on explanations for historical events. Peter Seixas has argued that when we ask students to do this, we misrepresent the nature of historical knowledge, because the products of historians are not settled conclusions but "provisional and tentative arguments in an ongoing dialogue within a community of scholars."[23] However, in addition to misrepresenting what knowledge is, this kind of reproduction-oriented history education deprives students of the chance to develop their powers of judgment. If there are no judgments to be made—because teachers, textbooks, or historians already have decided on the right answers—then students will be no more capable of reasoning after studying history than they were before. For history education to develop reasoned judgment, students must learn to reach their own conclusions about the causes of historical events, their consequences, and their significance.

A second characteristic of the humanistic study of history is that it promotes an expanded view of humanity. Eisner notes, "There is a shared agreement that humanistic studies shed light on what it means to be a human being." They do this, in part, by taking us beyond the narrow confines of our present circumstances and confronting us with the cares, concerns, and ways of thinking of people different than ourselves. History is particularly well suited to this goal, because studying other times and other civilizations demonstrates that our own society represents not a timeless or universal standard but simply one set of alternatives among many. Even young children have learned that people in the past looked, acted, and believed differently than they do. What well-planned history education can do—along with anthropology or cultural geography—is help them understand the logic of these alternative ways of thinking and acting, so that they don't conclude cultural differences are due to a lack of intelligence. This ability to recognize, understand, and even embrace the range of human diversity is critical to participatory democracy. As Parker notes, one of the chief obstacles to a pluralist political community is the refusal by some to "walk the path" of democratic action with others. This path, as Barber points out, requires listening—receiving, hearing, empathizing—and that is possible only if we truly believe the views of others are potentially as sensible as our own, if we understand that there are ways of being human other than those to which we are accustomed. Only when we accept that those we disagree with might have a reasonable basis for their beliefs can we engage in meaningful dialogue.[24]

For history to develop this expanded perspective on humanity, students must learn about people different than themselves and societies different than their own. This means studying a wider range of topics than is currently the norm in the United States, where the curriculum typically focuses almost entirely on national history—in other words, on those people most likely to be similar to the students themselves. Students in the United States have few opportunities to study Incan civilization, Mesolithic people, medieval heretics, or the thousands of other times and places from world history that have little direct connection to their own national past. Yet it is precisely because these eras are so different than their own that they are worth examining. By studying the social institutions and cultures of people far removed in time and space, students should be better able to understand the multiple ways of being human. We believe this understanding will better prepare students for the demands of life in a pluralist democracy than a repeated emphasis on their own country's past.

The final characteristic of the humanistic study of history—and the most controversial—is that it involves deliberation over the common good. This has not been a significant part of either the classical or romantic humanist traditions, both of which emphasize individual judgment rather than joint deliberation, and individual standards of moral and ethical behavior rather than collective visions of the common good. However, our view of humanity is a more social one, and we believe both the format and objective of humanistic study should be social in nature. Dewey argues that "'humanism' means at bottom being imbued with an intelligent sense of human interests," and he equates such interests with the good of society. For Dewey, a study of humanity that simply involves the accumulation of knowledge "is on a level with the busy work of children." For any study to be truly humane, he argues it must produce "greater sensitiveness to social well-being and greater ability to promote that well-being."[25] Similarly, Benjamin Ladner suggests

> It is the special task of the humanities to sustain a community of discourse that fosters thinking not only as an isolated, private activity but also as convivial, collective, public deliberation. This is the concern for civility—those cooperative efforts which insure the care of the public realm in which we all exist. In cultivating an educated citizenry, which is the foundation of civility, the humanities not only foster a common language that *enables* us to speak and make decisions together, but they hold in focus what it is *important* to be talking about and deciding.[26]

Discussions about how to promote social well-being and how to care for the public realm are at the heart of participatory democracy, and we believe history has an important role to play in preparing students to take part in such deliberation.

This has not been a role history education has traditionally embraced, however, nor is it one that leads to easily predictable results. We cannot count on history to produce a concern with the common good nor to guarantee students will be inclined to take part in collaborative judgments. We can, however, ensure that they have the chance to consider the common good and the opportunity to reason together with others. We have noted that schools cannot hope to cover all possible historical topics and that choices must be made based on some criteria. We would suggest that one of these criteria should be the extent to which given topics promote consideration of the common good. Toward that end, students should be exposed to historical topics that force them to consider issues of justice—the impact of racism, for example, or gender roles, dictatorship, warfare, colonialism, economic relations, and so on. In addition, students should have the chance to discuss the justice of past events or social arrangements, as well as the justice of their legacy.

We realize that some teachers, and some historians, believe students should not make these kinds of judgments; they often resort to the claim, "That's not real history." We consider that argument shortsighted. All of us repeatedly make judgments about history. The Holocaust, slavery, suffrage, the Vietnam War, the Civil Rights movement, the Crusades, the end of apartheid, the Ku Klux Klan, the bombing of Hiroshima, September 11—surely all of us have made judgments about whether these contributed to or detracted from the common good. Children certainly have: In our interviews with them, they consistently point to justice (or "fairness," as they say) as one of the principal reasons for their interest in the subject. (We discuss this at greater length in chap. 5.) However, they usually have not systematically examined any particular definition of justice—much less competing conceptions—nor have they discussed its relationship to issues of the common good. Students' preexisting ideas about fairness provide an important starting point for such considerations, but deliberation about historical topics should be designed to help them develop more coherent perspectives and a clearer sense of how they apply to concrete circumstances (whether historical or contemporary). Rather than ignoring or downplaying issues of justice and the common good, history educators should use deliberation to promote judgments that are reasonable and publicly justifiable, and they should help students understand how to make and defend those judgments in the context of a pluralist democracy. If our goal is to educate students for citizenship, omitting such discussion would be an outrageous example of missed opportunity.[27]

However, engaging students in discussions of fairness or justice is not the same as leading them to predetermined conclusions about what should or should not have taken place in the past or what should or should not be done today. The purpose of deliberation is to enable students to work with others to reach such conclusions, not to reproduce the beliefs of teachers, textbooks, historians, or politicians. This is the danger of history that focuses on questions of the common good: Those in positions of authority may think they already know what the common good is and that their role is to reproduce their opinions in students—to tell them what to think about The New Deal or Vietnam or the War in Iraq. In a pluralist democracy, we cannot impose a single vision of the common good on students or teach them a single set of judgments about history. However, we can engage them in discussions in which they work together to develop their own judgments and their own visions.

CONCLUSIONS

The goal of history education can remain vague and unarticulated, or it can be explicitly formulated and brought into the open for public discussion. In either case, the subject will be guided by some underlying rationale, because from a sociocultural perspective, human activity invariably is influenced by socially determined goals, whether we like to admit it or not. From our perspective, history's place in the curriculum must be justified in terms of its contribution to democratic citizenship—citizenship that is participatory, pluralist, and deliberative—and its practices must be structured to achieve that end. This kind of citizenship is a journey more than a destination, and it requires that students be prepared for "the heat and jostle of the crowd," as Jane Addams put it. The humanistic study of history is especially well suited for such preparation because it allows students "to drink at the great wells of human experience"—a process that has the potential both to develop reasoned judgment and to promote an expanded view of humanity. The extent to which history may lead to "identification with the common lot which is the essential idea of Democracy" is less certain, but this uncertainly makes it all the more important that we carefully assess the content and method of history education, so that students have the chance to take part in deliberations over the common good. In the remainder of this book, we use the criteria developed in this chapter to evaluate both the variety of purposes and activities involved in history education and the tools used in teaching and learning the subject.

ENDNOTES

1. Jane Addams, *Democracy and Social Ethics* (Cambridge, Mass.: Harvard University Press, 1964), 11.
2. Recent case studies of history teachers in Britain, however, indicate that they embrace moral and political goals for history education as well as purely academic ones; see Chris Husbands, Alison Kitson, and Anna Pendry, *Understanding History Education: Teaching and Learning About the Past in Secondary Schools* (Philadelphia: Open University Press, 2003), 116–37.
3. One version of the argument that history should be studied for its own sake comes from Arthur M. Schlesinger, Jr., who equates such study with content that has not been influenced by political, economic, religious, or ethnic pressure groups; the fact that no content can be free of such influence is illustrated by Schelesinger's own recommendation, immediately following his admonition that it be studied "for its own sake," that "above all, history can give a sense of national identity." Arthur M. Schlesinger, Jr., *The Disuniting of America: Reflections on a Multicultural Society* (New York: W. W. Norton, 1992), 136–37; Schlesinger's equation of identity and

objectivity is noted in Joseph R. Moreau, "Schoolbook Nation: Imagining the American Community in United States History Texts for Grammar and Secondary Schools, 1865–1930" (Ph.D. diss., University of Michigan, Ann Arbor, 2002), 16.

4. Some of the more well-known examples of this effort include Bernard R. Gifford, Ed., *History in the Schools: What Shall We Teach?* (New York: Macmillan, 1988); Paul Gagnon and the Bradley Commission on History in Schools, Eds., *Historical Literacy: The Case for History in American Education* (New York: Macmillan, 1989); and Charlotte Crabtree, Gary Nash, Paul Gagnon, and Scott Waugh, Eds., *Lessons From History: Essential Understandings and Historical Perspectives Students Should Acquire* (Los Angeles, Calif.: National Center for History in the Schools, University of California, Los Angeles, 1992).

5. Stephen J. Thornton, "Subject Specific Teaching Methods: History," in *Subject-Specific Instructional Methods and Activities*, Vol. 8, *Advances in Research on Teaching*, Ed. Jere Brophy (New York: Elsevier Science, 2001), 309; "Educating the Educators: Rethinking Subject Matter and Methods," *Theory Into Practice* 40 (Winter 2001), 75.

6. Carl. F. Kaestle, *Pillars of the Republic: Common Schools and American Society, 1780–1860* (New York: Hill and Wang, 1983), 75–103; Lawrence A. Cremin, "Horace Mann's Legacy," in *The Republic and the School: Horace Mann on the Education of Free Men*, Ed. Lawrence A. Cremin (New York: Teachers College, Columbia University, 1957), 6–15; Lowell C. Rose and Alec M. Gallup, "The 32nd Annual Phi Delta Kappa/Gallup Poll of the Public's Attitudes Toward the Public Schools," *Phi Delta Kappan* 80 (September 2000): 47. On the pervasiveness of citizenship education as a rationale for schooling in the United States, see Walter C. Parker, "'Advanced' Ideas about Democracy: Toward a Pluralistic Conception of Citizen Education," *Teachers College Record* 98 (Fall 1996): 104, and "Introduction: Schools as Laboratories of Democracy," in *Educating the Democratic Mind*, Ed. Walter C. Parker (Albany, N.Y.: State University of New York Press, 1996), 1–22. Works on the relationship between schooling and democratic citizenship include Jane Addams, *Democracy and Social Ethics*; Michael W. Apple and James A. Beane, *Democratic Schools* (Alexandria, Va: Association for Supervision and Curriculum Development, 1995); Benjamin R. Barber, *An Aristocracy of Everyone: The Politics of Education and the Future of America* (New York: Oxford University Press, 1996); George S. Counts, *Dare the Schools Build a New Social Order?* (New York: John Day, 1932); John Dewey, *Democracy and Education: An Introduction to the Philosophy of Education* (New York: Free Press, 1966); Amy Gutmann, *Democratic Education* (Princeton, N.J.: Princeton University Press, 1988); bell hooks, *Teaching to Transgress: Education as the Practice of Freedom* (New York: Routledge, 1994); and Hilda Taba, Elizabeth Hall Brady, and John T. Robinson, *Intergroup Education in Public Schools* (Washington, D.C.: American Council on Education, 1952).

7. Parker, "Introduction," 11. Some people avoid the word *citizenship* in discussions of education because they feel it implies public schools exist only to serve those who are legal citizens of the nation; as will become clear in this chapter, though, our view of citizenship includes all participation in the public life of a democracy, not just formal interactions with the state, and as a result, we retain the term and use it in this broader sense. We also recognize that not all educational endeavors are geared toward citizenship and that not all political systems are democracies.

Even within democratic societies like the United States, many people withdraw
their children from public schooling precisely because they want education to
serve goals other than (or at odds with) preparation for democratic citizenship.
However, we have little expertise with nondemocratic political systems or educational structures, and we do not presume to outline the purposes of history in
such contexts.

8. The public outcry over the 2002 decision by the Ninth Circuit Court of Appeals,
   which declared school-sponsored recitation of the pledge unconstitutional, illustrated the deeply ingrained nature of this practice; Oliver Libaw, "Pledging Religious Allegiance? Supreme Court Likely to Have Final Say on First Amendment
   Issue," available from http://abcnews.go.com/sections/us/DailyNews/pledge_
   effects020626.html, accessed 9 April, 2003.

9. R. Freeman Butts, *The Revival of Civic Learning: A Rationale for Citizenship Education in American Schools* (Bloomington, Ind.: Phi Delta Kappa Educational Foundation, 1980); Center for Civic Education, *Civitas: A Framework for Civic Education*
   (Calabasas, Calif.: Author, 1991). Limitations to this perspective on civic education are discussed in Walter C. Parker, *Teaching Democracy: Unity and Diversity in
   Public Life* (New York: Teachers College Press, 2003), 18–19. Students in a nondemocratic society can also learn how their government operates, but this kind of
   civic information is somewhat superfluous, because it cannot be used to make political decisions. On the other hand, even within democratic societies, civic education cannot be taken for granted. In Britain, for example, students have not
   traditionally been exposed (until recently) to instruction related to the British political system.

10. Shirley H. Engle and Anna S. Ochoa, *Education for Democratic Citizenship: Decision
    Making in the Social Studies* (New York: Teachers College Press, 1988), 18, 25;
    Donald W. Oliver and James P. Shaver, *Teaching Public Issues in the High School*
    (Boston: Houghton Mifflin, 1966); Parker, *Teaching Democracy*, 18–20.

11. Fred M. Newmann, Thomas A. Bertocci, and Ruthanne M. Landsness, "Skills in
    Citizen Action," in *Educating the Democratic Mind*, Ed. Walter C. Parker (Albany,
    NY: State University of New York Press, 1996), 226. A more extensive treatment
    of this proposal can be found in Fred M. Newmann, *Education for Citizen Action*
    (Berkeley, Calif.: McCutchan Publishing Corporation, 1975).

12. Newmann, Bertocci, and Landsness, "Skills in Citizen Action," 226–7.

13. Robert D. Putnam, *Bowling Alone: The Collapse and Revival of American Community*
    (New York: Touchstone, 2001); Michael Walzer, "The Civil Society Argument," in
    Dimensions of Radical Democracy: Pluralism, Citizenship, Community, Ed. Chantal
    Mouffe (New York: Verso, 1992), 90; Parker, *Teaching Democracy*, 35–40; Nancy
    Fraser, "Rethinking the Public Sphere: A Contribution to the Critique of Actually
    Existing Democracy," in *Between Borders: Pedagogy and the Politics of Cultural
    Studies*, Eds. Henry A. Giroux and Peter McLaren (New York: Routledge, 1994),
    92; Jane Bernard-Powers, "The 'Woman Question' in Citizenship Education," in
    Educating the Democratic Mind, Ed. Walter C. Parker (Albany, NY: State University
    of New York Press, 1996), 287–308; Wendy Sarvasy, "Social Citizenship From a
    Feminist Perspective," *Hypatia* 12 (Fall 1997): 54–73; Petra Munro, "'Widening
    the Circle': Jane Addams, Gender, and the Re/Definition of Democracy," in
    "Bending the Future to Their Will": Civic Women, Social Education, and Democracy,

Eds. Margaret Smith Crocco and O. L. Davis, Jr. (Lanham, Md.: Rowman and Littlefield, 1999), 73–92.

14. Newmann, Bertocci, and Landsness, "Skills in Citizen Action," 228. Benjamin Barber provides a comprehensive critique of this competitive approach to politics in *Strong Democracy: Participatory Politics for a New Age* (Berkeley, Calif.: University of California Press, 1984).

15. Barber, *Strong Democracy*, 117–118, 171.

16. Barber, *Strong Democracy*, 42, 152; Parker, *Teaching Democracy*, 20–28; Craig Calhoun, "Introduction: Habermas and the Public Sphere," in *Habermas and the Public Sphere*, Ed. Craig Calhoun (Cambridge, Mass.: MIT Press, 1992), 35.

17. Parker, *Teaching about Democracy*, 20.

18. David Mathews, "Reviewing and Previewing Civics," in *Educating the Democratic Mind*, Ed. Walter C. Parker (Albany, N.Y.: State University of New York Press, 1996), 279, 283; Barber, *Strong Democracy*, 174; Craig Calhoun, "Introduction," 29; Amy Gutmann and Dennis Thompson, "Why Deliberative Democracy is Different," in *Democracy*, Eds. Ellen Frankel Paul, Fred D. Miller, Jr., and Jeffrey Paul (New York: Cambridge University Press, 2000), 161–180.

19. John Dewey, *Democracy and Education*, 87.

20. Nimrod Aloni, "A Redefinition of Liberal and Humanistic Education," *International Review of Education* 43 (1997): 89. The two other schools of thought identified by Aloni are existentialist humanism (such as the work of Martin Buber) and radical humanism (as found in the work of Paolo Freire or Michael Apple). For other reviews of competing definitions of humanistic education and the humanities, see James L. Jarrett, *The Humanities and Humanistic Education* (Menlo Park, Calif.: Addison-Wesley, 1973), 47–62, and Ralph Barton Perry, "A Definition of the Humanities," in *The Meaning of the Humanities*, Ed. Theodore Meyer Green (Princeton, N.J.: Princeton University Press, 1938), 43–87.

21. Amy Gutmann, "Democratic Citizenship," in *For Love of Country: Debating the Limits to Patriotism*, Eds. Martha C. Nussbaum and Joshua Cohen (Boston, Mass.: Beacon), 70.

22. Elliot Eisner, "Can the Humanities Be Taught in American Public Schools?" In *The Humanities in Precollegiate Education: Eighty-Third Yearbook of the National Society for the Study of Education*, Part II, Ed. Benjamin Ladner (Chicago: University of Chicago Press, 1984), 115; William B. Stanley and James A. Whitson, "Citizenship as Practical Competence: A Response to the New Reform Movement in Social Education," *International Journal of Social Education* 7 (Fall 1991): 59; Barber, *Strong Democracy*, 138. Stanley and Whitson argue for *phronesis*, or "practical competence," as the core of social education, and their argument is parallel to our emphasis on reasoned judgment, particularly in its rejection of instrumental rationality.

23. Peter Seixas, "The Community of Inquiry as a Basis for Knowledge and Learning: The Case of History," *American Educational Research Journal* 30 (Summer 1993): 313.

24. Eisner, "Can the Humanities Be Taught," 115; Parker, "'Advanced Ideas about Democracy," 119; Barber, *Strong Democracy*, 174. Sam Wineburg, following Carl Degler, makes a similar point about history's role in expanding our understanding of what it means to be human. Sam Wineburg, "Historical Thinking and Other Unnatural Acts," in *Historical Thinking and Other Unnatural Acts: Charting the Future of Teaching the Past* (Philadelphia: Temple University Press, 2001), 6;

Carl N. Degler, "Remaking American History," *Journal of American History* 67 (June 1980): 23. For an example of a primary-grades curriculum project aimed at helping students understand the reasons for other ways of life, see Janet Alleman and Jere Brophy, *Social Studies Excursions, K–3*, 3 vol. (Portsmouth, N.H.: Heinemann, 2001–2003).

25. Dewey, *Democracy and Education*, 288.

26. Benjamin Ladner, "Introduction: The Humanities and the Schools," in *The Humanities in Precollegiate Education: Eighty-Third Yearbook of the National Society for the Study of Education*, Part II, Ed. Benjamin Ladner (Chicago: University of Chicago Press, 1984), 5.

27. Andra Makler, "What Does Justice Look Like?," in *Teaching for Justice in the Social Studies Classroom*, Eds. Andra Makler and Ruth Shagoury Hubbard (Portsmouth, N.H.: Heinemann, 2000), 209–222.

Chapter 3

The Identification Stance

When the Stranger says: "What is the meaning of this city?

Do you huddle close together because you love each other?"

What will you answer: "We all dwell together

To make money from each other"? or "This is a community"?

— *T. S. Eliot[1]*

When students learn about the past, they are often asked to identify with what they are studying—that is, they are expected to associate themselves, either as individuals or as members of larger social groups, with specific people, events, or institutions in history. This process is not the same as exploring how the past has led to the present; that activity falls within the analytic stance, which we discuss in the next chapter. Identification is a more subjective, even partisan, act. To some extent, identification is a leap of faith: It requires students to affirm that their lives in the present mirror elements of the past in at least some important respects. This activity is common not only in schools but in the wider society, and it serves multiple purposes. Family history, for example, can be used to develop feelings of personal continuity with the past, stories of national origins and historic turning points can create a sense of group membership and allegiance, and historic societal achievements can be used to justify contemporary social arrangements or political actions. Whenever we hear that history "tells us who we are," we are dealing with some version of the identification stance.

Yet although identification may be one of the most common historical activities, it is also one of the most reviled. The "wrong" sides of the dichotomies we mentioned in the first chapter—heritage, amateur history, the abuse of history, and so on—almost always include some version of identification, because the suggestion that history can tell us who we are threatens the discipline's posture as an objective and scholarly enterprise, separate from and above earthly political or social concerns. From such a perspective, using history as a source of identification is an outdated and counterproductive undertaking, one that renders the subject a servant of

45

contemporary concerns and thus impedes more proper and intellectual attempts to make sense of the past.

However, this stance is not going to go away simply because some scholars consider it outdated or insufficiently "disciplinary." The belief that history should provide a source of identification is a popular one in modern Western thought, and it is at the core of much of the historical activity in U.S. schools. Rather than dismiss identification, we need to ask how and when it might contribute to a pluralist, participatory democracy—and when it might stand in its way. Some form of identification is necessary for democratic life, because without attachment to community, individuals would be unlikely to take part in the hard work of seeking the common good. If we have no community with which to identify, our lives together may amount to little more than an attempt "to make money from each other," as T.S. Eliot worries, and we may find that we "live dispersed on ribbon roads, and no man knows or cares who is his neighbour." If we hope, on the other hand, to bring people together with one another, historical identification provides a powerful means for doing so.

However, identification does have its drawbacks. When we link ourselves to one community, we often cut ourselves off from others, sometimes with ruinous consequences. Throughout the world, historical identifications serve as the basis for repression or violence: Inequitable social arrangements are explained by age-old traditions, long-standing community conflicts are used as justification for new rounds of hostility, ancient defeats and victimization become an excuse for terrorism, and glorification of national history leads to wars of aggression. T.S. Eliot himself, so much concerned with community, had a very limited image of how communities of identification should operate: No proponent of either pluralism or democracy, he was a racist, elitist, and misogynist who supported authoritarian political structures and hereditary privilege.[2] Is this the way it must be? Does identification always entail exclusion? If so, does it have any role in preparing students for democracy?

IDENTIFICATION WITH PERSONAL AND FAMILY HISTORY

One of the most basic forms of historical identification occurs when we look back at the events we have experienced in our lives and equate our present selves with those of our personal pasts. We do not imagine that those events happened to someone else just because they took place months or years ago. Instead, we think of ourselves as having a stable identity that endures through time; we remember growing up, going to school, getting a job, and so on, and we draw on these memories to construct a historical self that endures over the course of our lives.[3] We may even think of major public events in terms of their effect on us as individuals rather than their social or political consequences. Roy Rosenzweig and David Thelen, for example, found that when their respondents reminisced about the Second World War, they usually talked about its influence on their own lives or careers rather than its impact on global political relations.[4] This kind of historical identification involves association of the personal past and present, whether the events involved are large or small.

History can also inspire identification that extends beyond personal experience. Gerda Lerner claims that history offers "a sense of perspective about our own lives and encourages us to transcend the finite span of one life-time by identifying with the generations that came before us and measuring our own actions against the generations that will follow."[5] One way of achieving this transcendence is through family history, which remains a powerful source of identification for many people throughout their lives. Relatives may point out familiar characteristics, pass on family heirlooms and artifacts, and share stories and jointly construct reminiscences; they may invoke the past to establish family traits, connect themselves to legacies of achievement or loss, or establish a sense of continuity and stability. Genealogical researchers report that their forays into family history provide both an enlarged sense of self and strength in the face of adversity, and Rosenweig and Thelen found that two thirds of their respondents considered this to be the most important kind of history. They conclude that "almost every American deeply engages the past, and the past that engages them most deeply is that of their family."[6]

Educators frequently recommend individual and family history projects as part of school history, particularly in the elementary and middle grades; in these projects, a student might bring in a chronological series of photographs of herself or her family, interview older relatives about their experiences in the past, or develop a family history chart or create a "coat of arms."[7] Such investigations can be feasible even for younger children, and they have the potential to expose students to history that is not only personally relevant and but also grounded in active investigation. It is difficult to assess how widespread such practices are, but in our experience, they appear relatively uncommon, and when they are used at all, their purpose may be to build self-esteem or develop language skills, or to serve as an introduction to the study of state, national, or world history. In general, using individual or family history as a source of identification seems to be more common outside schools than within.

Research on students' ideas about the purpose of history bears out this observation: Although they may recognize that people are interested in their own pasts, and that adults often research family history, students do not usually point to this as a central purpose of learning history. When Bruce VanSledright asked elementary, middle, and secondary students why they thought history was taught at school, for example, none of the younger students, and only a few of the older ones, suggested that history helped them form a sense of individual identity.[8] Similarly, in our own work at the elementary and middle levels, students have only occasionally commented on the role of individual or familial pasts in constructing a sense of self. An exception, though, came when one of us talked to a group of fourth and fifth graders who were in the midst of individual and family history projects; those students often pointed to personal and family identification as a reason for studying the subject. After making timelines and giving presentations about the most important events in their lives (a project known as the "History of Me"), several students explained that it was interesting to learn about "special moments in your life" or events they hadn't remembered. As one girl put it, "You could find out things that you didn't even know about yourself"; clearly, she associated her present self with her personal past, even though she hadn't remembered some of the events in that past.[9]

Other times, these students identified with the histories of their families. After completing family history charts and interviewing grandparents, several noted the importance of finding out about their relatives and ancestors. As one girl explained, "If you didn't have history, how would you know who's related to you and who's not?" Others emphasized learning not just who their ancestors were but how they lived; one suggested history was important because it "tells you about your relatives, what your relatives might have done when they were children," while another noted that "you want to know how people in your family lived and why they lived that way." Like many adults, these students were interested in the history of their own families, and they considered that an important reason for studying the past. By the end of the school year, though, after they had turned from individual and family history projects to other investigations—focused on the North American colonies, the American Revolution, and immigration to the United States—these explanations largely disappeared, and students emphasized identification with larger social groupings, as well as purposes unrelated to identification. The role of history in providing a sense of individual identification with personal and familial pasts seems to have been a temporary one, or at least one superseded by other concerns.[10]

NATIONAL IDENTIFICATION

Most people identify with social groups larger than their families, and history is often used to promote identification with one group in particular—the nation. Such identification may involve politically defined states (the United States, Finland, Tanzania, etc.) or groups that aspire to recognition as independent states (Kurdistan, Chechnya, the Tamil region of Sri Lanka, etc.). Such nations are neither "natural" nor self-evident, and identification with them must be constructed and maintained; as Benedict Anderson has put it, nations are "imagined political communities." Imagining such communities into existence takes many forms, but one of the most important ways of legitimating claims to nationality is through history. Anderson suggests that nationalism aims at continuity over generations in a way that other ideologies do not; to identify with a nation—as opposed to a political or economic program such as socialism, free trade, or the various forms of globalism—means to identify with the past. Rogers Smith refers to the accounts that establish this kind of identification as "constitutive stories": Such stories proclaim that factors like ancestry and history constitute the very identities of persons. By defining who community members and their ancestors "have always been," these stories "imply that such people and their heirs cannot authentically choose to belong to any other political community."[11]

Nationalism has been an important political program for most of the last 2 centuries, and during that time, the past has been used to promote national identification in many different ways—by reviving languages and dialects that have fallen into disuse; collecting and disseminating folk songs and stories; excavating and displaying archeological remains; and promoting unique forms of dress, dance, music, and recreation. So important are such traditions for developing an imagined national community that when they do not already exist, they must be invented; indeed, any equation of tradition with a particular national identity involves an element of invention, because a vast array of potential practices must be narrowed down to those deemed sufficiently virtuous to take their place in the public past, whereas other, equally historical practices are forgotten or discarded.[12]

For many years, however, these forms of historically grounded nationalism were relatively unimportant in the United States, because the country's most common languages, literary traditions, and social practices originated in Europe and thus provided little basis for identification with the new nation. (For many years the most distinctly "American" cultural practices were those of Native Americans, and these were hardly acceptable as a basis for widespread national identification, given that the rest of the country was more or less continually at war with the native population.) Moreover, by the late 19th century, when efforts to promote national identity reached their zenith, claims that Americans were united by a single language, religion, ethnic origin, or set of cultural elements clearly were inaccurate. As in other countries, history was used to bind the diverse residents of the United States into an imagined national community, but folktales and rustic costumes weren't up to the task. Instead, Americans looked to a different sort of history to tell them who they were—stories of their nation's origin and development. Such stories have been used throughout U.S. history to create a sense of national identification, with major consequences for educational practice.[13] We deal with the specific content of these stories and their impact on student's understanding of the country's historical development in chapters 8 and 9, but here we are concerned primarily with how they promote identification with the nation.

The primary years of schooling in the United States—from kindergarten through third grade—often are criticized for failing to acquaint children with history, but this criticism is only partly valid. There are certain episodes in history that children in these grades do encounter, not once but repeatedly. Nearly every student in the United States will learn the story of the Pilgrims and the so-called First Thanksgiving year after year after year. They also are likely to learn about Columbus and his "discovery" of the Americas, about George Washington and Abraham Lincoln, about Betsy Ross and the first U.S. flag, and about Martin Luther King, Jr. and Rosa Parks. Far from a random assortment of stories, these historical episodes all function to promote identification with the nation. They tell children how "we" began and how we got where we are today: Columbus initiated European exploration, the Pilgrims established English settlements, George Washington was the father of our country (and Betsy Ross its mother, as Michael Frish puts it), Abraham Lincoln preserved our nation, and Parks and King brought about racial equality.[14]

The fact that some of these interpretations are farfetched and some of the stories outright fabrications is beside the point. These stories are not told because they match the evidence; that's not their purpose. These stories are told so that students will identify with the United States as a national entity. In later years of schooling, the stories become more complex (perhaps only slightly) and less associated with famous individuals, but the emphasis on national origins and development remains. History and civics textbooks convey a clear and consistent national story that emphasizes the founding people, events, and documents of the nation; only wars compete with national origins as a source of content in textbooks. Non-Western countries and cultures, meanwhile, generally appear only if they are current or former enemies of the United States.[15] Throughout their school careers, students repeatedly study exploration and settlement, the American Revolution and the establishment of the Constitution, the Civil War and emancipation (and often, the Civil Rights movement); they only occasionally, if ever, study topics not related to their national past, such as ancient civilizations, the medieval world, African or Asian history, or modern Europe.

By learning stories about how the nation began and how it got to be where it is today, students are expected to associate themselves with the country as a whole—all the citizens of the United States can trace themselves, as members of a national polity, back to Columbus, the Pilgrims, Washington, Lincoln, and King. As Anderson puts it, "The son of an Italian immigrant to New York will find ancestors in the Pilgrim Fathers."[16] On the other hand, simply exposing students to these stories might not necessarily lead to identification; after all, a resident of the United States could study Chinese history for years without feeling personal connections with it, and a student from Germany could learn about U.S. history without feeling any kinship with Americans. However, students here also encounter methods of presentation that promote identification. In the early years, they may dress up as Pilgrims or reenact stories from the lives of Washington, Lincoln, King, and others, thus establishing a direct and physical link between themselves and these national heroes. References to George Washington as "the father of our country" or to Pilgrims and other early settlers as "our forefathers" represent another way of associating students with the past, although such terms seem dated and may be falling out of use.

In later grades, teachers promote identification through their use of first-person plural pronouns: They talk about the origin of *our* country, how *we* became independent from Britain, how immigrants came to *our* country, why *we* fought in the Second World War, and so on. To residents of the United States, this language seems obvious and natural, and we are apt to assume that teachers everywhere discuss their national past this way. Yet in fact, such language is not universal. In Britain, teachers would never say, "*We* entered the Second World War in 1940"; they would say, "*Britain* entered in 1940." Using words like *we* and *our* to discuss the national past would be considered unprofessional, because promoting identification is not a core purpose of the curriculum. In the United States, however, the use of such language is an ever-present feature of history education.[17]

And it works. Students in the United States, like their teachers, associate themselves with the people and events of the national past even when they do not approve of them. A colleague of ours who grades International Baccalaureate examinations in London tells us he can pick out papers written by U.S. students in the blink of an eye, because only they use the word *we* when writing about the past. Our own research with elementary and middle-school students corroborates this pattern. When they discuss national history, they constantly use first-person plural pronouns: They talk about how *our* country became independent, how the Civil War nearly split *us* apart, how *we* mistreated Native Americans. Just as important, however, their judgments of historical significance revolve around issues of national identity; when asked to evaluate the most important people, events, or trends in history, they emphasize precisely those they believe tell them "who we are" as a nation—namely, national origins and turning points. VanSledright found that students frequently referred to the need to understand national origins as the reason for studying U.S. history at school, and this theme has also been prevalent among the elementary and secondary students with whom we have worked.[18]

We first noticed the importance students attached to such events in the classroom study of fourth and fifth graders mentioned earlier. Toward the end of the school year, after students had studied a wide variety of topics, they were asked which they considered most important. Two topics stood out: the American Revolution and the evolving rights of African Americans. In both cases, students made explicit connections between themselves and the events they had studied. In discussing the Revolution, for example, one student explained, "If we didn't fight that or anything, then we would still be a part of England, and we wouldn't be called the United States of America, and we wouldn't actually be completely free." Another student suggested, "If they didn't fight, England would still be ruling us, and we'd have to do everything that they want us to do," and still another noted that the war "helped us get free from England, be ourselves over here in America, North America, and not over there." This last student went on to explain that "if it wasn't for that war, we wouldn't be free to make our own choices now, and let England rule us, and I think it was a big time, a big event in our history, because we wouldn't be here today, talking about our freedom if it wasn't for that."[19]

Several students justified the entire subject of history by pointing to the need to know about such national origins; when asked why history was important enough to study at school, for example, one girl suggested, "If we didn't know there was a Revolutionary War, then we'd be like, 'We were alive the whooooole time that the world was alive.'" Asked to clarify, she explained, "If we didn't have a Revolutionary War, and people didn't fight, then we would still belong to Britain.... We should know that we belong to ourselves, and *how* we belong to ourselves." This student, along with most of her classmates, was deeply attached to the importance of the American Revolution in establishing her country's political independence, and the use of words like *we*, *us*, and *our* was an inescapable feature of their explanations.[20]

In discussing issues related to African American history, particularly slavery and the Civil Rights movement, students emphasized the origins of contemporary social relations in the United States. One student, for example, said the most important event in history was "when we changed slavery," whereas another noted, "If Lincoln wasn't elected president or anything, then we would still have slaves and whip them and stuff." Another student thought knowing about the Civil Rights movement was important "because we don't want to treat black people like that today," whereas another pointed to the importance of "getting Martin Luther King to stop the prejudice and stuff—there are still some—but if he didn't, then everybody would like be prejudiced, and then like a species of humans would be extinct, a race."[21]

The importance of national identification also was clear when we investigated middle graders' views of historical significance. In that study, we interviewed 48 students from a variety of ethnic and economic backgrounds in Grades 5 through 8. Working in groups of three or four, they were presented with a set of 20 captioned pictures depicting events from the last 400 years of North American history and asked to select the 8 they considered most important. Because they had studied more history at school, many could draw on a greater range and depth of knowledge than those in the earlier study, but like their younger counterparts, they focused largely on the origin and development of the United States as a social and political entity. Several groups, for example, noted that pictures of Hernando de Soto or the First Thanksgiving represented the exploration and settlement of North America; as one student put it, the

Thanksgiving picture showed "the start of the United States, when we all became possible, because we all came from over there, and a bunch of immigrants came over here, and that's basically how we started our nation." Similarly, students who chose a picture of Ellis Island noted the role of immigration in shaping the nation's current population; one girl considered it important "because we're supposed to be a country made out of a melting pot.... And if we didn't have immigration, then we wouldn't have as many people in our country, and that's what makes our country different from other countries."[22]

These students also consistently selected the American Revolution as one of the most important events in history; every group placed it among their eight pictures, and they did so automatically, without debate or discussion. Their explanations were familiar ones, as they pointed to the war's importance in establishing the United States as a separate country. One student explained that it "kinda started our country," while another noted that without the Revolution, "we would have no country," and still another suggested, "we'd still be part of England." Students used these pronouns in talking about the country's origins regardless of their own ethnicity or the recentness of their families' immigration; African Americans—as well as Hispanic students and European immigrants in the United States for only a few years—described the nation's origins as their own. In their interviews with eighth and ninth graders, Carole Hahn and her colleagues found the same pattern: Students identified with the nation's past even when their direct ancestors were not part of the events they were discussing.[23]

This is not to say everyone in the United States identifies with the national past in the same way. Research with both adults and adolescents suggests that ethnicity plays an important role in shaping ideas about the nature and direction of the country's past, and we will address those differences in greater detail in chapter 9, when we discuss how students use narratives of progress to understand U.S. history. However, the available evidence suggests that schools are most likely to promote identification with the nation—rather than other groupings such as class, ethnicity, religion, or gender—and that their efforts are to large degree successful. This conclusion seems inconsistent with many educational debates over the past decade, during which critics assumed that multicultural approaches to history would encourage identification based on ethnicity rather than national citizenship and that the country would fragment (or had already fragmented) as a result. Based on our experiences, these alternative sources of identification are not often encouraged at school, and to the extent that students accept them, they do not necessarily preclude students' identification with the nation as a whole; even when teachers and students are critical of the U.S. past, this criticism refers to *our* history, understood as that of a shared nation.

Yet we recognize that some people do embrace other identities and that in many cases, these provide alternatives to identification with the United States as a political entity. Research with children and adolescents is far from comprehensive, and we still need much more insight into variations among students from diverse backgrounds. Although identification with the national past appears widespread, it seems unlikely to be found universally across all ethnicities and geographic regions. Native Americans, for example, often see themselves as existing outside of and apart from the U.S. national past, and African Americans frequently incorporate African heritage into their sense of self. Some White Southerners, meanwhile, may feel regionally distinct experiences are a more appropriate source of identity than dominant national stories, and members of certain religious groups may feel more connections with their counterparts in other countries than with Americans of other religions. We hope future research will provide a clearer picture of the development of these identities and their intersection with national ones.[24]

IDENTIFICATION OF THE PRESENT WITH THE NATIONAL PAST

In the first type of identification discussed in this chapter, individuals associate themselves with their personal past or that of their families; in the second, they connect themselves to a country's origins and the story of its development. A third type of identification is less personal and individual but grows out of the first two; it takes place when current public events are linked with the national past. Just as people affirm basic similarities between their lives today and in the past (extended in time through their families), they may connect the nature of their country today with its character in the past. The identification of personal present and past, that is, provides a model for one way of understanding the nation in historical context.

Social theorists have long characterized this as one of the most basic functions of history, whether in small-scale societies or complex civilizations. When past and present are connected in this way, history becomes a warrant or charter for present practice: Contemporary cultural patterns or social arrangements are justified because they were established by founding ancestors or because their practice dates back to dim antiquity. If past and present are the same, then the way things were long ago provides the most appropriate model for life today.[25] In the United States, one manifestation of this identification is the quest to uncover the beliefs and intentions of the country's "founding fathers." If the framers of the Constitution assumed that gun ownership was a fundamental right of individuals, then the Second Amendment must protect such ownership today; if, on the other hand, they thought in terms of collective military efforts, then more stringent controls are defensible. Similarly, if George Washington and other icons of U.S. history were devout Christians, government-sanctioned expressions of Christianity seem justified, whereas if they were deists and agnostics, separation of church and state may rest on firmer ground than Supreme Court decisions. Because the past is so widely accepted as a foundation for the present, issues like these have resulted in long-standing and acrimonious debates; they have even inspired some people to fabricate historical anecdotes, quotations, and other evidence, or to charge others with having done so.[26]

This use of history is usually a conservative one, because the past is most often portrayed as worthy of respect and admiration, and it therefore serves as sanction for the status quo. The "constitutive stories" described by Smith aim not only to root people in a shared history, that is, but to inspire a sense of worth by portraying the traits of their community as inherently valuable.[27] Under these circumstances, change can be justified only by making the argument that the old ways have been forgotten. The identification of past and present, however, can also be used by those with more radical perspectives. This occurs when the nation's past mistakes— slavery, imperialism, massacre of native people—are equated with its character today: In the past, the United States has sought to control other countries, therefore, it must be doing so today; in the past, the United States has sanctioned structural racism and inequality, therefore, it must be doing so today. Again, there is an equation of past and present, but rather than using the assumed legitimacy of past events and social arrangements to justify those in the present, the assumed illegitimacy of the past is used to criticize the nation's present.

Not surprisingly, research suggests the conservative function of identification predominates in both classroom teaching and students' thinking. Catherine Cornbleth's study of history classes at the elementary, middle, and secondary levels revealed an image of the United States as "imperfect but best": The country was portrayed as the best in the world despite past problems or current difficulties. Although prejudicial, selfish, or dishonorable acts in the past were acknowledged, teachers suggested these wrongs had been righted and were no longer a significant part of the nation's legacy; in addition, the United States was presented as a country that has historically won the respect and admiration of other countries through its "can-do" attitude and tradition of solving problems.[28]

This is similar to the perspective we found in our interviews with middle school students, who were much more likely to emphasize "best" than "imperfect." We have already noted that these students identified with the nation's founding events and documents, such as the American Revolution and the U.S. Constitution. Yet students saw these as more than the foundation for their own identity within a shared national community; they also thought of them as a basis for their country's unique moral superiority. Every group of students we interviewed, for example, chose the Bill of Rights as one of the most important items in U.S. history, and they pointed to its role in establishing what they perceived as uniquely American freedoms. One student explained that "unlike other countries we have freedom of speech, and other countries didn't have that kind of right, and the Bill of Rights is important because it reassures us that we have these rights and the law cannot take them away from us." Another noted that the Bill of Rights is important "to distinguish us from other countries, because we have more freedom than they do," and still another noted that it was "a big part of why everybody loved America … 'cause American's known around the world as the place for freedom." As one student succinctly put it, "America's known for its freedom and stuff, and I think that's part of what makes it good."[29]

These students also consistently chose items related to the extension of political rights, such as the Emancipation Proclamation, the Civil Rights movement, and women's suffrage. In each case, they explained their selections by noting the importance of extending rights and freedoms already enjoyed by other Americans. One student, for example, noted that the Emancipation Proclamation was "another step toward freedom," while another suggested that it "helped enforce" the Bill of Rights. Similarly, one student explained that "the Constitution says that all people are equal," and the Emancipation Proclamation "made it all true because before that they were slaves and didn't have privileges like White people do." Yet another student explained that suffrage was "kind of like" the Emancipation Proclamation for women, and still another suggested that the Civil Rights movement was important because it benefited "the last *major* group of people that hadn't gotten their rights." The progressive development and extension of rights and opportunities was the most frequently mentioned theme in students' responses regardless of their age, gender, or ethnic background. They clearly were aware that inequities and injustices had existed in the past—and still do, to some extent—but their emphasis on the expansion of rights and freedom revealed their concern with establishing that in the United States, such hardships and injustices invariably are corrected and overcome.[30]

Students' belief in their country's moral rectitude and superiority was especially evident when they discussed wars, particularly those in the 20th century. For some students, wars demonstrated the military might of the United States; one, for example, explained that the Second World War showed that "you don't mess with America," while another thought "it showed that American was a great world power." Other times, students interpreted wars in terms of their beneficial effects on people in other countries. As one put it, the United States goes to war to "help people … we were fighting for other people." One student suggested that the Second World War demonstrated that "we stand up for people," while another noted that during the war, "We were just basically helping other countries." Similarly, one student thought that the United States was fighting the Vietnam War "for the Vietnamese people," and another explained that the war "helped Vietnam be different. Well, it helped the north and south or something."[31] Although we did not ask about more recent military conflicts such as the Gulf War, students' attempts to make sense of Vietnam and World War II—events that they had not studied at school—indicates their attempt to assimilate the nation's recent past to their understanding of its enduring qualities: The United States is historically a strong nation that helps others.

Students used history to establish "who we are" not only by providing a community of identification, but by positioning that community as a uniquely powerful and morally superior one.

IDENTIFICATION, PARTICIPATION, AND PLURALISM

This chapter has focused on identification with the past, an action found both within and outside of schools, and arguably one of the most common of historical activities. However, although identification involves, by definition, some association of past and present, the historical connections that result from identification serve three distinct purposes in our society: They can be used to provide a sense of self extending throughout one's own life and back to relatives and ancestors, they can be used to create shared connections to the nation or other groups through stories of origins and development, and they can be used to link a nation's past and present to legitimize or criticize contemporary affairs. These three purposes overlap both conceptually and in practice, but they have very different implications for students' development as members of a pluralist, participatory democracy.

We noted that personal and familial identification, although critically important for many adults, does not seem to be a significant component of history for children and adolescents. A number of factors may explain this lack of salience: Students may be too young and inexperienced to see their personal pasts as important influences on their present circumstances, they likely have not felt the existential yearnings that lead adults to search for meaning beyond their own lives, and they may simply have never had the chance to study personal and family history in any systematic way, because these are not the most common activities in history classrooms. When given the opportunity to investigate their own pasts and those of their families, students find the experience interesting and rewarding, but their identification with such history wanes when they begin to study topics that are more national in scope.

As preparation for participatory democracy, this is as it should be. Identifying with an individual past, or the history of a family, is a perfectly appropriate and understandable activity, but its impact on public participation is limited. Although it may be personally gratifying to think of our present-day activities as part of a tradition that stretches throughout the lives of ourselves and our family, this kind of identification is ultimately too inward looking to contribute to common deliberation; it associates us only with people to whom we already feel close, and it excludes those with whom we need to connect as part of the public sphere. Indeed, Rosenzweig wonders whether these privatized versions of the past may actually reinforce, rather than break down, barriers between people.[32] Feeling proud and secure in one's family heritage is a laudable goal, but if identification never moves beyond the narrow confines of family, our society may become increasingly atomized, with few commitments among those who are not related to each other. Margaret Thatcher, in fact, once suggested that such a state of affairs had already arrived; she approvingly announced, "There is no such thing as society. There are individual men and women, and there are families."[33]

Yet of course there is such a thing as society, and a major purpose of schools is to help students develop the capacity to sustain their society in healthy and productive ways (and to engage in deliberation about what constitutes "healthy and productive"). This effort requires identification with larger social groups, particularly those that can mobilize to bring about social change or maintain current institutions. The common good that students will be working toward throughout their lives is one that extends beyond themselves and their families—thus the phrase *common good*, not *individual good* or *family good*. Moreover, students will be deliberating with people outside their own families, and they must feel some identification with them—at the very least, enough to regard them as part of the same community of discourse. If we encourage students to identify with their individual and family pasts, then we also need to go a step further and promote identification with groups larger and more diverse than their families.

Such identification has been a major preoccupation of history education in the United States. Students have been encouraged to identify with one particular social grouping—their country—and the suitability of this effort has been at the core of debates over education and multiculturalism throughout the past decade and more. Many people insist that promoting a single national identity serves to maintain the status and authority of those who already wield political and economic power in our society, and that such attempts invariably degrade the identities of the country's diverse cultural groups. Others maintain that the country cannot abide such diverse cultural identities and that the nation can be held together only if we share a single vision of what it means to be an American; embracing "hyphenated" identities, they maintain, weakens and ultimately disunites the nation.[34] We believe this dichotomy is too sharply drawn and that history education has an important role to play in resolving the tension between unity and diversity.

It seems evident to us that participation in a pluralist, participatory democracy requires a fundamental attachment to one's country. Nations enjoy a privileged position in today's world: They can compel actions of their residents and bestow rights and benefits on them that other groups cannot. A nation like the United States can demand that its residents pay taxes and obey the law (or suffer the consequences), and it can guarantee their freedom of speech and right to privacy. Religions, ethnicities, and voluntary associations can do none of these; to the extent that we follow the demands of non-state organizations, we do so voluntarily, and to the extent they provide us with privileges, they do so contingently. Our relationship with the state, on the other hand, is one of mutual responsibility: We cannot ignore the nation's demands nor can it disregard its obligations to us. Someday nations may cease to exist, replaced by larger political groupings, global capitalism, or postapocalyptic anarchy, but for today, they are an inescapable part of our public life.[35]

The legitimacy of the state's demands and benefits—at least in a democratic nation—rests on a shared sense of identity among its citizens. We accept taxation not just because we derive advantages from government services but because we know those advantages will be shared among people who are in some fundamental sense like us, because they are members of the same nation. We accept the results of elections even when we disagree with them, because we know the decisions were made by people like ourselves, people we believe have the same right to vote and direct the course of the nation that we do. By providing assistance to our fellow citizens and accepting their right to make decisions affecting our lives, we show a partiality that does not extend to those in other countries, and this partiality depends on the creation of a shared national identity.[36]

In chapter 2 we emphasized the importance of participation in a wide variety of non-state communities, but in most such groups, the role of identification is unproblematic. Identification with a religious denomination, a neighborhood association, or a political party, for example, typically precedes participation—we take part in these groups because we identify with them. However, except for immigrants, the fact of our participation in national life is determined by law and birth, not choice, and thus our sense of national identity must be created. Without it, we would be unlikely to accept the nation's sovereignty—and yet we would have no alternatives open to us, because nations are the only sovereign entities. National identity is necessary both for the state's continued legitimacy and for our own sense of political belonging.

In theory, national identity need not be couched in historical terms. Citizens of a given country might feel connected to each other because of their shared commitment to a set of political principles, economic institutions, or cultural practices; that is, they might be willing to work together as part of a system of mutual decision making and assistance, because they know other citizens subscribe to the same standards and assumptions about how their country should be run, even if these commitments have no history behind them. From this perspective, national identity could be grounded solely in contemporary concerns, and schools could focus on developing attachment to the here and now rather than the past. Indeed, citizens of a nation might even choose to work together for purely pragmatic reasons: They might affirm their community with others because they believe there are direct advantages—social, material, or spiritual—to be gained from shared participation. In this case, the nation would simply be an efficient institutional shell for the pursuit of individual, family, or other subnational benefits, and national identity would be an instrumental means for achieving those goals.[37]

In reality, there are no nations in which identification rests on concerns such as these. Although contemporary and pragmatic concerns may figure into national identity, by themselves they do not provide a stable or enduring basis for political participation. No matter how much we share the convictions of our fellow citizens, sometimes they will make decisions with which we disagree—decisions that may conflict with the convictions we thought we shared. No matter how much we think can be gained in the short run from participation in the nation's institutions, sometimes those institutions will fail us—the economy will founder, crime will increase, or social practices will take unexpected and unwelcome turns. If we were bound to our fellow citizens only by contemporary commitments, we would have little motivation to weather such storms; we might reject our shared identity and either pursue other remedies (survivalism, revolution, anarchy) or cease to participate in the nation's public sphere altogether.

Identity anchored in history provides a more durable commitment to our nation and our fellow citizens. "Achieving our country," as Richard Rorty puts it, is obviously not a short-term prospect but one requiring the sustained commitment of many people over a very long period.[38] When we see ourselves as part of a community extending through time, we gain a broader perspective on the present: We may believe our nation has serious problems today, but people like us—those with whom we share a national identity—have been at this for a very long time. For us to give up now would be shortsighted at best, a betrayal of our ancestors at worst. Among the U.S. students we have talked to, such identification involves an optimistic assessment of the nation's progress: They are confident we will overcome our problems just as we have in the past. However, identification with national history need not be so cheery; even if the past provides no guarantee of success, the very fact that so many of us have taken part in the nation's public life over the years can sustain our efforts in the present. Those dedicated to confronting racism, sexism, or social inequality, for example, can draw strength from the knowledge that many others have confronted these issues before, sometimes succeeding, sometimes failing. To give up on such causes in the event of setbacks today would be to disrespect and disregard our ancestors. Similarly, but from a different political perspective, failing to participate in military action today because of the fear of failure would be an insult to those who fought before. Regardless of our political inclinations, when our identity is grounded in the nation's history, we have incentives for shared action and public responsibility that would be lacking if we lived only in the present.

Yet we all know there is a dark side to national identity. Establishing who we are also means establishing who we aren't, and this process has had disastrous effects for most of the last two centuries. U.S. citizenship has long been tied to certain forms of exclusion—principally based on race and ethnicity but also related to gender and class. One of the most prevalent themes in U.S. history has been the attempt to exclude certain groups of people from the full benefits of citizenship—African Americans, Native Americans, the unpropertied, women, Chinese and Japanese immigrants, Southern and Eastern European immigrants, non-Christians, Christians of the wrong kind, labor activists, communists, homosexuals, and anyone else who failed to conform to the prevailing norms for national identity during a given time period. No wonder attempts to promote national identity in schools are viewed with suspicion as little more than thinly veiled attempts to legitimate racial, gender, and class privilege—that is just what they often have been. Nor is it any wonder that for many people, ethnicity provides a more appealing source of identification than the exclusionary tales so often told in school.

The predicament that besets history education, then, is this: The subject is uniquely privileged to provide the shared sense of national identity necessary for democratic participation, and yet the vision of identity offered in schools is, for many students, exclusionary and unappealing. We believe this dilemma can be resolved. If history is to promote identification with a nation whose public sphere is pluralist and participatory, then those are the principles that should form the basis for its constitutive stories: The earliest and most enduring historical themes students encounter at school should revolve around the varied peopling of what is now their country and the efforts at full participation by those diverse groups. At the same time, history educators should avoid promoting identification with stories that encourage exclusion. Students should learn about immigration from Asia, Latin America, and Europe (and not just during the Colonial Era); about slavery, emancipation, Jim Crow laws, and the Civil Rights movement; about Native Americans and their relationships with Europeans; and about the Bill of Rights, women's suffrage, the labor movement, and antiwar protests. Some of these topics would be more appropriate for primary children and some for older students, but themes of pluralism and participation should form the basis for the history curriculum from an early age. Stories of Columbus and Thanksgiving, George Washington and Betsy Ross, meanwhile, should take a back seat or be discarded altogether. Americans will never fully share a national identity so long as their earliest history lessons extol European conquest and praise slaveowners.

To some extent, the curriculum already encourages a pluralist and participatory conception of national identity: Primary students are likely to learn about Martin Luther King and Rosa Parks, and older ones about Native American cultures or immigration at the beginning of the 20th century. Also, as we have noted, students regard the progressive expansion of rights and opportunities as a central theme in U.S. history. Often times, however, these topics are included in such a way that their pluralist and participatory elements are muted. In studying immigration (or forced migration during slavery), for example, students rarely study the cultural backgrounds of people who came to North America; instead, immigrants are portrayed almost as though they were waiting to be transformed into "real" Americans. Native Americans, meanwhile, remain in the distant past, predecessors to White civilization but not its contemporaries, and violence against minorities, except during slavery, remains practically invisible. By and large, diversity exists in the school curriculum only when it doesn't really matter.

Similarly, extension of the right to public participation is hailed as the crowning glory of the nation, but only when such participation is consensual and nonthreatening. In studying the Civil Rights Movement, for example, students learn about individual efforts but not collective action, about Martin Luther King but not Malcolm X, and about the "old, tired" Rosa Parks, who was actually a young activist. Other forms of participation, such as labor activism and war protests, rarely make it into the classroom at all. Given the limited nature of the stories we currently tell about pluralism and participation, students are likely to develop narrow ideas about how these play out in public life. For such stories to become the foundation of our national identity, students will need to learn about them in much richer and more complex ways. Only then might the tension between national and other identities be resolved and diversity become the basis of our unity.

Before we close this discussion, we must address one other drawback to national identity—the tendency to regard one's own social group as inherently good, moral, and strong, and to believe the worst about other groups.[39] Even if the residents of a nation achieve a widely shared sense of identification among themselves, they might still be likely—perhaps more likely than ever—to exalt their own country's virtues and to view others with suspicion. Such comparative evaluations breed violence and warfare, and millions of people have died because their leaders could so easily manipulate nationalist sentiments. This aspect of nationalism derives, in part, from the third kind of identification discussed in this chapter—the tendency to equate past and present. If our national ancestors were so powerful or righteous that they deserve our adulation, and if past and present are the same, then we are justified in attributing such power and righteousness to ourselves today. If the United States was a uniquely good and moral society in the past, for example, then it must be so today, and our actions in the world are easily defended. As the students we interviewed suggested, the United States is the kind of country that goes to war to help people, not to hurt them.

After the September 11 attacks, this justification for studying history was all the rage among conservative commentators, who renewed their efforts to justify history teaching as a way of inspiring patriotism. By learning that the United States has always been the greatest nation on Earth, they argued, and by learning to worship the great patriots of our country's past, students would be more likely to understand and support the need to "defend ourselves." Lynne Cheney, for example, noted that children should know about American history "as we set out to defend America, 'assured of the rightness of our cause,' in our President's words, 'and confident of victories to come.'"[40] This connection between history and national chauvinism is not new, of course, nor is it unique to the United States. History is frequently used to inspire patriotic enthusiasm in general, and militarism in particular, and it has often been implicated in nationalist rivalries. After World War II, for example, the United Nations sponsored efforts to reduce the nationalism found in history textbooks in hopes the subject would be less likely to contribute to future military conflicts.[41]

The equation of national past and present is the least productive variation on the identification stance, and indeed, it destroys participation in democratic decision making because it robs us of the need—or ability—to judge our actions today. It's one thing to identify with the nation's past and to see ourselves as part of a story that extends through time; it's quite another to use that story to short-circuit judgments in the present. Neither domestic nor international policies can be justified—or rejected, for that matter—solely in terms of historical identification. The intentions of the Constitution's framers tell us nothing about whether we should adopt more stringent gun control laws, and the country's motivations in World War II tell us nothing about its military actions today. Similarly, if the nation's leaders were racist in the 19th century, it tells us nothing about our leaders today, and if the Spanish-American war amounted to imperialist aggression, it tells us nothing about the war in Iraq. To the extent that these historical events have implications for today, it is not because they allow us mythically to join past and present but because they serve as analogies that can alert us to possible causes and consequences of contemporary events, which can then be analyzed in the light of supporting evidence (a topic to be taken up in the next chapter).

As our interviews with students suggest, however, this mythic view of the past is a strong one, and it no doubt derives from a wide variety of influences, including family, community, and the media. History educators in school may have difficulty addressing such a commonly accepted use of the past, but for the sake of democracy, they must do so nonetheless. Rather than simply discounting (or ignoring) such mythic identifications, educators might treat them as open questions, suitable for investigation by students in the intermediate grades and beyond. Students could become engaged in sophisticated and motivating research if they were asked to marshal evidence for or against propositions such as, "The United States fights wars only in defense of freedom," "The Supreme Court has always supported the interests of the rich," or other beliefs chosen by students themselves. Such inquiry should, at the very least, add complexity and nuance to their understanding of the relationship between past and present by alerting them to the fact that few historical trends are absolute—and that any evaluation of those trends depends on the use of evidence, not on a priori assumptions about the moral rectitude or wickedness of the nation.

CONCLUSIONS

Identification is one of the most common historical activities. It connects people to the personal past as well as that of family and nation; it also promotes association between the national present and past. Although these diverse forms of identification all involve some connection between history and the contemporary world, they have very different implications for the development of citizenship in a pluralist, participatory democracy. Identification with personal and family history can be fulfilling and rewarding, but it is largely neutral with regard to public participation; if students are to take part in deliberation over the common good, they must move beyond such inward-looking identifications. Ultimately, identity contributes to democracy to the extent that it encourages people to feel a sense of community with larger social groups.

One of the most important such groups is the nation, and history education in the United States devotes a great deal of attention to developing national identity in young people. This effort begins from an early age, as children are encouraged to identify with events and individuals from "our" national past. These efforts are largely successful: For students from a wide variety of backgrounds, the national past provides a story of where "we" began as a nation and of how the nation has developed since then. However, many of the elements in this vision are exclusionary ones, as students are encouraged to identify with conquerors and slaveowners; even when diverse individuals are included in the story of the national past, they are assimilated into a narrow conception of what it means to be an American. As a result, many students will be forced either to deny competing elements of their identity (such as their ethnic background) or to turn their backs on national identity. We have suggested that this tension can be resolved, at least in part, by constructing national identity around historical examples of the key elements of our democracy—pluralism and participation—rather than the traditional pantheon of European founders.

The third type of identification—equation of the national past and present—has little role to play in democratic deliberation. In fact, it positively undercuts deliberation, because it seeks to justify present day actions (or sometimes, to denounce them) not by reasoned judgment but by appeal to the eternal verities of the past. In a democracy, though, there are no eternal verities, either positive or negative; we are part of a tradition that stretches back in time, and we are affected in important ways by that tradition, but history can neither condone nor condemn our actions today. To say that history tells us who we are is only true to the extent that it provides a way of thinking about where our community has been in the past. In considering the present and future of that community, history cannot tell us what to do. It can, however, nourish our ability to engage in analysis and moral judgment—the subjects of the next two chapters.

ENDNOTES

1. T. S. Eliot, "Choruses From 'The Rock,'" in *T.S. Eliot: The Complete Poems and Plays, 1909–1950* (New York: Harcourt, Brace, and World, 1971), 101, 103.

2. Lois A. Cuddy, *T. S. Eliot and the Poetics of Evolution: Sub-Versions of Classicism, Culture, and Progress* (Lewisburg, Pa.: Bucknell University Press, 2000), 218–236; Anthony Julius, *T. S. Eliot, Anti-Semitism and Literary Form* (New York: Cambridge University Press, 1995); Cynthia Ozick, "T. S. Eliot at 101," *New Yorker,* 20 November, 1989, 119–54; Christopher Ricks, *T. S. Eliot and Prejudice* (Berkeley, Ca.: University of California Press, 1994), 25–40.

3. Eric T. Olson, "Personal Identity," in *The Stanford Encyclopedia of Philosophy,* Fall 2002 ed., Ed. Edward N. Zalta, available from http://plato.stanford.edu/archives/fall2002/entries/identity-personal, accessed 17 April, 2003; Marcel Mauss, "A Category of the Human Mind: The Notion of Person; the Notion of Self," in *The Category of the Person: Anthropology, Philosophy, History,* Eds. Michael Carrithers, Steven Collins, and Steven Lukes (New York: Cambridge University Press, 1985), 1–25; Alfred I. Hallowell, "The Self and Its Behavioral Environment," in *Culture and Experience* (Philadelphia: University of Pennsylvania Press, 1955), 75–110. The concept of personal identity, however, is not necessarily a universal construct, and the use of the term *identity* in this way has been common only since about the 1950s; L. L. Langness and Gelya Frank, *Lives: An Anthropological Approach to Biography* (Novato, Calif.: Chandler and Sharp, 1981), 90, 101–05; Philip Gleason, "Identifying Identity: A Semantic History," *Journal of American History* 69 (March 1983), 910–31; Richard Handler, "Is 'Identity' a Useful Cross-cultural Concept?", in *Commemorations: The Politics of National Identity,* Ed. John R. Gillis (Princeton, N.J.: Princeton University Press, 1994), 27–40.

4. Roy Rosenzweig and David Thelen, *The Presence of the Past: Popular Uses of History in American Life* (New York: Columbia University Press, 1998), 22, 37–38, 93, 124, 127.

5. Gerda Lerner, *Why History Matters: Life and Thought* (New York: Oxford University Press, 1998), 201.

6. David Lowenthal, *Possessed by the Past: The Heritage Crusade and the Spoils of History* (New York: Cambridge University Press, 1998), 32–34; Rosenzweig and Thelen, *The Presence of the Past,* 22.

7. M. Gail Hickey, *Bringing History Home: Local and Family History Projects for Grades K–6* (Boston: Allyn & Bacon, 1998); Linda S. Levstik and Keith C. Barton, *Doing History: Investigating With Children and Elementary School* (Mahwah, N.J.: Lawrence Erlbaum Associates, Inc., 2001); Carole Chin, "The Berkeley Children's History Trunk," *Social Education* 50 (April/May 1986): 280–282; Stacy Schwartz, "My Family's Story: Discovering History at Home," *Social Studies and the Young Learner* 12 (January/February 2000): 6–9; Mary E. Haas and Wilson Wylie, "The Family History Coat of Arms," *Social Education* 50 (January 1986): 25–26; Joan Skonick, Nancy Dulberg, and Thea Maestre, *Through Other Eyes: Developing Empathy and Multicultural Perspectives in the Social Studies* (Toronto, Ontario, Canada: Pippin Publishing, 1999), 38–47.

8. Bruce A. VanSledright, "And Santayana Lives On: Students' Views on the Purposes for Studying American History," *Journal of Curriculum Studies* 29 (September/October 1997): 539–540.

9. Keith C. Barton, "Historical Understanding Among Elementary Children" (Ed.D. diss., University of Kentucky, Lexington, 1994), 99.

10. Barton, "Historical Understanding Among Elementary Children," 99, 102–07.

11. Benedict Anderson, *Imagined Communities* (New York: Verso, 1991), 6, 9–11; Anderson suggests that nationalism shares this concern with the past with religion. Rogers M. Smith, "Citizenship and the Politics of People-Building," *Citizenship Studies* 5 (February 2001): 79–80.

12. Eric Hobsbawn and Terence Ranger, Eds., *The Invention of Tradition* (Cambridge: Cambridge University Press, 1983); Elizabeth Crooke, *Politics, Archaeology and the Creation of a National Museum in Ireland: An Expression of National Life* (Dublin: Irish Academic Press, 2000); Joshua Searle-White, *The Psychology of Nationalism* (New York: Palgrave, 2001), 53–56; Ernest Gellner, *Nations and Nationalism* (Ithaca, N.Y.: Cornell University Press, 1983), 55–58.

13. Joyce Appleby, Lynn Hunt, and Margaret Jacob, *Telling the Truth About History* (New York: W. W. Norton, 1994), 91–125; Michael Kammen, *Mystic Chords of Memory: The Transformation of Tradition in American Culture* (New York: Vintage Books, 1993), 228–253 and passim; David D. Van Tassel, *Recording America's Past: An Interpretation of the Development of Historical Studies in America, 1607–1884* (Chicago: University of Chicago Press, 1960), 87–94 and passim.

14. Michael Frisch, *A Shared Authority: Essays on the Craft and Meaning of Oral and Public History* (Albany, N.Y.: State University of New York Press, 1990), 47.

15. Patricia G. Avery and Annette M. Simmons, "Civic Life as Conveyed in United States Civics and History Textbooks," *International Journal of Social Studies* 15 (Fall/Winter 2000/2001): 105–30.

16. Anderson, *Imagined Communities*, 145.

17. Further illustration and discussion of this pattern can be found in Linda S. Levstik, "Articulating the Silences: Teachers' and Adolescents' Conceptions of Historical Significance," in *Knowing, Teaching, and Learning History: National and International Perspectives*, Eds. Peter N. Stearns, Peter Seixas, and Sam Wineburg (New York: New York University Press, 2000), 284–305, and Catherine Cornbleth, "An American Curriculum?," *Teachers College Record* 99 (Summer 1998): 622–46.

18. VanSledright, "And Santayana Lives On," 538–39.

19. Barton, "Historical Understanding Among Elementary Children," 90–91.

20. Barton, "Historical Understanding Among Elementary Children," 90–92.

21. Barton, "Historical Understanding Among Elementary Children," 92, 103.

22. Keith C. Barton and Linda S. Levstik, "'It Wasn't a Good Part of History': National Identity and Ambiguity in Students' Explanations of Historical Significance," *Teachers College Record* 99 (Spring 1998): 483.

23. Carole L. Hahn, "Challenges to Civic Education in the United States," in *Civic Education Across Countries: Twenty-Four National Case Studies from the IEA Civic Education Project*, Eds. Judith Torney-Purta, John Schwille, and Jo-Ann Amadeo (Amsterdam: International Association for the Evaluation of Educational Achievement, 1999), 597; Barton and Levstik, "'It Wasn't a Good Part of History,'" 484–85; the middle grade students we studied also pointed to the impor-

tance of events in African American history, as well as other episodes in U.S. history, and these explanations will be discussed in more detail in the next section and in chapter 9.

24. Some of these alternative identifications are evident in the interviews reported in Rosenzweig and Thelen, *Presence of the Past*, 18, 120–123, 128–129, 147–176. Interestingly, Rosenzweig and Thelen found that national history was rarely emphasized by White Americans, who focused instead on individual and family history; only when asked what they thought children should learn about history did they turn to more national and public events. They suggest this lack of attention may be due to the fact that "the conventional narrative of national history is so much a part of American consciousness that most people don't comment on it unless it is threatened or questioned—as it was when we asked about what children should learn." The pervasiveness of identification with the national past in our interviews with children and teachers lends support to this interpretation.

25. John Bodnar, *Remaking America: Public Memory, Commemoration, and Patriotism in the Twentieth Century* (Princeton, N.J.: Princeton University Press, 1994), 13–20; Mary Douglas, *How Institutions Think* (Syracuse, N.Y.: Syracuse University Press, 1986), 69–80; Bronislaw Malinowski, "Myth in Primitive Psychology," in *Magic, Science, Religion and Other Essays* (New York: Doubleday, 1955), 93–148; E. E. Evans-Pritchard, *The Nuer* (London: Oxford University Press, 1940), 104–108, 234; Edward Shils, "Tradition," *Comparative Studies in Society and History* 13 (April 1971): 122–159; Raymond Williams, *Marxism and Literature* (New York: Oxford University Press), 115–120.

26. For works including quotations that suggest George Washington, James Madison, Thomas Jefferson, and others were devout Christians who intended to found the nation on Christian principles, see David Barton, *The Myth of Separation: What is the Correct Relationship Between Church and State? A Revealing Look at What the Founders and Early Courts Really Said*, 3rd. ed. (Aledo, Tex.: WallBuilder Press, 1992), and John Eidsmoe, *Christianity and the Constitution: The Faith of Our Founding Fathers* (Grand Rapids, Mich.: Baker Book House, 1987); for contrasting quotes as well as arguments that Barton and Eidmoe rely on fabricated sources, see Rob Boston, *Why the Religious Right is Wrong About Separation of Church and State* (Buffalo, N.Y. : Prometheus Books, 1993), "Words of Our American Founding Fathers: Refuting the Notion that the U.S. was Founded on Christianity," available from http://www.stephenjaygould.org/ctrl/quotes_founders.html, accessed 9 April, 2003; Gene Garman, "Essays in Addition to *America's Real Religion*," available from http://www.stephenjaygould.org/ctrl/garman_arr.html, accessed 9 April, 2003. On the controversy surrounding Michael A. Bellesiles' *Arming America: The Origins of a National Gun Culture* (New York: Knopf, 2000), see Danny Postel, "Did the Shootouts over 'Arming America' Divert Attention From the Real Issues?," *Chronicle of Higher Education*, 1 February 2002, sec. A, p. 12, and the collection of essays in *Williams and Mary Quarterly* 59 (January 2002).

27. Smith, "Politics of People-Building," 81.

28. Cornbleth, "An American Curriculum?," 628–632.

29. Barton and Levstik, "'It Wasn't a Good Part of History,'" 484–85.

30. Barton and Levstik, "'It Wasn't a Good Part of History,'" 485–87.

31. Barton and Levstik, "'It Wasn't a Good Part of History,'" 489–90, 496–99.

32. Rosenzweig and Thelen, *The Presence of the Past*, 186–87.

33. Cited in Oliver Letwin, "For Labour There is No Such Thing as Society, Only the State," in *There is Such a Thing as Society: Twelve Principles of Compassionate Conservatism*, Ed. Gary Streeter (London: Politico's Publishing), 39.

34. For a succinct discussion of these debates, see Walter Feinberg, *Common Schools/Uncommon Identities: National Unity and Cultural Difference* (New Haven, Conn.: Yale University Press, 1998), 1–30.

35. Richard Rorty, *Achieving Our Country: Leftist Thought in Twentieth Century America* (Cambridge, Mass.: Harvard University Press, 1998), 98; Smith, "Politics of People-Building," 74–80; Walter C. Parker, *Teaching Democracy: Unity and Diversity in Public Life* (New York: Teachers College Press, 2003), 26. Because we are primarily concerned with the United States and other long-standing political entities, we use the words *nation, state,* and *country* interchangeably. In some parts of the world, on the other hand, a group of people may consider themselves a nation but be subsumed in one or more states (e.g., Kurds or Chechnyans); in other cases, a nation may have its "own" state but aspire to control portions of other states that it considers rightfully part of the same nation (as in the attempt to establish a "greater Serbia").

36. Feinberg, *Common Schools/Uncommon Identities*, 31–58.

37. Rogers M. Smith develops a similar argument in *Stories of Peoplehood: The Politics and Morals of Political Membership* (New York: Cambridge University Press, 2003), 72–125.

38. Rorty, *Achieving Our Country*, 51.

39. A large body of research, derived from social identity theory, has investigated how people categorize themselves and others as members of groups; see Henri Tajfel and John C. Turner, "An Integrative Theory of Intergroup Conflict," in *The Social Psychology of Intergroup Relations*, Eds. William G. Austin and Stephen Worche (Monterey, Calif.: Brooks/Cole, 1979), 33–47; Dominic Abrams and Michael A. Hogg, Eds., *Social Identity Theory: Constructive and Critical Advances* (New York: Springer-Verlag, 1990); and on social identity theory and nationalism, Searle-White, *The Psychology of Nationalism*, 12–24.

40. Lynne V. Cheney, "Teaching Our Children About America" (speech to the Dallas Institute of Humanities and Culture, 5 October, 2001), available from http://www.whitehouse.gov/mrscheney/news/20011005.html, accessed 9 April, 2003; see also Diane Ravitch, "Now Is the Time to Teach Democracy," *Education Week*, 17 October, 2001, 48; Chester Finn, "Patriotism Revisited," October 2001, available from http://edreform.com/mom/patriotism.html, accessed 9 April, 2003; and William J. Bennett, *Why We Fight: Moral Clarity and the War on Terrorism* (New York: Doubleday, 2002).

41. Joseph A. Lauwerys, *History Textbooks and International Understanding* (Paris: UNESCO, 1953); UNESCO, *Better History Textbooks: UNESCO and Its Program VI* (Paris: n.p., 1951).; UNESCO, *The Brussels Seminar: Findings and Studies* (Paris: n.p., 1951). On the role of history teaching in developing support for French militarism between the world wars, see Mona Siegel, "Lasting Lessons: War, Peace, and Patriotism in French Primary Schools, 1914–1939" (Ph.D. diss., University of Wisconsin, Madison, 1996).

The Analytic Stance

- *Third-grade children cut out pictures of old cars, trucks, ships, and other forms of movement and arrange them on a visual timeline illustrating the development of transportation.*
- *Fifth graders meet in small groups to read and analyze primary and secondary source material about the "starving time" at Jamestown Colony. They develop arguments in response to the question, "Why did the inhabitants of Jamestown starve if they had enough food to last the winter of 1609–1610?"[1]*
- *After a series of disturbances in Cincinnati, students in local high school history classes study other instances of racially motivated riots—Wilmington in 1898, Tulsa in 1921, Los Angeles in 1943, 1965, and 1992—and develop presentations with their recommendations for preventing such clashes in the future.*

Although the preceding examples include a variety of topics and approaches, they share a common activity—analysis. In Benjamin Bloom's venerable definition, *analysis* involves breaking material down into its constituent parts, detecting the connections and interactions of those parts, and identifying the arrangement or organizational structure that holds them together. In history, such analysis involves searching for connections among disparate events to identify some developmental trend, causal pattern, or argumentative structure—the causes and consequences of race riots, how cars and trucks have changed over time, or how evidence can be used to produce accounts of the Jamestown colony.[2] Analysis predominates when we focus on the common characteristics of particular time periods (the Cold War or the Colonial Era), patterns of historical change (the development of modern medicine or the waning of the Middle Ages), or the causes and consequences of historical events (What caused the American Revolution?, What went on during the Cuban Missile Crisis?). Analysis is also prominent when working with evidence to construct historical explanations or accounts. In each case, history consists primarily of the use of analysis to identify the connections, relationships, and structures that tie together individual events or pieces of evidence.

Analysis is the activity most often promoted, defended, and justified by historians and other educators. We must admit we have a particular fondness for it ourselves. With few exceptions, when scholars seek to differentiate the "use" of history from its "abuse," or meaningful study from misguided, their ideal is some form of the analytic stance. Its emphasis on the logical, rational elements in historical study makes it particularly appealing to those of us who earn our living from scholarship, and its focus on higher cognitive activities—such as examining the causes and consequences of historical events—seems attractive as an apparently hard-nosed alternative to the more emotive history sometimes emphasized in other stances. The analytic stance is at the center of nearly every proposal for reform of the curriculum (including most of our own previous work) and has always been the standard for the best "academic" history education in the United States and elsewhere.

Yet the widespread appeal of historical analysis can lead us to miss some important distinctions. There is no single way of studying history analytically, and educators who agree that students should look for causal relationships or use evidence to construct arguments may disagree on other matters of fundamental importance. As with each of the stances, analysis can serve more than one purpose, and these differing purposes have significant implications for the selection of content. In addition, history taught in accordance with any of these purposes may contribute to or detract from education for a pluralist democracy—depending on the nature of students' learning opportunities and on how teachers represent content. In this chapter, we attempt to pull apart these differing purposes and to suggest how they might best contribute to the kinds of humanistic education we have identified as the ultimate goal of learning history.

THE HISTORY OF THE PRESENT

One of the most recognizable reasons for studying history is to understand how present-day society came to be. In this view, the need to understand the contemporary world—its politics, economics, culture, and so on—is taken for granted, and history is seen as an indispensable means for developing that understanding. Proponents of this perspective hold that we can only understand the institutions, attitudes, or cultural patterns we live with today by tracing their origins and developments in the past. Indeed, this is sometimes taken to be the unique contribution of history, the single characteristic that separates it from sociology, economics, or other social sciences: Instead of analyzing social patterns at a single moment, history traces the development of those patterns over time, as a way of explaining how they came to be.

From this perspective, if we want to understand contemporary gender roles, it is not enough to know about patterns of work or civic participation today. We also need to know about women's roles in domestic labor in the

19th and 20th centuries, the post-World War II emphasis on norms of femininity, the feminist movements of the early and late 1900s, and many other historical topics. This background is necessary to understand how current roles for women came into existence. Similarly, if we want to understand the present-day conflict in Northern Ireland or Maori land claims in New Zealand, we will gain only a superficial understanding from following the news or examining the latest statistics. To more fully comprehend the situation in Northern Ireland, we need to know about the Plantation of Ulster in the 16th century, the Act of Union and the move for Home Rule in the 19th, and the Easter Rising, Partition, Bloody Sunday, and Enniskillen Bombing in the 20th. In the case of New Zealand, we need information on early patterns of contact between Europeans and Maori, the Treaty of Waitangi, and subsequent land appropriations. The origins of the present always lie in the past, and those roots cannot be ignored.

This perspective on historical analysis is firmly rooted in academic scholarship, even if not all historians would subscribe to it unconditionally. Leibniz noted in the 17th century that one of the benefits of historical study is the recognition of "the origins of things present which are to be found in things past; for a reality is never better understood than through its causes." Scholars throughout the 20th century returned to such observations as the basic justification for their profession. Frederick Jackson Turner, for example, maintained that the aim of history "is to know the elements of the present by understanding what came into the present from the past." For Turner, studying the past without connecting it to the present was antiquarianism, not history: "The goal of the antiquarian is the dead past; the goal of the historian is the living present." Similarly, John Dewey argued that history is significant only when it helps explain the present and that "the way to get insight into any complex product is to trace the process of its making—to follow it through the successive stages of its growth." More recently, British historian G. Kitson Clark observed that only a "very stupid" person would fail to realize that current affairs cannot be understood without knowledge of the events leading up to them.[3]

As Carl Becker noted, if the purpose of history is to illuminate the present, the most important topics are those related to contemporary issues—regardless of how significant they may have seemed in their day. Much of the work of historians is guided by precisely this perspective, even if they do not always acknowledge or articulate such a position. Peter Novick's *The Holocaust in American Life*, for example, takes an issue of clear contemporary importance—the role of the Holocaust as a source of Jewish identity and its position in current political and academic debates—and shows how the form and substance of such discussions have developed since the end of the Second World War. Similarly, David W. Blight's *Race and Reunion: The Civil War in American Memory* examines how popular perceptions of the Civil War were shaped in the 50 years after 1865. Although Blight's history ends in the early 20th century, it derives its importance precisely from the role of these perceptions in framing enduring national debates. If Blight had chosen to write about perceptions of the War of 1812 or some other event with little connection to contemporary issues, his work would merely constitute, in the view of someone like Turner, "antiquarianism." (Indeed, historians who investigate seemingly obscure events in history often justify their work by establishing that these events actually have had an impact on the present, even though this impact has been overlooked previously.) To take a less weighty example, Stephen Nissenbaum's *The Battle for Christmas* describes how developments in the late 18th and early 19th centuries shaped our modern celebration of the holiday. Like Blight, Nissenbaum ends his narrative long before the present, and he has little to say about modern culture directly. However, if he had chosen a holiday less important to contemporary society—Arbor Day, for example—his book would have stimulated much less interest.[4]

Implicitly or explicitly, historical works like these seek to explain elements of the present by exploring their origins and development in the past. This approach has had an important influence on school history in the United States. It is no accident that students repeatedly encounter the national past during their school careers or that they study world history much less often. This focus on national history results not only from the need to create a community of identification, as we discussed in chapter 3, but also from the assumption that the nature and functioning of U.S. society today can best be understood by tracing its origins. Students are unlikely to encounter the kinds of scholarship found in works like those by Novick, Blight, or Nissenbaum, but they do study the origin and development of many characteristics of the contemporary United States, particularly its legal, constitutional, economic, and demographic features. The eras of the American Revolution, the ratification of the Constitution, and the Early Republic figure so prominently in school history both because they serve as our own "origin myth" and because developments in these periods are assumed to be crucial to understanding the current political structure of the United States. Gordon Craig nicely combines these purposes when he notes, "We need to provide ourselves and our students with an account of the American past that describes where we came from and how we developed our national identity and particularity, our form of government, and our characteristic institutions."[5] Like many proponents of increased attention to history in schools, Craig argues that understanding American society today means understanding its historical development.

Many students come away from the study of history with precisely this message. When Bruce VanSledright asked elementary, middle, and high school students why they thought American history was taught in schools, many of their responses reflected Craig's conception of the subject's purpose. One fifth grader, for example, said it was important "so you'll know about how the country came to be and how you got to where you were. It's important to know how you got where you are because that's the country you live in and you want to know a lot about the country you live in." Similarly, an eighth grader remarked that history is important "so you can learn about the past and how the United States was discovered. If you live in a certain place, how it was discovered, how everything started, what special events happened." Another eighth grader put it succinctly: "So we can know what led up to us being here now." High school students in VanSledright's study also provided explanations based on the need to understand the present, such as "so we learn about our roots, kind of like where we came from and how we came to be," "how things got started ... how my ancestors [got here] and just how the country got started," and "how your government came to pass."[6]

We found a similar pattern in our own work, when we asked fourth and fifth graders why history was important. One particularly articulate student noted that whenever he began watching a hockey game on television, he had to go to bed before it was over, and so the next morning, he was always curious to find out who won. However, his curiosity about history was different:

> It's just the opposite of watching a hockey game, because you couldn't see the whole thing, but you see how it ended; you want to know how it got started and stuff. It's just like seeing half of everything, I mean, you just want to get that other half, and when you find that other half, it answers millions of questions that changed the world.

This student recognized that he already knew the "end of the game," the state of the world today, and that he still needed to find out how it got that way. Few of the students in these interviews were able to express their ideas about history so abstractly (or with such unique imagery), but many of them explained the importance of knowing how the present-day world came about.[7]

This approach to history has enormous potential for contributing to a pluralist, participatory democracy. If we hope to prepare students to engage in thoughtful discussion of public issues, then we must help them understand how the decisions of the past led to current patterns, structures, or situations. Without knowing what produced an issue under discussion, students would be doing little more than debating in the dark. And indeed, this kind of relevance has often been cited as a chief justification for studying the past. David Hackett Fisher, for example, argues that we cannot intelligently comprehend any major problem facing the world today without "an extended sense of how it has developed through time." This is clearly a prerequisite to meaningful discussions of current policy issues. As British historian Arthur Marwick notes, "If there is to be any possibility of changing 'the way things have always been done' there must be reasoned appraisal of how and why they came to be done in this way." Those historians most closely associated with the use of the past to solve practical problems—"progressive" historians such as James Harvey Robinson, Charles Beard, and Carl Becker—argued that the utility of history lay in its potential for illuminating aspects of the present.[8]

Perhaps the most influential example of this kind of history is C. Vann Woodward's *The Strange Career of Jim Crow*. Appearing in 1954, at a time of resistance to the system of legal segregation then in place throughout the South, *Strange Career* challenged the widespread Southern belief that Jim Crow laws and other forms of segregation were of such remote origin and so deeply ingrained in Southern culture that resistance was doomed to failure. Many Southerners assumed that segregation was "the way things had always been"—it was simply part of Southern life, and little could be done to change it. Woodward argued, to the contrary, that the "rigid and universal" form segregation had taken by 1954 actually appeared around the end of the 19th century and had been preceded by experimentation and variety in race relations. He maintained that it was only in the 1890s, as a political response to economic decline, that legal segregation crystallized into the form that continued into the 1950s. He intended his work to contribute to policy debates concerning desegregation; he noted later that "since the historian lives in the present he has obligations to the present as well as to the past he studies," and this obligation involves "exposing myth and overcoming cultural amnesia." Woodward's challenge to received beliefs about segregation were so influential that Martin Luther King, Jr., was quoted as calling his work "the historical Bible of the civil rights movement." It is important to note, though, that although Woodward was personally committed to desegregation, his purpose was not to provide support for a given policy position, but to provide a more accurate historical background against which policy debates could take place.[9]

In the years since the initial publication of *The Strange Career of Jim Crow*, other historians have produced evidence contradicting many of Woodward's conclusions, but as John Hope Franklin has noted, these findings have done little to damage the overall thesis. Their limited impact may reflect the differing purposes other historians have brought to their work. Many have had little interest in providing a context for discussion of policy issues; Woodward, with his goal of trying to understand the development of patterns of segregation, simply incorporated most of this conflicting research into each new revision of his work. One historian whose conclusions are most at odds with those of Woodward nonetheless shares his view of history's purpose. Joel Williamson, who argues that development of segregation had more to do with attitudes than legal restrictions and thus might prove resistant to legal change, has—like Woodward—sought to uncover the historical origins of modern practices. His work aims to show when and how racial attitudes hardened into the forms that we still live with today. Writing of the goals of historical research, he notes, "We are, of course, not responsible for what our ancestors did, but they are responsible for us and much of what we do."[10]

Williamson's quote also points to an important limitation of this approach to history. Recognizing that our ancestors are responsible for what we do may lead to the belief that they determine what we do—that is, the past happened the way it had to happen, and there were no alternatives open to our ancestors or ourselves. If history is thought of as a series of unavoidable events that leads inexorably to the present, then we are left with no room to maneuver. The present is simply the inevitable outcome of all that went before, and any attempt to bring about change in politics, economics, or society is doomed to failure. Indeed, history is sometimes used for precisely this purpose—to justify the status quo by convincing people that the way things are is the way they must be. As David Landes and Charles Tilly put it, "History has been misused as a stick to beat reformers and to block change."[11] This, of course, is antithetical to participatory democracy. Understanding how the past led to the present is useful as a basis for contemporary decision making only when it acknowledges the free will both of people in the past and of ourselves. Our ancestors made decisions in their own time that led to governmental institutions, economic structures, or social patterns that we live with today, but they could have made other decisions with other consequences.[12] Also, if people in the past made choices that affected their future (and our present), then we too are free to make decisions that support, modify, or overturn these historical legacies.

LEARNING LESSONS FROM THE PAST

Historical analysis can assume contemporary relevance in another way: by providing lessons for the present. This is perhaps the most commonly asserted rationale for studying history and the most commonly derided. Both children and adults say they expect history to provide them with lessons that can guide their actions today, and they often point to this as the basic reason for studying the subject. However, many historians are eager to assert—often with palpable condescension—that there are no lessons in history and that attempting to find any is a fruitless and misguided endeavor, contrary to the subject's true purpose. Henry Steele Commager, for example, argues that history "will not solve problems; it will not guarantee us against the errors of the past; it will not show nations how to avoid wars, or how to win them; it will not provide scientific explanations of depressions or keys to prosperity; it will not contribute in any overt way to progress."[13] Given this list of what history cannot do, many people are likely to view history (or historians) with a justifiable condescension of their own and to move on to subjects aiming at some contemporary applications—such as the natural and social sciences. The disparity between popular perception and professional pronouncement suggests this is a topic in need of more careful examination, as well as consideration of the varying conceptions people may attach to what it means to learn lessons from the past.

The term *lessons of history* is a popular one. An internet search for the phrase yielded over 47,000 hits, and the expression is bandied about regularly in the media. However, this seemingly simple construction covers a range of potential meanings. For some people, the lessons of history derive from the kind of identification we discussed in the last chapter: Studying history not only tells us what happened in the past, it teaches us what we must do today. Because the United States supported Britain in World War II, for example, Britain should support the United States in the Mideast today. The analytic version of this approach, though, focuses more on the attempt to produce empirical generalizations—regular and predictable patterns of historical change and human behavior that provide the basis for predicting what will happen in the future. In the 19th and early 20th centuries, this often involved identifying "stages" of social evolution through which all societies were assumed to progress. A later approach sought more limited generalizations of the "If x, then y" variety, and this perspective was the subject of considerable academic debate during the middle decades of the 20th century, although it inspires much less interest today.[14]

The chief objection leveled against the search for generalizations is that in human history (unlike in the natural sciences), no two situations are ever identical or even close to it—and hence, the "independent variable" under study will never be the only factor influencing the outcome of events. Each historical situation is unique, and thus, no general laws can ever be induced from them; as Peter Geyl puts it, history yields no practical lessons because of the "inexhaustible novelty of circumstances and combination of causes."[15] When historians reject the possibility of learning lessons from history, they often are objecting to the quest for universal generalizations. However, we have come across little or no evidence that this perspective has had a significant impact on history education in the United States, or that students see it as part of history's purpose.

Less rigid ways of thinking about history's lessons are more popular both in academia and in precollegiate education. Such approaches also look for generalizations, but in less mechanistic terms. Those working from this perspective recognize that historical situations are so widely varied that hard-and-fast rules are unlikely ever to emerge, but they nonetheless maintain that there are some regularities (however limited and conditional) that are worth noting, and that can provide insight into the possible consequences of contemporary actions. Just as we use our own personal experiences to help guide our individual actions, we can look to the past for some suggestions as to the likely consequences of actions at the societal level. Gustaaf Renier, for example, argues that history is useful for practical problem solving because of the resemblance of past situations to those in the present and that "the narrative of past experiences ... is for societies what memory is for their individual members." However, just as our own personal experiences can never directly predict what will happen as a result of the actions we undertake today, so history is never perfectly predictive. It simply suggests some likely consequences of contemporary decisions or perhaps some possible outcomes. As Peter Lee puts it, history opens up "new possibilities for action, by changing a chaos of practical pasts into rational history, and, through vicarious experience, giving us some purchase, however slight, on the future—not so much by predicting what it will be like as by preventing it from ambushing us."[16] Those who accept this perspective on history's purpose often avoid the phrase *lessons of history*, perhaps because of its negative connotations among historians or because they don't want to give the mistaken impression that they think universal laws are possible. Nonetheless, one of the most common ways of justifying the study of history is by suggesting the past can provide vicarious experience, however limited, as a basis for decision making in the present.[17]

Howard Zinn, a historian closely associated with the use of the past to shed light on contemporary politics, provides some examples of what such limited generalizations might look like. History, he claims, "can expose the pretensions of governments to either neutrality or beneficence"; "can expose the ideology that pervades our culture" by "recalling the rhetoric of the past, and measuring it against the actual past"; "can show how good social movements can go wrong, how leaders can betray their followers, how rebels can become bureaucrats, how ideals can become frozen and reified."[18] The limitations of such observations are evident in Zinn's repeated use of the word *can*. Few people would suggest that when the U.S. government claims its military interventions are in the best interests of democracy at home and abroad, it is always and invariably masking support for brutal dictatorships and global capitalism. Yet knowing about a string of such occurrences in history makes us more likely to suspect that the government's actions in each new situation might reflect such interests. Although this is a weak form of generalization, it could sometimes protect us, as Lee puts it, from being "ambushed" by the world around us.

A similar perspective on the lessons of history is expressed in terms of analogies rather than generalizations. Here, the basis for decision making is not a general pattern abstracted from many discrete cases but the particular circumstances of specific events that are taken to be highly similar to the present situation. The underlying premise is the same—that past experience can point to possible or likely consequences of current events—but only one or a small number of events are used as the reference point. One such analogy that periodically impinges on national consciousness is Chamberlain's appeasement of Hitler at Munich. When Iraq invaded Kuwait in 1990, public discussion of potential responses often returned to Munich as an example of what happens if a dictator, bent on expansion, is not stopped at the earliest opportunity. Similarly, many people thought of U.S. involvement in Kuwait (and later, the Balkans) as analogous to Vietnam: Because the situations were similar (entailing unclear military goals played out on unfamiliar terrain), one might expect the results to be the same.[19]

Yet although historians are sometimes willing to endorse at least the weaker versions of this quest for historical generalization and analogy, it is important to recognize that this is often disavowed as the aim of historical research itself. As Lee notes, historical generalizations "are valid and useful, so long as it is realized that they are not distillations of, or formal 'results' of, historical research."[20] From this perspective, discussion of historical generalizations and analogies generally takes place outside the professional discipline of academic history, in classrooms, among policymakers, or in the media, and professional historians do not undertake their investigations with the explicit purpose of developing generalizations or analogies that will provide predictions related to current policy making. Historians do not set out to discover the lessons of history, and few would end their research with a set of recommendations. This is perhaps why historians so often disavow this approach to historical study or even deny that history has any use whatsoever—because it is not what they do with history.

However, the assertion that historical research does not or cannot directly lead to such generalizations is not entirely convincing. Historical scholarship often does attempt to establish generalizations that provide lessons for present-day public policy. *The Road to Poverty: The Making of Wealth and Hardship in Appalachia*, by Dwight Billings and Kathleen Blee, for example, examines how capitalist markets, state coercion, and cultural strategies have interacted over the past two centuries to produce distinct forms of poverty in a rural community in Central Appalachia. Part of the study's purpose is to move beyond perspectives on Appalachian poverty that focus only on external economic forces or the supposedly deficient culture of mountaineers. Billings and Blee provide a more complex view of the region's history by addressing the impact of local politics, culture, and capitalism on economic development there. However, the authors make it clear that they are not simply attempting "to get the 'story' of Central Appalachia 'right.'" Their aim, rather, is to contribute to policy discussions of the alleviation of chronic rural poverty by identifying lessons (their word) in the historical experiences of the communities they studied. One such lesson, for example, is that patterns of reciprocity among kin and neighbors have enabled rural Appalachians to survive during times of scarcity, transition, or political and economic struggle. They note, "The public policy implication is clear. Cultural strategies that sustain social capital in impoverished communities should be strengthened, not weakened." Other lessons revolve around the limits of market-driven economic development, the role of local elites in mobilizing clients in support of narrow factional interests, and the subordination of economic development to political concerns. In each case, Billings and Blee identify the economic strategies that have and have not been effective in reducing poverty over the past two centuries, and thereby reach conclusions about what is likely to be effective in the future.[21]

Billings and Blee are hardly unique in their use of history to guide recommendations for social action in the present. Any number of scholars have developed careful, thoughtful, and evidence-based historical generalizations or analogies relevant to contemporary society. Robert Putnam, for example, in *Bowling Alone: The Collapse and Revival of American Community*, suggests that the Progressive Era can serve as a model for revitalizing civic engagement in modern America. In a chapter titled "Lessons of History: The Gilded Age and the Progressive Era," Putnam documents the similarities of those times and our own; he then describes how 19th-century fraternal and cultural groups, originally geared toward the private concerns of their members, "gradually turned their attention to community issues and eventually to political reform." One of the lessons to be learned from this, according to Putnam, is that the creation of private social networks "was not an alternative to, but a prerequisite for, political mobilization and reform"—and presumably might be in our day as well. Putnam is also careful to note the less positive lessons of the Progressive Era: how control by elite "experts" demobilized public participation, how social reform served as a mask for social control, and how an emphasis on community led to racial segregation and social exclusion. In this view, historical experiences—whether positive or negative—can serve as lessons for how we might increase civic involvement during a time of social, economic, and technological change.[22]

This kind of scholarship stands in direct contrast to the assertion that historical research does not directly lead to generalizations. Historians might object that these researchers, however, are not historians: Billings and Blee are sociologists, and Putnam is a political scientist. Indeed, we have no doubt that social scientists are more likely to look for lessons in the past than are scholars who have academic appointments in history departments. However, that doesn't mean that the work of such scholars is not historical: *The Road to Poverty* is built on systematic analysis of primary source evidence, and the conclusions in *Bowling Alone* represent a carefully documented synthesis of other historians' scholarship. These clearly are works of history, and the suggestion that looking for lessons in the past is either the product of a deluded mind or a misleading popularization of "real" history is simply incorrect. Identifying historical lessons is not only part of society's commonsense understanding of what history is about, but also a respected component of academic scholarship.

Also, there is no question history actually is used as a source of lessons, regardless of the protestations of some historians. Arthur M. Schlesinger, Jr., has pointed out that all public policy decisions are essentially historical, because they always imply "a guess about the future derived from the experience of the past"; such decisions imply "an expectation, or at the very least a hope, that certain actions will produce tomorrow the same sort of results they produced yesterday." Without such expectations, we would be incapable of making any choices at all about how to direct our individual or collective actions. The most famous statement of this perspective on the utility of history comes from the philosopher George Santayana, who argued that "those who cannot remember the past are condemned to repeat it."

Whether people actually do learn lessons from the past or act in demonstrably more rational ways because of their knowledge of history is debatable, but certainly the expectation that they should do so is a commonly acknowledged expectation for the subject's utility.[23]

Moreover, when history's place in the school curriculum is justified in terms of its contribution to citizenship—as it almost always is in the United States—the lessons of history are typically a part of that justification. Paul Gagnon and the Bradley Commission on History in Schools, in their manifesto for increasing the scope and quality of school history, chose as their epigraph Thomas Jefferson's famous observation: "History, by apprizing them of the past, will enable them to judge of the future." A somewhat more complete quote also appears as the rationale for history education in the forerunner to the national history standards, the aptly titled *Lessons From History: Essential Understandings and Historical Perspectives*: "It [history] will avail them of the experience of other times and other nations; it will qualify them as judges of the actions and designs of men."[24] For Jefferson, future possibilities could be judged by using the experience of "other times and other nations"—knowing what has happened in the past enables us to judge what is likely to happen in the future. Similarly, history helps us judge the "actions and designs of men" because by analyzing how people have behaved in the past, we can reach some conclusions about how they might behave in the future.

We don't know how common it is for students to directly encounter this perspective on the purpose of history, either in schools or out. However, we do know that many of them see this as the basic reason for studying the subject, whether anyone has suggested it to them or not. In VanSledright's study of students' ideas about the purposes of history, some variation on the "Santayanan purpose" was one of the most common responses to the question, "Why do you think they teach you American history in school?" One fifth grader, for example, explained, "Something major happened in the past and they want you to know about it ... in case it happens again. If it happened again, you would know what to do." Similarly, an eighth grader suggested, "We can learn from our ancestors' mistakes, so we won't make the same mistakes," and a high school student noted, "We can be sure we learn from our mistakes by knowing what our mistakes were and how they came out, so we don't do the same thing wrong again, at worst, and so we can do the same thing right. We can know what was done wrong, how it was done wrong, and how it can be made right." In our own work with middle-school students, we found this rationale was often invoked to explain the importance of inglorious events in U.S. history. Some students, for example, explained the Vietnam War was important because of the lessons the nation had learned from it. One said the war taught us we "shouldn't go slowly into a war," whereas another suggested it "taught us that we weren't invincible, that there are other people who are willing to give up more than us to get what they needed." One student thought all wars are important to study because of "the mistakes you made in a war and stuff so it doesn't happen again."[25]

The expectation that lessons can be learned from studying the past, then, is an element of both children's understanding of the subject and broader public expectations for history, and such expectations can certainly contribute to education for a pluralist, participatory democracy. We accept Schlesinger's argument that all public policy decisions are to some extent historical, because they are always made with an eye toward the consequences of past decisions. Learning about other times and other nations should enable us to "judge of the future," in Jefferson's words, by providing a repertoire of vicarious experience that can widen our understanding of the causes and consequences of human actions. Particularly in its more limited formulations, which acknowledge the great variability of circumstances that can influence the course of history, the quest for generalizations or analogies should enable us to more intelligently discuss the outcomes—both intended and unintended—of the actions we undertake.

However, this perspective is not without its drawbacks, even in its most conditional and qualified version. The problem with looking for lessons in history is not that there are too few lessons to be learned but too many, all of them so ambiguous that their application is never entirely clear. Herbert Butterfield pointed out many years ago that the lessons of history may simply amount to ratification of the prejudices people already have; he noted that "one of the dangers of history lies in the ease with which these apparently self-evident judgments can be extracted from it, provided one closes one's eyes to certain facts."[26] Is the lesson of Vietnam really that we shouldn't "go into a war slowly," as our middle-school student concluded, or is it that we should stay away from the internal politics of other countries? Or maybe that the U.S. government is willing to terrorize the developing world in pursuit of its own economic and strategic interests? If students are presented with any of these lessons as facts to be learned and repeated, then their history education will amount to little more than indoctrination. If, on the other hand, they engage in debate and discussion over the lessons that can be learned from the past, as well as their applicability to the present, then they will be better prepared for the kinds of discourse suitable for participatory democracy.

There are no a priori grounds—no strictly "historical" procedures—for deciding among the competing lessons that might be learned from Vietnam or any other historical event. The only way of reaching such decisions is through the messy and contentious arena of public discussion. On the eve of military action in Afghanistan, any number of competing historical analogies were suggested: Would such action be like the Russian intervention in Afghanistan in the 1980s, or like British imperialism there in the 1800s, or like U.S. actions in Kuwait, or Kosovo, or Somalia, or Vietnam? No single analogy can ever be compelling enough to decide the issue for us or tell us in simple-minded terms what policies we should support. However, a discussion that involves awareness of a range of historical analogies and their potential application will be a better discussion than one that ignores them. Even when government action fails to take such historical precedents into account, we can still do so as citizens by either supporting or protesting such actions, and we can base our positions on our own conclusions about history. Any public action will inevitably be justified on some historical grounds, and as citizens in a participatory democracy, we must be able to evaluate those justifications—to determine if the particular generalizations or analogies in use are the most appropriate ones.[27]

LEARNING HOW HISTORICAL ACCOUNTS ARE CREATED

The final version of the analytic stance involves learning how historical accounts are created and in particular, how those accounts are grounded in evidence. From this perspective, the purpose of history education is not to learn a particular set of substantive propositions about the past (although it will necessarily include such learning) but rather to learn how knowledge about the past is arrived at in the first place. At the risk of oversimplification, this approach can most easily be equated with learning about the process of historical research rather than the specific content that such research produces. As such, it focuses on the disciplinary nature of the academic subject of history and is frequently justified by pointing to the necessity of acquainting students with the unique "way of knowing" that characterizes history as an academic subject. From this perspective, the purpose of learning history is not to retain specific interpretations constructed by historians or found in textbooks but to understand the process of developing historical accounts.

This perspective has a long heritage in history education, but in its present form, it derives primarily from two sources: the New Social Studies movement, which rose to some prominence in the United States in the 1960s and early 1970s, and the rethinking of the history curriculum in Britain around the same time, particularly as it coalesced into the Schools Council *History 13–16* project. Both these movements were concerned with the structure of history as a discipline, and both resulted in curriculum projects that emphasized the process by which historical accounts are developed. In the United States, the Amherst Project's *What Happened on Lexington Green? An Inquiry into the Nature and Methods of History*, and in Britain, the Schools Council's *What is History* unit, exposed students to a range of evidence and engaged them in answering questions through the evaluation of conflicting or problematic sources. Response to the New Social Studies materials in U.S. schools was mixed at best, but the principles embedded in such efforts remain an important component of most suggestions for reforming the subject today. In Britain, meanwhile, this perspective has been well received among teachers and has been incorporated into national standards for curriculum and assessment.[28]

In later chapters, we will examine some of the tools—such as narrative, inquiry, and empathy—that are part of these approaches. At this point, though, we are concerned primarily with the aims of history education and with how teaching students about evidence might contribute to democratic participation. It can do so, first of all, by developing students' understanding of the basis for claims to knowledge. Decision making in a democracy requires knowledge—we have to know something to make intelligent decisions—but also requires understanding the grounds on which such knowledge is constructed; as Lee notes, "It is generally held that if I can be said to *know* something, I have good grounds for what I believe."[29] If students simply encounter assertions about the past and then remember those assertions without understanding how they were arrived at in the first place, it is difficult to say that they actually know anything at all. Their only grounds for believing those statements are true is that they heard them from a supposedly authoritative source—the teacher, textbook, television, or other point of reference.

However, historical claims specifically are not grounded in authority; they are grounded in evidence that has been held up for public inspection. If students simply remember a body of information, and they think that information is true because someone in a position of authority said it was, then from a disciplinary standpoint, they don't actually have any knowledge, only a memory of baseless assertions. Just as important, from our perspective, they have no way of distinguishing historical claims that are based on evidence from those that aren't—such as myths, legends, or outright lies. The inability to distinguish between a myth and a grounded assertion about the past destroys the foundation for participatory democracy, because students will be susceptible to any outrageous story they may be told. Were millions of Jews killed during the Holocaust or not? The most reliable answer to a question like this will result from the use of evidence. If students don't understand that, they will have no way of deciding which claims can be believed and which cannot, and if they think that historical knowledge is based on authority, then they will have no way of adjudicating the claims of competing authorities. Faced with conflicting information about the past, they are likely to throw their hands up in the air and declare that "one opinion is as good as another." Neither unquestioning acceptance of historical assertions nor disaffected rejection of every claim as "just an opinion" provides the kind of knowledge that will serve students well as citizens of a democracy. To use history to understand the present or to solve modern problems, students must be able to analyze the creation of historical accounts so that they will be able to determine how well supported a claim is by the available evidence.[30]

This kind of analysis is especially important in a democracy characterized by extreme disparities in access to knowledge and education. Individuals who have greater access to historical information—those who have a wealth of books and computer resources at home, those whose families go to museums and historic sites, those who grow up engaging in discursive styles similar to the ones used in historical scholarship—are well positioned to impose their historical interpretations on others, in many cases not because their claims are better grounded but because they are more adept at using their positions of power to overwhelm those with fewer resources at their disposal. Similarly, when the combined institutional force of school systems, curriculum mandates, statewide testing systems, and publishing companies conspire to present an officially sanctioned interpretation of the past, students who do not understand how historical accounts are created may be powerless to resist. Yet when students have learned that claims must be backed up with evidence, that historians regularly disagree over interpretations, and that asking different questions of the past will yield different accounts, they should be better positioned to challenge dominant interpretations and to develop their own conclusions. This was an explicit goal of much of the work within the New Social Studies tradition; Allan Kownslar, for example, argued that when students learned that written history was an interpretation based on primary sources, they became better able to develop and defend their own generalizations as well as "less likely to be fooled or misled by vague statements, myths, or stereotypes in textbooks, or those advanced by some politicians, journalists, salesmen, teachers, neighbors, or friends, and, equally important, by the students themselves." More recently, this perspective has been echoed by Bruce VanSledright and by Sam Wineburg.[31]

Only one thing is still missing in our account of this perspective on history's purpose—the voices of students. Recall that in each of the first two approaches to the analytic stance, there was evidence that students themselves understood and accepted those rationales for studying the past: Some thought that history helped explain the present, and some thought lessons could be learned from the past (and some thought both). However, very little research suggests that they think of history's purpose in terms of learning how historical accounts are created. We have never heard U.S. students explain history's significance in terms of familiarizing them with the structure of the discipline or with history's unique form of knowledge—using either these or simpler terms—despite the fact that some of our interviews have taken place among students who were immersed regularly in historical evidence and the construction of accounts (nor have we seen such evidence in our colleagues' research). Even in Britain, where students encounter evidence-based approaches to history from the earliest years of study and where they recognize that knowledge of the past is constructed from incomplete evidence, students do not usually talk about history's purpose in terms of a way of knowing. They focus instead on the content of the subject, just as students in the United States do.[32]

There is, however, one important exception to this pattern. In research that one of us conducted together with Alan McCully, secondary students in Northern Ireland (the equivalent of middle-grade students in the United

States), often explained that the reason for studying history at school was so "we can make up our own minds." In Northern Ireland, historical events have powerful contemporary significance, and they are interpreted very differently depending on political loyalties. Secondary students there are aware that much of their exposure to history outside school is highly selective and is likely to reflect the partisan bias of a single community, and many of those we interviewed explained the purpose of school history in terms of helping them overcome this limitation. At school, they noted, teachers presented "both sides" of history and thus provided them the information they needed to reach their own, supportable conclusions about the past. Students did not often describe this process in the way history educators might—they didn't talk about "grounding interpretations in evidence," for example—but many of them clearly explained that school history allowed them to move beyond the ungrounded perspectives they encountered outside school and toward more supportable positions that took account of varied perspectives.[33]

Two factors may help to explain why these students were more likely to talk about history's purpose in terms of helping them make up their own minds. The first is that they were secondary students who had been exposed to history as an interpretive, inquiry-oriented subject for many years. Other studies have focused on students with much less experience with this version of the analytic stance, either because they were in the elementary grades or because their history courses had been oriented primarily toward the transmission of information. In addition, secondary students in Northern Ireland (unlike primary students there) study a number of historical topics that remain at the center of contemporary controversy—the Plantation of Ulster, the Battle of the Boyne, the Home Rule Movement, Partition, and so on. Although links to the present are not necessarily highlighted while studying these topics, students are nonetheless aware that such issues retain symbolic importance in the present and that perspectives on them differ widely. When school history presents conflicting evidence and viewpoints on issues of contemporary significance, it seems logical for students to conclude that the purpose of the endeavor is to help them make up their own minds about historical accounts. If students were to engage in activities similar in structure but involving topics of limited relevance or interest, they might be less inclined to formulate the subject's purpose in these terms.

CONCLUSIONS

At a superficial level, the analytic stance may be the least controversial approach to history: Practically everyone agrees that students should be engaged in some form of analysis rather than in memorization and repetition of names or dates. However, superficial agreement may mask some fundamental differences over the kinds of analysis in which students might be expected to engage. These are not simply matters of definition or arguments with only academic importance. Each of the varieties of the analytic stance can directly contribute to students' preparation for citizenship in a participatory democracy, but none can guarantee it. To make such a contribution, we have argued that certain conditions must obtain in each of the three varieties of this stance. Studying history as the development of the present, for example, can provide students with the knowledge of society necessary to preserve contemporary institutions or bring about needed changes. For this knowledge to have an effect on the present, however, students must be given the chance to consider the indeterminacy of historical developments and the agency of people in the past, rather than being presented with a past that seems to have unfolded naturally and inevitably—one that simply justifies the present state of affairs and negates the ability of people to intervene in their own destiny.

Similarly, studying history can lead to lessons for the present in the form of generalizations and analogies, at least when these take into account the variety and novelty of historical circumstances rather than posit universal stages of development or causal laws. However, lessons cannot simply be fed to students, for such conclusions are never obvious or unproblematic; instead, students must have the chance to engage in the same kind of discussions over the applicability of historical lessons that inspire debate in the wider public sphere. Finally, learning how historical accounts are grounded in evidence should enable students to move beyond biased and unsubstantiated stories, but students may be better positioned to utilize this understanding if their studies directly address controversial or deeply symbolic historical people and events. If exposure to the interpretation of historical sources is limited to remote, abstract, or uncontroversial topics, then formal education may have little impact on students' ability or inclination to challenge received opinion.

ENDNOTES

1. Bruce VanSledright, *In Search of America's Past: Learning to Read History in Elementary School* (New York: Teachers College Press, 2002), 24–52.
2. Benjamin S. Bloom, Max D. Engelhart, Edward J. Furst, Walker H. Hill, and David R. Krathwohl, *Cognitive Domain*, Handbook 1, *Taxonomy of Educational Objectives: The Classification of Educational Goals* (New York: David McKay, 1956), 144–45. In a previous discussion of stances toward history, we referred to this as the "rationalistic stance"; Linda S. Levstik and Keith C. Barton, "Committing Acts of History: Mediated Action, Humanistic Education, and Participatory Democracy," in *Critical Issues in Social Studies Research for the 21st Century*, Ed. William Stanley (Greenwich, Conn.: Information Age Publishing, 2001), 119–148.
3. Leibniz cited in Maurice Bloch, *The Historian's Craft* (New York: Knopf, 1953), 35; Frederick Jackson Turner, "The Significance of History," in *The Early Writings of Frederick Jackson Turner* (Madison, Wisc.: University of Wisconsin Press, 1938), 51,

53; John Dewey, *Democracy and Education* (New York: Macmillan, 1966), 214; G. Kitson Clark, *The Critical Historian* (New York: Basic Books, 1967), 195. See also Peter Geyl, *Use and Abuse of History* (New Haven, Conn.: Yale University Press, 1955), 85; Edward H. Carr, *What is History?* (New York: Vintage Books, 1961), 29.

4. Peter Novick, *The Holocaust in American Life* (Boston: Houghton Mifflin, 1999); David W. Blight, *Race and Reunion: The Civil War in American Memory* (Cambridge, Mass.: Harvard University Press, 2001); Stephen Nissenbaum, *The Battle for Christmas* (New York: Knopf, 1996).

5. William H. McNeill, Michael Kammen, and Gordon A. Craig, "Why Study History? Three Historians Respond," in *Historical Literacy: The Case for History in American Education,* Eds. Paul Gagnon and the Bradley Commission on History in Schools (New York: Macmillan, 1989), 114.

6. Bruce A. VanSledright, "And Santayana Lives On: Students' Views on the Purposes for Studying American History," *Journal of Curriculum Studies* 29 (September/October 1997): 538–39.

7. Keith C. Barton, "Historical Understanding Among Elementary Children" (Ed.D. diss., University of Kentucky, Lexington, 1994), 101–02.

8. David Hackett Fisher, *Historians' Fallacies: Toward a Logic of Historical Thought* (New York, Harper and Row, 1970), 315; Arthur Marwick, *The Nature of History* (London: Macmillan, 1970), 13; James Harvey Robinson, *The New History: Essays Illustrating the Modern Historical Outlook* (New York: Macmillan, 1912), 18, 21, 24; Carl Becker, "Some Aspects of the Influence of Social Problems and Ideas Upon the Study and Writing of History," *American Journal of Sociology* 18 (March 1913): 666–67, 670.

9. C. Vann Woodward, *Thinking Back: The Perils of Writing History* (Baton Rouge, La.: Louisiana State University Press, 1986), 82–83, 87, 92, 98, 137–38. See also C. Vann Woodward, *The Strange Career of Jim Crow,* 3rd rev. ed. (New York: Oxford University Press, 1974), v–xvii; John Herbert Roper, *C. Vann Woodward, Southerner* (Athens, Ga.: University of Georgia Press, 1987), 171–200.

10. Roper, *C. Vann Woodward, Southerner,* 171–200; Howard N. Rabinowitz, "More Than the Woodward Thesis: Assessing The Strange Career of Jim Crow," in *C. Vann Woodward: A Southern Historian and his Critics,* Ed. John Herbert Roper (Athens, Ga.: University of Georgia Press, 1997), 167-182; Joel Williamson, "C. Vann Woodward and the Origins of a New Wisdom, in *C. Vann Woodward: A Southern Historian and His Critics,* Ed. John Herbert Roper (Athens, Ga.: University of Georgia Press, 1997), 219.

11. David S. Landes and Charles Tilly, *History as Social Science* (Englewood Cliffs, N.J.: Prentice-Hall, 1971), 6.

12. Gordon Craig makes a similar point in "History as a Humanistic Discipline," in *Historical Literacy,* 134.

13. Henry Steele Commager, *The Nature and the Study of History* (Columbus, Ohio: Charles E. Merrill, 1965), 73. On historians' rejection of the "lessons of history," see also Peter J. Lee, "Why Learn History?" in *Learning History,* Eds. A. K. Dickinson, P. J. Lee, and P. J. Rogers (London: Heinemann Educational, 1984), 5; Gustaaf Renier, *History, Its Purpose and Method* (London: Allen & Unwin, 1950), 27.

14. Examples of the "stages of evolution" approach include Friedrich Engels, *The Origin of the Family, Private Property and the State* (Chicago: C. H. Kerr, 1902); Georg Hegel, *The Philosophy of History* (New York: Dover, 1956); Lewis H. Morgan, *Ancient*

Society (Cambridge, Mass.: Harvard University Press, 1964). Oswald Spengler, *The Decline of the West* (New York: Knopf, 1939); Arnold Toynbee, *A Study of History*, 12 vols. (London: Oxford University Press, 1935–1955). The debate over more limited generalizations is represented in Carl G. Hempel, "The Function of General Laws in History," in *Theories of History*, Ed. Patrick Gardiner (Glencoe, N.Y.: Free Press, 1959), 344–356, and Morton White, "Historical Explanation," in *Theories of History*, Ed. Patrick Gardiner (Glencoe, N.Y.: Free Press, 1959), 356–373.

15. Geyl, *Use and Abuse of History*, 84; see also Robinson, *The New History*, 21.

16. Renier, *History, Its Purpose and Method*, 14; see also A. L. Rowse, *The Use of History* (London: Hodder and Stoughton, 1946), 19; Peter Lee, "History in School: Aims, Purposes and Approaches: A Reply to John White," in Peter Lee, John Slater, Paddy Walsh, and John White, *The Aims of School History: The National Curriculum and Beyond* (London: Tufnell Press), 27.

17. This is at the core of Carl Becker's argument that history pushes back the "specious present." Carl Becker, "Everyman His Own Historian," *American Historical Review* 37 (January 1932): 221–236.

18. Howard Zinn, *The Politics of History*, 2nd. ed. (Urbana, Ill.: University of Illinois Press, 1990), 42, 47, 51. Zinn does not formulate these observations as generalizations per se, but their wording can easily be rearranged in terms of the lessons the past might yield: Sometimes government actions are neither neutral nor beneficent; sometimes people's actions are guided by ideology that is inconsistent with public rhetoric, sometimes idealistic social movements have negative consequences, and so on.

19. On the use of historical analogies, see Peter J. Rogers, "Why Teach History?" in *Learning History*, Eds. A. K. Dickinson, P. J. Lee, and P. J. Rogers (London: Heinemann Educational, 1984), 20–38; Lester D. Stephens, *Probing the Past: A Guide to the Study and Teaching of History* (Boston: Allyn & Bacon, 1974), 115–119; John Tosh, *The Pursuit of History: Aims, Methods and New Directions in the Study of Modern History* (New York: Longman, 1984), 13–14.

20. Peter J. Lee, "Why Learn History?," 9.

21. Dwight B. Billings and Kathleen M. Blee, *The Road to Poverty: The Making of Wealth and Hardship in Appalachia* (New York: Cambridge University Press, 2000), 320, 324.

22. Robert D. Putnam, *Bowling Alone: The Collapse and Revival of American Community* (New York: Simon & Schuster, 2000), 367–401; quotes from p. 399.

23. Arthur M. Schlesinger, Jr., "The Inscrutability of History," *Encounter* 27 (November 1966), 10; George Santayana, *The Life of Reason; or, Phases in Human Progress*, Vol. 1, *Introduction and Reason in Common Sense* (New York: Scribner's, 1905), 284. G. Kitson Clark also makes the observation that historical assumptions "are implicit in most language and in all political judgments," in *The Critical Historian*, 8.

24. Gagnon and The Bradley Commission on History in Schools, *History Literacy*, v; Charlotte Crabtree, Gary Nash, Paul Gagnon, and Scott Waugh, Eds., *Lessons from History: Essential Understandings and Historical Perspectives Students Should Acquire* (Los Angeles, Calif.: National Center for History in the Schools, University of California, Los Angeles, 1992), 3; Thomas Jefferson, *Notes on the State of Virginia*, Ed. William Peden (Chapel Hill, NC: University of North Carolina Press, 1995), 148. Jefferson concludes by noting that history "will enable them to know ambition under every design it may assume; and knowing it, to defeat its views."

25. VanSledright, "And Santayana Lives On," 529–30; Keith C. Barton and Linda S. Levstik, "'It Wasn't a Good Part of History': National Identity and Ambiguity in Students' Explanations of Historical Significance," *Teachers College Record* 99 (Spring 1998), 490.

26. Herbert Butterfield, "The Dangers of History," in *History and Human Relations* (London: Collins, 1951), 162, 180. On the problem of deciding which lesson applies in a given circumstance, see also Peter J. Lee, "Why Learn History?," 8–9; Schlesinger, "The Inscrutability of History," 312; *Simone A. Schweber, Making Sense of the Holocaust: Lessons from Classroom Practice* (New York: Teachers College Press, 2004).

27. Allan Lichtman and Valerie French, *Historians and the Living Past: The Theory and Practice of Historical Study* (Arlington Heights, Ill.: AHM Publication Corporation, 1978), 1–2.

28. On history education within the New Social Studies, see Edwin Fenton, *The New Social Studies* (New York: Holt, Rinehart & Winston, 1967); Richard H. Brown, "Learning How to Learn: The Amherst Project and History Education in the Schools," *The Social Studies* 87 (November/December 1996): 267–73; Allan O. Kownslar, "Is History Relevant?" in *Teaching American History: The Quest for Relevancy,* Ed. Allan O. Kownslar (Washington, D.C.: National Council for the Social Studies, 1974), 3–15; Eunice Johns and Warren L. Hickman, *Ahead of Us ... The Past: History and the Historian, A Concept Study* (New York: Macmillan, 1975); Peter S. Bennett, *What Happened on Lexington Green? An Inquiry into the Nature and Methods of History* (Menlo Park, Calif.: Addison-Wesley, 1970). On history education in Britain, see Robert Phillips, *History Teaching, Nationhood and the State: A Study in Educational Politics* (London: Cassell, 1998), 12–22; Richard Aldrich and Dennis Dean, "The Historical Dimension," in *History in the National Curriculum,* Ed. Richard Aldrich (London: Kogan Page, 1991), 93–113; Dennis Shemilt, *Evaluation Study: Schools Council History 13–16 Project* (Edinburgh: Holmes McDougall, 1980), 4–5; Qualifications and Curriculum Authority, "The Importance of History," available from http://www.nc.uk.net/servlets/NCFrame?subject=Hi&KeyStage=2, accessed 9 April, 2003. On earlier evidence-based approaches to history, see Stephen J. Thornton, "Legitimacy in the Social Studies Curriculum," in *Education Across a Century: The Centennial Volume, One Hundredth Yearbook of the National Society for the Study of Education,* Ed. Lyn Corno (Chicago: University of Chicago Press, 2001), 185–204, and Aldrich, "The Historical Dimension"; for a comparison of *History 13–16* and the Amherst Project, see Stephen J. Thornton, "Subject Specific Teaching Methods: History," in *Subject Specific Instructional Methods and Activities,* Vol. 8, *Advances in Research on Teaching,* Ed. Jere Brophy (New York: Elsevier Science, 2001), 298–302. The former is now referred to as the *Schools History Project;* see Schools History Project, "What is the SHP?" available from http://www.tasc.ac.uk/shp/whatis/whatis.htm, accessed 9 April, 2003.

29. Peter Lee, "Historical Knowledge and the National Curriculum," in *History in the National Curriculum,* Ed. Richard Aldrich (London: Kogan Page, 1991), 48.

30. Peter Lee, "Historical Knowledge and the National Curriculum," 48–49; Keith C. Barton, "'I Just Kinda Know': Elementary Students' Ideas About Historical Evidence," *Theory and Research in Social Education* 25 (Fall 1997): 407-08.

31. Kownslar, "Is History Relevant?," 5; Bruce VanSledright, *In Search of America's Past, Learning to Read History in Elementary School* (New York: Teachers College

Press, 2002), 153; Sam Wineburg, *Historical Thinking and Other Unnatural Acts: Charting the Future of Teaching the Past* (Philadelphia: Temple University Press, 2001), 83.

32. Keith C. Barton, "'You'd Be Wanting to Know about the Past'": Social Contexts of Children's Historical Understanding in Northern Ireland and the USA," *Comparative Education* 37 (February 2001): 89–106; "Primary Children's Understanding of the Role of Historical Evidence: Comparisons Between the United States and Northern Ireland," *International Journal of History Teaching, Learning and Research* 1 (June 2001), 21–30; Paul Goalen, "'…Somone Might Become Involved in a Fascist Group or Something…': Pupils' Perceptions of History at the End of Key Stages 2, 3, and 4," *Teaching History* 96 (August 1999), 34–38; Mike Huggins, "An Analysis of the Rationales for Learning History Given by Children and Teachers at Key Stage 2," *The Curriculum Journal* 7 (Autumn 1996): 307–321.

33. This research is currently in the analysis stage and has not yet been published.

Chapter 5

The Moral Response Stance

History says, Don't hope

On this side of the grave.

But then, once in a lifetime

The longed-for tidal wave

Of justice can rise up,

And hope and history rhyme.

—Seamus Heaney[1]

History often calls up strong moral responses, as we regard some aspects of the past with admiration, others with condemnation, and still others with simple remembrance: Martin Luther King was admirable, Hitler reprehensible, and September 11 tragic. In recognition of these responses, we erect memorials and monuments, dedicate plaques, and set aside days for remembrance, mourning, or celebration. When artists address historical topics, meanwhile, morality is never far from the surface: Spike Lee recalls the moral character of Malcolm X in film, Bruce Springsteen captures the grief and determination of September 11 in *The Rising*, and Picasso portrays the horror of war in *Guernica*. In schools, too, the moral response stance is common. Although we may not often speak in terms of morality, we nonetheless expect students to celebrate the good things in history and condemn the bad: We want them not only to look to Abraham Lincoln and Harriet Tubman as part of their national identity but as people they should admire; we want them not only to analyze the causes and consequences of slavery or the Holocaust but to condemn them. In fact, we would probably be shocked, and even offended, if they did not demonstrate such responses.

Although moral responses can be directed toward a variety of ends—remembrance, condemnation, and admiration are the three we will discuss in this chapter—all revolve around notions of right and wrong, of what should and should not happen. Such questions are a central part of participatory democracy because the decisions we make in the public sphere are not simply instrumental ones designed to achieve predetermined ends in an efficient manner; we are not just trying to hit on the most cost-effective means of providing health care to the poor or the least disruptive way of managing relations between employers and employees. Public issues are invariably about the ends themselves, about our vision of the common good, and about what we hope to achieve as a society. As we discussed in chapter 2, these hopes cannot be taken for granted or discovered in some consensus that exists prior to public participation; still less can we impose them on each other or on our students. In a pluralist democracy, we hold differing visions, and a major purpose of public schooling must be to help students compare those differences and, where possible, transcend them. When people move beyond their old, narrow visions to new, more inclusive ones, hope and history can rhyme, as Seamus Heaney puts it. The study of the past can never tell students what to hope for, but it can provide the context for discussing and working out those hopes so that if it should happen in their lifetimes that the "longed-for tidal wave of justice can rise up," they will recognize it and become part of it.

REMEMBRANCE AND FORGETTING

One of the most basic forms of moral response is remembrance: We honor the people who have gone before us, not necessarily for any specific achievement but simply because we feel that it is somehow right to hold them in memory. This form of moral response was particularly clear in research with students in Northern Ireland. Recall that in chapter 3, we discussed a U.S. study in which we asked students in the middle grades to choose the historical events they considered most important and to explain their choices, and that their responses focused primarily on the origin and development of the United States as a social and political entity. (They also emphasized the importance of technological progress, a topic we will take up in chap. 9.) One of us conducted a similar study in Northern Ireland with students in the equivalent of Grades 6 through 10. These students gave very different responses than did their counterparts in the United States, and one of the most notable differences lay in the importance they attached to remembrance.

The most common reason students in Northern Ireland gave for selecting an event as historically significant was that it involved death or hardship. This justification was used by both Catholics and Protests, by boys and girls, and by students at all grade levels. In fact, only 1 pair of students (out of 20 pairs interviewed) did not use this rationale, and most used it multiple times. Students especially mentioned the extent of death when they explained the importance of the world wars (two of the three events they chose most frequently). A Protestant boy, for example, thought the First World War was important because "so many people were involved in it, and there were so many tragedies and all," while one Catholic girl explained that it was important because "there was a lot of people killed and lost lives, and suffered a lot," and another noted that "there's so much death and destruction." Several students also considered the sinking of the Titanic (which was built in Belfast) one of the most important events in history, and those who did so typically pointed to the number of deaths involved; one girl, for example, explained that it was important because "it was the worst ever disaster on the sea that there has ever been—and maybe going to be—and it was a terrible thing the way it just sank in the sea and killed a whole lot of people." Students also pointed to widespread suffering as well as death when discussing the significance of the Irish Famine; students explained their choice of this event by noting, "It was a time of hunger," "It shows you how unfortunate people were in that time," "The Great Famine starved many thousands of families," and "Everyone went through a terrible time, starvation and hunger, and there's a lot of people who died."[2]

Many students connected the importance of death and suffering to the need for remembrance, and again, this was particularly clear when students talked about the world wars. One Protestant boy, for example, thought World War I was important "because a lot of people died and you have to remember them by saying it was very important," and a Catholic girl noted that it was important "because a lot of people died, and myself, I had a great-uncle, he was killed in World War I, and I thought it was very brave, the people that was in World War I, they shouldn't be forgotten." This same girl, though, made it clear that personal connections were not the only basis for remembrance. She also thought the Irish Famine was important and explained, "It should be remembered because a lot of people died during the Famine, and they should be remembered for the hard times they had, and best not to forget them." Another Catholic girl described the importance of remembrance in discussing the Enniskillen bombing: "It was on the news this weekend, because we were all remembering it, and it showed you people—actually showed you people—how they remembered it, and you saw them crying and all, so you remember it." When asked why such remembrance would be important to those who were not directly affected, she explained, "Because they should remember people died in it as well, and they were all injured, and they were only there like to show they're sorry for what happened." Later in the interview, in discussing why remembrance of those who died in the world wars is important, she explained, "Well, I think you should remember them for what they done, like all the soldiers might have fought for what they thought was right, and we shouldn't just forget them, just because it's over."[3]

Students' responses reflect the significance of remembrance throughout the wider society in Britain and Ireland, where it is taken for granted that people in the past should be remembered because of the hardships they endured or because they tragically lost their lives. In Britain, for example, Remembrance Day (the Sunday in November devoted to commemorating those who died in the world wars) is one of the most important dates on the calendar: People wear poppies (the symbol of remembrance) for several days beforehand, ceremonies are held at war memorials throughout the country, and the nation watches on television as the Queen places a wreath on the Cenotaph at Whitehall. These symbols and ceremonies carry far more emotional weight than counterparts like Memorial Day or Veterans Day do in the United States, and they also are less focused on achievement; in the United States, many people revere and honor the bravery or determination of veterans, but in Britain, the occasion is more somber and more focused on loss than triumph—it is a time for remembrance, not celebration.

In Northern Ireland, Remembrance Day itself is more controversial, because many regard it as a specifically Protestant occasion. However, remembrance is just as important among Catholics, who are more likely to focus on the memory of Irish martyrs—either distant historical figures or those who have died in sectarian incidents in recent decades, such as the Hunger Strikes or Bloody Sunday. Both communities, meanwhile, mourn the innocent victims of bombings and other violent incidents. Similar examples of public remembrance can be found in the United States. As visitors pass the Vietnam Wall, for example, they may gently touch a name, leave a memento, or weep. They are not necessarily there to admire or condemn; rather, they simply want to recognize and remember the individuals involved in a historic—and tragic—moment. Similarly, the victims of the terrorist bombing in Oklahoma City are honored with a memorial park, the masses of immigrants who came through New York harbor are recalled at the Ellis Island memorial, and the experiences of Japanese Americans relocated to Gila River, Manzanar, and Tule Lake are documented in print and film. Yet in general, remembrance is much less a part of our public culture than it is in Britain and Ireland, and tributes here are more often tied to character and achievement; note, for example, how public commemoration of September 11 focuses on the fire fighters and police officers who lost their lives rather than on the office workers or airline passengers who died that day.

Given that remembrance has a somewhat modest public profile in the United States, it is not surprising that students here do not usually talk about history in such terms. Moreover, the contribution of remembrance to participatory democracy is not altogether obvious. The greater attention in Northern Ireland to mourning those who have suffered and died seems an interesting, even touching, cultural difference, but there are no obvious implications for public deliberation of the common good—at least not until we consider that the opposite of remembrance is forgetting, and that forgetting is something we are very good at in the United States. As we discussed in chapter 1, there is no evidence that children or adults in the United States are less interested in history than people anywhere else; our interests, however, can be highly selective, and we are much more likely to remember some historical events than others. As Jane White notes, "Historical, geographic, economic, or political events that do not reflect the United States and its inhabitants at their finest hour, embodying the ideas for which we stand, tend to be ruthlessly edited out when 'what is or was' meets the filter of 'what should be.'"[4]

This editing (or forgetting) was particularly clear when one of us asked teachers in the United States to participate in the same task as middle-schools students—choosing the most important items from a set of captioned historical pictures and explaining their choices. Students had been particularly interested in events they recognized as presenting a challenge to their progressive and consensual understanding of U.S. history—wanting to know more about the Vietnam War and why people protested against it, for example—but teachers suggested such incidents should be omitted from the curriculum. Although they were not as convinced as students that the United States only enters wars for altruistic purposes, they did not see Vietnam as a part of "who we are" as a nation, and they worried about including it as one of the most important events because "it was a negative thing."[5]

In general, these teachers rejected any incident that illustrated a lack of unity and consensus in U.S. history; they suggested that coercive or divisive elements of the past were developmentally inappropriate in the elementary and middle grades (because they were negative), that they represented aberrations rather than patterns in the nation's past (Vietnam was a problem at the time, but it had no long-term consequences), and that they would undermine children's sense of national identity. Thus, they considered the Civil Rights movement significant, because it sought to join minorities with European Americans in civic life, but not instances of ethnoracial repression (such as Indian removal or Japanese American relocation), collective resistance (antiwar protests), or movements challenging basic social and economic conditions (labor movements or the Great Depression). Although they were aware that injustices had happened in the past, they were terrified of what they might unleash by speaking about them in the present, and in response, they chose silence.[6]

Any consideration of history is selective, but we need to think carefully about the consequences of the particular selections we make. In the United States, the story of national unity and progress is so strong that it sweeps away all else, and the experiences of dissent and repression are forgotten. This is destructive for democracy, particularly if participation and pluralism are to be at the heart of our national identity. Forgetting such recurrent features of our national past also makes it more difficult to analyze the causes and consequences of historical events or to understand how we got to where we are today. If we have no duty to remember those who suffered and died, if we are free to pick and choose from history at will, there is little to stand in the way of this story of unity and consensus, and we become the amoral historical censors described by George Orwell and Milan Kundera—airbrushing the past to satisfy our power and authority in the present.[7]

However, if we have a duty to someone other than ourselves, if we should remember those who have suffered and died just because it is right to do so and "best not to forget them," then we cannot be so cavalier in forgetting inconvenient truths. In Northern Ireland, it is notable that the pull of remembrance led students to take seriously the lives of people on the other side of the community divide: Protestants mourned the suffering and loss of the Irish Famine, often regarded as the historical territory of Nationalists, and Catholics thought it was important to remember victims of the Enniskillen bombing and soldiers in the world wars, generally thought of as Unionist causes. We have even seen a Catholic teacher in Northern Ireland, in the midst of a lesson on the First World War, stop to lead the class in prayer for the memory of those who died at the Battle of the Somme—one of the most emotionally charged events for the other community. Recognition by each community of the other's suffering is one of the strongest counterweights to sectarian division in Northern Ireland, and if peace comes to the region someday, such remembrance is likely to play a key role in reconciliation.

In U.S. schools, the study of history features two topics whose inclusion seems to be motivated, in part, by feelings of remembrance. One is the Holocaust. Many students learn about this topic even in elementary school or at grade levels that would not normally cover European history or the recent past; in fact, it is one of the first historical topics outside the national past that students are likely to study, and for many it remains the only such topic for several years. The rationale for studying the Holocaust is no doubt related to the magnitude of the tragedy; when an event is this catastrophic, it demands our attention, even if it fails to fit into the traditional curriculum. A second such topic is slavery; again, even in elementary school, many students will learn about the brutal treatment of those who were enslaved in the antebellum United States. The proximity of slavery, as well as its magnitude, seems to promote remembrance—these things happened right here among many of our own direct ancestors, and we cannot ignore it. Neither of these topics, however, fundamentally challenges our narrative of national unity and progress. The Holocaust happened far away and was carried out by people from other nations, so it has few implications for our own character, particularly if we ignore U.S. racism and anti-Semitism during the same period. Slavery, meanwhile, fits snugly within our national story: It was a tremendous problem, but we solved it, just as we solve all problems.[8]

However, if we extended this remembrance to other instances of death and suffering, it might force us to confront issues we would rather forget—issues whose consideration would strengthen our democracy. If we believe that it is right to remember death and suffering even when such remembrance fails to bolster our identity as a unified and uniquely moral nation, then we would be forced to reflect on the 58,000 U.S. soldiers and millions of Vietnamese who died during the Vietnam War; on the tens of millions of Native Americans eradicated as a result of European conquest and settlement, on the hundreds of labor activists killed by police and strikebreakers in the late 19th and early 20th centuries, and on the hundreds of African Americans lynched by White mobs at about the same time. Those are examples just from our own past; if we took world history seriously, we would also have to remember those who suffered at Stalin's hands, or under apartheid, or during the reign of Augustus Pinochet and the Shah of Iran. And, if we remembered them—just because we thought it was right to do so—that remembrance might lead us to wonder why they had to suffer and die, and to begin discussing how we might avoid such tragedies today and in the future.

FAIRNESS AND JUSTICE

Moral responses to history often revolve around issues of justice: We become outraged when we learn about people who were robbed of their life or liberty, who suffered brutality or oppression, and who were denied rights to which we believe they were entitled. Most of the examples of remembrance we have discussed involve just such issues—for one reason or another, people suffered or died when they should not have, and the value of remembrance is that it can force consideration of such issues. When we come face-to-face with misery and tragedy, we respond by condemning the forces that brought about these circumstances and, it is to be hoped, try to avoid replicating them in the present and future. Less extreme occurrences can also provoke condemnation, as when we denounce Orville Faubus for trying to bar African Americans from attending Little Rock's Central High or when we deplore the blacklisting of entertainers for supposedly "un-American" activities. This condemnation is a routine part of our moral response to history, and children and adolescents are also quick to express outrage over human rights violations, to condemn the perpetrators of what they perceive to be historical wrongs, and, sometimes, to call for retaliation or redress. They usually refer to these issues not in terms of "justice" or "injustice," though, but by words like "fair" and "unfair."

In our classroom study of fourth and fifth graders, students were fascinated by topics that involved unfair treatment of people in the past. They were outraged, for example, when they learned that English settlers in North America either intentionally deceived Native Americans or disregarded the treaties they made with them. In one discussion of Native–European relations, the teacher asked students which side they would be on, given what they had learned about the period, and all sided with Native Americans. One pointed out that they were there "a long time before everybody else" and explained that "if someone was not from your house, they couldn't just break in there." Another student agreed and added, "The English like took them over; they didn't know what the paper was, so how would they *not* sign?" During this discussion, students consistently pointed to the unfairness of taking land from those who already occupied it.[9]

Discussions of fairness in these classrooms also centered on issues of gender and ethnicity. Students reacted strongly when they learned about women's lack of rights in the past, and they frequently noted the unfairness of their not having been allowed to vote. Similarly, their interest in slavery revolved primarily around the unfairness of slaves' treatment. Two girls, during an interview, noted that they found a picture of an enslaved family particularly interesting because, as one explained, "It shows how badly these people were treated, because their home is like battered down, because they don't get like a lot of good food or anything because they're just like slaves and I think that, it's so, I think it's horrible that people actually treated other humans like that." Similar concerns were evident in discussions of immigration in the late 19th and early 20th centuries. In developing reenactments of immigrants' processing at Ellis Island, many students focused on treatment they considered unfair, such as separation of parents and children. In class discussions, students also brought up current issues they considered parallel to this kind of unfairness, such as when people "go around and try to beat up gay people," as well as examples of racist incidents they had learned about in the media.[10]

Students in other countries also are interested in questions of fairness. When one of us asked students in New Zealand to choose historically significant events, for example, many of their answers related to the same kinds of issues U.S. students considered salient. They thought women's suffrage was one of the most important events in history because it corrected the injustice of allowing only men to vote; as one student put it, "Women getting to vote, that's only fair!" Similarly, students of Maori, Pacific Islander, and European backgrounds all agreed the Treaty of Waitangi was significant because it was about fairness—"how Maori would be treated." In Northern Ireland as well, fairness was a common refrain in students' responses, particularly among Catholics. One noted, for example, that the Battle of the Boyne was important because "they were trying to take land off the Catholics," whereas another pointed out, "I don't think it's right that Protestants should have control of Ireland." Another student thought the plantation of English and Scottish settlers "was a bit unfair to Ireland," and several pointed out the unfairness of the Penal Laws that placed restrictions on Catholics in the 18th century: One explained, "It should be even, Catholics should be allowed to do the same things as Protestants"; another noted, "I think Catholics *and* Protestants should have a say in everything, it's not right that Protestants should have the say of what the laws is"; and still another pointed out, "It wasn't fair that these laws were being brought in; Catholics felt as if, like, Catholics weren't important."[11]

As we suggested in chapter 2, if we are concerned with issues of the common good, then we should choose topics of study, at least in part, because of their ability to promote discussion of such issues. We all know that children and adolescents are quick to attend to fairness in their own treatment by peers or adults; in fact, educators frequently are advised to build on this inclination to develop students' interest in wider social issues. Our research in the United States, New Zealand, and Northern Ireland suggests that a concern with fairness is widespread, and that it applies as much to historical topics as contemporary ones. This is surely good news for anyone hoping to develop students' ability to participate in pluralist democracies, because public deliberation often centers on issues of fairness—just the kinds of questions students find fascinating.

However, for students' concern with fairness to contribute to democratic citizenship, we need to help them develop their ideas in two important and related ways. First, we need to provide a chance for them to move beyond their preexisting, common-sense ideas about what counts as fair and unfair and toward consideration of a broader and more inclusive conception of justice. Note that students in the United States considered actions unfair if they involved trickery (as in Native–European relations), maltreatment (as in brutality toward slaves or separation of immigrant families), or differential status (as in the lack of suffrage for women or violence against gays). These are certainly important components of any conception of justice, and they go a long way toward providing students with a foundation for moral responses to historical events. Yet each is essentially a negative perspective on what counts as fair or unfair: Unfairness occurs when something goes wrong, when there is some aberration in our relations with others: We should not trick other people, mistreat them, or deprive them of their rights based on ethnicity, gender, sexual orientation, and so on. When we do these things, it is unfair; to ensure fairness, we need to stop such things from happening.

Students would be better equipped for public deliberation, though, if they also were able to consider how positive steps could be taken to ensure justice. The United Nation's Universal Declaration of Human Rights, for example, not only identifies the kinds of negative rights students are already familiar with—prohibition of slavery, freedom from torture, right to movement, and so on—but also asserts that all people have the right to an education, to protection against unemployment, and to a standard of living adequate for health and well-being. If students were to consider which historical developments contributed—or failed to contribute—to these rights, they would have a broader basis for notions of what is fair or unfair. In New Zealand, many students took exactly this view when they talked about the historical significance of public education. It was only fair, students argued, for the government to operate public schools "because it gave everyone, rich or poor ... the right to read, and to an education, so when they grow up to get jobs, they would know how to read and write." Before that, one student noted, "just the people who could afford it could go to school, [but] then, like, everyone could." Another student, like many of his peers, pointed out that public schooling made it possible for "everyone to get an equal education. Most schools in New Zealand now are pretty much equal."[12]

These students agreed, too, that an equal education meant an equal chance at employment; in fact, every group interviewed mentioned this as an argument for the importance of education, whether they eventually chose that as one of the most historically significant events or not. As one student in an economically depressed area noted, without public education, "a lot of people, especially in this area, wouldn't be able to go to school.... It's like we're the next generation, and we need to be able to work so we make money and so we can bring up our families." Although U.S. students sometimes noted the importance of an expanded system of public schooling, they justified their choices in terms of individual opportunity and development, not by reference to standards of fairness or equity. The power of government to promote justice through positive action—not just through the removal of barriers—was not part of their basis for judging historical significance.[13] U.S. students would be better served, as would our society in general, if they had the chance to consider alternative ways of looking at justice and how to achieve it. They might ultimately reject these alternatives, of course, but such rejection should be the result of careful consideration rather than lack of exposure.

Students also need experience considering the intersection of historic injustices and contemporary concerns—particularly when their own concerns are at stake. In Northern Ireland, for example, students were quick to note injustices against the Catholic community—plantation of settlers, Penal Laws, killing of protestors on Bloody Sunday—but it was only Catholic students who did so; to the extent that Protestant students thought such events were important, it was because they established Protestant ascendancy in Ireland, not because they represented examples of unfairness to others. Indeed, Protestants were less likely to mention the theme of fairness, and they were primarily interested in injustices to their own community. Similarly, over half the girls interviewed chose women's suffrage as one of the most important topics in history, but no boys did so. Unlike remembrance, which was a theme that cut across all groups in Northern Ireland, justice was a partisan concern reflecting contemporary positions and concerns.[14]

The complexity of reconciling contemporary concerns and moral responses to historic injustices—particularly among those benefiting from injustice—also was apparent in interviews with students in New Zealand. One student of European background, for example, suggested that it "would be fair" to give the land back to Maori but that it would be very complicated to do so; ultimately, he used the language of equality to reject redress of historic injustice: "I reckon everyone should have the same, like, should all be equal. You shouldn't get anything just because you're Maori, or you shouldn't get anything just because you're Pakeha [non-Maori]." One group of students of European ancestry laid out the terms of the debate even more starkly. One noted, "The Maori, when their ancestors signed the treaty, they said they could have that land.... They could have said, 'We don't want you on our land, it's ours,' but they let us come here." "Yes," another student said, "and then we took all their land." Frustrated, the first student responded, "I think we should all just live peacefully." When asked how that might be accomplished, this lively exchange ensued:

Reed:	Send them all to Auckland!
Robert:	No!
Frederick:	Give them back what's rightfully theirs!
Interviewer:	And that would be?
Reed:	It was all theirs before Cook came.
Robert:	So they should have?
Reed:	All of it? Maybe not all of it, but quite a bit of it?
Robert:	More than fifty percent.
Frederick:	No.
Reed:	No, they didn't have to let us take it.
Frederick:	Now they want it back.
Reed:	Now that we've taken over.

These students were dealing with difficult issues, as they tried to balance their moral response to the past with their understanding of what would be fair today, particularly for their own ethnic group. Interestingly, none of the Maori or Pacific Islander students even framed the question in this way. Although they thought the Treaty of Waitangi was important and that it represented an occasion when Maori were dealt with unfairly, they did not mention returning land to Maori people. Instead, they suggested that the treaty represented an opportunity lost to greed and that non-Maori could have learned to use the land more wisely. Like many members of dominant groups, the European students in this study not only had trouble reconciling their own interests with the perspectives of other groups, they had a limited sense of what those other perspectives were in the first place.[15]

If students pay attention to some injustices but not others, their participation in the public sphere will do little to advance the common good. In some respects, our research with students in the United States is encouraging in this regard, because they demonstrate little of the partiality evident in Northern Ireland and New Zealand: Boys and girls are equally likely to consider women's suffrage important, students from all ethnic backgrounds consider the expansion of rights the central theme in U.S. history, and those from European backgrounds are quick to condemn injustices against Native Americans. This is not entirely surprising, given the repeated emphasis of the history curriculum on freedom and equality as defining American values. Students appear to accept these values and to use them as one basis for their moral response to history.

Public deliberation among adults in the United States, however, rarely reflects such unanimity. Unwillingness to confront historic injustices, attention to some questions of fairness but not others, and failure to appreciate other groups' perspectives on issues of justice all contribute to significant divides over public policy. Students' early embrace of fairness for all, that is, seems to have a limited legacy as they enter adulthood. Their belief that historic injustices have already been overcome, combined with their lack of attention to positive means for promoting justice (rather than simply removing unfair restrictions on rights), may render them ill-prepared to engage such issues more fully in adulthood. As history educators, we might better capitalize on students' interest in fairness if we exposed them to a wider variety of ways of assessing justice, and if we engaged them in difficult consideration of those injustices that endure into contemporary society and whose resolution might conflict with other deeply held values. Again, there is no way to control students' responses, nor would such control be desirable. The point is to give them the chance to engage in reasoned judgment through public deliberation, not to determine the outcome of that deliberation.

HEROES AND HEROISM

Heroes are frequently recommended as a focus for historical study, especially in the elementary grades. Magazines for classroom teachers offer a steady stream of ideas for incorporating heroes into the curriculum ("Hooray for Heroes!" one article proclaims), and more serious professional journals also advise teachers to expand their attention to such historical figures. Traditionally, lists of heroes have been somewhat exclusive (focusing primarily on rich White males), but some recent articles—though by no means all—aim to expand the set of available heroes to reflect a greater range of diversity. Teachers who want to make heroes the focus of their students' exposure to history will have no trouble finding a wealth of resources to aid them.[16]

The study of heroes, though, does not just involve learning about historic individuals. Studying famous people can be used for many purposes and as part of each of the four stances; George Washington or Martin Luther King, Jr., could be used to promote national identification, for example, and Hitler or Napoleon could be the subject of analytic approaches to military strategy. However, designating people from the past as heroes is usually meant to call forth a moral response: To refer to someone as a hero is to say something about how people should be. After all, it is this equation of what people *should be* and what particular individuals *were* that qualifies them as heroes. Often, heroes serve as counterweights to the injustices we discussed in the last section: We condemn slavery but approve of Abraham Lincoln and Harriet Tubman, we condemn the Holocaust but approve of resisters and rescuers, we condemn apartheid but approve of Nelson Mandela.

Heroes are not just people we think students should know about but people we expect them to admire.

The same individuals frequently serve double duty as objects of identification and admiration; if we expect students to identify with national figures, we want to make sure they are worthy of their admiration as well. Martin Luther King, Jr., is an obvious candidate for this role, because not only did he play a role in changing race relations in the United States, but he was a courageous man who fought for what he believed. Other times, stories about national heroes are invented to illustrate their virtues—such as the tale of Washington and the cherry tree. Occasionally, though, we ask students to admire people who are not part of their national story (in the United States, Nelson Mandela and Mother Teresa are popular figures in this role), and sometimes heroes need not even be individually famous, as the admiration for the fire fighters and police officers who responded to the tragedy at the World Trace Center makes clear. Some recommendations for teaching about heroes specifically suggest focusing on "everyday" heroes rather than only the famous.[17]

This admiration is usually accompanied by another purpose—imitation. We hope students will not only affirm the goodness of heroes but model their own lives after them. Recommendations for including heroes in the curriculum often are explicit in their advocacy of this purpose: Heroes are a source of character development. We select individuals in history who had positive character traits, hold them up for admiration, and reap the benefits when students develop those traits themselves. Students are exhorted to be as honest as Abe Lincoln, to make King's dream of better relations between the races come true, or to serve their community in ways similar to New York fire fighters. As Tony Sanchez puts it, "The hearts and minds of children and youth can be engaged by heroes and heroines. There are lessons to be learned, hearts to be moved, and imaginations to be stimulated."[18]

One problem with this perspective on the purpose of history is that it's far more popular among adults than children. In all our interviews with elementary and middle-school students, we cannot recall a single instance in which one said the purpose of learning history was to find heroes, role models, or people they could look to for the development of character. Bruce VanSledright, in his study of students' views of the purposes for studying history, also fails to report a single such example.[19] Students we have talked to are certainly familiar with famous people in history, and they can explain their impact on the present; sometimes they even admire them. What they do not do, however, is refer to them as heroes or suggest they provide a means of developing their own character.

On the other hand, we have never specifically asked students about their heroes; we can only note that they never brought the subject up in discussing history. Other researchers, however, have investigated this question more directly. Steven White and Joseph O'Brien, for example, asked 600 students from kindergarten through 12th grade who their heroes were. At all grade levels other than kindergarten, most students pointed to parents or other family members. (Kindergarteners chose cartoon characters most often.) The second most common response was for students to say they did not have a hero or did not know who it was (or not to answer the question at all); following that were sports and entertainment figures, and only a small portion of students mentioned anyone from history. Similarly, Kristin Anderson and Donna Cavallaro asked 179 children, ages 8 to 13, who they looked up to or admired. Thirty-four percent of the students choose their parents, followed by entertainers (20%), friends (14%), professional athletes (11%), and acquaintances (8%). Fewer than 1% of the children chose historical figures. These studies do not show that students have no historical heroes—maybe people from history are just further down the list—but the infrequency with which they mentioned them certainly suggests that they are not very salient role models.[20]

Some people might argue that this is precisely the problem: Students' heroes derive from the wrong sources, such as pop culture, and as history educators we need to begin supplying better alternatives (or supplying them again, as those who assume a mythical golden age of heroism in the curriculum suggest).[21] However, from the standpoint of participatory democracy, that may not be a particularly effective way of engaging students in moral response. The problem is not that the pantheon of heroes is insufficiently pluralistic; classroom teachers, curriculum developers, and publishers already are well aware of the need to diversify the historic individuals students learn about. Although we may not be as far along in this endeavor as we wish, it seems unlikely that the celebration of diversity will disappear from education, no matter how often political forces produce short-term bumps in the road. We believe the problem is deeper than that and stems from the very idea of holding up famous people as character models for students.

Anytime we idolize historical figures, we open ourselves up to disappointment, because all individuals have their flaws. All the heroes of U.S. history—both traditional and contemporary—had their shortcomings: Some were racists or misogynists; others were selfish or dishonest; still others mistreated family, peers, or subordinates. (Those who have escaped such characterizations probably just didn't produce enough historical evidence to allow their behavior to be probed more carefully.) Advocates of the heroic approach to history education are well aware that these blemishes can no longer be ignored, but they suggest two strategies for retaining the importance of heroes in spite of such drawbacks. The first is to point out that the attitudes and behaviors of historic individuals must be put into the context of their time. This is true enough, but in its most simplistic form—a form we often hear from educators—it means that any behavior can be excused so long as it results from a prevailing cultural belief. This leads some people to conclude, for example, that slave owners cannot be condemned because slavery was an accepted practice at the time, or that relocation of

Japanese Americans in World War II simply reflected widespread bias, and its advocates cannot be denounced for having gone along with it. This view assumes a consensual past in which everyone held the same beliefs and attitudes—a profoundly mistaken conclusion that ignores the diversity of views that existed at any given time. Enslaved people, after all, did not accept the practice (nor did abolitionists or many others), and Japanese Americans were not biased against themselves.

In its more nuanced form, the view that historical beliefs and actions must be put into the context of their time aims not to exonerate racism or other prejudices but to help students understand how they arose from social contexts different than their own.[22] Analytically, that makes perfect sense, but it also undercuts the use of historic individuals as heroes, because if they can only be understood within a time period that differs from our own, they are meaningless as role models for our time. The underlying assumption of the use of historic figures as heroes is that students today could be like them, but if attitudes and behaviors arise from cultural context, then students literally cannot be like people in history, because our context is a different one; we do not live in their time periods, and thus, they have little to say to us. Advocates of contextualizing racism or other flaws sometimes imply that the virtues of heroes are eternal, but their shortcomings are a product of their times. We can't have it both ways: If the virtues of heroes are timeless enough to imitate, then their failings must also be timeless enough to condemn.

A second way of dealing with the blemishes of historic individuals is to incorporate those into the very study of heroes itself. A number of authors advocate that we should learn about the flaws of famous people as well as their more admirable achievements. This more complete and complicated view of heroes would be even more beneficial to students than simplistic portrayals of uniform goodness, so that they can see that heroes were ordinary people, not models of perfection.[23] Again, we agree with this perspective in a general way, but it also seems to undercut the role of famous people specifically as heroes. If the purpose of learning about heroes is for students to admire them and become like them, then presenting their good and bad sides seems counterproductive. Do we want students to develop all their character qualities, both positive and negative? Obviously not, but how can we ask students to be like someone in history, but only partially?

We believe the answer to this lies in dropping the concept of heroes and replacing it with a focus on heroic actions. Throughout history, many people whose personal flaws disqualify them from being considered heroes have nonetheless behaved in ways worthy of admiration and imitation. Many supporters of women's rights in the 19th and early 20th centuries, for example, worked tirelessly to expand the opportunities available for women, and they often acted bravely in the face of opposition and intimidation. We can certainly regard these attempts to bring about a more just and equitable society as heroic. On the other hand, many of these women were inveterate racists, and they often justified women's suffrage by arguing that it would strengthen the voting power of the White majority. Some of their actions were heroic, but in light of their prejudice, we cannot hold them up as heroes for our students. Similarly, Lyndon B. Johnson will never be a hero of ours (for reasons too numerous to mention), but we can admire the determination with which he brought about passage of the Civil Rights Act. That action resulted in monumental benefits for our democracy, and we would not hesitate to suggest to students that they also pursue justice despite seemingly insurmountable odds; they do not have to take on the ruthless character qualities of Johnson to admire his persistence in promoting equality. Also, consider the example of Oskar Shindler, a man of unsavory character and questionable business practices who nonetheless took great risks to protect his Jewish employees during the Second World War: His actions were heroic, but his overall character was not that of a hero.

Focusing on heroic acts rather than the personal qualities of heroes provides a more appropriate preparation for democratic participation. Such participation, especially in a pluralist society, cannot depend on our conclusions about the character of individuals, because the very fact of pluralism ensures that some people will always regard others with suspicion or even hatred. Some will never be able to consider homosexuals, or Muslims, or Whites, to be good people who are worthy of their admiration. Yet democracy requires that we work together anyway, that we do things with each other for the benefit of society—participation is about action, not about character. If we want students to admire some aspects of history and if we want them to imitate that which they admire, we would be better served by emphasizing virtuous acts than virtuous people. Interestingly, this may even accord more closely with students' own definition of what constitutes a hero; when White and O'Brien asked students, "What is a hero?," the vast majority responded by pointing out the acts in which heroes engage—saving someone, helping someone, or "doing good"—and only a small proportion noted personal characteristics.[24]

CONCLUSIONS

Responding morally—affirming what we believe should or should not be the case in human affairs—is an inescapable part of our encounter with the past. It also forms a major component of history education in schools, although its role is generally unacknowledged and, as a result, unanalyzed. Although we rarely phrase our objectives in moral terms, we invariably expect students to admire some people or events and to condemn others. If we hope to prepare students for democratic life, this is as it should be: Our hopes for the future are necessarily rooted in our moral visions, and history provides the opportunity to apply those visions to the real world of human action. The past not only serves as a source of analytic examples—a way of examining causes and consequences—but as the training ground for moral response. Although some aspects of morality will vary among groups, others are rooted in the nature of the democracy we envision.

We have suggested that history education in the United States would benefit from a greater concern with remembrance—the duty to remember and reflect on those who have suffered and died in the past. If we do not feel such obligation, then the mistakes of the past are likely to disappear from view and leave us with a glorious—and inaccurate—perspective on national progress, one that provides little preparation for either reasoned judgment or the consideration of experiences different than our own. Reflecting on those who have suffered and died when they should not have, though, calls attention to issues of justice, or "fairness," as children and adolescents put it. This is a topic students find highly motivating, and history provides a wealth of examples that can prepare them for deliberations over justice in public life today. Such preparation should include attention to difficult and controversial issues, though; students need to be exposed to multiple perspectives on what constitutes justice and how to achieve it, and they need to confront instances where justice and self-interest—particularly for privileged groups—may conflict. Many of history's examples will be negative ones; as Seamus Heaney observes, history tells us not to hope on this side of the grave. However, throughout history, there have been encouraging examples, times when people have made the effort to work together for the common good or to embrace those who are different than themselves. By focusing on such heroic actions, students might have more room for hope and a better sense of themselves as agents of that hope.

ENDNOTES

1. Seamus Heaney, "Voices From Lemnos," in *Opened Ground: Selected Poems, 1966–1996* (New York: Farrar, Straus & Giroux, 1998), 305–06.
2. Keith C. Barton, "'Best Not to Forget Them': Positionality and Students' Ideas about Historical Significance in Northern Ireland," paper presented at the annual meeting of the American Educational Research Association, 19–23 April, 1999. The importance of most historical events in Northern Ireland are perceived differently by Protestant and Catholic communities, but these differences were relatively insignificant in the responses of students in this study. Remembrance of those who died in the world wars, for example, is generally considered more salient in the Protestant community, but as these quotes indicate, students of both religious backgrounds thought victims of the wars were worthy of being honored. Similarly, the Irish Famine figures more prominently in Catholic representations of the past, but students from both traditions regarded the suffering that it produced historically significant.
3. Barton, "Best Not to Forget Them."
4. Jane J. White, "Teaching Anthropology to Precollegiate Teachers and Students," in *The Teaching of Anthropology: Problems, Issues, and Decisions*, Eds. Conrad P.

Kottak, Jane J. White, Richard H. Furlow, and Patricia C. Rice (Mountain View, Calif.: Mayfield Publications, 1997), 291.

5. Linda S. Levstik, "Articulating the Silences: Teachers' and Adolescents' Conceptions of Historical Significance," in *Knowing, Teaching, and Learning History: National and International Perspectives*, Eds. Peter N. Stearns, Peter Seixas, and Sam Wineburg (New York: New York University Press, 2000), 293–94.

6. Levstik, "Articulating the Silences," 296–97.

7. George Orwell, *1984: A Novel* (New York: New American Library, 1983); Milan Kundera, *The Book of Laughter and Forgetting* (New York: HarperPerennial, 1996).

8. The way in which focusing on slavery as the central experience of African American history limits students' ability to see connections to the present is discussed in John S. Wills, "Who Needs Multicultural Education? White Students, U.S. History, and the Construction of a Usable Past," *Anthropology and Education Quarterly* 27 (September 1996): 365–389.

9. Keith C. Barton, "Historical Understanding Among Elementary Children" (Ed.D. diss., University of Kentucky, Lexington, 1994), 185–86.

10. Barton, "Historical Understanding among Elementary Children," 185, 186–87.

11. Linda S. Levstik, "Crossing the Empty Spaces: Perspective Taking in New Zealand Adolescents' Understanding of National History," in *Historical Empathy and Perspective Taking in the Social Studies*, Eds. O.L. Davis, Jr., Elizabeth Anne Yeager, and Stuart J. Foster (Lanham, Md.: Rowman and Littlefield, 2001), 80–81, 84; Barton, "Best Not to Forget Them."

12. Levstik, "Crossing the Empty Spaces," 83–84.

13. Levstik, "Crossing the Empty Spaces," 83–84; Keith C. Barton and Linda S. Levstik, "'It Wasn't a Good Part of History': National Identity and Ambiguity in Students' Explanations of Historical Significance," *Teachers College Record* 99 (Spring 1998): 486.

14. Barton, "Best Not to Forget Them."

15. Levstik, "Crossing the Empty Spaces," 85.

16. "African-American Heroes," *Instructor* 110, No. 5 (January/February 2001): 49–52; Jacqueline Clark, "Hooray for Heroes," *Instructor* 112, No. 2 (September 2002): 68–70; Joseph H. Fairbanks, Jr., "Heroes and Villains: Suggestions for a Classroom Activity on the Nature of History," *The Social Studies* 81 (January/February 1990): 6–9; Judy Freeman, "Books About all Kinds of Heroes," *Instructor* 107, No. 7 (April 1998): 26–8, "New Books That Celebrate the Triumphs of Real-Life Heroes," *Instructor* 107, No. 3 (October 1997): 24–7, "Real-Life Heroes," *Instructor* 110, No. 4 (November/December 2000): 17–21; Carol S. Holzberg, "Web Sightings: Heroes and Role Models," *Technology and Learning* 21 (August 2000): 56; Guy Larkins, "Transescents, Heroes, and Democracy: Social Education Through Biography," *Middle School Journal* 15 (May 1984): 12–13; Rahima Wade, "Heroes," *Social Studies and the Young Learner* 8, No. 3 (January/February, 1996): 15–17; Andrew Wales, "Heroes: Paper People Worthy of Admiration," *Arts and Activities* 130, No. 2 (October 2001): 38–39.

17. For example, Brenda A. Dyck, "Heroes Among Us: An Exercise in Evaluation," *Social Studies and the Young Learner* 13 (March/April 2001), 3–4.

18. Lori L. Kebetz, "Looking at Our Heroes: Does Character Really Count?," *School Library Media Activities Monthly* 16, No. 5 (January 2000), 12–15; Tony R. Sanchez, "It's Time Again for Heroes—Or Were They Ever Gone?," *The Social Studies* 91

(March/April 2000), 58–61,"Learning by Example," *Schools in the Middle* 9, No. 3 (November 1999), 38–41; Thomas Lickona, *Educating for Character: How Our Schools Can Teach Respect and Responsibility* (New York: Bantam, 1991), 310–11.

19. Bruce A. VanSledright, "And Santayana Lives On: Students' Views on the Purposes for Studying American History," *Journal of Curriculum Studies* 29 (September/October 1997): 529–557.

20. Steven H. White and Joseph E. O'Brien, "What Is a Hero? An Exploratory Study of Students' Conceptions of Heroes," *Journal of Moral Education* 28 (March 1999): 88–89; Kristin J. Anderson and Donna Cavallaro, "Parents or Pop Culture? Children's Heroes and Role Models," *Childhood Education* 78 (Spring 2002): 166.

21. L. Dunn, "Teaching the Heroes of American History," *The Social Studies* 82 (January February 1991): 26–30; Peter H. Gibbon, "Making the Case for Heroes," *Harvard Education Letter* 18, No. 4 (July/August 2002): 8; Sanchez, "It's Time Again for Heroes," 58–61.

22. Penny Clark, "Heroes and Canadian History," *Canadian Social Studies* 34 (Fall 1999), 136–7; Dunn, "Teaching the Heroes"; Sanchez, "It's Time Again for Heroes," "Learning by Example."

23. Dunn, "Teaching the Heroes"; Sanchez, "It's Time Again for Heroes," "Learning by Example," "Heroes and Heroines: Biographies to Live By," *Social Studies and the Young Learner* 13 (September/October 2000): 27–29.

24. White and O'Brien, "What is a Hero?," 88.

The Exhibition Stance

After looking at the enlarged photographs

of obsolete rural crafts, the bearded man

winnowing, the women in long skirts

at their embroidery,

the objects on open display, the churn,

the snuff-mill, the dogskin float,

in the Manor House galleries,

we walked among the trees to the half-dozen

re-erected workshops and cottages

transported from the edge of our region,

tidy and white in the mild April sun.

Passing between the archetypal round pillars

with the open five-barred gate,

my friend John said:

'What they need now, somewhere about here,

is a field for the faction fights.'

—*John Hewitt[1]*

Many years ago, as a freshman in college, one of us enrolled in an introductory history course—History of Europe to 1713, Tuesdays and Thursdays from 3:00 to 4:15. This was a special section of what would otherwise be a large lecture course, and enrollment was limited to 15 students. The course promised everything that had been lacking in high school—a knowledgeable instructor, readings from primary sources, and motivated students. However, once class started, it became clear these would be overshadowed by the dominant pattern of discourse in the classroom. Two days a week, for 1 hour and 15 minutes each day, the instructor tried to involve students in discussion while two know-it-alls blathered incessantly about historical trivia. These two had attended a local high school together, and they were playing out a long-established pattern of competition: The instructor directed a question toward the entire group, one of the two challenged him on some tangential point ("Excuse me, but historians think it may have been *pneumonic* plague rather than *bubonic!*"), and the other countered the challenge. These two students and the professor then engaged in a long debate over insignificant historical details while the rest of the class remained silent. We were neither knowledgeable about nor interested in such trivia. For many of us, though, this experience led to a compelling conclusion: Studying history meant exhibiting encyclopedic knowledge of insignificant factual information and should be avoided at all cost.

That may have been an overgeneralization, but it contained an element of truth: On many occasions, history is simply exhibited, and no further action is involved. Of course, any use of history necessarily involves some exhibition. If academics, or politicians, or veterans discuss the Vietnam War or its legacy, historical knowledge will be displayed along the way. However, what we describe in this chapter are instances in which exhibition of historical information is not a means to an end or an incidental outcome of other uses of history but constitutes an end in itself. This is common practice, and both children and adults repeatedly take part in these displays. At first glance, such exhibition might seem a benign practice, but in some cases it can detract significantly from the demands of participatory democracy, as when important issues such as the "faction fights" in John Hewitt's poem remain hidden from view. Other times, displays of historical information can make important contributions to education for democracy, but only when they are consistent with principles that are too often absent in practice.

EXHIBITION AS PERSONAL FULFILLMENT

Many people take part in the exhibition of historical knowledge because they find it personally fulfilling. Several hobbies and leisure activities involve the display of historical information, and people who engage in these pursuits do so because they find them personally enriching. Many antique collectors, for example, take pride in showing off their possessions and describing how they were produced or when they were used. Classic car enthusiasts do the same: They gather periodically in parking lots to display their vehicles, and they are happy to describe the fine points of their cars' engines, bodies, or detailing. Other people take part in historical recreations—of Civil War battles, frontier settlements, Colonial villages, and so on—and they spend their weekends traveling from one exhibit to another. Still others like to read books or watch documentaries about historical events and relate what they have learned to friends and family. Even genealogists, who may have a variety of purposes for their research, sometimes just like to display a family tree, an ancestor chart, or a copy of an old will. In each of these cases, historically accurate details take on a great deal of significance. Authentic finish, original parts, closely documented lines of descent—all of these lead to greater esteem for those who can pull them off. Reenactment clubs even give awards to those whose costumes demonstrate the greatest authenticity.

Although students have few opportunities to take part in historical hobbies like these at school, many know that adults are involved in them. Some have told us about relatives who visit old graveyards in search of their family's history, others have noted parents' or grandparents' interest in telling them about wars or other aspects of the past, and still others have mentioned annual parades of classic cars; children are also aware that displaying historical knowledge can have materials benefits, such as appearing on television quiz shows. Many times, they are willing participants in these activities: They go along on family outings, check out books on history from the library, and proudly relate giving the correct response while watching *Jeopardy*. In talking about such uses of history, children don't focus specifically on the exhibition aspect of knowledge, but they have begun to understand one of the underlying reasons for such displays: They know that some people find the quest for historical information personally rewarding.[2]

Displaying antiques, parading classic cars, and placing coats of arms above fireplaces probably don't advance participatory democracy in any noticeable fashion, but neither do they stand in its way. Although enacted in company with others, these are activities carried out for the rewards they bring to individuals, and they have little direct connection to the common good or to public action. They are neither more nor less relevant to democracy than an interest in basketball, gardening, or small engine repair. Yet other times the display of historical information for personal reward has more public consequences. The two students in the class we described at the beginning of this chapter were also seeking fulfillment, but for them, it depended on establishing their superiority in the eyes of the professor and their peers. They wanted to show how much they knew, presumably because they believed it would make others think more highly of them. As a result, the class was silenced. Those of us who had not subscribed to *Strategy and Tactics* magazine (one of their favorite sources of information) felt incapable of taking part in the discussion. Eventually, we lost interest in doing so.

Unfortunately, these students are not unusual. Our colleagues who teach history at the university level have told us they often have students whose prior experiences with history have consisted of accumulating information, and that these students see university coursework as the perfect opportunity to display their prowess in retrieving it. Conversations about Vietnam get bogged down in details about the effectiveness of specific models of helicopters, discussions of the American West become discussions of rifle manufacture, and so on. The result is always the same—the other students in the class stop talking. They often tell the professor they don't feel "smart" enough to keep up with these discussions. Instructors face the problem often enough that many have developed strategies to prevent these grandstanding students from derailing their courses. One colleague asks them to explain the significance of the details they bring up or to connect them back to the larger point of discussion. Another raises her hand like a traffic officer and says, "Stop! Hold that thought!"—and then never returns to it.

Those obsessed with historic details have long been accused of self-absorption. Over 400 years ago, Philip Sidney referred to the historian as the "tyrant of table talk," "better acquainted with a thousand years ago than with the present age," and "laden with old mouse-eaten records." More recently, David Hackett Fisher has suggested that memorized facts are displayed as "empty emblems of erudition."[3] Although few people are so fixated on antiquarian details, those who do like to display information can easily become "tyrants" and squelch the contributions of anyone whose knowledge is less encyclopedic. Experienced teachers will be able to put a lid on these shenanigans, but the danger is that some instructors, whether at the collegiate or precollegiate levels, will be less skilled at involving students in more substantial discussions—or worse, that they will actually validate the exhibition of knowledge as an end in itself, perhaps even making it a precondition of classroom participation. History then becomes the preserve of pedantic blowhards, and "discussion" focuses on the knowledge easiest to display—namely, discrete factual details. When the exhibition of historical information limits the extent and content of participation in this way, it detracts significantly from the inclusive discourse necessary for participatory democracy.

EXHIBITION AS ACCOUNTABILITY

One of the most common purposes guiding exhibition of historical information in school settings is accountability. Children are expected to display what they know about history as a way of holding them accountable for learning and their teachers and schools accountable for delivering a required curriculum. In the first instance, students have to answer questions at the end of a chapter, write definitions of vocabulary words, answer questions posed by the teacher in class, and take classroom tests over the material they are expected to have mastered. The second kind of accountability, however, has become increasingly important in recent years; in fact, it dominates teaching in many locations and practically overwhelms all other discussions of educational practice. In this kind of exhibition, students take mandated, standardized tests so that state-level agencies can determine whether schools have effectively delivered the required curriculum. In both forms of exhibition, students are expected to display historical knowledge, but the object of accountability differs—students themselves in the first instance, primarily teachers and schools (and sometimes students) in the second.

The first practice—requiring that students display their knowledge of history as proof they have mastered the material—is a time-honored one, but like many time-honored educational practices, it has little to recommend it as a way of promoting either learning or citizenship. Having students look up the answers to textbook exercises provides evidence that they have looked up the answers to textbook exercises, having them recall information in classroom recitations provides evidence that they can recall information in classroom recitations, and having them answer questions on classroom tests provides evidence that they can answer questions on classroom tests. If the goal of history education were to have students complete exercises, recall information, or answer questions, then the display of knowledge in these ways might be an appropriate method of holding them accountable, and students who wanted to accomplish those goals would presumably be motivated to engage in the preparation that would enable them to succeed in such displays. However, even if these were the goals of history education, there would be no reason to believe that the learning that goes into such displays would transfer in any meaningful way: Memorizing information on Hittites does not make students more knowledgeable about Etruscans. Displaying information in these ways allows teachers to determine whether students have retained specific information, but it does little else.

Moreover, if the purpose of history education is to prepare students for participatory democracy, these displays have no particular relevance. Being able to display historical information does not demonstrate that students have an expanded view of humanity, that they are able to make reasoned judgments, or that they can deliberate about the common good. In the course of engaging in a discussion about the common good, students might well display a great deal of historical information—indeed, any good discussion would necessitate such display. However, holding students accountable for that display of information rather than for the educational goals of history would be misguided. Long experience with children and adults suggests that many can display historical information without having any particular interest in the common good or any notable ability to make reasoned judgments. If teachers want to hold students accountable for learning history in the ways we have mentioned, they will have to evaluate their judgments and deliberation as they engage in such activities. There's no point in asking students to come to the front of the class and saying, "Give me a reasoned judgment!" or "Show me your expanded view of humanity!" when these can be more carefully evaluated in the context of meaningful classroom activities. Exhibition as an isolated activity does not seem well suited for classroom accountability when history is taught in a humanistic fashion.

However, it is the second kind of accountability that may be more important—and more problematic—in today's world. Since the 1980s, the discourse of "raising academic standards" and the practice of creating "standards documents" has come to dominate educational policy.[4] These efforts initially involved the development of national guides to curriculum and instruction in each content area, but more recently, the emphasis has been on state-level standards accompanied by systems of reward and punishment tied to measures of students' learning. In states that have implemented these "high-stakes" testing programs, evidence of improvement in student performance can result in financial rewards for districts, schools, principals, or even individual teachers, whereas lack of such improvement sometimes can lead to dismissal of faculty or intervention into the administration of entire districts. (In some places, student promotion and graduation also are tied to state tests.) These sanctions are meant to provide powerful incentives for schools to ensure that students perform well on the required measures, and as a result, state-level standards are increasingly driving expectations for classroom instruction.[5]

Can requiring students to display knowledge on state-mandated tests improve history education? Ten years ago, we thought that it could, at least to some degree. Although these displays would not necessarily have benefited the students taking part in them, we hoped that mandated, high-stakes tests could lead to positive and significant changes in the teaching of history. We thought the entire field of social studies was poorly taught, relying as it did on textbooks and requiring memorization of a narrow body of factual information. In the primary grades, the subject was virtually absent. Students in most districts took achievement tests, but these typically covered only math, reading, and language, and so social studies (along with science) had low status and was often omitted under the pressures of time. We believed that if students were tested on historical content, schools would be more likely to include the subject in the curriculum and to do so from the first years of schooling.

We also expected that these tests would go beyond evaluating retention of discrete bits of factual information. The early 1990s were heady times in the world of assessment, in both practitioner and academic circles; the air was full of talk of writing portfolios, performance assessments, and multiple forms of evaluation.[6] We knew it was possible to assess more sophisticated intellectual skills than those that traditionally had been tested, and we worked in a state that was briefly at the forefront of such innovations.[7] We thought new assessments would engage students in group deliberation, involve them in deep and sensitive reasoning, and even focus on issues of the common good. Also, if the assessments did this, we believed, so would teachers: To prepare for tests of reasoning, they would have to spend time giving students the chance to reason; to prepare them for assessments that involved group deliberation, they would have to engage them in deliberation throughout the year. We had no problem with teaching to the tests as long as the tests were worth teaching to. We accepted the premise that tests drive instruction, as well as its corollary that good tests would lead to good instruction.[8] If the goals of history education were clearly articulated, and if high-stakes tests matched these goals, we had every reason to think that instruction would begin to change accordingly.

There has indeed been some evidence that state-level tests can lead teachers to adopt more challenging and authentic instructional practices, at least in some subjects (notably mathematics and writing) and at some grade levels (mainly those in which students are tested).[9] For several years, our work in schools also suggested that the notice given to social studies (including history) was increasing, as primary teachers began to request workshops on using literature to teach the subject, upper elementary teachers gave the topic more systematic attention, and middle school history teachers seemed to enjoy new status and respect. Just as important, outstanding teachers had their instructional practices validated; instead of bucking the trend when they had students work in groups to compare primary sources, they now found that these activities directly prepared students for high-stakes testing and ultimately led to financial rewards for themselves and their colleagues. We expected the "wisdom of practice" these teachers brought to their job would be recognized as such and that they would become role models for peers who sought to improve their practice. We hoped the reforms we saw taking shape locally were about to take off on a national scale.

However, events did not continue to live up to our hopes. For one thing, some states omitted science and social studies from the topics assessed, and as a result, these subjects received no more attention than they ever had—and sometimes they received less, as all teachers were expected to drop what they were doing and focus on the content of the tests. Even in states where social studies was part of the mandated evaluation system, the early promise of new tests became compromised, as performance assessments and group tasks were replaced by paper-and-pencil items that could be scored easily. Questions that might address such topics as the common good, meanwhile, were quickly ruled off the table in an effort to remove any content that smacked of "values." Also, in many schools, curriculum content became limited to the specific items known to be covered on the tests (rather than the larger subject areas they were meant to sample), and instructional practices came to reflect the format of the required tests—as writing, research papers, and discussion were replaced by disjointed information, short reading passages, and multiple choice questions. Some world history teachers in New York noted that new state tests, although they did not result in wholesale changes in instructional practice, nonetheless led to reductions in both the number and scope of student projects assigned, increases in the use of lectures and textbooks, and a focus on covering content and helping students produce narrow and literal "right" answers, even when working with primary source material.[10]

Even when tests have not focused solely on discrete pieces of factual information, and even when they have not been limited to machine-scorable multiple choice items, they sometimes have had a negative impact on curriculum and instruction. In both Kentucky and Ohio, for example, the form and content of the mandated tests go well beyond the trivial, and they retain at least the vestiges of a concern with higher order thinking. They do not involve performance assessments of group discussions about the common good, and they contain a much higher percentage of multiple choice items than we would like, but they do include at least a small portion of open-ended, constructed-response items that ask students to display their reasoning about important historical content. One released item from the 11th grade Kentucky test, for example, asks students to choose two examples of post-World War II U.S. foreign policy, to explain how each example was related to the objective of "containing" communism, and to evaluate whether each was successful. In Ohio, a sixth-grade item lists reform activities in which Eleanor Roosevelt was involved; students are then directed to choose two of the movements and explain how each affected the lives of Americans, as well as to explain how another woman, of their own choosing, contributed to American society.[11]

These questions require some judgment, and the topics are related to the demands of citizenship. Such tests should be useful for holding schools accountable for teaching students how to engage in reasoning about historical content and thus for improving instruction. Yet in fact, many educators have responded to these tests in the same way as their colleagues in other states—by limiting instruction to a few specific topics, engaging in lecture and recitation, using ineffective test preparation materials, and focusing on isolated pieces of information. The tests ask students to make judgments about cause and effect, but schools require them to memorize factual details; the tests call for written responses, but schools require circled answers on worksheets; most distressingly, the tests require understanding, but schools focus on coverage. We do not fully grasp the mechanisms that lead to the adoption of instructional practices so distinctly at odds with the measures used to hold schools accountable, but we find merit in Sandra Cimbricz's suggestion that the perceptions of tests may exert a greater impact on practice than the tests themselves. If educators assimilate current tests to their prior images of low-level, multiple-choice tests, or if they fail to recognize the difference between the content of the test and that found in textbooks or ditto books, they will be unlikely to modify instruction in ways intended by policymakers. Our observations are certainly consistent with S. G. Grant's argument that state-level tests are but one influence among many on teachers' practice and that tests therefore represent, at best, an "uncertain" lever of change.[12]

Both research evidence and our own experiences in schools, then, suggest that the drawbacks of requiring students to display historical information to hold schools accountable are likely to outweigh the potential advantages. There is little evidence that such testing increases students' experience with reasoned judgment, expanded views of humanity, or deliberations over the common good. In fact, there is evidence that in some cases, such features of humanistic education are being pushed further from the curriculum than ever and are being replaced with practices that expose students to a narrow range of content, taught in an ineffective manner. Far from contributing to participatory democracy, exhibition for the purpose of accountability may be undermining the potential benefit of history education for democratic citizenship.

EXHIBITION AS SERVICE TO OTHERS

When exhibition of history is used for personal fulfillment, the beneficiaries are those who exhibit the information themselves: People display antiques, family crests, or trivia because they enjoy doing so. When exhibition is used for accountability, the beneficiary is more collective and abstract: Students display what they've learned so that the entire educational system will benefit, because schools will be held accountable for ensuring that students are learning. In a third type of exhibition, though, it is the recipients of the exhibited information who are expected to benefit. That is, those who see or hear historical displays are assumed to be better off for the experience—not because they have been told how to interpret the displays or what lessons to draw from them, but simply because they have come into contact with the information. Although at first glance this might appear to be a simplistic use of history, it actually involves complicated social processes and has important implications for the humanistic study of history and, ultimately, for participatory democracy.

We have encountered this use of historical exhibition repeatedly, both in our interviews with children and in our own lives within and outside academia. However, we began to understand its significance more fully when an undergraduate student completed a classroom research project in which she interviewed one of her former high school history teachers. She knew that he was an avid participant in Civil War battle reenactments. In her interview, she asked him why he took part in these. He didn't note his personal enjoyment of the experience, but instead explained

> The horror of the Civil War is the 600,000 battle deaths, but many people that lived were amputees, many arms and legs were removed, and of course surgery at that time was sort of primitive, so you can imagine the horror that happened at that time. War, *all* war, is terrible. There is no glory in war, but we must remember what they did to sacrifice, and why we are standing here today, and why we're free.

This reenactor's view of the purpose of knowing history was complex and multifaceted. In his view, history involved rational analysis (allowing him to conclude that war leads to physical suffering), identification (note the repeated use of the word *we*), and moral response (in the importance he attaches to remembering the sacrifices of the past). Each of these purposes motivated his participation in these exhibitions. However, the displays themselves—the battle reenactments—did not directly involve any of these. The immediate purpose was to present historical information and let others analyze, identify, and respond. He had developed his own interpretation of why these things were important to know about, and he expected spectators to draw similar conclusions; the goal of the display, however, was not to present his conclusions but to present the information on which they were based. The purpose, as he saw it, was to serve others.

Students' experience with this kind of exhibition takes place in two principal contexts: discussions with relatives and other adults, and visits to historical museums and sites. As we noted in chapter 1, students repeatedly point to parents, grandparents, and siblings as sources of their historical knowledge, and they occasionally mention other children or adults as well. Children's experiences in these settings are probably familiar ones for most of us: They hear about what it was like in the "old days," about differences in technology and household appliances, about how locations were different long ago. They also hear about participation in wars and political movements and about the history that others have learned from books, movies, television, and school.[13]

The likelihood that this exhibition will be accompanied by some explanation of its meaning probably is greater than with more impersonal displays; grandparents, for example, may explain that life was harder when they were growing up and that children should be grateful for what they have. Other times, though, information may be passed along because of the belief that someone else will be better off for knowing it, with no particular "lesson" attached. Children may be told that nickels were made of lead during World War II, that "I used to shoot rabbits in that field" where the mall is now, or that the local golf course is where Magnus Barefoot, the King of Norway, was killed in 1103. In Northern Ireland, children often note that older siblings have told them about the historical topics they are studying at school—they know about the Vikings, or Romans, or Victorians because their brothers or sisters already studied those topics and told them about them. Presumably, their siblings thought that if the Vikings were important enough to learn about at school, they should go ahead and pass the information along to the rest of the family. There is a kind of selflessness about such displays—they are done for someone else's benefit. Moreover, many students are consciously aware that this is one of the purposes that guides history, and they look forward to fulfilling the same role themselves one day: They plan to tell their own children and grandchildren about life when they were in school or about the historical topics they've studied.[14]

Exhibiting historical information as a service to others is also one of the principle purposes of museums and historic sites, and these are among the most common locations in which children learn about the past. Restored homes, antique farm implements, glass cases full of artifacts, Archie Bunker's chair—these are on display, at least in part, because some private or public agency has decided they should be seen. Their popularity indicates that visitors agree. Sometimes these sites go beyond simple display and aim at producing a particular effect among visitors, whether identification, moral response, or analysis of historical trends. However, other times they display objects with little explicit purpose beyond making them available for viewing. We saw an extreme example of such display when we visited a Scottish "folk museum" that included shelf after shelf of unlabelled household appliances from the 18th and 19th centuries. Few museums are as lacking in interpretation as this one, but many are nonetheless devoted primarily to displaying available materials or accurately recreating historical times rather than any of the other "acts" of history. At the heart of such exhibition is the belief that visitors will benefit from having witnessed these displays.

This service to others is the way in which exhibition is most likely to contribute to participatory democracy. Reasoned judgment, an expansive view of humanity, and deliberation about the common good all require accurate and accessible information. Sometimes citizens will acquire such information from books, sometimes from electronic media, and sometimes from archives. Other times, the most accessible sources will be people or museums. Who better to ask about life 50 years ago than one's grandparents? Where better to find out what farming was like in the 19th century than a recreated farm community? Where else could one see Viking jewelry other than in a museum? For that matter, who could better explain topics like Woodland Indian life or the Industrial Revolution than older siblings who have already studied them? The willingness to display such information is critical for participatory democracy to operate.

This selfless exhibition of historical information could even be a model for classroom assignments: Rather than displaying information for teachers or accountability agencies, students could display information for each other. In one of our classroom studies, for example, fourth and fifth graders worked in groups to create presentations for a "history museum" that younger children visited. In the class Bruce VanSledright taught, groups of students chose different colonies to research and then wrote up their findings for other members of the class.[15] Similar projects might include posters, videos, dramatizations, or magazines aimed at displaying historic information for others inside or outside the school community; the older students get, the more varied and sophisticated these exhibitions could become. Also, in creating such displays, students would have to engage in each of the components of humanistic history education—making judgments about the synthesis and representation of historical content, taking into account the perspectives of each other and of their audience, and deliberating about how best to accomplish their goals. Ultimately, these assignments would provide teachers with more of the information needed for classroom accountability than tests and worksheets, and they would do so within a more authentic—and humanistic—context.

However, providing service to others is not an unproblematic undertaking. For the exhibition of historical information to contribute to humanistic education, it must involve information that other people want and need. This is a tricky proposition. Those who have information to display typically control the form and content of its presentation, and they may have the power and resources to impose their conception of "needed information" on others. This dominance is a particular problem within the exhibition stance because it is less obvious: Analysis, identification, and moral response are easily recognized as social constructions, but information that is simply displayed can take on the appearance of a natural, inevitable, or objective representation of the world. It appears to "mirror" historical reality rather than to interpret it. This reaction was particularly clear in the interviews conducted by Roy Rosenzweig and David Thelen. They found that respondents placed more trust in historic sites and museums than any other source and that they believed such locations transported them "straight back to the times when people had used the artifacts on display or occupied the places where 'history' had been made." They felt these encounters provided them with direct and undistorted access to the experiences of people in the past; as one person noted, a museum "isn't trying to present you with any points of view."[16]

However, the exhibition of historical information is inseparable from interpretation, and museums and historic sites reflect a host of social, cultural, economic, and ideological underpinnings.[17] The simple fact that interpretation is involved does not constitute a drawback, because interpretation-free displays cannot exist. Even the Scottish folk museum, for example, had to make decisions about what to display: Why exhibit five kinds of iron kettle, for example, instead of five kinds of eviction notice? When such interpretations are not acknowledged, the variety of information that could be displayed is pushed out of view and becomes almost unimaginable, but sometimes it is those alternative sources of information that are most important.

In Northern Ireland, for example, the Ulster Folk and Transport Museum (subject of the poem at the beginning of this chapter) is dedicated to displaying details of folk life in the region. As Hewitt observes, visitors see restored homes, shops, and other buildings (far more than the "half dozen" at the time the poem was written), all with authentic furnishings, tools, implements, and the ongoing activities of a living history museum. What is missing, as his friend points out, is "a field for the faction fights." Visitors will not see items related to historical conflicts involving Catholic and Protestant communities. Indeed, the museum was established with the explicit intention of creating a depiction of Northern Ireland's material culture that spanned the two communities. Its intent was to display what they had in common rather than what separated them. As a former director of the museum suggested, such locations should provide "oases of calm" and a vision around which "people of all persuasions could unite."[18]

The search for common ground is an admirable objective not only in Northern Ireland but in all divided societies; as we discussed in chapter 3, people are unlikely to care about the common good unless they perceive themselves as having a common identity. We wonder, though, whether such common ground can be established by displaying details of material life without acknowledging the historical circumstances that have led to conflict—conflicts that in the case of Northern Ireland continue to this day. Of course, no individual museum can be charged with the task of solving society's deep-seated historical conflicts. The Ulster Folk and Transport Museum has a specific mission that it addresses very capably. However, in Northern Ireland, virtually no museums address the history of religious and political conflict; nearly all are devoted to displaying uncontroversial details of social and material life. Visitors to the vast majority of museums and historic sites there come away without encountering any suggestion that the country is beset by fundamental and ongoing conflict with deep roots in history. A number of museum professionals, though, are beginning to question whether such "neutral" or "passive" approaches are appropriate, given the region's deeply conflicted history and its continuing discord. One museum curator, for example, suggested to us that among the reasons for Northern Ireland's continuing troubles is the unwillingness of public institutions, such as schools and museums, to address the conflict directly.[19]

A similar example can be found closer to home, at Colonial Williamsburg. Richard Handler and Eric Gable note that visitors are constantly reminded of the accuracy of the many details of material culture they encounter there—architecture, furnishings, tools, decorations, patterns of land use, and so on. Inaccurate features are also brought to visitors' attention, and this practice further reinforces the impression that the staff is devoted to a faithful presentation of life as it existed in Colonial Williamsburg. This concern with accurate detail is also evident when interpreters address the social life of the town: They limit discussion to the specific time represented in the reconstruction (the 1770s) and steadfastly avoid comparison to later time periods or the present. Anachronisms are avoided at all costs, whether they relate to architectural details or the larger narrative of American history. As a result, a topic like slavery can be discussed only as it existed in Colonial Williamsburg. The nature of slavery in other times and places, its role in the Civil War, its legacy in the present—all of these are avoided as anachronistic, despite the fact that, according to Handler and Gable, these are what visitors most want to know about. They argue that the obsession with presenting the past as it "really was" at Williamsburg serves to erase the relationships between history and our own time: Visiting a museum that strives so faithfully to recreate a single moment in time makes it difficult to see connections between the structural conditions and cultural patterns of past and present. Just as in Northern Ireland, the display of extensive and authentic historical detail may result in avoidance of larger social concerns.[20]

To live up to its potential for service to others, then, the exhibition of historical information must follow two key principles. First, any exhibition should include attention to how it was created, and in the process lay bare its own assumptions, perspectives, and omissions. That is, it should call attention to the choices made in its creation (both what to display and how to display it) as well as the consequences of those choices and potential alternatives. As Gaynor Kavanah points out, when the experiences of some groups of people—such as those of women, children, minorities, or workers—are left out of museum displays, it becomes difficult for visitors to struggle against the dominant representations found there; she notes that "visitors can only do so much to fill in the blanks."[21] Audiences would be better able to conceptualize and pursue alternative information if the limitations of displays were frankly admitted; rather than pretending that a given exhibition is the only way of approaching the subject—thereby implying that the audience need not ask for anything more—exhibitions should be open and reflective about the constructed nature of their representations. Even in school assignments, students could explain to their audience the choices they made, the consequences of those choices, and how they could have displayed information differently.

Exhibitions also would be more useful if they allowed audiences to relate the displayed information to their own ideas, perspectives, and questions. This is a basic tenet of contemporary theories of education, and George Hein suggests that museums should be guided by a similar principle: For visitors to learn from displays, museums must allow them to "connect what they see, do and feel with what they already know, understand and acknowledge."[22] This seems to be precisely the element missing at Colonial Williamsburg: If visitors come with questions about the role of slavery throughout U.S. history but are presented only with information on a given time and place, the learning that results may be minimal. From an educational perspective, then, simply presenting children with displays of historical information—whether from historic sites, teachers, books, or peers—may be ineffective, particularly if the goal of history education is to enable students to deliberate over matters of the common good. For displays to constitute service to others, there must be some attempt to identify what historical information others truly need. Again, classroom assignments could follow this same principle: Students working on historical displays might begin by finding out what their audience already knows about the topic and what questions they have about it.

CONCLUSIONS

When we began this work, the exhibition stance was our least favorite, and we held it in thinly disguised contempt, despite our avowed purpose of trying to understand the potential contribution of each of the four principal acts of history. In fact, we dreaded deciding which of us would write what we thought must be a depressing chapter. Indeed, some uses of historical display are depressing—its self-glorifying use by "tyrants of table talk" and its destructive effect on teaching and learning when used as a means of presumed "accountability." In both these cases, the display of information constitutes a potential obstacle to humanistic history education, and we believe educators must be diligent in developing strategies to overcome these obstacles. However, in its role of providing service to others, we find an admirable use for the exhibition of historical information, and we believe such displays can be an important part of educational endeavors, whether inside or outside formal institutions. Providing information that other people need to make judgments, understand humanity, and deliberate about the common good is indispensable for democracy, and students can learn from an early age that they too can take part in such displays—by sharing what they know with younger children, with peers, or with people outside the school. In fact, this is one of the uses of historical information with which children are already familiar: Many explain that the purpose of learning history is to pass on information themselves someday. To live up to this potential, however, students must have the opportunity to actually take part in such other-oriented displays and to construct them according to the principles we have discussed.

ENDNOTES

1. John Hewitt, "Cultra Manor: The Ulster Folk Museum," in *The Collected Poems of John Hewitt*, Ed. Frank Ormsby (Belfast, Northern Ireland: Blackstaff Press, 1991), 187. Reprinted by permission of Blackstaff Press on behalf of the estate of John Hewitt.
2. "Historical Understanding among Elementary Children" (Ed.D. diss., University of Kentucky, Lexington, 1994), 77–84; Linda S. Levstik and Keith C. Barton, "'They Still Use Some of Their Past': Historical Saliences in Children's Chronological Thinking," *Journal of Curriculum Studies 28* (September/October 1996): 558–560. See also Bruce A. VanSledright, "'I Don't Remember—The Ideas are all Jumbled in My Head': 8th Graders' Reconstructions of Colonial American History," *Journal of Curriculum and Supervision* 10 (Summer 1995): 335.
3. Sidney quoted in Nicholas P. Canny, *Making Ireland British, 1580–1650* (New York: Oxford University Press, 2001), 20; David Hackett Fisher, *Historians' Fallacies: Toward a Logic of Historical Thought* (New York, Harper and Row, 1970), 311.
4. The case for standards can be found in Diane Ravitch, *National Standards in American Education: A Citizen's Guide* (Washington, D.C.: Brookings, 1995); National Council on Education Standards and Testing, *Raising Standards for American Education: A Report to Congress, the Secretary of Education, the National Education Goals*

Panel, and the American People (Washington, D.C.: U.S. Department of Education, 1992); and Marc S. Tucker and Judy B. Codding, *Standards for Our Schools: How to Set Them, Measure Them, and Reach Them* (San Francisco: Jossey-Bass, 1998). Critical perspectives on this movement include Alfie Kohn, *The Schools Our Children Deserve: Moving Beyond Traditional Classrooms and "Tougher Standards"* (Boston: Houghton Mifflin, 1999); Linda M. McNeil, *Contradictions of School Reform: Educational Costs of Standardized Testing* (New York: Routledge, 2000); Susan Ohanian, *One Size Fits Few: The Folly of Educational Standards* (Portsmouth, N.H.: Heinemann, 1999). For discussion of the development of national standards in history, see Linda Symcox, *Whose History? The Struggle for National Standards in American Classrooms* (New York: Teachers College Press, 2002) and Gary B. Nash, Charlotte Crabtree, and Ross E. Dunn, *History on Trial: Culture Wars and the Teaching of the Past* (New York: A. A. Knopf, 1997).

5. S. G. Grant, *History Lessons: Teaching, Learning, and Testing in U.S. High School Classrooms* (Mahwah, N.J.: Lawrence Erlbaum Associates, Inc., 2003), 129–148; Sandra C. Cimbricz, "State-Mandated Testing and Teachers' Beliefs and Practices," *Education Policy Analysis Archives* 10, No. 2, 9 January, 2002 [journal on-line], available from http://epaa.asu.edu/epaa/v10n2.html, accessed 24 January, 2002.

6. For example, Doug A. Archbald and Fred M. Newmann, *Beyond Standardized Testing: Assessing Authentic Academic Achievement in the Secondary School* (Reston, Va.; National Association of Secondary School Principals, 1988); Randy Elliott Bennett and William C. Ward, Eds., *Construction versus Choice in Cognitive Measurement: Issues in Constructed Response, Performance Testing, and Portfolio Assessment* (Hillsdale, N.J.: Lawrence Erlbaum Associates, Inc., 1993); Linda Darling-Hammond, Jacqueline Ancess, and Beverly Falk, *Authentic Assessment in Action: Studies of Schools and Students at Work* (New York: Teachers College Press, 1995); Bill Harp, Ed., *Assessment and Evaluation in Whole Language Programs* (Norwood, Mass.: Christopher-Gordon, 1994); Diane Hart, *Authentic Assessment: A Handbook for Educators* (New York: Addison-Wesley, 1994); Robert J. Tierney, Mark A. Carter, and Laura E. Desai, *Portfolio Assessment in the Reading-Writing Classroom* (Norwood, Mass.: Christopher-Gordon, 1991).

7. Jean Fontana, "Portfolio Assessment: Its Beginnings in Vermont and Kentucky," *NASSP Bulletin* 79 (October 1995): 25–30; Thomas R. Guskey, *High Stakes Performance Assessment: Perspectives on Kentucky's Educational Reform* (Thousand Oaks, Calif.: Corwin Press, 1994); Kentucky Institute for Education Research, *The Implementation of Performance Assessment in Kentucky* (Louisville, Ky.: School of Education, University of Louisville, 1995), ERIC Document Reproduction Service, ED 394978; Linda G. Esser, "Writing Assessment Portfolios in Kentucky: Owned by the Students or Owned by the State?," paper presented at the annual meeting of the American Educational Research Association, 8–12 April, 1996, ERIC Document Reproduction Service, ED 405634; Brian M. Stecher, Sheila Barron, Tessa Kaganoff, and Joy Goodwin, *The Effects of Standards-Based Assessment on Classroom Practices; Results of the 1996–97 RAND Survey of Kentucky Teachers of Mathematics and Writing* (Los Angeles: Center for the Study of Evaluation, University of California, Los Angeles, 1998), ERIC Document Reproduction Service, ED 426070.

8. This perspective is reflected in Grant P. Wiggins, *Assessing Student Performance: Exploring the Purpose and Limits of Testing* (San Francisco: Jossey-Bass Publishers, 1993) and "A True Test: Toward More Authentic and Equitable Assessment," *Phi Delta Kappan* 70 (May 1989): 703–13; Linda Darling-Hammond, "Setting Standards for Students: The Case for Authentic Assessment," *NASSP Bulletin* 77 (November 1993): 18–26; James W. Popham, "Circumventing the High Costs of Authentic Assessment," *Phi Delta Kappan* 74 (February 1993): 470–73; Dennie Wolf, JoAnne Eresh, and Paul G. LeMahieu, "Good Measure: Assessment as a Tool for Education Reform," *Educational Leadership* 49 (May 1992): 8–13.

9. Brian M. Stecher, Sheila Barron, Tessa Kaganoff, and Joy Goodwin, "The Effects of Standards-Based Assessment on Classroom Practices: Results of the 1996–97 RAND Survey of Kentucky Teachers of Mathematics and Writing," Center for the Study of Evaluation Technical Report 482 (Los Angeles: National Center for Research on Evaluation, Standards, and Student Testing, University of California, Los Angeles, 1998), available at http://www.cse.ucla.edu/CRESST/Reports/TECH482.PDF, accessed 9 April, 2003; Hilda Borko and Rebekah Elliott, "Tensions Between Competing Pedagogical and Accountability Commitments for Exemplary Teachers of Mathematics in Kentucky," Center for the Study of Evaluation Technical Report 495 (Los Angeles: National Center for Research on Evaluation, Standards, and Student Testing, University of California, Los Angeles, 1998), available at http://www.cse.ucla.edu/CRESST/Reports/TECH495.PDF, accessed 9 April, 2003; Shelby A. Wolfe and Monette C. McIver, "Writing Whirligigs: The Art and Assessment of Writing in Kentucky State Reform," Center for the Study of Evaluation Technical Report 496 (Los Angeles: National Center for Research on Evaluation, Standards, and Student Testing, University of California, Los Angeles, 1998), available at http://www.cse.ucla.edu/CRESST/Reports/TECH496.PDF, accessed 9 April, 2003; Brian M. Stecher and Sheila I. Barron, "Quadrennial Milepost Accountability Testing in Kentucky," Center for the Study of Evaluation Technical Report 505 (Los Angeles: National Center for Research on Evaluation, Standards, and Student Testing, University of California, Los Angeles, 1999), available at http://www.cse.ucla.edu/CRESST/Reports/TECH505.PDF, accessed 9 April, 2003; Sheila L. Barron, Tammi Chun, and Karen Ross, "The Effects of the Washington State Education Reform on Schools and Classrooms," Center for the Study of Evaluation Technical Report 525 (Los Angeles: National Center for Research on Evaluation, Standards, and Student Testing, University of California, Los Angeles, 2000), available at http://www.cse.ucla.edu/CRESST/Reports/TECH525.PDF, accessed 9 April, 2003; Brian Stecher and Tammi Chun, "School and Classroom Practices During Two Years of Education Reform in Washington State," Center for the Study of Evaluation Technical Report 550 (Los Angeles: National Center for Research on Evaluation, Standards, and Student Testing, University of California, Los Angeles, 2001), available at http://www.cse.ucla.edu/CRESST/Reports/TECH550.PDF, accessed 9 April, 2003.

10. Stecher and Barron, "Quadrennial Milepost Accountability Testing," 31–33; Barron, Chun, and Ross, "Effects of the Washington State Education Reform," 72–73; Stecher and Chun, "School and Classroom Practices," 27–28; Cimbricz, "State-Mandated Testing"; McNeil, *Contradictions of School Reform*, 205–11,

234–43, 246–49; Wayne E. Wright, "The Effects of High Stakes Testing in an Inner-City Elementary School: The Curriculum, the Teachers, and the English Language Learners," *Current Issues in Education* 5, No. 5, 2002 [journal on-line], available from http://cie.ed.asu.edu/volume5/number5/, accessed July 8, 2002; Audrey L. Amrein and David C. Berliner, "High-Stakes Testing, Uncertainty, and Student Learning," *Education Policy Analysis Archives* 10, No. 18, 28 March, 2002 [journal on-line], available from http://epaa.asu.edu/epaa/v10n18/, accessed 6 August, 2002; S. G. Grant, Alison Derme-Insinna, Jill Gradwell, Ann Marie Lauricella, Lynn Pullano, and Kathryn Tzetzo, "Juggling Two Sets of Books: A Teacher Responds to the New York State Global History Exam," *Journal of Curriculum and Supervision* 17 (Spring 2002): 232–255, and "Teachers, Tests, and Tensions: Teachers Respond to the New York State Global History Exam," *International Social Studies Forum* 1, No. 1 (2001): 107–125. Moreover, some researchers suggest that there is little evidence that state-level testing has improved achievement and that in some cases, it may have been accompanied by a decrease in scores on independent measures of achievement; others have argued that the negative consequences of such tests fall disproportionately on poor and minority students. Walt Haney, "The Myth of the Texas Miracle in Education," *Education Policy Analysis Archives* 8, No. 41, 9 August, 2000 [journal on-line], available at http://epaa.asu.edu/epaa/v8n41/, accessed 6 August, 2002; McNeil, *Contradictions of School Reform*, 246–249, 252–255, 258–260; Amrein and Berliner, "High-Stakes Testing."

11. Kentucky Department of Education, "Containment," 1999–2000 CATS Assessment Open-Response Item Scoring Worksheet (Frankfort, Ky: Kentucky Department of Education); available from http://www.kde.state.ky.us/oapd/ttp/ri/99OR/Social%20Studies/Containment.pdf, accessed 13 August, 2002; Ohio Department of Education, "Practice Test: Citizenship," Proficiency Tests, Sixth-Grade Test Materials (Columbus, Ohio: Ohio Department of Education); available from http://www.ode.state.oh.us/proficiency/sample_tests/sixth/6ptcitz.pdf, accessed 13 August, 2002.

12. Cimbricz, "State-Mandated Testing"; S. G. Grant, "An Uncertain Lever: Exploring the Influence of State-Level Testing in New York State on Teaching Social Studies," *Teachers College Record* 103 (June 2001): 398–426; Grant et al., "Juggling Two Sets of Books."

13. Barton, "Historical Understanding Among Elementary Children," 79–84, "You'd be Wanting to Know About the Past," 93–94; Levstik and Barton, "They Still Use Some of Their Past" 555–60; Keith C. Barton and Linda S. Levstik, "'It Wasn't a Good Part of History': National Identity and Students' Explanations of Historical Significance," *Teachers College Record* 99 (Spring 1998): 490–99.

14. Barton, "Historical Understanding among Elementary Children," 104–107, "You'd be Wanting to Know about the Past," 97; see also Bruce A. VanSledright, "The Teaching-Learning Interaction in American History: A Study of Two Teachers and Their Fifth Graders," *Journal of Social Studies Research* 19 (Spring, 1995): 21.

15. Linda S. Levstik and Keith C. Barton, *Doing History: Investigating with Children in Elementary and Middle Schools*, 2nd ed. (Mahwah, N.J.: Lawrence Erlbaum Associates, Inc., 2001), 77–105; Bruce A. VanSledright, *In Search of America's Past:*

Learning to Read History in Elementary School (New York: Teachers College Press, 2002), 53–77.

16. Roy Rosenzweig and David Thelen, *The Presence of the Past: Popular Uses of History in American Life* (New York: Columbia University Press, 1998), 32, 105–06.

17. John Elsner and Roger Cardinal, *The Cultures of Collection* (London: Reaktion Books, 1994); Eilean Hooper-Greenhill, *Museums and the Shaping of Knowledge* (London: Routledge, 1992); Ivan Karp and Steven D. Lavine, Eds., *Exhibiting Cultures* (New York: Smithsonian Institution Press, 1992); Sharon MacDonald, *The Politics of Display* (London, Routledge, 1998); Sharon MacDonald and Gordon Fyfe, Eds., *Theorising Museums* (Oxford, England: Blackwell, 1996); Daniel J. Sherman and Irit Rogoff, *Museum Culture* (London: Routledge, 1994); John Willinsky, *Learning to Divide the World: Education at Empire's End* (Minneapolis: University of Minnesota Press, 1998).

18. Brian Graham, "Ulster: A Representation of Place Yet to Be Imagined," in *Who are "the People"? Unionism, Protestantism and Loyalism in Northern Ireland*, Eds. Peter Shirlow and Mark McGovern (Chicago, Pluto Press, 1997), 39; Anthony Buckley and M. Kenny, "Cultural Heritage in an Oasis of Calm: Divided Identities in a Museum in Ulster," in *Culture, Tourism and Development: The Case of Ireland*, Ed. Ullrich Kockel (Liverpool: Liverpool University Press, 1994), cited in Elizabeth Crooke, "Confronting a Troubled History: Which Past in Northern Ireland's Museums?," *International Journal of Heritage Studies* 7 (June 2001): 127.

19. Elizabeth Crooke, "Inclusion and Northern Ireland," in *Including Museums: Perspectives on Museums, Galleries and Social Inclusion*, Eds. Jocelyn Dodd and Richard Sandell (Leicester, United Kingdom: Research Center for Museums and Galleries, University of Leicester, 2001), 69–72, and "Confronting a Troubled History," 119–136; Felicity Heywood, "Across the Divide: Can Museums Help Heal the Wounds of Northern Ireland?," *Museums Journal* 100 (June 2000): 16–19. One exception to this focus on uncontroversial history is the Tower Museum in Londonderry, which devotes attention to the city's role in Northern Ireland's political troubles. In addition, some recent exhibits in the region have focused on symbols of division, although they have taken pains to provide balanced presentations that are unlikely to provoke controversy.

20. Richard Handler and Eric Gable, *The New History in an Old Museum* (Durham, N.C.: Duke University Press, 1997), 46–49, 53–59, 70–77, 84–101, 220–226. Similarly, David Blight argues that the recollections of Civil War veterans in the late 1800s were so dominated by "petty realism" focused on trivial, everyday details of battlefield life that larger issues related to the causes of the war and the role of race in national life were effectively avoided in public memory. David W. Blight, *Race and Reunion: The Civil War in American Memory* (Cambridge, Mass.: Harvard University Press, 2001), 108, 185, 191.

21. Gaynor Kavanagh, "Making Histories, Making Memories," in *Making Histories in Museums*, Ed. Gaynor Kavanagh (London: Leicester University Press, 1996), 7.

22. George E. Hein, *Learning in the Museum* (New York: Routledge, 1998), 153.

Narrative Structure
and History Education

In September, 1939, a dentist in Viceroy, Louisiana, placed a human tooth into a jar of Coca-Cola and let it stand overnight. The next morning Hitler invaded Poland.

—*David Mamet[1]*

We cringe when the word *narrative* comes up in educational settings, for we fear we're about to be assaulted with claims that are simplified, overstated, or unreflective—or all three at once. Narrative has been credited with being a "fundamental structure of human experience," a "solution to a fundamental problem in life ... creating understandable order in human affairs," "the most fundamental way of grappling with new experience," and a "primary act of mind." Given such grand claims, it is hardly surprising that some educators equate history with "a story well told" or that they argue children's earliest exposure to the subject should be in the form of stories.[2]

However, whenever a cultural practice is credited with being this fundamental, universal, and transhistorical, some caution is in order. Narrative may well be an important feature of human understanding, and it may have an important role to play in teaching history, but we should pause before rushing into an uncritical acceptance of its virtues. In particular, we might benefit from slowing down to consider exactly what historical narratives are (and are not), what varieties of narrative find their ways into educational settings, and how these may influence students' understanding. In this chapter, we address the general role of narrative structure as a cultural tool; later, we will assess one class of narratives (those that emphasize individual motivation and achievement) as well as one particular narrative—the story of U.S. freedom and progress. Throughout chapters 7, 8, and 9, our emphasis will be on the affordances and constraints provided by narrative in helping students engage in historical activity.

THE MEANING OF NARRATIVE

"Everyone knows," Thomas Leitch observes, "what stories are—fortunately; for it is excessively difficult to say just what they are." Dictionaries aren't much help. *Webster's New Collegiate Dictionary* defines *story* as "a fictional narrative shorter than a novel" and characterizes *narrative* as synonymous with *story*. Similarly, the *American Heritage Dictionary* defines *story* as "an account," *account* as "a narrative," and *narrative* as "a story."[3] This interchangeable use of story, narrative, and account is common in both academic scholarship and everyday usage, but it doesn't move us much closer to the defining features of the concept. Nor have literary theorists pinned down its meaning with any precision. Despite the massive amount of scholarship on narrative—Leitch suggests it would take a lifetime to survey such work—clear definitions are rare. Literary theorists talk about the topic, and they talk around the topic, but they don't often stop to say just what they mean by the term *narrative*. Often they appear to mean "anything and everything" or "whatever I happen to be talking about at the moment."

Even when advocating the use of narratives to teach history, many educators avoid supplying a precise definition—perhaps they assume everyone really does know what stories are. Grant Bage, in his insightful and highly useful book *Narrative Matters: Teaching and Learning History Through Story*, examines a wide variety of advantages, disadvantages, and complications related to the use of narratives in the classroom, but he steadfastly refuses to limit the concept to any defining set of characteristics. Although we understand the desire to keep the concept open to varying interpretation of diverse readers, our purpose here is to analyze narrative as a cultural tool, and we believe that requires some clarity about what that tool involves. Many discussions of narrative in history education have suffered from the conflation of narrative structure with particular kinds of narratives or from the equation of narrative with all literature. Although we are not about to provide a conclusive discussion of the subject, we are going to suggest an operational definition that we hope will help educators think through the implications of narrative for teaching and learning history.

David Bordwell's and Kristin Thompson's definition of narrative is clear and succinct: "a chain of events in cause–effect relationship occurring in time and space." Although they are writing about film, their definition applies just as well to written texts, and to historical texts as much as to fictional ones. As they explain in somewhat more detail, "Typically, a narrative begins with one situation; a series of changes occurs according to a pattern of cause and effect; finally, a new situation arises that brings about the end of the narrative." Similarly, with regard to history, Tom Holt observes that narratives involve "some temporal order that is inherently causal."[4] We consider this a useful way of characterizing narrative not only because of its congruence with many historical works, but also because of its consistency with important patterns in children's comprehension and recall of text. To further specify the components of narrative, we would add the elements of Kenneth Burke's pentad: actor, action, goal or intention, scene, and instrument. Combined with the definition of narrative as a chain of causally linked events, these elements call attention to how our expectations for narrative are shaped, and thus they help us think through the affordances and constraints of narrative as a tool for teaching history.

The first aspect of Bordwell's and Thompson's definition that bears note is its characterization of narrative as a "chain of events." Particularly when applied to history, narratives are fundamentally about grouping events into a sequence (or "chain"). Historians don't try to record the entire history of the world either in its breadth or its depth—that is, they don't begin with the first appearance of humans and work their way up through today, nor do they try to describe everything that went on in a given period in time. Rather, when writing narrative history, historians select some events as belonging together as part of a coherent sequence, and they arrange those events so that their coherence is clear—whether that sequence is about the Industrial Revolution, the spread of Islam, or the life of Helen Keller. A narrative of the women's suffrage movement in the United States, for example, will not mention the building of pyramids in ancient Egypt, or the Black Death in Europe, or the demise of the East African Railway; the story isn't about those things, so historians writing the story of women's suffrage don't include them.

Leaving out the pyramids, of course, is an easy call—but there are other events that require more judgment: When does the story of women's suffrage in the United States start—the Colonial Era, the antebellum period, or the early 20th century? When does it end—with the ratification of the 19th amendment, with gender-related changes in voting patterns in the 1990s, or has the end of the story not yet arrived? Does the story include links with suffrage movements in other parts of the world, or are these unimportant? In answering each of these questions, historians impose order on the infinite variety of facts from which they could draw, and in narrative history, this ordering consists specifically of arranging the selected facts into a sequence—deciding when the story begins, when it ends, and the order of events in between. Nor is this sequencing mere window dressing or some "literary" attempt to make history engaging and readable: It is at the very heart of what many historians do. Historians' claim to present truthful accounts of the past lies not just in getting the facts themselves right but in getting their arrangement right.[5]

Questions of selection and arrangement inevitably lead to consideration of the next component of narrative: causality. A narrative is not a random listing of events, no matter how carefully selected and arranged. Narratives (and certainly narrative histories) aim at causal explanation—they attempt to lay out how one event caused another, as well as the factors that influenced those links. A narrative account of the First World War, for example, will note that on June 18, 1914, Serbian nationalists in Sarajevo assassinated Archduke Francis Ferdinand, heir to the throne of Austria-Hungary. Encouraged by its ally Germany, Austria-Hungary declared war against Serbia, whose ally Russia then declared war against Austria-Hungary, ultimately resulting in Germany's declaration of war against Russia. France supported its ally Russia, leading Germany to move through Belgium in hopes of quickly conquering France and avoiding a war on two fronts; Belgium's ally Britain then went to war against Germany. More complicated accounts will point to long-standing military, nationalist, and economic rivalries in initiating the conflict, and more extended ones will detail the end of the Russian government, the entry of the United States into the war, the formation of the League of Nations, the roots of the Second World War, and so on. All such accounts, though, will arrange events into a causal chain.

Even when authors do not make these causal links explicit, they imply them through the sequential ordering of events; we assume that if the events occur in order, they must be related. The quote at the beginning of this chapter (from a dramatic monologue) is absurd precisely because the first sentence leads the audience to expect a narrative. It includes all the elements of Burke's pentad—an actor (the dentist), an action (putting the tooth into a jar of soda), a scene (Viceroy, Louisiana, 1939), an instrument (empirical science), and an intention (presumably, the desire to uncover the effect of soda pop on dental health). The audience fully expects the next sentence to describe the outcome of this experiment, but those expectations are undercut when we hear instead that Hitler invaded Poland—an event we know could not possibly be causally related to the first. As he so often does, Mamet manipulates the audience by refusing to give them what he has led them to expect—in this case, the causally related events of a narrative. In sum, when we discuss narratives, we will be referring to constructed sequences of events that are both causally related and chronological; these sequences typically include a setting, actor, agent, goal, and instrument.

STUDENTS AND HISTORICAL NARRATIVES

As noted earlier, we consider our definition of narrative useful not only because of its applicability to many historical works but also because of its consonance with studies of how people comprehend and recall fictional narratives. This body of research initially was rooted in attempts to develop story grammars (sets of rules for how stories are structured) and the observation that many traditional folktales from a variety of cultures have a common structure—namely, they contain a setting, beginning, reaction, attempt, outcome, and ending. Research by Jean Mandler and others has shown that these elements have "psychological reality"—that is, people have a mental "story schema" structured around these common components, and this schema affects how they understand and remember the stories they hear. For example, they remember stories better (and judge them more positively) when all these essential components are included. When people hear a story in which elements are missing, they have trouble remembering the story accurately, and they often go so far as to fill in the missing parts based on their overall understanding of the story and their own assumptions about how the world works. In addition, they expect these elements to occur in a particular order: When they do not, people read more slowly and have more trouble recalling the stories accurately. Also, when people make mistakes in their retellings, they tend to leave the overall story structure intact—that is, they misremember the details, but they don't retell the story in the wrong order, nor do they leave out essential elements.[6]

These findings suggest that comprehension and recall of narratives are influenced by specific, preexisting expectations—expectations related not to the content of stories but to their structure. There is also evidence that this kind of story schema influences students' understanding of history. As we have already noted, children begin to pick up information about the past from a very early age; this information involves a variety of people, places, events, and trends and comes from a wide spectrum of sources—relatives, cartoons, movies, books, historic sites, artifacts, and so on. Yet this information doesn't simply clutter students' minds like so much mismatched furniture; rather, students mentally structure information in ways that make sense—and one of the ways that makes most sense is narrative.

Bruce VanSledright and Jere Brophy, for example, interviewed fourth and fifth graders to find out what they knew about common topics in the fifth-grade curriculum—the colonies, the American Revolution, the Civil War, and so on. They found that students often conflated information from more than one source (mixing together details of the Civil War and the French and Indian War, for example) or combined accurate details with misconceptions or "fanciful elaborations"—logical but historically inaccurate details they made up to fill in the gaps in their knowledge. However, despite the numerous inaccuracies in their description of historical events, students' accounts made sense when viewed as narratives—that is, they contained all the elements of a story grammar, even when the historical details were wrong. They often explained causal relationships or attributed motivations, for example, based not on any specific knowledge of historical events but simply on their understanding of human nature—such as the student who thought that during the Civil War, the North and South fought over "the West," which was "unknown land."[7]

Margaret McKeown and Isabel Beck found a similar pattern when they interviewed fifth and sixth graders about their knowledge of the American Revolution. They found that students' knowledge was "often vague, disorganized, or inaccurate." Students had little understanding of the governmental relations between England and the colonies or of why the war was fought, and they often mixed together a variety of historical details into broad and undifferentiated categories that McKeown and Beck call "stews." Students confused the Declaration of Independence, for example, with the Constitution, the Mayflower Compact, and the Emancipation Proclamation as part of a "document stew." Yet it's clear from their description of patterns in students' responses that however inaccurate the details, students recognized that the overall structure of their historical knowledge had a narrative structure. As McKeown and Beck explain

Many students seemed to have constructed the understanding that the United States was once a new and boundless land that beckoned people from many countries to come in search of freedom. There was evidence of a realization that freedom was a goal, something that had to be fought for, and that various phenomena—wars, documents, celebrations—were milestones in achieving that goal.

Although Beck and McKeown do not use the concept of story schema to explain these findings, the essential elements of story grammar are apparent in their description of students' thinking.[8]

We have also found narrative "simplifications" in our own studies of children's understanding of change over time. In our classroom study of fourth and fifth graders, students were asked not only what they knew about particular events they had studied but why they thought various aspects of society had changed over time—technology, fashion, social roles, and so on. It became clear they often used elements of narrative to make sense of a variety of historical topics. Many times, for example, they conceived of history in terms of the goal-directed activity that forms the basis for narratives. One group of students, in captioning artifacts used in a display on the history of household technology, noted that a candle "was like a substitute for awhile for the light bulb." Similarly, another group suggested that milk once came in bottles because "they didn't have cardboard" and that people had milk delivered to their homes because "they didn't have that many stores back then." In cases like these, students seemed to think of historical developments as having the same teleological nature as fictional narratives: The outcome was already known, and events led inexorably toward that outcome—the past, for these students, was just the present waiting to happen.[9]

Students also simplified the past into a minimal number of characters and events. When studying the American Revolution, for example, they did not recognize that there were many thousands of participants engaged in many different conflicts throughout the colonies. Instead, they thought there were simply two bodies of troops who kept meeting each other in battle, and that all the colonists were closely involved with major political figures and events. They thought of long-term historical processes, meanwhile, as having consisted of a small number of happenings, each of which took place at one point in time. One student explained the origin of slavery in North America, for example, by suggesting that "during the Revolutionary War and stuff, people sailed down to Africa ... to like get away from the war, and they found these black people, and they thought they were monkeys or animals, and they thought they were really neat, and they crowded them up on boats and stuff, and sold them."[10] This is much the same kind of fanciful elaboration noted by VanSledright and Brophy. However, notice that the student is not simply inventing details to add interest to a historical episode; rather, he is collapsing a gradual and long-term historical process into a single discrete event.

This simplification of the duration and extent of historical process was particularly noticeable when students talked about immigration to the United States. Rather than recognizing immigration as a process that took place over several centuries and involved millions of people, most students described it as though it happened all at once with a limited number of ships. In looking at a picture of an immigrant ship from 1906, for example, one student suggested that "this is one of the main ships that brought everybody over to America," while another noted that "it looks like it was when the queen and king went over to sail to get like more people." When asked to put the picture in chronological order as part of a set of pictures from the past 400 years, many students thought it must be the oldest in the set because it showed people coming to America—and people had to come here before anything else in the pictures could have happened. One thought it was older than a picture of Abraham Lincoln because "the people had to come over here before Abe Lincoln, before they had presidents, 'cause nobody would elect them, you know. They had to have people over here to elect the president."[11]

In a related way, students often simplified historical change by characterizing it as a rational process: They thought the world changed because people had figured out how to do things correctly. They explained that technological changes took place because of "new inventions" or "coming up with new ideas," and they also thought that styles and fashion had changed for rational reasons—new materials were invented, and new dyes were discovered. For these students, history could not simply be a succession of unrelated states—people once dressed one way, now they dress another—but must reflect the kinds of causal connections found in narrative. Beliefs, too, changed for rational reasons, and students confined these changes to simple and straightforward episodes: People no longer believe in witches because that belief was disproved in a single court case or through the discoveries of medical science; Martin Luther King, Jr., gave a speech, and Whites realized that they shouldn't be prejudiced; women gained equal rights because people "figured it out" that women were equal to men. In yet another example of fanciful elaboration, one student explained declining prejudice by suggesting that at some point in the past, people realized African Americans are humans due to

> Tests and research and stuff, and like maybe a Black person got hurt and they took them to the hospital, and while they were at the hospital, maybe a doctor took a, took maybe a part of the skin, they had to do it in surgery, so they cut off part of the skin, and maybe took it to a lab, and got it tested.

The student didn't present his description as though it were an actual historical event, but he thought it was the kind of event that probably occurred. Not only did these students expect history to be composed of causal links, then, they expected those links to be quick, clean, and obvious—not long-term, complicated, or ambiguous. History, for them, was a narrative, and a very simple one at that.[12]

AFFORDANCES AND CONSTRAINTS OF NARRATIVE

Narrative is one tool students use to make sense of history, as they take the variety of historical people and events they have learned about, both in and out of school, and collapse them into a simplified cause-and-effect chain with each of the expected elements. Perhaps the most important affordance of this tool is that it aids students in their search for coherence in history. Whether trying to understand specific events in the past or broader historical changes, students use narrative to make sense of how disparate items go together. Far from thinking of history as "just one damn thing after another," children expect history to have a pattern, and so they look for logical and chronological sequences, for causes and consequences, for agents and their motivations—all the components of a simple story grammar. Historians use narrative structure for much the same reason: It enables them to make sense of the past. The purpose of a historical narrative, after all, is to identify a meaningful pattern out of the massive array of facts that can be established for any given time. Students and historians, then, use narrative in fundamentally similar ways.

From a practical, pedagogical standpoint, perhaps the chief advantage of narrative is its familiarity. Children are exposed to narrative from their earliest encounters with bedtime stories and picture books, as well as through cartoons, movies, television, and the everyday stories of peers and relatives. The pervasiveness of these formats attests to their popularity for children and adults, and the story schema research discussed earlier indicates that people have a clear, if tacit, understanding of the structure of narrative (at least of simple ones). Using narrative to make sense of history, then, does not require developing expertise with a new tool—it's not like learning how to write a five-paragraph essay, apply algorithms for long division, or dissect a frog. Children can be expected to know something about how narrative works even before they first study history at school, and it thus serves as a kind of scaffolding for the subject.[13] Their knowledge of the range of narrative types should expand through increased exposure to both history and literature, but they can be counted on already to understand the basics—setting, agents, causality, and so on (even though they are unlikely to know those terms). As a result, teachers can focus their attention on the content of the subject rather than its procedures: Students only need to learn particular historical stories, not what stories are all about in the first place.

With such compelling arguments in favor of narrative, we may be classed as a couple of Cassandras for failing to endorse it wholeheartedly. However, like any cultural tool, narrative not only helps solve the problems of life (in this case, making meaning from the past) but also limits the range of solutions by narrowing perceptions of reality. Narrative limits—and thus distorts—our understanding of the past in two particularly important ways. The first of these derives from its very familiarity. Because narratives are so common, so widely used in our attempts to make meaning of the world, it is easy to forget that they have been intentionally constructed—that someone has sifted through the evidence and made decisions about where the story begins and ends, who the agents are, and how the actions are causally related. Rather than seeing any particular historical narrative as one way of making sense of a period in history, it is tempting—for children or adults—to regard that narrative as history itself.[14] Because narratives are such powerful cultural tools, we may forget that they are only tools and that they mediate our access to history. That is, we may think of the structure found in narratives as being a part of the past rather than a structure that has been imposed—in the quest for meaning—on a limitless number of discrete happenings. Also, if children only encounter the products of historical narration—if the process of constructing the narrative is not transparent—then they are particularly unlikely to recognize that the story could be told other ways or that people, events, and time periods might be analyzed through formats other than narrative. We found this in our own work, when students who had read historical narratives were confident they knew the truth or "what really happened," particularly in instances where people responded with extraordinary bravery or outrageous inhumanity. Students did not seek alternative explanations or viewpoints; the narratives they encountered were so powerful that they were not spontaneously critical of them.[15]

The second important drawback of narrative also relates to its constructed nature, but it revolves less around the fact that narratives are constructed than around the actual substance of that construction: Any historical narrative simplifies what went on in the past. A narrative necessarily includes some things and omits others (whether agents, events, or causes), and there are gains and losses with each of these inclusions and omissions. In terms of agents, for example, historical narratives for many years included elite White men and omitted women, minorities, and the poor. This kind of narrative may have had the advantage of helping us understand, at least in part, the actions of those who held political, legal, and economic power in society, but it had the distinct disadvantage of providing little insight into the lives of the majority of the population. Once historians began to pay closer attention to marginalized groups, they sometimes still treated them less as the agents of history than as objects of manipulation by those in power—thus, the list of characters in historical narratives expanded to create a more complex narrative, but the casual links still exhibited many of the same simplifications and limited our insight into the past. Recently, a great deal of historical writing has examined the agency of such marginalized groups—moving them from the margins to the center of the narrative—but such works have also been criticized for attributing too much agency to those who lacked formal power and thus for neglecting the larger structural constraints on their lives. No matter where we focus our attention, then, it seems that we will miss out on some other, potentially significant part of the situation.

Although we may prefer to focus attention in one place rather than another, no single story of the past is uniquely privileged, for no historical account can be comprehensive. Without simplification, there would be no coherence. This is simply another way of saying that a narrative is, in Roland Barthes' terms, "without noise"—without items that might distract from the overall story being told.[16] However, one of the chief drawbacks to narrative in history is precisely the fact that the "noise" of one historical narrative is central to the action of another. There is no solution to this problem, no correct way to establish the "proper" content of any historical narrative (beyond demonstrating that the events narrated did in fact occur), but the dilemma must be recognized and confronted: We have to examine the impact of telling any particular narrative, or any set of narratives, as well as the consequences of students' narrative simplifications. Does it matter, for example, that elementary children think two groups of soldiers continually met each other in battle during the Colonial Era rather than recognizing that conflicts took place between many different troops? Does it matter that they think immigration happened at one point in time rather than extending over centuries? Just as important, we have to examine whether we are creating these simplifications through instruction. Are we encouraging students to make certain kinds of simplifications when we emphasize Abraham Lincoln and the Emancipation Proclamation rather than the abolitionist movement, or when we engage students' curiosity through stories of famous inventors rather than teaching them about the social and economic conditions that underlie technological change? We have to simplify history to teach it, and we can hardly be surprised that students simplify it even further when they learn it—but do these simplifications matter?

This is no easy question. Historians are motivated by their personal interests and aspirations and by the concerns of their own academic community—they will make decisions about their work based on the extent to which it supplies narratives previously lacking in the field, adds detail or nuance to existing narratives, fulfills personal interests, or results in publications that lead to employment, tenure, or other recognition. However, our concern in this book is not primarily with the community of professional historians but with the much broader arena of participatory democracy. In thinking about the value of narrative in history, we have to ask ourselves what is gained and what is lost—as a pluralist, democratic society—in the particular historical narratives that we tell. Like language generally, narrative works as a cultural tool at multiple levels, and thus we have to examine the affordances and constraints not only of narrative structure in general but of the specific narratives (or classes of narratives) to which children are most often exposed. These are questions we will take up in the next two chapters.

NARRATIVE STRUCTURE AS A CULTURAL TOOL

Narrative structure often has been credited with being a fundamental property of the mind, and some scholars regard it as an inescapable component of historical research and writing. The prevalence of these conceptions forces us to defend our characterization of narrative as a tool, a historical and cultural creation that is neither "natural" nor inevitable. If narrative is defined broadly enough, of course, all history (and all human experience) is a narrative, but if everything is narrative, then the concept serves little purpose. If we limit narrative to a temporally and causally linked chain of events, though, it seems clear that much published history is not primarily narrative in format. Many works do not attempt to tell a story of causally related changes but instead set out to analyze what life was like at a given time in the past. Victoria Bynum's *Unruly Women: The Politics of Sexual Control in the Old South*, for example, describes the experiences of women in antebellum and wartime North Carolina who were considered deviant or disorderly, and she analyzes how race and class affected both their behavior and the reactions of the patriarchal power structure. There are many small narratives within the book, but the overall work does not have a narrative structure; Bynum is not trying to trace changes in patterns of women's behavior over an extended time but to describe and analyze those patterns during a single period in which they remained relatively stable. Similarly, Eugene Genovese's *Roll, Jordan, Roll: The World the Slaves Made* describes and analyzes just what the title implies—the "world" of slaves in the American South. It is not about the origin and development of slavery nor about the circumstances that led to its overthrow; it is about how slaves lived, worked, worshipped, celebrated, and so on during a particular period of the past.[17]

Works like these, and perhaps any work of history, can be thought of as parts of a narrative. We know that expectations for women's behavior have changed over the past 200 years, and so Bynum's book can be seen as one component of that story. Similarly, we know that culture and social relations have changed since the first Africans were brought to North America, and so a description of slave life in the 1800s can be seen as a portion of the overall narrative of African American life. In fact, Genovese often comments on the historical roots and enduring impact of the patterns of life he describes. Yet just because works like these illustrate portions of a historical narrative, their internal structure is not necessarily narrative. As we read them, we may mentally slot them into our own historical narratives, but the books themselves do not take the form of a story. This kind of nonnarrative history is common: Many of the most important and well-respected works of academic historians set out to describe life at a given time in the past rather than to tell a story, and other kinds of historical representation—museums, documentary films, personal reminiscences—also frequently focus on static portrayals of life in the past. Nonnarrative history sometimes shows up even in elementary school: Children may study historic Native American peoples by learning about their "way of life" (usually at the moment of contact with Europeans), and when studying the British colonies in North America, they usually learn about purportedly stable social and economic patterns rather than narratives of the growth and development of the colonies. Clearly, narrative is not the only format for representing historical information nor the only one to which children have access.

Yet still, one might argue that such nonnarrative formats are inherently more difficult for children to make sense of, particularly if narrative is some kind of universal property of the mind, a "built-in" cognitive limitation, or a developmental stage for children at a particular age. If narrative is universal, then its constraints and affordances hardly matter, for there would be nothing educators could do about them. We might lament the shortcomings of stories, but trying to overcome those would amount to tilting at windmills—there is little point, after all, in trying to change the architecture of the human mind. Interpreting narrative in terms of the mind's structure is tempting, because stories are so common both within and outside of schools; a number of theorists, in fact, have argued that young children find narratives more accessible than expository forms of discourse or that there is a developmental progression from one to the other.[18] Many teachers, meanwhile, would point out students seem much better able to understand and recall stories than the nonnarrative content of science or mathematics. However, even if such differences exist, the assumption of a natural or developmental preference for narrative may not be warranted. Perhaps narrative is a "primary act of mind," as Barbara Hardy claimed, an inherently and uniquely accessible format, but perhaps schools (and other settings) simply develop familiarity with this genre at the expense of alternatives.

Christine Pappas suggests that the elementary curriculum, heavily geared toward the use of a narrow range of fictional narratives, may be based on "an unexamined, unacknowledged ideology about young children and their cognitive/linguistic development"—namely, that narrative is a superior format for instruction in the early grades. To test this assumption, Pappas read kindergartners a series of picture books and asked them to retell or "pretend read" their contents; half the books used in the study were fictional stories (such as *The Owl and the Woodpecker* and *Poppy the Panda*), and half were nonfictional, nonnarrative books (such as *Squirrels* and *Tunnels*). She found that students were successful in reenacting both genres (showing equal fluency with their distinctive features), that they improved in their ability to read each genre over the course of multiple sessions, and that they learned vocabulary from both. Perhaps most surprisingly, students showed a marked preference for the nonnarrative works. Pappas concludes that narrative may be less "primary" than many educators believe and that an emphasis on stories in the first years of schooling may hinder children's mastery of a wider range of texts. Other researchers who have investigated students' experience with varied text genres have reached much the same conclusion.[19]

If students in their first year of schooling find nonnarrative texts as interesting and comprehensible as narrative ones, then older student's reliance on narrative as a way of making sense of history may be the result of instructional practices that emphasize stories, rather than an indication of some primal attachment to the format. VanSledright and Brophy make a similar observation: They note that students they interviewed relied more heavily on narrative after studying history in fifth grade than they had the previous year, and they speculate that this may have resulted from their teacher's extensive use of historical fiction.[20] As suggestive as such studies are, though, they provide little direct evidence for the relative accessibility of narrative and nonnarrative texts in history. What we need are studies that directly compare children's understanding of historical information presented in differing formats. Only then could we determine the extent to which narrative understanding might be independent of the mode of instruction.

Unfortunately, there are no such studies, at least as far as we are aware. However, one of us has examined the historical understanding of children in a region where historical narratives are far less prominent than they are in the United States. In Northern Ireland, children are exposed to history in many of the same contexts as in the United States—at school, from relatives, at historical sites, in museums, and through the media—but very little of the content they encounter in these settings is narrative in form. In school, for example, students in the primary grades (the equivalent of U.S. second through fifth grades) study the way of life of people at various times in the past—Mesolithic people, the Vikings, the Victorians, Ancient Egyptians, and so on. They do not learn about these topics as narratives but instead study how each group of people lived at a given time and place in the past, just as many historians do. Outside school, children visit prehistoric burial sites or the ruins of castles and abbeys, and they go to museums and historic parks. Rarely do these settings present connected narratives of historical developments; instead, they depict the social and material life of people who lived decades, centuries, or millennia ago. Parents and grandparents, meanwhile, often tell children about their lives in the more recent past—focusing on chores, technology, and so on. Even media depictions of history are less narrative than in the United States. Children there often watch documentaries about life in the past rather than the comedies and dramas that are so important to U.S. children. Historical fiction, meanwhile, is much less popular than in the United States, and children in Northern Ireland are more likely to read nonnarrative works like *The Vikings* or *Life in a Medieval Village*.[21]

There are two principal reasons, mutually reinforcing, for this pattern of history education in Northern Ireland. As discussed in chapter 4, history teaching in Britain focuses on developing students' understanding of how historical knowledge is created rather than on the details of specific narratives. Particularly at the primary level, this is most easily accomplished through studying particular time periods: Students can more easily examine the evidence (artifacts, photographs, and so on) for how the Vikings lived or what daily life was like in the 1950s than the complicated diplomatic correspondence or statistical data needed to establish narrative historical accounts. Narratives are not entirely absent from history education in England—even in primary school, students may learn stories of Florence Nightingale or Guy Fawkes. Yet in Northern Ireland, a second factor—more political than pedagogical—forestalls even these occasional forays into narrative. There are two competing narratives of history in Northern Ireland, one Nationalist and one Unionist, and arguments over their relative significance strike at the heart of the region's ongoing conflict. Nearly any story from the history of Ireland, Northern Ireland, or Britain could be seen—implicitly or explicitly—to support either a Nationalist or Unionist political stance and would therefore be too controversial to include in the primary curriculum. Institutions outside formal schooling reinforce this pattern. Museums and historic sites, for example, are constrained both by their desire to avoid controversy and by an explicit aim to support the teaching of the national curriculum, and thus they are no more likely to present history in narrative form than are schools.[22]

In working with students in Northern Ireland, it became clear that they employed certain aspects of narrative less often than did those in the United States. One research project there was designed to parallel previous research with children in the United States: Students in the equivalent of Grades 2 through 6 were shown pictures from different times in history, asked to put them in chronological order, and to talk about how they knew which were older and which were newer. These interview tasks were combined with observations of classroom history activities over the course of approximately three months. Both interviews and observations provided ample opportunities to explore students' ideas about how and why life had changed over time. Two aspects of their responses were striking. First, students in Northern Ireland were less likely than those in the United States to simplify the past into a linear sequence. Recall that many U.S. students thought a picture of immigrants had to be earlier than one of presidents because people had to come to North America before they could start having elections. In a similar way, most thought a family moving West must be older than an antebellum city (because people had to explore an area before developing cities), and a colonial mansion must be older than a log cabin (because it took time to build larger homes).[23] (See Fig. 7.1.)

As noted previously, U.S. students had reduced the noise of history so that images stood in a simple, chronological order. They showed little rec-

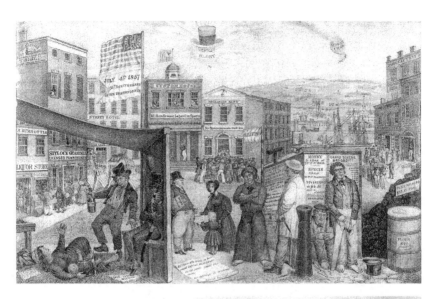

FIG. 7.1.   Pictures used in research with students in the United States. Most U.S. students thought the photograph of settlers was older than that of the antebellum city because people had to explore an area before they developed cities. Library of Congress, Prints and Photographs Division, Reproduction No. LC-USZ62-8844. National Archives and Records Administration, NAIL Control number NWDNS-69-N-13606C.

ognition that different ways of life coexisted at any given time in the past or that historical processes like immigration extended over lengthy periods, even while other events were taking place. Students in Northern Ireland, though, often made exactly the opposite observation: When arranging pictures, they frequently noted that very different images (such as an urban street scene in Belfast and a thatched cottage in rural Donegal) could be from the same time, and that they simply represented different economic classes or different geographic regions (See Fig. 7.2.) One student even explained that a way of life might continue to exist while new ways were developing. Although many also simplified history in the same ways as the U.S. students, overall they were less wedded to the idea that the past had the contours of a narrative sequence.[24]

Students in Northern Ireland also differed in their explanations of why life had changed over time. U.S. students described historical change as a highly rational process in which the causal links between different time periods were clear and simple: A medical test proved that African Americans were human, a court case established that there were no witches, and inventors solved technological problems and made life better. As noted earlier, sometimes students' explanations had an almost teleological cast, as when one noted that candles were "like a substitute for awhile" until the light bulb was invented. They even assimilated changes in fashion to their image of rational progress, as when they asserted that clothes were different in the past because people didn't have the material (like leather) to make the clothes we have now. For these U.S. students, historical change represented the same kind of causally related, goal-oriented actions found in narratives. Students in Northern Ireland often gave similar explanations, but other times they talked about change as though it were not always a rational process with clear causal connections. Many students there, for example, explained that clothes have changed because people's ideas about what looks good have changed—they didn't suggest that clothes had improved, as U.S. students did, but simply that "people don't like the same things all the time," and thus, fashions change. Although such explanation retained the sequence found in narratives, there was no clear attribution of causation; these students thought that some aspects of life—notably fashions—could change without following the logical dictates of a connected narrative. Thus, modern clothes or hairstyles might simply represent differences compared to 100 years ago, not the results of unfolding technological mastery or rational problem solving.[25]

Narrative, then, seems to play a much less pervasive role in the historical understanding of students in Northern Ireland than in the United States. Students there sometimes see history as linear and rational progress, and sometimes they do not; in the United States, they almost always do. Also, because U.S. students are more wedded to narrative as a tool for making sense of the past, they are much more susceptible to its constraints: Because they are so concerned to find the "plot" of history, they

FIG. 7.2. Pictures used in research with students in Northern Ireland. Students in Northern Ireland noted that pictures like these might reflect differing economic circumstances or geographic regions at the same point in time. Reproduced with the kind permission of the Trustees of the Museums and Galleries of Northern Ireland (Collection Ulster Museum, Belfast, Record No. WO4/13/6, Record No. HO5/22/1).

systematically omit those features of the past that fail to conform to what they think of as history's overarching story. Ultimately, this reliance on narrative simplification diminishes the potential of history as preparation for democratic citizenship within each of the four stances: It can lead students to narrow their conception of what counts as a "true" American, to dismiss the suffering of victims of progress, to omit important information from historical displays, and to misconstrue the causes and consequences of historical events. As Eric Foner warns, in discussing overly simplified and narrativized stories of "freedom" in U.S. history, "such an approach too often fails to recognize how dissenting voices, rejected positions, and disparaged theories have also played a role in shaping the meaning of freedom."[26] Yet any serious preparation for a pluralist and participatory democracy would require that we engage students in the consideration of just such voices, positions, and theories. To do so, we need to make students more aware of the ways in which narrative structure leads to simplifications and omissions.

CONCLUSIONS

Narratives are powerful cultural tools. We grow up surrounded by them, and we develop expectations for how they work—the elements that should be included and the way they should be structured. This makes them particularly convenient as a method of instruction. Because we can assume that children already know quite a bit about them, we can get on to dealing with the content, rather than the format, of the history we want them to learn. Try teaching students to engage in an inquiry project on the American Revolution, and it will quickly become apparent just how much easier it is to tell them a story about it instead. Yet however pervasive narratives are and however convenient as a form of instruction, they are not the only vehicle students have for making sense of the world, as the studies discussed in this chapter show. They may be "primary," but they certainly aren't exclusive. Rather than capitulating to the power of narrative and accepting it as the default mode of history instruction, we need to evaluate its affordances and constraints in promoting the goals of education in a pluralist democracy.

Narrative has important advantages apart from its obvious familiarity. First and foremost, it promotes the search for meaning by encouraging students to look for causal connections and to examine relationships. In our view, this quest for meaning is critical to any worthwhile perspective on the past, regardless of the historical stance taken—the best uses of identification, analysis, moral response, and even exhibition all strive to make sense of the flow of history rather than simply presenting it as an incidental sequence of unconnected events. However, the drawbacks of narrative also are clear. Narratives may help us understand history, but in their selectivity, they also stand between us and history. Out of the past's unlimited expanse of people and actions, narratives necessarily set limits—they tells stories about these people and not others, and they group actions into these events and not others. In itself, that is no constraint, because selectivity is unavoidable. Constraints arise when narrative is confused with history itself, so that alternative stories and alternative ways of conceptualizing history appear illegitimate. Precisely because stories are so powerful, we tend to think they are true in and of themselves rather than representing the outcome of choices people have made about how to organize a set of (selectively) true statements. Also, when certain types of narrative are dominant—as we will argue in the next two chapters—it becomes difficult to think of history in any other way.

ENDNOTES

1. David Mamet, "A Sermon," in *Goldberg Street: Short Plays and Monologues* (New York: Grove Press, 1985), 157.
2. F. Michael Connelly and D. Jean Clandinin, "Stories of Experience and Narrative Enquiry," *Educational Researcher* 12 (June/July 1990): 2; John A. Robinson and Linda Hawpe, "Narrative Thinking as a Heuristic Process," in *Narrative Psychology: The Storied Nature of Human Conduct,* Ed. Theodore R. Sabin (New York: Praeger: 1986), 112; Gordon Wells, *The Meaning Makers* (London: Hodder and Stoughton, 1986), 206; all cited in Grant Bage, *Narrative Matters: Teaching and Learning History Through Story* (London: Falmer Press, 1999); Barbara Hardy, "Narrative as a Primary Act of Mind," in *The Cool Web: The Pattern of Children's Reading,* Eds. Margaret Meek, Aiden Warlow, and Griselda Barton (London: Bodley Head, 1977), 12. On the use of narrative in teaching history, see California State Department of Education, *History-Social Science Framework for California Public Schools, Kindergarten Through Grade Twelve* (Sacramento, Calif.: Author, 1988); Elaine Wrisley Reed, *Helping Your Child Learn History: With Activities for Children Aged 4 Through 11* (Washington, D.C.: U.S. Department of Education, Office of Educational Research and Improvement, 1993); Kieran Egan, "Layers of Historical Understanding," *Theory and Research in Social Education* 4 (Fall 1989), 280–294. For a more balanced treatment of the role of narrative in history education, see Bage, *Narrative Matters.*
3. Thomas M. Leitch, *What Stories Are: Narrative Theory and Interpretation* (University Park, Pa.: Pennsylvania State University Press, 1986), 3; *Webster's New Collegiate Dictionary,* 8th ed. (1977), s. v. "story," "narrative"; *The American Heritage Dictionary of the English Language,* 3rd ed. (1992), s. v. "story," "account," "narrative."
4. David Bordwell and Kristin Thompson, *Film Art: An Introduction,* 5th ed. (New York: McGraw-Hill, 1990), 90; Tom Holt, *Thinking Historically: Narrative, Imagination, and Understanding* (New York: The College Board, 1995), 13.
5. The role of narrative in the interpretation of history is the subject of a vast literature, but two of the most important sources of our perspective on this issue are Louis O. Mink, "Narrative Form as a Cognitive Instrument," in *The Writing of History: Literary Form and Historical Understanding,* Eds. Robert H. Canary and Henry Kozick (Madison, Wisc.: University of Wisconsin Press, 1978), 129–49, and Hayden White, "The Value of Narrativity in the Representation of Reality," in *The*

Content of the Form: Narrative Discourse and Historical Representation (Baltimore: The Johns Hopkins University Press, 1987), 1–25. For an overview of some of these issues and their implications for education, see Avner Segall, "Critical History: Implications for History/Social Studies Education," *Theory and Research in Social Education* 27 (Summer 1999): 358–74.

6. Jean Matter Mandler, *Stories, Scripts, and Scenes: Aspects of Schema Theory* (Hillsdale, N.J.: Lawrence Erlbaum Associates, Inc., 1984), 31–73.
7. Bruce VanSledright and Jere Brophy, "Storytelling, Imagination, and Fanciful Elaboration in Children's Historical Reconstructions," *American Educational Research Journal* 29 (Winter 1992): 850.
8. Margaret G. McKeown and Isabel L. Beck, "The Assessment and Characterization of Young Learners' Knowledge of a Topic in History," *American Educational Research Journal* 27 (Winter 1990): 709, 720.
9. Keith C. Barton, "Narrative Simplifications in Elementary Students' Historical Thinking," in *Advances in Research on Teaching*, Vol. 6, *Teaching and Learning History*, Ed. Jere Brophy (Greenwich, Conn.: JAI Press, 1996), 56–60.
10. Barton, "Narrative Simplifications," 67.
11. Barton, "Narrative Simplifications," 63–64, 67–68.
12. Barton, "Narrative Simplifications," 59, 68.
13. Matthew T. Downey and Linda S. Levstik, "Teaching and Learning History: The Research Base," *Social Education* 52 (September 1988): 338. One version of this position has been developed by Kieran Egan, who argues that students' first exposure to history should come in the form of the "mythic" story, which he claims is the format children find most interesting and comprehensible; Egan, "Layers of Historical Understanding."
14. Bage, *Narrative Matters*, 89.
15. Linda S. Levstik, "The Relationship Between Historical Response and Narrative in a Sixth-Grade Classroom," *Theory and Research in Social Education* 19 (Winter 1986): 17; Linda S. Levstik, "Historical Narrative and the Young Reader," *Theory Into Practice* 28 (Spring 1989): 118.,
16. Roland Barthes, "Introduction to the Structural Analysis of Narrative," in *Image-Music-Text* (New York: Hill and Wang, 1977), 89.
17. Victoria E. Bynum, *Unruly Women: The Politics of Social and Sexual Control in the Old South* (Chapel Hill: University of North Carolina Press, 1992); Eugene D. Genovese, *Roll, Jordon, Roll: The World the Slaves Made* (New York: Pantheon Books, 1974).
18. Nell K. Duke, "3.6 Minutes per Day: The Scarcity of Informational Texts in First Grade," *Reading Research Quarterly* 35 (April/May/June 2000): 207–08.
19. Christine C. Pappas, "Is Narrative 'Primary'? Some Insights from Kindergartners' Pretend Readings of Stories and Information Books," *Journal of Reading Behavior* 25 (March 1993), 126; Duke, "3.6 Minutes per Day," 206–08.
20. VanSledright and Brophy, "Storytelling, Imagination, and Fanciful Elaboration," 851. The paucity of informational text in primary schooling is documented in Duke, "3.6 Minutes per Day," 202–24.
21. Keith C. Barton, "A Sociocultural Perspective on Children's Understanding of Historical Change: Comparative Findings From Northern Ireland and the United States," *American Educational Research Journal* 38 (Winter 2002): 899–905; "History Education and National Identity in Northern Ireland and the United

States," *Theory into Practice,* 40 (Winter 2001)*:* 49–50; "'You'd Be Wanting to Know about the Past': Social Contexts of Children's Historical Understanding in Northern Ireland and the United States," *Comparative Education,* 37 (February 2001) 98–100.

22. The one context in which children may learn narratives of the past is in their own homes and neighborhoods from family, friends, or other community members. Indeed, many people assume that children in Northern Ireland consume stories of their national past—particularly sectarian ones—from an early age. The available evidence, however, suggests that these narratives may not be salient for children until later in adolescence. Even if students are learning narratives at home, however, they are not reinforced at school or in most of the public forums in which children report learning about the past. Keith C. Barton and Alan W. McCully, "History, identity, and the school curriculum in Northern Ireland: An empirical study of secondary students' ideas and perspectives." *Journal of Curriculum Studies* (forthcoming); Barton, "Children's Understanding of Historical Change," 902; "'You'd Be Wanting to Know about the Past,'" 100.

23. Barton, "Narrative Simplifications," 60–66.

24. Barton, "Sociocultural Perspective," 892–96.

25. Barton, "Narrative Simplifications," 56–60; "Sociocultural Perspective," 887–92.

26. Eric Foner, *The Story of American Freedom* (New York: W. W. Norton, 1998), xiv.

Chapter 8

Narratives of Individual Achievement and Motivation

> *Men make their own history, but they do not make it just as they please; they do not make it under circumstances chosen by themselves, but under circumstances directly encountered, given and transmitted from the past. The tradition of all the dead generations weighs like a nightmare on the brain of the living.*
>
> —*Karl Marx[1]*

For many educators, the term *narrative* implies a particular type of story, one focusing on the struggles and triumphs of individuals and emphasizing personal perceptions and interpretations. This concern with individual consciousness has been an integral part of the development of contemporary Western literature, particularly as reflected in the novel, and so it is hardly surprising that educators prefer such narratives. The literary works used from kindergarten through 12th grade almost always feature the experiences of individuals, and students learn to interpret behavior in terms of individual motivation and achievement. Even when educational researchers use narrative methods, they are concerned primarily with engaging participants in reconstruction of their individual experience as a way of making meaning out of their lives and careers.

Yet although this is a common type of narrative, it is by no means the only one, particularly within history. Narratives can be told about nations, about social groups, or about institutions; they can even be told about landscapes or the weather. Much traditional school history, in fact, has focused on just such nonindividual entities. More recently, though, practitioners have been advised to emphasize individuals—through historical fiction, biographies, and response activities—as a way of increasing students' interest in the subject and helping them understand the "human dimension" of the subject. This approach has several advantages: It builds on students' prior experience in making sense of human behavior, motivates them to learn about distant time periods and remote events, and alerts them to the role of human agency in historical developments. From the standpoint of participatory democracy, this last point is particularly important: If the study of history never makes it to the personal level, students might come to regard humans as little more than pawns in a cosmic game of chess. For them to take responsibility for the common good, they must believe they have a role to play in creating the future. History can help them see how individuals influence the course of events.

However, interpreting history too exclusively in terms of individual motivation and achievement also has its drawbacks. It can deflect attention from the larger structural conditions that provide the context within which human action takes place, and as a result, students may be misled into thinking that individuals can bring about whatever changes they desire, regardless of the cultural, economic, or political forces that have an impact on their lives. As Marx observes, people do make their own history, but "they do not make it just as they please"—their actions take place within a context inherited from the past, and this inheritance involves societal institutions that exist apart from and independent of any individual life. Changing such institutions—or preserving them—requires more than individual effort; it requires collective action as people work together to undertake tasks they could not accomplish on their own. To prepare students for democracy, history education must not only acquaint them with human agency but help them better understand the context within which such agency operates.

THE ROLE OF INDIVIDUAL NARRATIVES IN HISTORY EDUCATION

In the last chapter, we pointed out that history need not take the form of a narrative. Yet even when history is narrative in format—as it so often is, especially in schools—it need not focus on the actions and intentions of individuals. Many historical narratives do not place individuals—or at least any particular individuals—at the center of their accounts. Narratives of political dynasties, of the rise and fall of a country's international power, of changing conditions of women's work, or of the end of slavery focus on sequences of events that involve large groups of people, and these groups are agents of those narratives. One way of telling the "story" of the Civil War, for example, is to narrate the conflict between two political structures known as the Union and the Confederacy, rather than the experiences of particular individuals (even though many individuals might show up in the story). Much traditional history—dealing with national legal and diplomatic affairs—is the story of politically defined groups such as states and nations, and contemporary social history often is about groups defined by class, ethnicity, or gender. More extreme examples of nonindividual narratives can be found in the work of the *Annales* school of historians; their narratives relate changes in social structure, agricultural systems, demographic patterns, and collective mentality. Because such histories focus on *la longue durée*—the long duration—they literally cannot be narratives of individuals, because the time period under consideration extends far beyond the lifetime of any one person. Cultural and material patterns or structures rather than individual people are the agents of such narratives.[2]

Of course, most of the actions that take place in these narratives (industrialization, imperialism, demographic shifts, or whatever) will be the aggregate outcome of many smaller actions undertaken by individuals, and those actions also will have an impact on the lives of individuals. Indeed, many narratives of this type will include stories of individuals as examples or illustrations of the larger changes being discussed. Jon Butler's *Awash in a Sea of Faith: Christianizing the American People*, for example, describes scores of individuals, but the agents of his narrative are characteristics of religion in the United States, not specific people: Religious beliefs and institutions change from the beginning of the book to the end, not the ideas of any particular people. Similarly, Charles Sellers, in *The Market Revolution: Jacksonian America, 1815–1846*, devotes attention to any number of influential individuals, but the agent of the narrative is the system of market relations: He analyzes changes in the economic system and related features of culture and society, not changes in any specific characters. No matter how many individuals are included in such stories, the agent of narratives like these remains a collective group (such as immigrants or coal miners), an abstract political or geographic entity (Canada, the Roman Empire), an element of social structure (landholding patterns, trade relations), or a cultural belief (witchcraft, racial attitudes).[3]

Such nonindividual narratives have long been a staple of school history texts. At the beginning of the 20th century, biographies were frequently recommended as the foundation for historical study, but by the 1930s, their role in the curriculum had come under attack. Mary Kelty, a leading theorist of elementary history education during the period, argued against biographies because of their inability to provide students with a picture of large-scale historical developments. Kelty recommended that history education should instead "trace the development of great *movements or forces*," each of which constituted "a 'significant phase' of the development of our civilization." For Kelty, "our civilization" was the agent of the narrative that students needed to learn, and historical episodes were grouped around movements affecting that civilization—not events in the lives of individuals. The titles of Kelty's elementary history texts, widely used in the United States for several decades, reflect that perspective: *The Story of the American People and Nation*, *The Beginnings of the American People and Nation*, and *The Growth of the American People and Nation*. Unit titles within these texts demonstrate a similar concern with agents and events beyond the individual level: "How the Nations Tried to Get Wealth From the New World," "How England Came to Own Most of North America," "How the English Colonies Came to Separate Themselves From the Mother Country," "How the United States Moved Westward to the Pacific," and so on. Similar perspectives were reflected in other history texts from the period, with titles like *America's March Toward Democracy*, *The Story of Our Country*, and *A History of*

American Progress. Individuals showed up in these works, but they were not the focus of the narrative.[4]

School history texts—at the elementary, middle, and high school levels—are still organized around such narratives, as typical unit titles make clear: "The Spread of Civilizations," "Global Exchanges," "Different Worlds Meet," "The Nation Expands," "The Nation Breaking Apart," "Becoming a World Power," and so on.[5] However, this focus on abstract entities and events—nations, economic systems, constitutional developments, economic relations—has also been blamed for producing students' apparent lack of motivation and achievement in the subject. As a result, reformers have emphasized the need to include both private and public history and to help students see historical events through the eyes of the people who experienced them. If a shared sense of humanity can be used to encourage students to see connections between themselves and people in the past, it is assumed they will be more likely to consider the subject meaningful and relevant. In some ways, these recommendations mirror those of 100 years ago, when biography was in ascendance, but they differ in emphasizing the everyday lives of ordinary people from a variety of backgrounds, rather than the public actions of a narrow range of world leaders and other famous individuals.[6]

This focus on the personal lives of people in the past has become increasingly popular—and much more feasible—over the last two decades. The explosion in children's book publishing has resulted in a wealth of easily available, well-written historical narratives on a wide variety of topics in U.S. history, and these include both picture books for the primary grades and chapter books for older students. Such works typically focus on narratives of individuals (real or fictional) participating in dramatic events like the American Revolution or the Civil Rights movement, or on those who were part of long-term social and demographic developments such as immigration or the westward movement.[7] Primary source collections, meanwhile, feature photographs, letters, diaries, and other documentation of daily life, and even textbook publishers have begun to include systematic attention to the words and deeds of ordinary people.

Such individual narratives have been easily adapted to the curricular patterns of elementary and middle schools. Although history has not usually been taught systematically before fourth or fifth grade, there has always been a place for stories of Columbus, George Washington, and Abraham Lincoln. (Despite her opposition to biography as a foundation for the history curriculum, even Kelty coauthored a collection of historical biographies for younger students.[8]) It has been relatively easy for teachers to expand this canon to include a more diverse set of individuals, including Harriet Tubman, Rosa Parks, and Martin Luther King, Jr. Elementary teachers also sometimes integrate history into their reading programs through popular works of historical fiction. Teachers in the intermediate and middle grades, although more burdened by requirements for chronological coverage, also frequently welcome the chance to humanize and personalize history, and so when studying events like the American Revolution or the Civil War, they may include works of historical fiction like *My Brother Sam is Dead* or *Across Five Aprils*.[9] Teachers may also ask students to imagine themselves in the place of people in history by writing simulated journal entries, engaging in dialogues, acting out events, and so on. It is difficult to reach broad generalizations on this issue, but based on our experience, individual narratives seem to be the dominant format for history in the early grades; in later grades, they often accompany, but do not usually replace, the less personal stories found in textbooks and curriculum guides.

THE APPEAL AND LIMITATIONS OF INDIVIDUAL NARRATIVES

Narratives that focus on the experiences of individuals can be very appealing to students. This became particularly clear in a classroom study one of us conducted several years ago. In that sixth-grade class, students were engaged in an individualized reading program as preparation for a History Day project. The teacher wanted students to become familiar with a range of historical topics before beginning to create their own displays, so over the course of several weeks, she gave them the chance to select, read, and respond to a variety of works of history, historical fiction, and historical biography from classroom and school libraries. In response to these books, students wrote journal entries and book reviews and took part in discussions with the teacher and other students.[10]

Most students in this study were interested in exploring historical events through the eyes of the individuals involved, as though they themselves were present or could relive the experiences of people in the past. They read about World War II, for example, not for stories of troop deployments or conflict among countries but to learn about brave children like Anne Frank or "madmen" like Hitler. They were particularly interested in the "border areas" of human experience: times when people had to respond to situations of fear, discrimination, or tragedy. Students often reflected on how they would have responded if put in the same situations, with comments such as "I would have run away! Why didn't they run away?" or "I would never have the guts to fly a plane across the Atlantic alone." They also speculated on the nature of bravery and inhumanity, and the motivations for each—exploring what might have led Hitler to undertake such insane actions or why ordinary people joined the Nazis' cause. The emotional relevance of the stories children read in this class and their personal identification with the characters in those stories were among the most salient characteristics of their interest in history.[11]

We found similar responses in a later study in which one of us worked with Jennifer, a fifth-grade girl who independently read eight works of historical fiction over the course of a school year. In discussing her response to each book, Jennifer consistently emphasized the importance of personal and individual elements in her reading. She was particularly interested in humanizing details about people in the past—how they felt about events, how they lived their daily lives, and what they wore and how they spoke. Like the sixth graders in the classroom study, Jennifer was fascinated by the reaction of historical characters to extreme situations—she wondered why they behaved as they did and what she would have done in their situation. In comparing these works to her textbook, she explained that with a text, "You don't imagine yourself there because they're not doing it as if it were a person. That would be a very interesting social studies book if they told a few things about the people as if it were from their own eyes." Her text actually was just as much a narrative as any of the works of historical fiction she was reading, but it was less interesting because it was not a narrative about individuals. What she wanted were readings that focused on emotion, morality, and individual judgment.[12]

These findings are consistent with reports from classroom teachers, both those we know personally and those who have published accounts of their practices. One of the chief advantages of history instruction that emphasizes individual narratives is its motivational power for children: They are captivated by stories that help them explore how people responded to dramatic situations or that give them the chance to imagine taking part in the events of the past. However, this focus on individuals also has significant disadvantages. In chapter 11 we consider the shortcomings of asking students to imagine the experiences of people in the past, but here we are concerned not with the ability of children to put themselves in other people's positions but with the drawbacks of overemphasizing individual choices, responses, and actions in the first place.

These drawbacks were apparent in our classroom study of fourth and fifth graders. As mentioned in previous chapters, that research involved observations and interviews in two classes (one a fourth grade, one a fourth and fifth combination) in which students were studying a variety of topics from U.S. history (Colonial Life, the French and Indian Wars, the American Revolution, Immigration, Women's Suffrage, Civil Rights) as well their own personal and family histories. These students were exposed to a range of historical materials—literature (fiction and nonfiction), reference books, primary sources and artifacts, and videos—and they often took part in the kind of response activities described previously. For example, they reenacted the trial of a woman accused of witchcraft in Salem, acted out meetings between French and English colonists, and wrote about how immigrants might have felt on arriving in the United States.[13]

As in our other studies, these students were interested in and motivated by learning about people in the past. Yet more disturbingly, they explained all historical events as though they were about individuals; they almost completely ignored the impact of collective action, as well as the role of societal institutions such as political, legal, and economic systems. When asked to explain why they thought people in the past treated women and minorities differently than they do today, for example, students pointed exclusively to individual attitudes: They suggested men were "bossy" and "wouldn't share," and that Whites were "lazy" and thought "Black people weren't as good as White people." These explanations may be true enough, but they are inadequate as explanations for racism or sexism because they leave out crucial factors such as socially sanctioned norms and beliefs, the role of the legal system in creating and sustaining systems of oppression, and the economic underpinnings of slavery or patriarchy.[14]

Similarly, when explaining why these practices have changed over time, students pointed to the impact of individuals in changing attitudes and beliefs: They thought famous people, particularly Abraham Lincoln and Martin Luther King, Jr., had single-handedly changed the lives of women and minorities in American society: "Abraham Lincoln set [slaves] free, and now we like them much better"; "Martin Luther King came along, and he stopped that"; "Famous people over the years have changed that and given other people their rights." As one student put it, Martin Luther King "said a speech, and then everybody started realizing that the Black people were the same as them … they needed to treat them how they would want to be treated." Almost completely lacking was any sense of the larger structural dimensions of such change, and entirely absent was any focus on collective action. History, for these students, was about a few famous individuals changing the minds of other individuals.[15]

Just as striking was students' interpretation of the American Revolution and the events leading up to it. In explaining the background to the conflict, their teachers emphasized sources of tension between England and the North American colonies, including the expansion of French and English settlements, wars in the colonies between France and England, taxes instituted to pay for protection of the colonies, and colonists' resentment at being taxed without direct representation in Parliament. However, as students discussed these issues and prepared for instructional activities, it became clear that they understood the events of the period very differently than their teachers. In particular, despite the emphasis on conflicts between political entities and over political principles, students' responses focused on individuals. When asked to explain the result of French and English expansion in North America, for example, students did not suggest that the two colonizing countries might go to war over territory, but rather that French and English settlers might get into a war because they "didn't like each other that much."[16]

Similarly, students consistently misinterpreted the English colonists' dispute with Britain as being about the amount and timing of taxes rather than with the lack of political representation in Parliament. The teachers could not rid students of their misconception that colonists were upset because taxes were too high and that they were being surprised in their homes by greedy tax collectors. A debate between students representing the colonies and England—despite seemingly careful preparation and scaffolding by the teacher regarding the political context—quickly degenerated into an argument about whether colonists should be free from their "mom's" control. As one student put it, the American Revolution was fought so that we wouldn't "be bossed around by the Queen."[17]

This same pattern is evident in studies conducted by other researchers. Jere Brophy and Bruce VanSledright, for example, conducted interviews with fifth graders before and after they studied topics such as the European exploration and colonization of North America. They found that at the beginning of their studies, students thought of explorers as individual hobbyists or entrepreneurs rather than as commissioned agents of government; even after instruction on the topic, they failed to understand the larger political economic contexts of their voyages, and although they recognized that these voyages were commissioned by European countries, they nonetheless attributed the reasons for exploration to personal motives of monarchs rather than to pursuit of national interests. Similarly, after studying colonization, most students still did not understand that colonies were governed by European nations, and they thought the process of colonization was the result of personal rivalry among individual monarchs. As in our own work, students focused on the motivations of individuals and neglected the political and economic contexts that shaped their actions.[18]

Interpreting the past solely in terms of individual motivation and achievement seriously limits students' understanding of many historical events. If students think that European colonization of the Americas took place because of the individual motivations of explorers or kings, or that the American Revolution was fought because people were surprised in their homes by tax collectors, then it could reasonably be said that they have not understood these episodes at all. Similarly, the lives of African Americans and other minorities in the United States did not change because a speech by King altered the attitudes of White people. To understand the history of civil rights, students need to understand changes in legislation and political representation, as well as the collective actions that brought about those institutional changes. Focusing on individual beliefs and actions fundamentally misrepresents those events and, perhaps more important, leaves students ill equipped to understand institutional racism and other forms of discrimination today, when individuals are less likely to publicly affirm personal prejudices.

These limitations were evident in John Wills' case study of middle-school history classrooms. In one class, students studied the Civil War period in depth (for 8 weeks), and a major emphasis of the unit was on the cruelties, indignities, and injustices that African Americans experienced under slavery. The unit included a variety of resources and response activities, and many of these focused on the experiences of individuals; students read from a collection of interviews with those who had experienced slavery firsthand, for example, and wrote personal responses. In these responses, students were sympathetic to the experiences of slaves and made an effort to identify with them, often imagining themselves in their place and speculating on how they would have felt—just as the students in our studies have done. Students repeatedly wrote about the abuse of slaves, including the cruelty of splitting up African American families, the brutality of masters who beat their slaves for small offenses, and their poor living conditions. Wills observes that they seemed sincere in their expressions of shock and outrage at such treatment, and he concludes that the unit was successful in sensitizing students—most of them White—to the lives and experiences of others.[19]

This teacher hoped students would be able to use their knowledge of the experience of African Americans to think about contemporary race relations, and during Wills' observations, a unique opportunity for discussion of the topic arose: the Los Angeles uprising/riots that followed the verdict in the trial of the police officers accused of beating Rodney King. For the teacher, the links between past and present were obvious, and they revolved around issues of equality, economic opportunity, brutality, equal protection, and rights under the law. However, these links were not obvious to students; in fact, they suggested that African Americans today had not taken advantage of economic opportunities, that remembering the history of their ancestors made them believe everyone was against them, and even that they had somehow brought discrimination on themselves. Because slavery was over, they thought, it had no relevance for understanding the present.[20]

Willis suggests students had difficulty seeing connections between past and present in part because they had not studied the experience of African Americans in any other time period, and so they were unaware of racism and inequality as enduring themes in the nation's past. Another reason he identifies, though, is that the focus on the brutal or inhumane treatment of slaves in their everyday lives provided students with a "moral discourse" but not a political one; issues of civil and political rights remain, even though the specific moral issues surrounding the mistreatment of slaves disappeared with the end of the practice. From our perspective, this is another way of saying that students' study of slavery had been limited to narratives of individual experience; these are the kinds of narratives that evoke the moral outrage that were so clear in this study and our own. What students had apparently not focused on was the institutionalization of racism in social norms, legal restrictions, and economic systems—"political" topics, in Willis' terms, that have relevance long after the specific brutality of slavery has disappeared.[21]

INDIVIDUAL NARRATIVES AS A CULTURAL TOOL

At this point, readers may wonder if we are being overly judgmental of children's understanding of history. After all, the 10- to 12-year-olds mentioned earlier were just beginning their systematic study of the subject, and so it is hardly surprising that their ideas did not coincide fully with those of professional historians or other adults. Indeed, we would not expect a fourth grader encountering the topic of colonization for the first time to develop a sophisticated analysis of European expansionism in the 17th and 18th centuries. However, what we are interested in is how such students do attempt to make sense of the history they encounter. When they come across narratives of colonization, or slavery, or suffrage (whether in school or out), they don't simply shut down and let the information pass through them like a sieve, nor do they develop a set of random misconceptions or incomplete understandings. Rather, their misunderstandings appear to be systematic and predictable. This is where we find the concept of tool use particularly productive, because it appears that in many cases, students turn to a tool they are already familiar with—that of the individual narrative.

The salience of this tool is especially clear in studies that have analyzed students' interpretation of written texts. When Margaret McKeown and Isabel Beck interviewed fifth graders who had read textbook passages on the topic of "no taxation without representation," for example, they noted that students interpreted their reading in terms of colonists getting angry, the strength of a British colonel, the ending of taxes by the King, and people "quieting down." McKeown and Beck refer to such responses as indicative of a "surface narrative," and they rightly fault textbooks for failing to adequately explain abstract concepts such as taxation and representation.[22] However, it is important to note that students' failure to understand the content of the text did not result in random responses or chaotic misconceptions—rather, students focused on individual actions and intentions rather than on political and economic structures and processes. When faced with text that was not entirely comprehensible to them, students imposed order on it—and the order they imposed derived from their familiarity with the actions and intentions of individuals.

Similarly, M. Anne Britt and her colleagues gave elementary students a passage about the building of the Panama Canal and asked them to retell what they had read. One of the most common problems in students' retellings was that they focused on a "substory" of the passage rather than the "main story." The researchers imply that this indicates a reading problem on the part of students, but from a sociocultural perspective, what was notable about these retellings was that every student retold the same substory—that of how workers at the canal overcame disease. The main story, the one they failed to retell, was about how the United States received permission to build the canal. Simply assuming that students had difficulty reading such historical passages would be misleading, for again, their problems were not random ones. They interpreted the text by using a tool with which they were familiar, the narrative of individual actions.[23]

However, it could still be argued that individual narratives are inherently easier for students to understand, just as one could argue that narrative representations of the past are more comprehensible than non-narrative ones. If students in the elementary grades consistently interpret historical events in terms of individual actions and intentions, the simplest explanation seems to be that this is the kind of explanation they are ready for. Margaret Donaldson and her colleagues have shown that young children attempt to make "human sense" of the world around them by putting novel situations into the context with which they are most familiar—the world of human motives and intentions.[24] Perhaps it is unreasonable to expect elementary children to do otherwise; perhaps this is the only tool they are capable of using. If some historical topics require an understanding of politics or economics, then maybe those are best left until a later age when students are ready and able to understand those features of society.

Once again, the differing patterns of history education in the United States and Northern Ireland give us a chance to evaluate the extent to which this focus on individuals is inevitable among students. Just as children's exposure to history in Northern Ireland is less narrative in structure than in the United States, it is also less focused on individuals. The elementary curriculum includes almost no attention to any specific people in history, again for both pedagogical and political reasons—pedagogically because history education emphasizes the social and economic elements of life in the past, and politically because nearly every individual from the history of Britain or Ireland would be identified as either Catholic or Protestant, and hence too controversial to study at school. Out-of-school experiences reinforce this emphasis, for many of the same reasons discussed in the last chapter. As a result, when young children learn about history in Northern Ireland, they learn, in simple terms, about the social structure of past societies—they study the economic patterns, material culture, and social relations of Mesolithic people, Vikings, Victorians, and so on. Although they may often be asked to imagine what it was like to a person at a certain time in the past, they almost never learn about the experiences of any specific individuals in history, either famous or common, real or fictional.[25]

When students in Northern Ireland were asked to explain why life had changed over time, their explanations also focused less exclusively on individual achievements and motivations than did those of U.S. students. Although many thought styles and fashions had changed for no particular reason, those who gave causal explanations pointed to differing social and economic contexts; some, for example, observed that clothes made in the home would look different than those from a store, and others pointed out the impact of rising affluence on the fashions available. They also sometimes explained changing social practices by identifying societal, rather than individual, factors. When asked why teachers no longer caned students, most pointed to precisely the kinds of factors missing in U.S. students' responses—collective action and changes in social institutions.

They explained that today caning is illegal, that it is against the regula-
tions of the education board, or that courts prohibit such practices. Several noted that these changes had come about because of the efforts of
human rights organizations.[26]

Similarly, in explaining why Viking women married much younger than
women today, most students placed marriage practices into a broader social
context: They noted changes in cultural norms and suggested a relationship between the age of marriage and the economic and demographic demands of Viking society. These explanations—given by the equivalent of
fourth graders—focused not on the decision-making processes of individuals but on the societal conditions that led to given cultural practices. This is
not to say that students never pointed to the role of individuals. In fact, they
often did so: Some thought that caning was common because people "just
didn't think" or that Vikings married early because they were stupid or
"thick." These explanations mirrored those of their U.S. counterparts who
thought slavery existed because Whites were lazy or women had fewer rights
in the past because men were bossy. Research in other countries has also
shown that students sometimes turn to individualistic explanations when
dealing with events in the past. Yet for U.S. students, this was essentially
their only way of explaining historical developments, whereas for those in
Northern Ireland, it was but one way of accounting for change, and by no
means the most common.[27]

These differences suggest that students' focus on individual motivation
and achievement is a cultural tool, rather than an inevitable way of making
sense of the past or a developmental stage best fitting those of a given age.
Individuals are a prominent part of U.S. students' exposure to history,
whether in the form of famous people like George Washington and Rosa
Parks or "everyday" figures in historical fiction or television programs, and
students make use of this familiarity when they try to account for historical
change. Roy Rosenzweig and David Thelen also found that within families,
the most common narratives people hoped to pass on to their children
"centered on the struggles of individuals to make a better world for themselves and those who came after them." Even when dealing with contemporary social relations, public discourse in the United States most often
focuses on individuals: Inequality, for example, is blamed on inadequate
personal drive, whereas structural constraints, group interests, and collective action are downplayed or dismissed. This stands in distinct contrast to
the United Kingdom, where discussions of social class and economic structure are an accepted part of public debate.[28]

Yet even within the United States, individual narratives are by no means
universal. Rosenzweig and Thelen, for example, found that both African
American and Sioux respondents were more likely than Whites to emphasize a collective past, and that African Americans focused on joining social
movements and other groupings to make a difference in the world.[29] We
still need to know much more about how students from varied backgrounds

think about historical developments, and conceptualizing their explanations in terms of tool use rather than individual cognition leads to a number of potentially productive avenues of research. Which students use the tool of individual motivation and achievement as a basis for historical explanations and under what circumstances? Are they more likely to use this tool to explain some events than others? What learning experiences influence use of the tool—does the prevalence of historical fiction in some classrooms, for example, make students more likely to rely on individualistic explanations? Also, to what extent does this tool interfere with understanding the nonindividual narratives found in textbooks? Investigation of these questions might lead to practical suggestions for enhancing students' ability to use a variety of tools in explaining the past. Students who consider multiple explanations will be better prepared for the demands of democratic deliberation than those who are limited to a single, dominant way of making sense of history.

CONCLUSIONS

Not all historical narratives focus on individuals, but such stories can be especially motivating for students, because they enable them to use their prior knowledge of human behavior as a way of understanding otherwise distant time periods and abstract topics. The wealth of historical literature for children and adolescents, and the popularity of response activities that ask students to imagine themselves as actors in historical events, provide opportunities to connect with the past in a way that textbooks, with their emphasis on the affairs of nations, have not traditionally been able to accomplish. Also, not only do stories of individuals increase students' interest and motivation, they may contribute to democratic citizenship: If students recognize that each person can play a role in directing the course of history, they may develop the sense of agency needed to take responsibility for the common good.

However, focusing on individual motivation and achievement as a driving force in history also places constraints on students' understanding of the social world, both now and in the past. If students fail to understand how individual actions and opportunities are shaped by cultural patterns and societal institutions—such as economic structures, legal and political systems, and religious denominations—then they will be poorly equipped to engage in reasoned judgments about matters of the common good. They may, for example, believe that social problems are caused solely by deficiencies in attitudes, rather than by inequitable or unproductive societal arrangements, and that solutions will result from changing those attitudes—making people more tolerant, more respectful of the environment, or whatever. They may also fail to apprehend that changing society often requires collective action rather than heroic efforts by a few powerful or charismatic individuals. Only by examining the role of the individual and society in history (and the frequent tension between the two) will students have the range of tools necessary for understanding how the social world operates.

ENDNOTES

1. Karl Marx, "The Eighteenth Brumaire of Louis Bonaparte," in *Karl Marx: Selected Writings,* Ed. David McLellan (New York: Oxford University Press, 1977), 300.
2. For example, Emmanuel Le Roy Ladurie, *The Peasants of Languedoc,* Trans. J. Day (Urbana, Ill.: University of Illinois Press, 1974); Marc Bloch, *French Royal History: An Essay on its Basic Characteristics,* Trans. J. Sondheimer (Berkeley, Calif.: University of California Press, 1996) and *The Royal Touch: Sacred Monarchy and Scrofula in England and France,* Trans. J. E. Anderson (London: Routledge & Kegan Paul, 1973); Fernand Braudel, *The Mediterranean and the Mediterranean World in the Age of Philip II,* 2 vols., Trans. S. Reynolds (Glasgow, Scotland: William Collins, 1972–73) and *Civilization and Capitalism 15th–18th Century,* 3 vols, Trans. S. Reynolds (Glasgow, Scotland: Willaim Collins, 1981–92); Lucien Febvre, *A New Kind of History: From the Writings of Febvre,* Ed. P. Burke, Trans. K. Folca (London: Routledge and Kegan Paul, 1973).
3. Jon Butler, *Awash in a Sea of Faith: Christianizing the American People* (Cambridge, Mass.: Harvard University Press, 1990); Charles Sellers, *The Market Revolution: Jacksonian America, 1815–1846* (New York: Oxford University Press, 1991).
4. Keith C. Barton, "Mary G. Kelty: The Most Important Social Educator No One has Heard of?," in *New Research in Curriculum History,* Eds. Sherry L. Field and O. L. Davis, Jr. (Greenwich, Conn.: Information Age Publishing, forthcoming); Mary G. Kelty, *Learning and Teaching History in the Middle Grades* (New York: Ginn and Company, 1936), 21–23; *The Story of the American People and Nation* (New York: Ginn, 1942); *The Beginnings of the American People and Nation* (New York: Ginn, 1931); *The Growth of the American People and Nation* (New York: Ginn, 1931); Wilbur F. Murra and others, *Bibliography of Textbooks in the Social Studies,* Bulletin No. 12 of the National Council for the Social Studies (Cambridge, Mass.: National Council for the Social Studies, 1939), 34–35. Joseph R. Moreau notes that the focus on heroic individuals and dramatic events in 19th century history textbooks worked against a coherent, overall narrative of historical change and that this approach was eventually supplanted by an emphasis on the development of institutions; "Schoolbook Nation: Imagining the American Community in United States History Texts for Grammar and Secondary Schools, 1865–1930" (Ph.D. diss., University of Michigan, Ann Arbor, 2002), 36, 42–50.
5. Houghton Mifflin, Level 6: *Discover Our Heritage,* http://www.eduplace.com/ss/wtp/level6/index.html; Houghton Mifflin, *Level 5: Build Our Nation,* http://www.eduplace.com/ss/wtp/level5/index.htmlHoughton; McDougal Littel, *Creating America,* available from http://www.classzone.com/books/ca_ww1/index.cfm
6. Joan W. Blos, "Perspectives on Historical Fiction," in *The Story of Ourselves: Teaching History Through Children's Literature,* Eds. Michael O. Tunnell and Richard Ammon (Portsmouth, N.H.: Heinemann, 1993), 13; Matthew T. Downey, "Reforming the History Curriculum," in *History in the Schools: What Shall We Teach?,* Ed. Bernard R. Gifford (New York: Macmillan, 1988), 198–213; Russell Freeedman, "Bring 'Em Back Alive," in *The Story of Ourselves:*

Teaching History Through Children's Literature, Eds. Michael O. Tunnell and Richard Ammon (Portsmouth, N.H.: Heinemann, 1993), 41–47; Linda S. Levstik, "History From the Bottom Up," *Social Education* 50 (February 1986), 1–7; Milton Meltzer, "On Teaching and Learning History," in *Milton Meltzer on Writing, History, and Social Responsibility,* Ed. E. Wendy Saul (New York: Teachers College Press, 1994), 30–36; "Ordinary People: In Their Own Words," in *Milton Meltzer on Writing, History, and Social Responsibility,* Ed. E. Wendy Saul (New York: Teachers College Press, 1994), 63–73; Carl M. Tomlinson, Michael O. Tunnell, and Donald J. Richgels, "The Content and Writing of History in Textbooks and Trade Books," in *The Story of Ourselves: Teaching History Through Children's Literature,* Eds. Michael O. Tunnell and Richard Ammon (Portsmouth, N.H.: Heinemann, 1993), 52–53.

7. Michael O. Tunnell, "Unmasking the Fiction of History: Children's Historical Literature Begins to Come of Age," in *The Story of Ourselves: Teaching History Through Children's Literature,* Eds. Michael O. Tunnell and Richard Ammon (Portsmouth, N.H.: Heinemann, 1993), 79–90.

8. Eleanor Thomas and Mary G. Kelty, *Heroes, Heroines, and Holidays* (New York: Ginn, 1947).

9. James Lincoln Collier and Christopher Collier, *My Brother Sam is Dead* (New York: Four Winds Press, 1974); Irene Hunt, *Across Five Aprils* (Morristown, N.J.: Silver Burdett Press, 1993).

10. Linda S. Levstik, "The Relationship Between Historical Response and Narrative in a Sixth-Grade Classroom," *Theory and Research in Social Education* 19 (Winter 1986): 1–19.

11. Levstik, "The Relationship Between Historical Response and Narrative," 6–8, 10.

12. Linda S. Levstik, "Historical Narrative and the Young Reader," *Theory Into Practice* 28 (Spring 1989): 114.

13. Keith C. Barton, "'Bossed Around by the Queen': Elementary Students' Understanding of Individuals and Institutions in History," *Journal of Curriculum and Supervision* 12 (Summer 1997): 290–314.

14. Barton, "Bossed Around by the Queen," 299.

15. Barton, "Bossed Around by the Queen," 299–300. G. Williamson McDiarmid found that students in a university historiography class gave explanations very similar to these; he notes, "They seemed to view the civil rights movement as the sum of individual heroic acts like those of Rosa Parks and Martin Luther King in the face of Southern bigotry and violence. None treated the movement as a culmination of a long struggle in which people had organized themselves to challenge discrimination." G. Williamson McDiarmid, "Understanding History for Teaching: A Study of the Historical Understanding of Prospective Teachers," in *Cognitive and Instructional Processes in History and the Social Sciences,* Eds. James F. Voss and Mario Carretero (Hillsdale, N.J.: Lawrence Erlbaum Associates, Inc., 1994), 169.

16. Barton, "Bossed Around by the Queen," 302.

17. Barton, "Bossed Around by the Queen," 303–305.

18. Jere Brophy, Bruce VanSledright, and Nancy Bredin, *Fifth-Graders' Ideas About European Exploration of the New World Expressed Before and After Studying This Topic Within a U.S. History Course,* Elementary Subjects Center Series No. 78 (East Lansing, Mich: Center for the Learning and Teaching of Elementary Subjects, Insti-

tute for Research on Teaching, College of Education, Michigan State University, 1992); Jere Brophy and Bruce VanSledright, *Teaching and Learning History in Elementary Schools* (New York: Teachers College Press, 1997), 128–131.

19. John S. Wills, "Who Needs Multicultural Education? White Students, U.S. History, and the Construction of a Usable Past," *Anthropology and Education Quarterly* 27 (September 1996): 365–89.

20. Wills, "Who Needs Multicultural Education," 370–74.

21. Wills, "Who Needs Multicultural Education," 370–80.

22. Margaret G. McKeown and Isabel Beck, "Making Sense of Accounts of History: Why Young Students Don't and How They Might," in *Teaching and Learning in History*, Eds. Gaea Leinhardt, Isabel L. Beck, and Catherine Stainton (Hillsdale, N.J.: Lawrence Erlbaum Associates, Inc., 1994), 1–26.

23. M. Anne Britt, Jean-François Rouet, Mara C. Georgi, and Charles A. Perfetti, "Learning From History Texts: From Causal Analysis to Argument Models," in *Teaching and Learning in History*, Eds. Gaea Leinhardt, Isabel L. Beck, and Catherine Stainton (Hillsdale, N.J.: Lawrence Erlbaum Associates, Inc., 1994), 47–84.

24. Margaret Donaldson, *Children's Minds* (New York: Norton, 1978), 16–17.

25. Keith C. Barton, "A Sociocultural Perspective on Children's Understanding of Historical Change: Comparative Findings From Northern Ireland and the United States," *American Educational Research Journal* 38 (Winter 2002): 899–905. Our experience in Ghana and New Zealand also suggests that the history curriculum in those countries is less tied to stories of individual achievement.

26. Barton, "Sociocultural Perspective," 888–92.

27. Barton, "Sociocultural Perspective," 892; Ola Halldén, "Learning History," *Oxford Review of Education* 12, No. 1 (1968): 53–66; Mario Carretero, Liliana Jacott, Margarita Limón, Asunción Lopez-Manjón, and Jose A. León, "Historical Knowledge: Cognitive and Instructional Implications," in *Cognitive and Instructional Processes in History and Social Sciences*, Eds. Mario Carretero and James F. Voss (Hillsdale, N.J.: Lawrence Erlbaum Associates, Inc., 1994), 357–376; Peter Lee, Alaric Dickinson, and Rosalyn Ashby, "Some Aspects of Children's Understanding of Historical Explanation," paper presented at the annual meeting of the American Educational Research Association, 18–22 April, 1995.

28. Roy Rosenzweig and David Thelen, *Presence of the Past: Popular Uses of History in American Life* (New York: Columbia University Press, 1998), 197; Barton, "Sociocultural Perspective," 903–04.

29. Rosenzweig and Thelen, *Presence of the Past,* 149–50, 158, 160, 162.

The Story of National Freedom and Progress

It was remembering, and it was also fantasizing: he imagined a drama in which he gave himself all the best lines, resonant lines of sad reasonableness whose indictments were all the more severe and unanswerable for their compression and emotional restraint.

—*Ian McEwan[1]*

History education in the United States—whether in school, at museums and historic sites, or in movies and cartoons—does not rely on just any old narrative. History is no random story of Greeks, Romans, Teutons, and Celts (much less Africans, Asians, or Native Americans). Nor are the narratives students learn at school necessarily related to the events that have had the most impact on the modern world. How much attention, after all, is given to the invention of the printing press, or the agricultural revolution, or the spread of Christianity or Islam? If taught at all, these are relegated to one-time-only coverage in a required middle-school course on world history or a high school elective in the subject. Except for these brief forays into world history, most of the required curriculum is devoted to episodes within one particular narrative: the "story of our country." Characters and events associated with the exploration, colonization, and settlement of North America, as well as the eventual independence of the colonies, are featured again and again and again, from kindergarten through college. This is hardly surprising, for as we discussed in chapter 3, one of the most common purposes of history is the creation of a shared national community.

Even given this obsession with the history of a single country, many kinds of narratives could be told. Students could learn, for example, about the diversity of people who have come to North America and the wide range of reasons that have brought them here. They could learn about attempts to establish utopian communities in the 19th century. They could learn about repression of labor unions. They could learn about the persistence of racism or patriarchy. All these narratives could illuminate the national experience of the United States—stories of varied agents and their motives, of failure and triumph, and of problems solved and unsolved. However, students do not learn these stories. Or more accurately, they may encounter them (at least some of them), but these encounters are so infrequent and ambiguous that they are overwhelmed by the dominant narrative of U.S. history—the story of freedom and progress. This is the story that students appropriate as their primary tool for understanding the past. Just as in Ian McEwan's novel *Amsterdam,* in which a character remembers having all the best lines in an argument with a friend, the story of U.S. freedom and progress is as much fantasy as memory.

APPROPRIATION OF THE U.S. NATIONAL NARRATIVE

Two themes are at the core of the story Americans most often tell themselves and their children about the nation's past. The first is freedom. As Eric Foner notes, "No idea is more fundamental to Americans' sense of themselves as individuals and as a nation than freedom," and this idea "has provided the most popular 'master narrative' for accounts of our past." As Foner himself demonstrates, this concept has varied enormously throughout U.S. history. However, despite its lack of decisive definition—or perhaps because of it—the notion of freedom has provided a long-standing object of pride, veneration, and aspiration for Americans otherwise separated by time, space, and social background. Its gradual unfolding is a central theme in public representation of the national past. A closely linked theme in the country's master narrative is the idea of progress—the belief that historical developments (in the United States, at least) have resulted in a steady improvement in social and material life. U.S. history texts in the 19th century portrayed material and moral progress as a fundamental law of history, one best illustrated by the country's own past, and James Loewen argues that this equation of change with progress remains dominant today—noting that "textbook authors present our nation as getting ever better in all areas, from race relations to transportation." Museums and other public historic sites display a similar reverence for progress in U.S. history.[2]

Yet these themes not only dominate the production of history in schools, museums, or other sites; they also dominate students' "consumption" of history; in the language of sociocultural theory, students have appropriated this particular narrative as one of their principal means of conceptualizing U.S. history. The importance of a narrative of freedom in understanding the national past is particularly clear in research described by James Wertsch. In that study, conducted by Kevin O'Connor, 24 college students were asked to spend 30 to 40 minutes writing an essay that would "provide an account of the origin of your country." In 23 of the essays, students relied on a single organizing theme—what Wertsch refers to as a "quest-for-freedom" narrative. Students explained the settlement of North America and the separation of the English colonies from Britain almost entirely in terms of colonists' desire to escape social systems (or rulers) that persecuted them or deprived them of freedom, or by referring to their intention to establish a social system based on individual freedom. Notably, students almost always framed these narratives around the actions of Europeans: Whites were mentioned over five times as often in these essays as Native Americans and over 12 times as often as African Americans. Moreover, Whites were more likely to be represented as agents—the driving force of the narrative—while Native Americans were portrayed as the recipients or victims of actions undertaken by others.[3]

In chapter 3 we noted that in our research with middle-school students—in which we asked them to explain which people, events, or documents from history they considered most important—participants not only identified with the United States as a national entity but also characterized it as morally superior. Their perception of the country's righteousness rested on the two pillars of the U.S. master narrative— freedom and progress. Like the college students in O'Connor's research, these middle schoolers repeatedly referred to the importance of freedom and to its role in defining the very nature of their country. Students thought the American Revolution was important, for example, because previously "we didn't have our rights, we weren't free," and without it, "we wouldn't have freedom." Similarly, the Bill of Rights was important because "it gave us all of our freedoms and rights," and "if we didn't have the Bill of Rights we wouldn't be as free, the country would be very much, so different."[4]

It is also important to note the importance of success in this quest for freedom. Joshua Searle-White, in his study of the psychology of nationalism, points out that in many places throughout the world, victimization is an important part of national identity; he notes that "one powerful way in which individuals can achieve a feeling of being right is to have been victimized, and to have others recognize that victimization." He suggests that this process extends to national groups as well, and that the tragedies of the past often take on more significance than triumphs. However, in the United States, success, not victimization, is at the heart of nationalism: Other people may desire freedom, but we have actually achieved it. Foner notes that foreign visitors are often struck by Americans' conviction that they alone among the nations of the world truly enjoy freedom, and the students in our study were no exception. Recall that they thought freedom was what set the United States apart from other nations. As one student put it, "Unlike other countries, we have freedom of speech, and other countries didn't have that kind of right." Another noted that the Bill of Rights is important "to distinguish us from other countries, because we have more freedom than they do," and still another pointed out that "America's known for its freedom and stuff, and I think that's part of what makes it good." Students recognized that neither the American Revolution nor the Bill of Rights resulted in freedom for everyone, but the overall story of U.S. history was nonetheless one of successfully securing freedom, even when repeated attempts were necessary to extend that success.[5]

   Belief in success highlights the second key feature of the master narrative these students used to understand U.S. history: progress. As we noted
in chapter 3, they described the United States as a country in which rights
and opportunities have repeatedly expanded, social relations have
steadily improved, and historic hardships and injustices have been corrected. Students mentioned this progressive expansion of rights, opportunities, and freedom more frequently than any other theme; they
consistently chose items such as the Emancipation Proclamation, women's
suffrage, and the Civil Rights movement as among the most important
events in the nation's past, and they explicitly described the changes
brought about by such events as part of an ongoing and significant process
in U.S. history, as the freedoms established at the nation's founding were
steadily expanded to include new groups of people. What was particularly
noticeable was the degree of reflection students had engaged in related to
the theme of national progress; our interpretation of their responses required little inference, because they so clearly and explicitly articulated its
importance in U.S. history. One girl, for example, suggested that the most
important thing she had learned about history at school was "the rights of
the people that were back then, that they had to fight for to get, and how
we have so much freedom now, and they hardly had any back in the 1900s,
or 1800s." Not only did students use the narrative of freedom and progress as a key tool for understanding national history, they were consciously
aware of its centrality.[6]
   This story of progress extended to others spheres of life as well, most notably technology. Students considered inventions like electricity, cars, air-
planes, and computers to be particularly important because of their
contribution to improved lifestyles: Without the light bulb, "we would have
been like in the stone age"; the computer "has really changed things, 'cause
you don't have to write things, you can just type them on a computer and
print it out"; and without the car, "we wouldn't be able to like travel, hardly
at all, we would have to walk." Sometimes students even considered more
ambiguous episodes examples of progress, because of the lessons that had
been learned. From the Great Depression, for example, the United States
learned that it wasn't "the god of all countries," whereas the Vietnam War
"taught us that we weren't invincible," that we "shouldn't go slowly into a
war," and that we shouldn't "waste men just trying to decide." Short-term
failures were simply the basis for long-term progress.[7]
   This emphasis on progress has also been evident in our work with elementary children. As we described in chapter 7, in our yearlong classroom
study of fourth and fifth graders, students appeared to think of past events
as having occurred in a rational sequence. Yet not only did they suggest that
the connection between historical episodes was rational, they almost always
equated these changes with progress. When asked to explain how life was
different than in the past, students repeatedly described not just differences
but improvements. One pointed to "better clothing, better houses, and

more money if you have a job, and there's better schools"; another noted that "telephones ... cars, beds, washing machines, houses, schools" had all improved; yet another explained that cars, ratios, and televisions all had "got better." It's hardly surprising that students considered technological changes to be improvements, but they also explained changing fashions in terms of progress; they thought current styles were better than in the past. Some even suggested that names change over time because "when other things change, people like to change too, so their names get better along with all the other things that get better." As one pointed out, "You don't want a really beautiful girl, and her name is Flossie, or a really cute boy, and his name is Oliver."[8]

Students also used perceptions of progress to arrange pictures in chronological order. We have already noted that students almost always placed a particular pair of pictures in the wrong order—one a drawing of a street scene situated in an antebellum city, the other a photograph of a family, with horse and carriage, traveling across a prairie in the 1880s. Students typically thought the pioneer family predated the city, and their explanations pointed to their belief that historical images could be arranged in a linear sequence; often, the basis for that sequence was what they perceived as progress in social and material life. One student noted that the antebellum picture "has lots of buildings," whereas the other "just has grass and fields and stuff like that"; another observed that the pioneer picture "doesn't have like any cities or anything around it, and these people, they have wagons, but it [the antebellum picture] has a city and nicer clothes and stuff." As one student confidently explained, "I *know* it didn't go from brick buildings to wagons and carriages *after* the brick buildings." Faced with the novel task of trying to arrange these pictures into a sequence—and not knowing the correct order—these students relied on a narrative of progress to make their decision.[9]

Sometimes this narrative even led students to misperceive the evidence in front of them. Most, for example, correctly placed a photograph from the 1970s after one from early in the 20th century. However, in explaining this placement, students "saw" progress even when none was evident. One, for example, pointed out that the streets were straighter in the more recent picture—despite the fact that the streets in the older pictured appeared straight, and the newer one included a cul-de-sac. That student also noted "the windows, look at the way they go out" in the recent picture, while the older houses "just have them plain"—this time in spite of the fact that both pictures showed houses with bay windows. Similarly, two other students thought the 1970s picture was more recent because the houses were bigger, even though both pictures included two-story homes. So powerful was the narrative of progress that it led students to distort the historical evidence to fit their preconceptions.[10]

This is not to say students never recognize that events or trends may fail to fit this narrative or even contradict it. In fact, in our work with middle-schools students, it was clear they were aware of enduring problems of racism and sexism: They knew such problems had not been completely solved, and this recognition came in large part from their own experiences or those of people in their families. They also knew that some events in U.S. history—the Vietnam War, in particular—had provoked dissent, and that episodes such as the Great Depression had resulted in widespread suffering. However, the narrative of progress and exceptionality was so strong that they had trouble understanding these perceived deviations. They knew some people were still prejudiced, but they did not know why; they knew some people opposed the Vietnam War, but they did not understand why. Similarly, elementary students occasionally recognized that some examples of historical change were difficult to reconcile with progress and that people in some geographic regions have experienced change differently than those in others, but this recognition existed in an uneasy tension with their belief in progress. For both elementary and middle-school students, these failures to conform to the ideal of progress remained idiosyncrasies in the national story, disjointed episodes that did not cohere into a larger narrative. Students had access to a tool for making sense of times when things went right, when problems were solved, and when life got better, but they had no alternative tools to help them make sense of discrepant events.[11]

Wertsch reports similar findings in the study of college students mentioned earlier. Although nearly all students in that study described the origins of the United States in terms of a quest-for-freedom narrative, not all cast that story in a positive light. In their essays, many made sarcastic, ironic, or openly critical remarks about the motivations or actions of Europeans, and they sometimes digressed from the master narrative into stories that related the oppression of minorities. Yet no matter how critical students were, they still voiced their criticisms within the framework of the same overarching narrative: Those who had reservations did not tell a different story, they just told the same story while interjecting their own comments on the side. Wertsch concludes, "No matter how much or how little the subjects seemed to accept and agree with this narrative tool, they all used it in one way or another.... In fact, no student even attempted to employ another narrative tool in any extended way."[12] As with our elementary and middle graders, these college students were limited by a tool that they recognized had limitations, but they had no alternative or more inclusive narrative at their disposal.

DIVERSITY IN USE OF THE NATIONAL NARRATIVE

It may be tempting to assume that stories of freedom and progress are universal features of national identity, but in many places these narratives have little salience. Groups that aspire to national sovereignty but have been unsuccessful in achieving it—Tamils in Sri Lanka, for example, or Palestinians in Israel—cannot point to freedom as a central feature of their experience.

For many such groups, as we noted previously, national identity may be based more on narratives of victimization than achievement. Also, in areas of longstanding and seemingly ineradicable conflict, stories of historical progress may have little resonance with the daily experiences of either children or adults. This was evident among students in Northern Ireland. We have already described how elementary students there were less likely than those in the United States to simplify history into a linear narrative premised on social and material progress. One 9-year-old, for example, recognized that later historical patterns do not necessarily displace earlier ones and asked if the pictures might be arranged other than in a linear order: He suggested overlapping one picture with another because older trends can continue even as new ones develop. Others suggested that differences between images might reflect economic circumstances or geographic diversity rather than progress from one time period to another.

The relative insignificance of progress as a tool for thinking about history in Northern Ireland was also evident when secondary students there were asked to make judgments of historical significance. Whereas most U.S. students chose examples of technological progress (the invention of the light bulb, or the car, or the computer) and explained their choices by pointing to the beneficial effects of these developments, few in Northern Ireland did so; in fact, many explicitly rejected the invention of the light bulb as historically significant, and several laughed derisively at the possibility of doing so. Examples of social progress, such as improved relations between groups or expanding rights and opportunities, were even less prevalent. This was the most frequently mentioned theme in the responses of U.S. students, but few students in Northern Ireland made such choices, and none described progress in social relations as a central theme in history. This is not to say that students were uninterested in social progress nor that they thought such progress was unimportant; in fact, they mentioned the need for improved community relations when discussing both historical and contemporary events, and without exception, they thought cooperation between Catholics and Protestants would be a good thing.[13]

Unlike students in the United States, though, who described progress as an enduring theme in their country's history, those in Northern Ireland considered examples of cooperation between the two communities salutary but isolated incidents—suggestive of the potential for a better future, perhaps, but unrealized in the present. This was especially clear in their reaction to a picture representing the Multiparty Talks, which had been agreed on shortly before the interviews took place. Over half the students chose this as one of the most important events in history, and all who did so explained its importance in terms of the potential for bringing about peace. However, despite their hopes for a better future, students were pessimistic about the talks' potential. Whenever they were asked if the talks would be successful, they said no—usually automatically, and in one case even laughing at the idea. Some pointed out that talks had taken place before with no success; one Catholic girl noted, "They have done it before.... There's still talks going on," and her interview partner added, "Still talks about talks." Ian and Craig, two Protestant boys in their final year of secondary school (about age 16) clearly explained the tension between hope and pessimism (or hope and history, in Seamus Heaney's phrase):

Craig: It's disappointing in a way, because people who want it, pray for it, hope for it—and people who don't think it will work, still *do* want it—but at the same time have to face the reality that it may not happen.

Interviewer: So if you don't think it's going to be successful, do you think there's ever going to be an end to terrorism in Northern Ireland?

Ian: Not really, 'cause if there's a united Ireland, the Protestants will just go out and do what the IRA's [Irish Republican Army] been doing for the past 28 years, and if there's no settlement, the IRA'll just resume with the violence against us.

Craig: We're stuck between a rock and a hard place. It's history repeating itself over and over again, and tit for tat. But we hope, you know, that's not to say I and Ian here are saying this [peace] will never happen, it could happen with the right attitude, but you have to be realistic and say it couldn't happen [i.e., might not happen], you have to face the world.

Ian and Craig display a familiar perspective on history in Northern Ireland; for many people in both communities, the past can be a kind of prison from which escape is unlikely, perhaps impossible. Terence Brown, echoing James Joyce, notes that "in both the Nationalist and Unionist version of the Irish past there is ... a profound sense of history as a given, as a nightmare from which it is impossible to awake." Students in the United States see history as the record of problem solving and continual progress; in this view, the present position of the United States as the perceived envy of the world results from having overcome historical challenges and having learned from any obstacles. Yet in Northern Ireland, history is a record of problems, failures, and missed opportunities; the present, as Craig notes, is "history repeating itself over and over again."[14]

Narratives of national progress, then, are not universally used as tools for understanding the past. This raises the question of whether, in a nation as diverse as the United States, a story of freedom and progress can really be as widely shared as we have implied. When not everyone has benefited from the nation's progress, how important can that story be? A great deal of contemporary political and academic discourse rests on the assumption that differing ethnic groups have distinct views of U.S. history, but we found only traces of these in our work with middle-school students. African Americans were aware of the persistence of racism, for example, but their narratives of the past were not noticeably different from their White counterparts; those we interviewed from other minority backgrounds, meanwhile, as well as those who were recent immigrants to the United States, focused almost entirely on the traditional narrative of freedom and progress. Our study, though, was not designed to distinguish among the views of students from different ethnic backgrounds. Our participants came from a variety of backgrounds, but our analysis was based primarily on aggregate data—we combined all students' responses and looked for overall patterns. Moreover, minority students' responses may have been constrained by their being interviewed along with members of other ethnic groups, or by the fact that each of the researchers was White. These factors may have made them less likely to deviate from the traditionally sanctioned national narrative. Even if they had another narrative at their disposal, they may have concluded that the setting called for a story that would not offend their peers or the adults who were interviewing them.

Terrie Epstein, however, has directly addressed racial differences in students' ideas about history in her research. In one study, she used questionnaires and interviews to collect information from nearly 50 students in an urban, Midwestern, working-class high school; students were divided nearly equally between those of African American and European American ancestry. Because this data was collected individually rather than in groups, Epstein was better able to compare the ideas of students of different ethnicities. In addition, African American students were interviewed by an African American graduate student, while Epstein interviewed the White students.[15] These procedures made it more likely that students from the two groups would articulate differences in their perspectives (if they existed) rather than submerge them for the sake of politeness or because of apprehension about how such ideas might be received.

Indeed, Epstein's study did reveal racial differences in students' historical perspectives. When asked to identify the three most important people in U.S. history, for example, African American historical figures accounted for three fourths of the answers of African American students (the top four being Martin Luther King, Jr., Malcolm X, Harriet Tubman, and John F. Kennedy), while European Americans accounted for over three fourths of the responses of White students (whose top choices were George Washington, John F. Kennedy, Martin Luther King, Jr., and Thomas Jefferson). Similarly, when asked about the three most important events in U.S. history, those associated with African Americans constituted two thirds of the responses of the African American students (led by the Civil Rights movement, the Civil War, slavery and emancipation, and the assassination of King) but only one third of the answers of White students (who most often mentioned the Civil War, the signing of the Declaration of Independence or the Constitution, 20th-century wars, and the American Revolution). Even when explaining the significance of the common items on their lists, students responded differently. African Americans were more likely to note the racial identity of historical figures and to emphasize the impact on African Americans of events such as the Civil War or the Civil Rights movement. White students, on the other hand, explained these events in more general terms and were less likely to note their connection to racial issues in history. No White student, for example, noted that King was African American, while 10 of 16 African American students did so.[16]

In summarizing both questionnaire and interview data from this study, Epstein emphasizes the differences in students' historical perspectives. She concludes

> European-American adolescents constructed historical perspectives that reflected dominant narrative themes about the expansion of democratic rights and rule to ever greater numbers of Americans. They viewed racial oppression as a historical aberration from the nation's progressive legacy, with no particular group or institution culpable for the causes of racial group inequality.

On the other hand

> The African-American students' perspectives were framed by another set of assumptions: the centrality of the historical experiences related to African Americans' struggles for equality, white people's or the government's responsibility for racial oppression, and the contradiction between the ideal and the reality of the inalienability of individual rights historically and in contemporary society.

In a later study based on in-depth interviews with 10 students, Epstein found a nearly identical pattern: White students constructed a national narrative in which European Americans were responsible for shaping the nation's development and in which the nation represented principles of individual rights and democratic rule; African American students, on the other hand, described the nation's story as being marked by racial domination and subordination, and they focused on African Americans' struggles for freedom and equality both within contemporary society and in the past.[17]

Epstein's research provides evidence for a proposition that many of us take for granted: Students of African American and European American backgrounds have different perspectives on the story of the nation's past. Obviously, these perspectives can be analyzed in terms of their narrative components; they include differences in setting (systematic institutional racism in one case, idiosyncratic and inexplicable prejudice in the other), actors (African Americans figuring more prominently for one group of students), actions (again, those involving African American more important for one), and instruments (with one group more likely to point to the struggles of African Americans, while the other focuses on the granting of rights by a benevolent government).

However, two critical elements of the country's traditional narrative were still important to the African American students in Epstein's study— freedom and progress. For these students, as for others, the motivating force in U.S. history is the desire for freedom. This is especially clear in Epstein's detailed profiles of students. One girl considered the Emancipation Proclamation important because it "freed the slaves," another chose the Bill of Rights because "it gave people rights," and a boy choose Harriet Tubman and King for "helping black people be free" and the Civil War because it represented "more freedom for blacks." For these students, the goal of historical action was freedom, and although they noted more resistance to such actions than did their European American counterparts, what mattered was success. All these people and events—the Emancipation Proclamation, the Bill of Rights, Tubman, King, and the Civil War—achieved what they set out to do: free slaves, give rights, help African Americans be free, and so on. This emphasis on success was especially notable in the comments of one girl who explained that Malcolm X was important because he "showed you can grow up being bad and turn into something good" and that Rosa Parks "wanted us to have the decision whether we wanted to sit in the front or the back or the middle. And I feel that she really made a difference." Indeed, all the historical figures on students' lists "made a difference"—there were no failures. The African American students in Epstein's study saw success as more difficult to achieve and much longer in coming than did White students, but the stories that mattered were nonetheless those resulting in freedom and progress.[18]

Roy Rosenzweig and David Thelen found similar perspectives among the adults in their national survey. African Americans focused on different aspects of the national past than Whites: They paid particular attention to slavery, civil rights, and Martin Luther King, Jr.; they emphasized oppression, discrimination, and racism; and they sometimes rejected the importance of traditional figures such as George Washington. Yet they nonetheless situated their views within an overall narrative of progress, in which African Americans had struggled, with some success, to overcome racism and oppression. Rosenzweig and Thelen conclude that the African Americans they interviewed found hope rather than despair in the national past and that they were "sustained by a progressive, enabling historical vision rooted in the story of emancipation and civil rights." Mexican Americans in this study also told a traditional story of progress, although they focused more on their attempt to partake in the "American dream" rather than on struggles to overcome oppression. One ethnic group in their survey, however, told a very different story: For the Oglala Sioux (who were interviewed as part of a purposively selected group), history was a story of survival and persistence in the face of oppression by Whites; the preservation of traditional culture, rather than freedom or progress, formed the central thread of their narrative.[19]

The story of freedom and progress, then, is not a universal means for conceptualizing the past, even within the United States. Racial, ethnic, religious, linguistic, and geographic background may have more impact on ideas about the U.S. past than we realize, and we hope that future research will shed light on the development of alternative narratives among young people from diverse backgrounds. Nonetheless, the story of U.S. freedom and progress is widely if not universally accepted by children and adults. Most students are exposed to this narrative at school, in the media, and in other public settings, and it exerts a powerful influence on their understanding of the past. Even when they are critical of events in the nation's history, when they deny the good intentions of traditional "heroes," when they lament the obstacles that have stood in the way of their ancestors or emphasize the ground yet to be gained, they still look for the same narrative threads—progress in social and material life and the desire for freedom.

AFFORDANCES AND CONSTRAINTS OF THE NARRATIVE OF FREEDOM AND PROGRESS

Interpreting U.S. history as a story of freedom and progress limits students' preparation for pluralist democracy in several fundamental ways. First, reliance on this narrative often stands in the way of understanding why historical events took place. Many of the colonists who came to the North America, for example, were not pursuing political or religious freedom but were seeking economic opportunity, and this continued to motivate immigration throughout the 19th and 20th centuries (and into the 21st). To think that European settlement in North America was motivated exclusively or even primarily by political or religious ideals is to misunderstand the reasons behind these historical migrations, and this kind of misunderstanding leaves students ill equipped to engage in reasoned judgments about either history or the present. Similarly, the country's foreign policy has not always been motivated by the desire to spread freedom throughout the world; to take just two examples, military interventions in Guatemala and Iran in 1954, although justified in the name of freedom, replaced elected leaders with dictators favorable to U.S. interests.[20] If students do not recognize that the government sometimes has opposed freedom rather than supported it, they will be incapable of making the informed judgments required of citizens. Any narrative simplifies, but this particular one—because it reduces the motivation for many historical episodes to the single, unobjectionable goal of freedom—simplifies the national past in a way that undermines students' ability to make sense of crucial matters of public policy.

If emphasizing freedom constrains students' understanding of the causes of historical events, then focusing on progress limits recognition of their consequences. When the events of the past are interpreted as progress—steady social and material improvement or at least the opportunity to learn from mistakes—then their negative or unintended results can be dismissed; for that matter, such consequences can scarcely be conceptualized, much less taken seriously. Colonization, Westward expansion, industrialization: All these must have been examples of progress—that's what history is in this country—so there is little reason to consider their potentially negative effects on American Indians, small farmers, or laborers. Indeed, if such groups appear within the country's national narrative, they do so as obstacles to progress, problems to be solved rather than historical actors at the center of U.S. history.[21] The narrative of progress then becomes the ultimate defense of the status quo, because it characterizes historical change as both beneficial and inevitable. As we have noted previously, students are aware that not all events in the past can be so easily assimilated to the story of progress, but that narrative so dominates their thinking that they have no alternative framework within which to make sense of these discrepant experiences. Without some way of considering both positive and negative consequences of events, the ability to deliberate over the common good will be seriously impoverished.

These first two drawbacks combine to create a third—a dismissal of alternative perspectives. If Americans have always been motivated by the noble desire for freedom, and if our efforts have always been successful, at least in the long run, then how could anyone call our actions into question? We imagine our national history the way McEwan's character remembers his own recent past, giving himself "all the best lines," lines both reasonable and unanswerable. Henry Kissinger, of all people, once remarked that what bothered him most in debates over Vietnam policy was that others questioned not our judgment but our motives. This sense of national purity and righteousness discounts dissenting viewpoints and dismisses aspirations not grounded in the quest for freedom (defined in contemporary U.S. terms).[22] It also results in a consensual view of the national past, one in which alternative viewpoints appear only if they are ultimately vindicated, as they were in the case of abolition or women's suffrage. Students rarely learn about Loyalists during the American Revolution, draft rioters during the Civil War, socialists during industrialization, or pacifists in the Second World War. More recent examples of dissent, such as protest over the Vietnam War, cannot be so easily erased from public memory, but students have no way of making sense of these viewpoints; how could protestors have been opposed to our attempt to extend freedom to the Vietnamese, after all? Participation in a pluralist democracy requires engagement with diverse viewpoints—not just recognition that they exist but an active attempt to understand them—and the story of U.S. freedom and progress does little to prepare students for such engagement.

The national narrative of the United States, then, might well be seen as a scourge on participatory democracy. By suggesting that the desire for freedom is the enduring motivation that drives both individual experience and public policy, it misrepresents the cause of many historical events and renders students incapable of making reasonable and informed judgments. Its emphasis on social and material progress, meanwhile, rules out consideration of the negative consequences of historical change—whether for specific groups or for society at large—and this blind spot limits students' ability to consider questions of the common good. Moreover, the combination of noble purposes and successful results makes dissent and alternative perspectives appear nonsensical; yet if students don't understand why people disagreed in the past, they won't be able to take part in the deliberations necessary for participation in a pluralist democracy. With so many fundamental drawbacks, what possible good could come from the story of national freedom and progress? What use could there be for a tool with so many constraints?

There is only one: It is a hell of a story! Throughout U.S. history, the narrative of freedom has been so strong and so pervasive that those excluded from full participation in the nation's politics, culture, or economy have consistently adopted the rhetoric of freedom to push for the extension of liberty to ever-widening segments of the population. The concept of freedom has been so powerful because, as Foner notes, it "exposes the contradictions between what America claims to be and what it actually is." If the master narrative of freedom is widely shared among Americans—and indeed, its position as the essence of our national past is almost unassailable—then social changes can be demanded on the basis of the country's failure to live up to its stated ideals. Abolitionists, suffragists, labor activists, Civil Rights advocates—all have used the language of freedom to pursue rights and opportunities long denied them. In 1919, for example, the labor activist Mother Jones was speaking to a group of striking steel workers in Pennsylvania. When ordered to appear in court, the judge asked if she had a permit to speak on the streets. "Yes, sir," she said, "I had a permit." The judge asked who had issued it, and she replied, "Patrick Henry; Thomas Jefferson; John Adams!" In calling forth these icons of American freedom, Jones laid claim to the country's master narrative and used it—consciously and reflectively—to pursue a new vision of the common good. A tool this powerful, with a track record of improving the lives of the dispossessed, disfranchised, and marginalized, is a tool worth keeping. As Richard Rorty puts it, "It would be a big help to American efforts for social justice if each new generation were able to think of itself as participating in a movement which has lasted for more than a century and has served human liberty well."[23]

Rorty's observation points to the other component of the nation's master narrative, the belief in progress. Not only have we tried to extend freedom, we actually have done so: Our effort "has served human liberty well." This belief provides hope that the struggle for a better future will one day be realized, and this too has been a part of the historic struggles of many different groups in our nation's past. David Blight, for example, argues that by the early 20th century, despite the persistence of lynching, poverty, and segregation, African Americans could not "afford the despair born of short-term defeats" and instead embraced "a faith that at least since 1863 time, God, and the weight of history might be on their side."[24] Compare this to the lack of belief in progress among students in Northern Ireland. For them, history is the record of tragedy rather than progress, and it provides little hope for a better future: If Ireland becomes united, they believe, Protestant paramilitaries will wage a campaign of terror; if the North remains part of Britain, the IRA will continue its own campaign.

Maybe this lack of hope is part of the reason for the intractability of Northern Ireland's problems, part of a vicious cycle of failure and despair. If there is no hope of a better future, then there is little reason to take part in deliberation over the common good, for its outcome is doomed to failure. As Rorty observes, "You cannot urge national political renewal on the basis of descriptions of fact. You have to describe the country in terms of what you passionately hope it will become, as well as in terms of what you know it to be now. You have to be loyal to a dream country rather than to the one to which you wake up every morning." To take political action, we must believe that our efforts will be rewarded, that our dreams will be realized. In the United States, history provides the grounds for such belief: Based on our success in solving problems, we can be confident that no matter how serious our current difficulties, we will one day work them out. This is the story we tell ourselves, one we want to believe; in Rorty's words, Americans "still want to feel part of a nation which can take control of its destiny and make itself a better place."[25]

Perhaps no other historical tool has such serious affordances and constraints. Our national narrative misrepresents the causes of historical events, deflects attention from their negative consequences, and dismisses alternative perspectives. Yet it provides a powerful foundation for those who seek social justice, and it offers hope for the future. The task for history education—perhaps its most difficult challenge—is to resolve the tension between these advantages and disadvantages, to enable students to use this tool for activism and hope without being blinded by its drawbacks. This will not be easy, but two approaches may contribute to such efforts.

The first centers on helping students understand that the narrative of freedom and progress, like all narratives, is a human construction rather than a mirror of reality. That is, students should learn how the story of freedom has been constructed throughout the nation's past—how the concept has been defined, how history has been used to illustrate and justify such definitions, and how these have changed over time. In addition to learning that the concept has been used in extending political rights to women and minorities, for example, students might also learn that in the nation's early years, freedom was construed as propertied independence, and that the notion of economic autonomy was later resurrected by labor radicals, populists, and socialists; that during World War II, freedom was used as a rallying cry in the struggle against fascism and that U.S. businesses capitalized on the concept's popularity through a major advertising campaign devoted to the virtue of "free enterprise"; that during the Cold War, freedom become equated with anticommunism and the defense of the status quo and that any nation allied with the U.S. immediately became a part of the "free world," without regard to its domestic liberties.[26] In sum, students should focus less on the history of freedom and more on the history of the concept of freedom; instead of pretending that freedom is a concrete and stable aspiration that has endured throughout our history, students would learn to historicize it—examining how it has been used for a range of purposes in differing contexts as well as the legacy of these varied interpretations in contemporary discourses (such as in history texts). Far from undermining the concept's vitality, this approach should enable students to engage in discussions of freedom and its role in the nation's past with greater reflection and flexibility—considering a range of possible interpretations—rather than having the meaning of freedom imposed on them by others.[27]

A second way of reducing the constraints imposed by the nation's master narrative is to involve students in continual consideration of the advantages and disadvantages of historical changes and events. Among the most basic questions students should learn to ask about any topic in history are, "Who benefited from this, and how? Who suffered from it, and how?" Whether studying long-term processes such as the rise and fall of bound labor, the transition from rural agriculture to urban industrialization, and the creation and expansion of rails and highways, or more bounded events such as the ratification of the U.S. Constitution, the passage of Jim Crow laws, and the war in Iraq, students should always be challenged to move beyond simplified perspectives that see such topics as uniformly positive or negative. Any historical event significant enough to study in the first place invariably impacted diverse people—and diverse groups of people—in different ways, and conclusions about the overall desirability of any such event must take into account this range of experiences.

This is one way in which the academic discipline of history does provide, at least in part, a useful model for democratic education, because few professional historians would engage in the unreflective cheerleading so often found in schools and the wider society; any contemporary work of history is likely to consider the range of experiences of multiple groups and individuals in the past. Such considerations also have long been a concern of African Americans. In *The Souls of Black Folk*, for example, W. E. B. Du Bois emphasized the endless tension between "the full range of suffering and the persistence of possibility in American history," and a long line of scholars, activists, and everyday citizens have engaged in similar analysis.[28] So too should students: If they are to make reasoned judgments about the common good, they will have to consider a wider range of evidence and interpretation than narrow stories of progress can provide. Passionate conviction that the nation will solve its problems cannot be accompanied by a mindless belief that everything that happens is for the best; a better future depends on more complex and nuanced understandings.

CONCLUSIONS

Anyone who believes the narrative of freedom and progress will disappear from U.S. history in the near future is seriously deluded. For over 200 years, this story has been our dominant tool for understanding the national past, and students encounter it at school, in museums and historic sites, and through the media. Predictably, they learn to use this tool from an early age, and this appropriation leads them to conceptualize historic change in terms of social and material progress and to identify the quest for freedom as the dominant theme in the nation's past. In some cases, this results in misinterpreting historical events and misunderstanding patterns of change, as when younger children think that settlement occurred at a single, discrete point in time or when older ones suggest that U.S. warfare must involve an attempt to "help" other nations. Even when students recognize that not all events in the past (or present) can be interpreted in terms of this narrative structure, they have little recourse to alternative frameworks, and so they have no way of bringing meaning to divergent perspectives or experiences.

The story of freedom and progress is not universal, though: Other nations do not always conceptualize their pasts using this tool, nor do all groups within the United States. Like any narrative, this one is only a tool, a human creation that has developed over time in one particular context, and its use is neither fixed nor inevitable. The fact that students in other countries are less likely than those in the United States to rely on notions of progress in thinking about historical change suggests that educators may be able to help students avoid some of this story's constraints. The challenge, however, will be to overcome those constraints without abandoning the narrative altogether; the story of freedom and progress will not and should not disappear from our national culture. The concept of freedom has provided inspiration for marginalized groups throughout U.S. history, and it might inspire continuing commitment toward a more just and equitable future; the belief in progress, meanwhile, provides hope that these aspirations will come to fruition. Balancing the affordances and constraints of the national narrative, we believe, depends on helping students understand the constructed nature of that story—including the ways in which it has changed over time, as well as its differing interpretations and uses—and directing their attention to the benefits and drawbacks of all historical events and patterns. Parroting a glorious story of the national past will not prepare students to participate in a pluralist democracy, but deliberating over multiple interpretations of that past just might do so.

ENDNOTES

1. Ian McEwan, *Amsterdam* (London: Vintage, 1998), 67.
2. Eric Foner, *The Story of American Freedom* (New York: W. W. Norton, 1998), xiii–xiv; Ruth Miller Elson, *Guardians of Tradition: American Schoolbooks of the Nineteenth Century* (Lincoln: University of Nebraska Press, 1964), 76–77, 166–68, 184, 258–61; Joseph R. Moreau, "Schoolbook Nation: Imagining the American Community in United States History Texts for Grammar and Secondary Schools, 1865–1930" (Ph.D. diss., University of Michigan, Ann Arbor, 2002), 47–49; James Loewen, *Lies My Teacher Told Me: Everything Your American History Textbook Got Wrong* (New York: New Press, 1995), 249–263; Christopher Lasch, *The True and Only Heaven: Progress and Its Critics* (New York: W. W. Norton, 1991); Mike Wallace, "Progress Talk: Museums of Science, Technology and Industry," in *Mickey Mouse History and other Essays on American Memory* (Philadelphia: Temple University Press, 1996), 75–85; Michael Kammen, *Mystic Chords of Memory: The Transformation of Tradition in American Culture* (New York: Vintage Books, 1991), 702–03.
3. James V Wertsch, *Mind as Action* (New York: Oxford University Press, 1998), 86–98; James V. Wertsch and Kevin O'Connor, "Multivoicedness in Historical Representation: American College Students' Accounts of the Origins of the United States," *Journal of Narrative and Life History* 4, No. 4 (1994): 295–309.
4. Keith C. Barton and Linda S. Levstik, "'It Wasn't a Good Part of History': National Identity and Ambiguity in Students' Explanations of Historical Significance," *Teachers College Record* 99 (Spring 1998): 484–85.
5. Joshua Searle-White, *The Psychology of Nationalism* (New York: Palgrave, 2001), 91; Foner, *Story of American Freedom*, xiii; Barton and Levstik, "'It Wasn't a Good Part of History,'" 484–85.
6. Barton and Levstik, "'It Wasn't a Good Part of History,'" 485–87.
7. Barton and Levstik, "'It Wasn't a Good Part of History,'" 487–90, 495–99. David Blight argues that Southerners' conversion of their Civil War defeat into a victory over Reconstruction instilled into the national culture the idea that "even when Americans lose, they win"; David W. Blight, *Race and Reunion: The Civil War in American Memory* (Cambridge, Mass.: Harvard University Press, 2001), 266, 272–73, 283–84, 291.
8. Keith C. Barton, "Narrative Simplifications in Elementary Students' Historical Thinking," in *Advances in Research on Teaching*, Vol. 6, *Teaching and Learning History*, Ed. Jere Brophy (Greenwich, Conn.: JAI Press, 1996), 56–62.
9. Barton, "Narrative Simplifications," 63.
10. Barton, "Narrative Simplifications," 62.
11. Barton and Levstik, "'It Wasn't a Good Part of History,'" 490–503; Barton, "Narrative Simplifications," 58, 65–66.
12. Wertsch, *Mind as Action*, 108.
13. Keith C. Barton, "'Best not to Forget Them': Positionality and Students' Ideas About Historical Significance in Northern Ireland," paper presented at the annual meeting of the American Educational Research Association, 19–23 April, 1999.
14. Barton, "'Best Not to Forget Them'"; Terence Brown, "Awakening From the Nightmare: Irish History in Some Recent Literature," in *Irishness in a Changing*

Society, Ed. The Princess Grace Irish Library (Gerrards Cross, Buckinghamshire, England: Colin Smythe, 1988), 66; "History, Stephen said, is a nightmare from which I am trying to awake"; James Joyce, *Ulysses* (New York: Random House, 1934), 35.

15. Terrie Epstein, "Deconstructing Differences in African-American and European-American Adolescents' Perspectives on U.S. History," *Curriculum Inquiry* 28 (October 1998): 397–423.

16. Epstein, "Deconstructing Differences," 403–07.

17. Epstein, "Deconstructing Differences," 418–19; "Adolescents' Perspectives on Racial Diversity in U.S. History: Case Studies From an Urban Classroom," *American Educational Research Journal* 37 (Spring 2000): 196–98, 202–03.

18. Epstein, "Deconstructing Differences," 409–12, 422. David Blight argues that in the "progress of the race" discourse found among African Americans in the early 20th century, emancipation was regarded "as a new creation, as the zero point of black racial development"; thus, the structure of the narrative of progress was embraced by establishing the story's beginning at a point in time other than that used by European Americans. David W. Blight, *Race and Reunion: The Civil War in American Memory* (Cambridge, Mass.: Harvard University Press, 2001), 319, 332–33.

19. Roy Rosenzweig and David Thelen, *The Presence of the Past: Popular Uses of History in American Life* (New York: Columbia University Press, 1998), 10, 13, 138, 151–161, 165–74.

20. Foner, *Story of American Freedom,* 254.

21. Foner, *Story of American Freedom,* 77; Shils, "Tradition," *Comparative Studies in Society and History* 13 (April 1971): 140; Wallace, "Progress Talk," 75–85.

22. Noam Chomsky, "The Responsibility of Intellectuals," in *The Chomsky Reader,* Ed. James Peck (New York: Pantheon Books, 1987), 59–82; Kissinger quote from p. 64.

23. Richard Rorty, *Achieving Our Country: Leftist Thought in Twentieth Century America* (Cambridge, Mass.: Harvard University Press, 1998), 51; Foner, *Story of American Freedom,* xvi, 79–80, 99,113; Mary Jones, *The Autobiography of Mother Jones* (Chicago: Charles H. Kerr, 1972), 213. Ironically, Mother Jones was in jail at the time, and she was encouraging strikers to go home rather than try to free her or lynch the jailor.

24. Blight, *Race and Reunion,* 304.

25. Rorty, *Achieving Our Country,* 99, 101.

26. Foner, *Story of American Freedom,* 113, 230, 254.

27. This approach is similar to that recommended by Segall, who suggests that the study of history should focus less on the nature of past events in and of themselves and more on the way in which those events—and the larger practices of history and history education—are constructed and interpreted; Avner Segall, "Critical History: Implications for History/Social Studies Education," *Theory and Research in Social Education* 27 (Summer 1999): 358–74.

28. Du Bois quoted in Blight, *Race and Reunion,* 253.

Inquiry

What doth it profit, my brethren, though a man say he hath faith, and have not works? Can faith save him? If a brother or sister be naked, and destitute of daily food, and one of you say unto them, Depart in peace, be ye warmed and filled; notwithstanding ye give them not those things which are needful to the body; what doth it profit? Even so faith, if it hath not works, is dead, being alone.

—James 2: 14–17

The use of inquiry as a tool for learning history demands particular attention. The word *history* comes to us via Middle English, Old French, and Latin from the Greek *historein*—meaning "to inquire."[1] Today when we hear the word we might think first of the products of historical study (books, articles, lectures, documentaries) or the object of those studies (life on the home front during World War II, Galileo's battles with the Catholic Church, the rise of imperialism). However, we all recognize that what happened in history does not show up magically in books or television series. Someone had to engage in an inquiry, an investigation, to find out what went on in the past. We can easily identify the most common sources for these investigations—old letters, diaries, and public documents; photographs, tools, and household objects; archaeological remains of buildings, towns, and burial sites; and not least, the memories of people still alive. These are not the exclusive preserve of professional academic historians. Genealogists, antique collectors, and filmmakers all use the same sources, and all engage in forms of historical inquiry. Inquiry is a basic part of what history is about in our society.

The use of inquiry as a tool for learning history (and other topics in social studies) has a long tradition—or more accurately, recommendations for using inquiry have a long tradition. From what we can see, the practice is not common in schools (at least in the United States) and never has been.[2] Both academic research and our own classroom experiences suggest that teachers and students have enormous difficulty carrying out some of the key components of historical inquiry. In this chapter, we try to sort out why these difficulties arise and how they might be overcome; some may not be inherent in the tool itself but may result, instead, from a lack of balance among the different components of the process, the "subtools" of inquiry. It may be that like faith without works, inquiry without each of its components is "dead," particularly as a means of preparing students for democracy.

INQUIRY AS REFLECTIVE THOUGHT

Educators are not always clear about the meaning of inquiry. Sometimes the phrase amounts to little more than a buzzword, and its use involves no attempt to specify its application or differentiate it from other kinds of instruction. Other times it refers to any hands-on, motivating activity (building a replica of the U.S. Capitol, taking a field trip to a Civil War battlefield) or involvement with primary sources (examining arrowheads, looking at old photographs)—anything that seems to be the opposite of plowing through the textbook or lecturing. This usage may reflect educators' tendency to characterize teaching approaches as polar opposites: On the one side is everything interesting, active, modern, and progressive, and on the other are boring, passive, old-fashioned, and entrenched strategies. One of the problems with these dichotomies is that they fail to distinguish among approaches on either side of the divide. Many classroom activities can be described as "hands-on" or "student centered," for example, but they do not necessarily involve inquiry; reenacting the battle of the Alamo or making soap from rendered hog fat may be more interesting than relying on textbooks and lectures, but to refer to them as inquiry (as some would) makes the term too vague to be useful.

Other times, educators use the term to refer to a set of curricular and instructional perspectives popular from the late 1950s through the early 1970s—namely, those that emphasized the "structure of the disciplines" and were known as the New Social Studies. These approaches shared a concern with teaching students the concepts, generalizations, and methods of investigation of the academic disciplines, and their origins often are traced to Jerome Bruner's famous observation that "any subject can be taught effectively in some intellectually honest form to any child at any stage of development" (although concern with teaching disciplinary structures predates Bruner by many years).[3] In social studies, proponents of this view advocated that students learn about each of the disciplines that make up the field—history, economics, sociology, geography, and so on. Because they recognized students would not learn disciplinary concepts and generalizations through memorization, their proposals were closely bound to inquiry as an instructional method. Because the unique insights of each discipline were thought to derive, at least in part, from its particular methods of investigation, students were expected to engage in the same procedures as its practitioners. That is, they would develop an understanding of economic concepts through analyzing data the way economists do, they would learn about geography by working as geographers do, and so on. These unique disciplinary methods usually were taken to be variations on a single, underlying process of investigation, though, and so "inquiry" was often touted as a generic instructional methodology that applied across disciplines.[4]

We find much to admire in the educational recommendations of the 1960s, but we are cautious about associating inquiry too closely with this set of innovations. First, it should be clear by now that we are not concerned primarily with history as an academic discipline; we do not believe history's contribution to participatory democracy depends on teaching students how historians as a professional community go about their investigations. Second, history has always been an uneasy fit with the structure of the disciplines approach because it lacks an easily identifiable set of concepts or generalizations; as we discussed in chapter 4, history has usually been more concerned with interpreting unique events than developing generalizations. Finally, the highly prescriptive and positivistic version of inquiry found in many proposals from this period may unduly limit the potential for students to engage in the kind of "deep and sensitive" reasoning we advocate. Thus, although we are sympathetic to many of the aims and methods of the New Social Studies, we would not want to see the process of inquiry linked exclusively to presumed disciplinary structures nor reduced to a set of procedures so narrow and specific that they become ends in themselves rather than tools for pursuing historical understanding.

Our view of inquiry is very traditional, and maybe even old-fashioned. Like many social educators over the years, we base our definition on John Dewey's analysis of reflective thought. In *How We Think*, Dewey argued that although beliefs about what is true (or at least reasonably probable) can rest on any number of foundations—tradition, authority, imitation, and so on—important beliefs should be grounded in evidence: They should result from "conscious inquiry into the nature, conditions, and bearings of the belief." This was what Dewey meant by reflective thought, and his definition of the process has become justly famous: "Active, persistent, and careful consideration of any belief or supposed form of knowledge in the light of the grounds that support it, and the further conclusions to which it tends."[5]

For us, inquiry is equivalent to Dewey's view of reflective thought. He described the process as beginning with a problem—a "felt difficulty" or "some perplexity, confusion, or doubt." This was followed by an attempt to define the problem clearly and to suggest a possible solution, hypothesis, or theory to resolve it—or better still, according to Dewey, a variety of alternative solutions. The implications of each of these solutions or hypotheses would then be considered, and empirical observation or experimentation would take place to see which best matched the evidence. This process provided the basis for conclusions—beliefs grounded in evidence. Dewey's description of this process is readily identifiable with the scientific method—identification and definition of a problem, generation of a hypothesis, collection of data, and the use of that data to evaluate the initial hypothesis.[6]

Dewey's formulation of reflective thinking matches the natural or behavioral sciences somewhat more closely than it does history, and many advocates of the New Social Studies assimilated Dewey's ideas to the deductive model of scientific investigation. However, the key components of inquiry are the same in any field. In history, for example, interest in the past begins with some "perplexity," something a person wants to know about, whether that person is an academic studying crowd behavior in Revolutionary France, a filmmaker interested in the development of baseball, or a third cousin trying to find out a distant ancestor's maiden name. To answer such questions, each of these historians must find evidence—primary and secondary sources like court records, newspaper articles, census schedules, or the work of previous researchers. Usually they employ the evidence they find as the basis for conclusions, whether presented in the form of an academic article, a popular film, or an ancestor chart. As different as these outcomes are, each can be publicly evaluated, at least in part, on its adherence to the process of inquiry. Failure to find relevant evidence or to base conclusions on the evidence that has been found can lead to rejection by colleagues, critics, or even relatives. Although historical inquiries differ from scientific ones, they nonetheless retain the critical components of reflective thought—asking questions, gathering and evaluating relevant evidence, and reaching conclusions based on that evidence. That, for us, is what historical inquiry is all about.

AFFORDANCES OF INQUIRY AS A TOOL

The process of inquiry can contribute to a humanistic study of history—and to participatory democracy—in at least three important ways. The first seems somewhat obvious, but it bears stating explicitly: People learn through inquiry. The process of gathering evidence to reach conclusions about important questions matches contemporary theories of human learning, in which people are seen as active constructors of meaning.[7] Given the match between inquiry as an instructional process and constructivism as a theoretical model, we can expect that students will know more if they have engaged in inquiry than if they have filled in worksheets in pursuit of grades, stickers, or teachers' praise. Having said that, though, we must point out that there are no comprehensive empirical investigations of the superiority of inquiry as a form of learning in history; that is, there are no large-scale experiments in which students in some classroom are rewarded for correctly mastering information related to the Civil War, while those in other rooms take part in inquiry-based investigations into the same subject. Indeed, such experiments probably are not possible, because what counts as knowledge in behaviorist and constructivist classrooms differs—retention of factual information in one case, judgment and conceptual understanding in the other. Because the two perspectives start with such different assumptions about the nature of knowledge, there is no common ground from which to judge the approach that leads to better understanding on the part of students. Moreover, there are a number of different perspectives on what it means to "construct knowledge," so even those educators who consider themselves constructivists may advocate a wide range of instructional practices. When we say that people learn through inquiry, then, we mean that inquiry is an approach consistent with current theory and research on human learning. When understanding is needed, inquiry appears to be one of the best ways to get there.

Such understanding is essential to democracy. In a society in which citizens govern themselves, they must have the understanding necessary to make decisions in line with their values and beliefs—they need to understand how the economy works, why people live the way they do, and how humans and the environment affect each other. They also have to understand history: how the world got to be the way it is, past consequences of group and individual actions, and alternatives to current arrangements. That kind of learning is most closely associated with the analytic stance toward history, but each of the other stances also depends on understanding: Engaging in moral response requires that people be familiar with historic triumphs and tragedies, identifying with a nation depends on knowing something about its past, and exhibition takes accurate and detailed knowledge as its very reason for being. One of the chief advantages of historical inquiry, then, is that it results in the learning critical to democratic life.

Moreover, by engaging students in the process of knowledge construction, inquiry has the potential to spread historical knowledge more equitably. As we have discussed, children begin to learn about history from a very young age, but what they learn may be heavily influenced by the settings in which they grow up—African American students, for example, do not always learn the same information and perspectives as those from European backgrounds. We still need to know much more about how ethnicity, class, gender, and geographic region influence students' understanding of history, but it seems likely that students develop both a core of shared knowledge (particularly related to national history) and a more particular body of information grounded in their unique backgrounds. Also, as we discussed in the last chapter, Terrie Epstein's research has shown that these initial perspectives may influence children's engagement with the content of the curriculum: African American and White students in the same classrooms do not always come away from their history lessons with the same ideas.[8]

Given that some students begin with prior knowledge more closely matching the historical perspectives sanctioned at school, it seems likely that some will be better positioned to understand and benefit from a curriculum delivered through textbooks, lectures, or other transmission-oriented methods. That is, those students whose prior knowledge already reflects the dominant historical narratives of school will be better able to comprehend and retain the new information they encounter at school, even if the instruction is poorly delivered. Meanwhile, those students whose prior knowledge conflicts with school history (or which is simply uncon-nected to it) will have more difficulty mastering a curriculum that does not meet them halfway. As a result, initial differences among students will in-crease the longer they are in school, with one group of students unlikely to encounter challenges that expand their perspectives, while other groups become increasingly alienated from the curriculum and are provided with little validation of their own ideas.

This widening gap is hardly consistent with the needs of a pluralist de-mocracy, and if inquiry can live up to its potential as a means of engaging students in the construction of knowledge, the impact of these initial dif-ferences may be lessened. By allowing students to pursue their own inves-tigations and reach their own conclusions, inquiry should enable those whose experiences have not traditionally been represented in the official curriculum to deepen and expand their historical understanding rather than simply to remain distanced from school history. Meanwhile, because inquiry can engage students with a variety of sources of evidence, those whose understandings have traditionally been privileged may be more likely to encounter conflicting perspectives that force them to question their beliefs. Again, at this point there is little empirical evidence that this is so; we can only suggest that one potential advantage of inquiry is that through its use, all students will be positioned to develop a more complete and nuanced understanding of history, and that this understanding may be more equitably distributed.

However, in addition to resulting in a useful product—more complete his-torical understanding—inquiry also engages students in a process critical to democratic pluralism: that of reaching conclusions based on evidence. Like Dewey, we recognize that people do not always base their conclusions on em-pirical data. Oftentimes people hold positions on important issues of public policy because of the influence of people in authority, or of their peers, or of the media—or just because they have always thought a certain way and are not about to let facts get in the way of long-held beliefs. Some people have no interest in moving beyond these patterns; they consider appeals to authority or tradition just as legitimate, if not more so, than appeals to reason. Yet these do not serve us well in a democracy, where we expect people to have reasons—good reasons—for the positions they advocate. Issues such as pro-viding access to quality health care, reducing crime, ending substance abuse, or educating our children are too important to leave to the forces of tradition, authority, or prejudice. They demand inquiry—"active, persistent, and care-ful consideration of any belief or supposed form of knowledge in the light of the grounds that support it, and the further conclusions to which it tends." Engaging students in inquiry should provide them with the skills necessary for their lives as active citizens—as well as, we hope, the disposition to use those skills in considering important issues.

This brings us to the third principal advantage of inquiry: It gives us some-thing to talk about. As we discussed earlier, the kind of pluralist democracy we envision depends on deliberation among equals in pursuit of shared knowledge and understanding. Without inquiry, this kind of communication is unlikely to take place, because the sources of knowledge and belief are either hidden or unquestioned. If attempts at discussion simply pit the knowledge some people have gained from their authorities and tradition against the knowledge others have gained from their authorities and tradition, the encounter is unlikely to result in meaningful communication or shared knowledge—more likely, the result will be frustration and hostility. Often the knowledge of the more powerful group will prevail, because those with power can use their resources and privilege to impose their positions on the less powerful (or at least coerce their acquiescence). However, inquiry makes the process of knowledge construction more transparent: By laying out questions, evidence, and conclusions (and the links among them) in clear view, inquiry allows ideas to be challenged without attacking anyone's identity or belief system. Also, although the powerful will always have an advantage in such deliberations, the process of inquiry will at least make these discussions somewhat more equitable, by requiring all participants to link conclusions to evidence and by providing them with the information necessary to do so. Not only does inquiry provide the knowledge and skills needed for discussions in a pluralist democracy, then, it creates the very conditions that allow such discussions to occur in the first place.

STUDENTS ENGAGING IN INQUIRY: PROBLEMS AND POSSIBILITIES

In our previous work, we have described teachers and students engaged in historical inquiry, and we have recommended inquiry as the basis for history education in the early grades and beyond.[9] However, many people question the effectiveness of such projects, and they doubt the ability of students—particularly in elementary school—to engage in meaningful inquiry; they suspect that students as young as 10 or 12 years old are incapable of taking part in activities as sophisticated as comparing sources or evaluating evidence for reliability. As a result, schools provide few opportunities to engage in such tasks. Asking fifth graders, or even eighth graders, to examine primary source documents from hundreds of years ago, with an eye toward evaluating how the perspective of their authors may have influenced their representation of events, and to compare their relative trustworthiness—well, this would seem to be a recipe for disaster. It's too complicated, students won't be able to do it, they'll get frustrated, and they won't learn anything. The experience of many teachers confirms that this is indeed a complicated undertaking.

Two recent studies illustrate the difficulty of implementing inquiry projects. Both examined classrooms in which students were taking part in WebQuests, structured inquiry projects involving Internet resources. Andrew Milson studied sixth graders who were creating "Time Travelers

Guidebooks" on Ancient Egypt; these included information on geography, culture, arts, science, and so on. George Lipscomb, meanwhile, worked with eighth graders who were assigned roles that corresponded with figures from the Civil War era (Confederate and Union Soldiers, Abolitionists, Northern and Southern women) and asked to write journal entries assuming their assigned identities. WebQuests like these have the potential to facilitate classroom inquiry because they provide technology-based guidance for each stage of the process—including description of the task to be accomplished, links to Web sites with relevant sources, and information on how to collect and analyze data from these sources. These projects thus promise to help teachers—and students—overcome some of the more difficult and time-consuming elements of inquiry, such as locating a variety of resources on a given topic.[10]

Yet in both of these classrooms, the results of students' engagement with inquiry were somewhat disappointing. In the sixth-grade classroom, strategies for gathering and organizing information were characterized by what Milson refers to as a quest for the "path of least resistance." That is, students often avoided reading the resources they located, and instead asked others to provide them with information to directly answer the questions they were investigating. They even ignored the links that had been provided and preferred instead to type queries into a search engine—a strategy they thought (at least initially) would lead them more directly to the answers. Lipscomb is even more skeptical about students' learning. He found that few of them developed a sophisticated recognition of the perspectives of people at the time of the Civil War; most simply wrote down factual information about dates and battles, copied information from Internet sources, or wrote journal entries as though they were passing notes like contemporary adolescents—rather than writing from the perspective of people at the time. Many students used a strategy similar to those in the classroom Milson studied: Rather than evaluating information from multiple sources, they went directly to search engines to find sites they thought would give them all the information to complete their task. Given these difficulties, it may seem simpler, more straightforward, and more in keeping with their abilities just to teach students what we already know about the past—what qualified historians have concluded from their own research.[11]

Neither Milson nor Lipscomb is quite as pessimistic about the prospects for inquiry as that. Both suggest ways of modifying classroom procedures so that students become more thoroughly engaged with the WebQuest process, and Milson describes how the teacher in his study made adjustments that improved students' ability to locate relevant information. Other studies have also shown that with careful teacher scaffolding and ongoing attention to the use of sources, students demonstrate a surprisingly advanced understanding of abstract concepts like perspective and reliability. Bruce VanSledright, for example, spent 4 months teaching history to fifth graders, so that he could find out what happened when they analyzed and evaluated multiple sources. During his semester in the classroom, VanSledright taught students how to be "historical detectives" while studying topics such as the Jamestown settlement, colonial development in North America, and the American Revolution. Within each of these units, students worked with multiple documents (both primary and secondary) and learned how to corroborate details across sources, judge their validity and reliability, and identify subtext and authors' intentions. In the unit on the Revolution, for example, VanSledright emphasized that events leading to the conflict had to be analyzed from perspectives rooted in opposing positions. To give students experience with this, he designed an activity in which groups of students were assigned to four imaginary newspapers, each with its own point of view (patriot, loyalist, etc.). Students used a packet of documents to create newspaper accounts and supporting illustrations consistent with the political perspective of their assigned group.[12]

These activities seemed successful within the classroom context—students were actively engaged in taking on different perspectives and debating with each other—but did their work with evidence have any impact on their understanding of the creation of historical knowledge? To test this, VanSledright asked a group of eight students, before and after their work as historical detectives, to read several written documents about a historical event and to examine two pictures representing each. The first set of sources dealt with the Boston Massacre, and students were asked to determine who did the shooting and why. The second set involved the Battle at Lexington Green, and students were to find out who fired the first shot. In both cases, documents were contradictory or inconclusive, and so it was impossible to reach a single, authoritative answer to either of these historical "riddles." As students reviewed these sources, VanSledright asked them to think aloud about their responses, and afterward he asked what differences they found in the sources, which they thought were most accurate, and how the authors (or artists) might have obtained their information.[13]

In the first task, before they had received any instruction in working with documents, students spent most of their time simply trying to understand what each source had to say about the event; they made almost no attempts to compare the sources or to evaluate which might be the most reliable. When specifically asked why the sources might be different, though, students gave sensible, if very basic, answers. They thought differences among the sources might be the result of different "points of view" (a concept they had learned about in language arts), but they had trouble elaborating what that might mean. They also thought the most accurate documents would be those whose authors were present at the events, but they made no effort to determine which those might be. These students seemed to have some ideas that might serve as a foundation for historical inquiry, then, but it was not clear if they could engage in more detailed and extensive evaluation of sources.[14]

Students' participation in the second task, after they had spent a semester learning how to be historical detectives, suggested that they were capable of precisely that. Compared to their responses in the first task, students spent much more time trying to identify the evidence they worked with (often distinguishing them on the basis of whether they were primary or secondary sources), corroborating details from one source to another, and judging their validity, reliability, and perspective. Their earlier, generic descriptions of the importance of point of view gave way to more specific judgments about particular pieces of testimony—for example, they noted that a British ensign might distort the truth to avoid being blamed for starting the conflict, that a colonial newspaper would be more likely to blame the British, and that the accuracy of an account written years after the event might suffer from the deficiencies of memory. Throughout the task, students continually compared documents to each other to reach an overall assessment of what happened rather than treating each source in isolation as they had done earlier in the year. Not all students were equally adept at these skills. However, based on students' participation in classroom activities and these interviews tasks, VanSledright concluded that children as young as fifth grade were intellectually capable of comparing and evaluating evidence and that they could be enthusiastic about doing so.[15]

VanSledright's findings are consistent with our own research. In our classroom study of fourth and fifth graders, students worked with a variety of historical sources; they collected information from relatives to create their own personal histories; they used physical artifacts, books, and other sources to create displays for a "history museum"; and they examined written documents as part of their study of the Colonial Era and the American Revolution. As in VanSledright's class, these students had little previous experience working with historical evidence at school, but they began with valid, common-sense ideas about how sources might be biased or incomplete. Near the beginning of the year, for example, as students were working on their personal histories, they were asked what they would do if they received conflicting information from different sources, such as if relatives disagreed in their memories of their children's first word. Several pointed out that some sources would be more reliable, for a variety of reasons: Their mothers probably would have been present to hear their first word, while their fathers were at work; some people get confused about what happened a long time ago or mix up siblings; and a "baby book" would be more reliable than memory because it was written down at the time. Some students also recognized that personal bias might affect the information they received—mothers might report that the first word was *mama*, whereas fathers would say it was *dada*. These 10- and 11-year-olds already were familiar with many of the factors critical to evaluating historical evidence—whether a person had firsthand knowledge of an event, their reliability in other settings, their vested interests, and how soon after an event their testimony took place.[16]

Students in these classrooms also had the chance to work with more traditional sources of historical evidence, including multiple accounts of the Battle at Lexington Green similar to those used in VanSledright's research. Students spent three class periods working in small groups to evaluate the reliability of 12 different accounts of the battle, with the ultimate goal of deciding, "Who fired the first shot?" Their work with these sources was impressive. Even before they saw the accounts, when the teacher first introduced the activity, they immediately wanted to know, "Were they written by colonists?" As they discussed each source, they showed a clear understanding of how a variety of factors might influence descriptions of the battle: An "onlooker" would be less biased than soldiers on either side, a diary entry would be more believable because it wasn't intended for the public, officers might change their accounts to avoid blame, an article in a London newspaper months later was removed in time and place, and a memoir written 50 years later would depend on unreliable memories. Like the students in VanSledright's study, these elementary children had no difficulty engaging in sophisticated evaluations of historical sources. They also enjoyed it: They remarked how quickly time flew during these lessons and how interesting it was to read the diaries of people involved in important historical events.[17]

However, there was one remarkable and unexpected problem. After 3 days of this activity, the teacher pulled students together to discuss their conclusions about who fired the first shot at Lexington Green. Each student had an opinion, and all were eager to share. Yet none of their opinions had any relationship to the evidence they had just spent 3 days evaluating. Students had not used the evidence to reach conclusions; they were just making up what they thought "must" have happened. After all, they pointed out, all the sources were biased in one way or another, so they couldn't rely on them. The teacher was shocked. The purpose of the exercise was to help students understand how historians go about their work, but when she asked whether they thought historians just write what they think must have happened, students agreed that they did. Despite their impressive ability to detect bias in sources, they missed the larger lesson related to the foundation of historical inquiry—that accounts must be based on evidence, however limited and incomplete.[18]

Other studies have noted the same problem—that students can analyze and evaluate sources without understanding the connection between evidence and historical accounts. In a study one of us conducted together with Dehea Smith, third graders diligently collected evidence, over the course of several weeks, to answer a series of questions they had developed about the history of their community. As soon as they began creating presentations on the topic, though, their evidence went out the window, and they began preparing accounts that amounted to little more than wholesale fiction. Although their teacher ultimately was successful in helping them establish the link between their research and their conclusions, this was no easy task. Similarly, VanSledright reports that students in his study often reached conclusions about antagonisms between colonists and British troops based not on the evidence they had reviewed but on their own allegiance to the colonial cause. Sometimes, their only justification for a particular judgment was, "This is what I think." Other times, they invented stories that were completely unconnected to the evidence—such as when one student maintained that a British sympathizer was hiding out at Lexington Green and secretly fired a shot in hopes of starting a war. Their confusion about how incomplete accounts can serve as a basis for historical knowledge is perhaps best summed up by the lament of a girl who explained her frustration that all evidence is uncertain: "I don't see how historians can do this," she said.[19]

Educators in Britain, where work with historical sources has been a prominent feature of the curriculum for two decades and more, have also recognized students' difficulty in making the connection between evidence and conclusions. Unlike the United States, Britain has a required national curriculum in history, and this curriculum mandates that teachers focus on the use of evidence in the creation of historical accounts. Moreover, students are examined on these topics rather than on their memorization of the details of historical narratives. As a result, classroom instruction frequently engages students in the kinds of activities described in the study by VanSledright and in our own previous work. Students throughout Britain are far more likely than those in the United States to be involved in analyzing and interpreting evidence. This naturally has led teachers and researchers there to look more closely at what happens when students undertake such work.

One of the most extensive British studies of children's understanding of historical concepts has been the "Project Chata" research carried out by Peter Lee, Rosalyn Ashby, and Alaric Dickinson. This study used multiple methods (both oral interviews and paper-and-pencil tasks) and involved hundreds of students from ages 7 to 14. In one portion of the research, students were given pairs of stories with differing accounts of the Roman occupation of Britain and asked to explain why they differed. Most students, except the very youngest, recognized that differences in the availability of evidence and its interpretation can lead to differing accounts, but for some, this meant that when historians do not know something with certainty, they simply make up what is missing. These students talked about interpretations as though they were synonymous with personal opinions—and because everyone is entitled to his or her own opinion, they thought all were equally valid. For these students, as Ashby and Lee put it, "Everything is up for grabs, because there is no way of deciding between competing opinions."[20] This is precisely the idea that has come up in our own work: Children conclude that historical sources are always biased and incomplete, so there is no way of deciding what happened—one idea is as good as another.

There are still many unanswered questions about students' understanding of the use of evidence to create historical accounts. For example, how do their ideas develop over time? How does classroom instruction influence those ideas? To what extent are their perspectives on evidence shaped by factors outside school? Do children always treat evidence in the same way, or are they influenced by the subject matter under consideration? Some of these questions have already been the subject of research, and some of the investigations we have covered here focused on a wider range of issues than those emphasized in our descriptions. Our intent, though, has been to call attention to two consistent—and seemingly contradictory—findings of research into students' participation in inquiry: (a) They have an impressive ability, from a young age, to consider key characteristics of the status of historical knowledge, including the incompleteness of historical evidence and the ways historical accounts and evidence can be influenced by bias or differing perspectives; and (b) they have a simplistic understanding of how historical accounts are created under circumstances of biased or incomplete evidence, an understanding that sometimes leads them to conclude that history can simply be made up or that one "opinion" is as good as another.

Where does this leave us? Does the research simply suggest that an understanding of the limitations of evidence develops in children before an understanding of how to use that evidence? Or that the latter is a more difficult idea, and hence fewer students grasp it? Perhaps that is so. However, we would like to suggest an alternative explanation, grounded in the concept of inquiry as a tool, that may better explain the findings from this research.

THE TOOL OF INQUIRY AND ITS COMPONENT PARTS

Students' difficulty understanding the connection between evidence and accounts may arise from the their exposure to only one portion of the tool of inquiry. When they are given sources to evaluate but are not engaged in the other components of inquiry—asking meaningful questions or reaching their own conclusions—we can hardly be surprised that their familiarity with the process is inadequate. It is as though we asked students to write an essay with a pencil but provided them with only the eraser! Just as a pencil achieves its full usefulness as a tool only when all its subparts (wood, lead, eraser) are present, inquiry may reach its full potential only when students engage in the entire process—using evidence to reach conclusions about meaningful questions.

Recall that Dewey's first step in reflective thinking was a "felt difficulty," "some perplexity, confusion, or doubt." He argued that "demand for the solution of a perplexity is the steadying and guiding factor in the entire process of reflection" and noted that trying to get anyone to engage in reflective thinking without the presence of some difficulty was as futile as telling them to lift themselves up by their own bootstraps.[21] This perplexity, this felt difficulty, is often missing in history classrooms both in the United States and elsewhere. The question of who fired the first shot at Lexington Green, for example, has little significance either in contemporary culture or in the discipline of history. It is not a question that historians debate, or one that comes up in political discussion, or in the media, or in families and communities. Teachers may be able to get students interested in such a question, but its lack of enduring significance means that the answer does not matter—one opinion really is as good as another, because nothing rests on the outcome. When students make up a story of what they think must have happened at Lexington Green, they may not be using the tool of inquiry very effectively, but neither have they been asked to use that tool—they have simply been engaged in an artificial exercise that simulates, in a decontextualized way, one of the components of inquiry.

This focus on just one component of inquiry—analysis of primary sources—has plagued not only educational research but also high-stakes testing and classroom practice. Both the New York Regents exams and Advanced Placement exams, for example, include "document-based questions" (DBQs) in history. The College Entrance Examination Board describes such items as emphasizing the "ability to analyze and synthesize historical data and assess verbal, quantitative, or pictorial materials as historical evidence." The College Board further explains

> The documents vary in length and are chosen to illustrate the interactions and complexities of the historical process. They may include charts, graphs, cartoons, and pictures, as well as written materials. The DBQ typically requires students to relate the documents to a historical period or theme and, thus, to focus on major periods and issues. For this reason, outside knowledge—information gained from materials other than the documents—is very important and must be incorporated into your essay if the highest scores are to be earned.

In 1999, the document-based question in U.S. history was, "To what extent had the colonists developed a sense of their identity and unity as Americans by the eve of the Revolution?," and sources of evidence included private correspondence, a speech in the British parliament, a declaration by the Continental Congress, published works from the 18th century, a list of relief donations, and the famous "Join, or die" illustration.[22]

Because tests like these carry so much weight, a minor industry has grown up to supply teachers with "document-based activities" to prepare students for exams. If students are to be given primary sources and asked questions about them on high-stakes tests, then of course they need experience with such activities as part of their ongoing instruction. State departments of education, nonprofit organizations, and private publishing companies all have developed teaching ideas and concrete materials for bringing primary source documents into the classroom. One advertisement for a packet of materials on World War II promises

> History comes alive when students analyze primary source documents! After evaluating and interpreting historical documents that they download from the Internet, students will discuss and debate issues and draw their own conclusions about history. Teacher's page contains objectives, discussion questions, and extension activities. Reproducible student pages include Web addresses and questions to be answered about the source.[23]

This is surely the form of inquiry without its substance, a tool without all its parts, faith without works. Where is the felt difficulty, the perplexity, confusion, or doubt in this kind of activity? When the questions arise from "reproducible student pages" rather than students' own concerns about the past, then the activity does not involve inquiry in any meaningful sense—it simply involves the analysis of documents. This advertisement illustrates the assumption at the heart of all such activities—that authorities rather than students are responsible for developing questions and identifying resources, and that the student's task is to generate a product (usually an essay) based on the assignments given them. Many such exercises fail to engage students even in the most minimal evaluation of the usefulness of sources they are examining, for their purpose is not to develop any kind of reasoned judgment, but to help students explain how given primary sources illustrate facts and concepts they have learned elsewhere.

Using primary sources in this way may be a worthwhile pedagogical practice, and it may be better than using a textbook, although we are not entirely convinced of either. However, there is certainly no reason to think that these document-based questions and activities contribute to participatory democracy in the way inquiry could. As we described earlier, these advantages include better comprehension of historical content, a more equitable distribution of knowledge, and familiarity with the process of using evidence to reach conclusions about significant social questions. We know of no theoretical argument (nor empirical evidence) that the analysis of preselected documents to answer predetermined questions leads to similar affordances. Questions such as "To what extent had the colonists developed a sense of their identity and unity as Americans by the eve of the Revolution?" could indeed take on some importance to students under the guidance of thoughtful teachers, and many students already have questions about World War II. However, when questions like these arise from reproducible student pages or other sources unrelated to students' concerns, they are not likely to inspire students to take part in careful evaluation of evidence or thoughtful development of conclusions. If the questions don't matter to students, why should they take anything other than the path of least resistance?

Yet some historical questions really do matter, and students want to investigate those. To take one obvious example: Why was the United States fighting in Vietnam, and why were some people opposed to it? Now that's a historical question worth asking. The specter of Vietnam still haunts foreign policy and public debate in the United States, as the discourse surrounding every international crisis reminds us. Many of us have very direct, personal involvement with the era—as veterans or as protestors, or as the relatives of such participants, and popular culture presents simplistic representations of the conflict through movies such as *Forrest Gump*. As a result, students are aware of the importance of Vietnam, they know there is some controversy over the war, and they want to know more about it.[24] If students were to use inquiry as a tool to learn more about this critical event in history, they might be more inclined to base their conclusions on evidence, precisely because they are in a state of perplexity, confusion, or doubt. They know there is something they do not understand, and they want to understand it. Dismissing the sources or making up stories (as they do so blithely with less relevant topics) would not serve their own purposes. Nor is Vietnam the only historical topic with contemporary significance; issues of race, gender, class, and religion provide enough enduring controversy to motivate a lifetime of inquiry.

Peter Seixas addresses this issue in his analysis of the difficulties facing teachers who hope to engage students in a community of inquiry in the classroom. On one hand, exposing students to the conclusions of professional historians (and expecting them to remember those conclusions) misrepresents the nature of historical knowledge by transforming a "provisional, dynamic, ongoing conversation to a static set of verities." Expecting students to engage in the same investigations as historians, on the other hand, is just as problematic, because students are not part of historians' professional communities—they do not know enough about historical content or the standards of research to produce knowledge with the same status as that of historians. Seixas suggests that this dilemma can be resolved in part by conceptualizing history "around students' questioning of their own culture and experience, an investigation of the past that questions its traces and theorizes its legacy and import for the present." In other words, students would be engaging in the process of historical inquiry, but they would be doing so with regard to the questions they find significant, rather than those that arise in a community of which they are not a part—the academic discipline of history. Seixas recommends that instruction begin with historical issues that will help students make sense of their own lives and their situation in the world, and that students be involved in the process of identifying events of historical significance.[25]

This is not to suggest, though, that historical inquiry be directed only toward questions students already have when they enter the classroom. In our experience, such questions may be very limited in both form and content. The critical task for the teacher is to help students develop questions that lead them toward inquiries that are meaningful and significant. To explore the development of slavery in North America, for example, David Gerwin and Jack Zevin describe how students can examine indenture certificates, property lists, colonial laws, advertisements for slave auctions, and other primary and secondary sources. From these, questions arise about the nature of slavery—What created the need for bound labor? Why were there different statuses for imported workers, such as slavery and indentured servitude? Who fell into each category, and why? Did racism cause slavery, or was it the outcome of the slave system? Students are likely to begin with preconceived ideas (equating Africans with slavery and Europeans with freedom, for example), but when teachers choose sources carefully and use them thoughtfully in the classroom, they can complicate students' ideas, develop their curiosity, and motivate them to engage in further study of the questions that interest them. Now that's inquiry.[26]

These examples should make it clear that inquiry does not require teachers to abdicate their responsibility for selecting materials or guiding students' investigations. Teachers must use their professional judgment to develop activities that inspire students' interest and motivate them to engage in inquiry, and their decisions will necessarily impose structure and limitations on students' work. This is as it should be, because history teachers have (we hope) a more developed and comprehensive understanding of history than their students. However, the teacher's selection of resources and activities is the beginning, not the end, of historical inquiry. Asking students to analyze selected documents on the Second World War or on American identity during the Colonial Era is a perfectly appropriate way of stimulating students' own questions, which they can then investigate through a variety of means. However, giving students materials, tasks, and questions ahead of time is a sterile undertaking, one likely to lead to a "technical formalism in which students apply skills to pseudoproblems," as William Stanley and James Whitson put it. Surely students will be better prepared for participatory democracy if they investigate problems they consider important than if they waste their time on pseudoproblems.[27]

CONCLUSIONS

There seems to be widespread agreement among history educators of all sorts—social studies professors, curriculum developers, educational psychologists, and academic historians—that analyzing primary sources is a good thing. There is less consensus as to why this should be so. In many cases, the practice of analyzing primary sources has become reified, as though it were an end in itself, or as though meaning could inhere in historical sources themselves rather than in the uses to which they are put. This has led to the unfortunate practice of asking students to evaluate historical sources apart from any guiding questions, or in connection with questions they have not themselves developed and that they may not consider important.[28] However, primary sources are merely a means to an end, and that end is inquiry—a process that necessarily involves a felt difficulty or some perplexity, confusion, or doubt.

If the goal of history education is to prepare students for a pluralist democracy, then inquiry has important advantages: It provides practice in the process of reaching judgments based on evidence, it makes the process of knowledge construction clear, and it may lead to deeper comprehension than transmission-oriented instructional strategies. Perhaps most important, the use of inquiry may contribute to greater equity in students' access to historical knowledge: Those whose ideas diverge from sanctioned versions of the past may be better able, through the use of inquiry, to integrate incongruous or even contradictory perspectives, whereas those whose prior knowledge better matches official versions may encounter information that complicates their previously unchallenged ideas. Research shows that even elementary students can take part in this complicated process, but they seem better able to evaluate the drawbacks of primary sources than to use such evidence to reach conclusions. Only if we recognize the role of sources within the broader process of inquiry are students likely to move beyond these limitations.

Primary sources can play two important roles in inquiry-oriented history education. First, they can inspire perplexity. Primary sources have an unparalleled ability to confront us with past reality: They are materials that come to us from the past and that cry out for interpretation and understanding; it is difficult to come into contact with even the simplest primary source without having questions, and these invariably are connected to our prior ideas about how the world works. As Tom Holt suggests, students' questions "arise in the space between the document itself and the reader's experience, what he or she *brings* to the material."[29] Such questions inspire further investigation, and this is the second role for primary sources—to provide evidence that answers our questions about the past. When we want to know what went on in history, primary sources are one way—although by no means the only one—of finding out. In both cases, the role of questions is critical, and without questions, the tool of inquiry is incomplete. Like faith without works, analyzing primary sources without questions is dead, being alone.

ENDNOTES

1. *The American Heritage Dictionary of the English Language*, 3rd ed. (1992), s. v. "history."
2. Stephen J. Thornton, "Legitimacy in the Social Studies Curriculum," in *One Hundredth Yearbook of the National Society for the Study of Education*, Part I: *Education Across a Century: The Centennial Volume*, Ed. Lyn Corno (Chicago, Ill.: University of Chicago Press, 2001), 192–94.
3. Jerome Bruner, *The Process of Education* (Cambridge, Mass.: Harvard University Press), 33. As early as 1933, Mary Kelty referred to the discipline-centered approach as one of the four dominant trends in social studies. Her description was nearly identical to that for which Bruner would later become famous: In this perspective, she wrote, each discipline "has a significant contribution to make in its

generalizations and understandings and in its ways of looking at life problems."
Mary G. Kelty, "The 'New' Content of the Social Studies in the Elementary
School," *Educational Method* 12 (May 1933): 465.

4. Two of the most comprehensive treatments of this approach are Byron G.
Massialas and C. Benjamin Cox, *Inquiry in Social Studies* (New York: McGraw-Hill,
1966) and Edwin Fenton, *The New Social Studies* (New York: Holt, Rinehart &
Winston, 1967). For a review of the use of recommendations for the use of inquiry
in history, see Thornton, "Legitimacy in the Social Studies Curriculum," 192–94.

5. John Dewey, *How We Think* (New York: D. C. Heath, 1910), 5–6.

6. Dewey, *How We Think*, 12, 72.

7. For example, John D. Bransford, Ann L. Brown, and Rodney R. Cocking, Eds., *How
People Learn: Brain, Mind, Experience, and School* (Washington, D.C.: National Acad-
emy Press, 2000); David J. Wood, *How Children Think and Learn: The Social Contexts of
Cognitive Development*, 2nd ed. (New York: Blackwell, 1998); John T. Bruer, *Schools for
Thought: A Science of Learning in the Classroom* (Cambridge, Mass.: MIT Press, 1994).

8. Terrie Epstein, "Adolescents' Perspectives on Racial Diversity in U.S. History:
Case Studies from an Urban Classroom," *American Educational Research Journal* 37
(Spring 2000): 185–214.

9. Linda S. Levstik and Keith C. Barton, *Doing History: Investigating With Children in
Elementary and Middle Schools*, 2nd ed. (Mahwah, N.J.: Lawrence Erlbaum Associates, Inc., 2001).

10. Andrew J. Milson, "The Internet and Inquiry Learning: Integrating Medium and
Method in a Sixth Grade Social Studies Classroom," *Theory and Research in Social
Education* 30 (Summer 2002): 330–353; George Lipscomb, "Eighth Graders' Im-
pressions of the Civil War: Using Technology in the History Classroom," *Education
Communication and Information* 2 (2002), 51–67. On the use of WebQuests more
generally, see Andrew J. Milson and Portia Downey, "WebQuest: Using Internet
Resources for Cooperative Inquiry," *Social Education* 65 (April 2001): 144–146.

11. Milson, "Internet and Inquiry Learning," 343–46; Lipscomb, "Eighth-Graders'
Impressions," 60–64.

12. Bruce A. VanSledright, "Fifth Graders Investigating History in the Classroom:
Results From a Researcher-Practiner Design Experiment," *Elementary School
Journal* 102 (November 2002): 131–160 .

13. VanSledright, "Fifth Graders Investigating History," 135–38.

14. VanSledright, "Fifth Graders Investigating History," 138–41.

15. VanSledright, "Fifth Graders Investigating History," 143–51.

16. Keith C. Barton, "'I Just Kinda Know': Elementary Students' Ideas About Historical Evidence," *Theory and Research in Social Education* 25 (Fall 1997): 407–430.

17. Barton, "'I Just Kinda Know,'" 413–17; materials for this research came from P.
Bennett, *What Happened on Lexington Green: An Inquiry into the Nature and Method
of History* (Menlo Park, Calif.: Addison-Wesley, 1970), and *What Happened on
Lexington Green: An Inquiry into the Nature and Methods of History* (teacher and student manuals; Washington, D.C.: Office of Education, Bureau of Research,
1967), Eric Document Reproduction Service, ED 032333.

18. Barton, "'I Just Kinda Know,'" 417–19.

19. Linda Levstik and Dehea B. Smith, "'I've Never Done This Before': Building a
Community of Inquiry in a Third-Grade Classroom," in *Advances in Research on*

Teaching, Vol. 6, *Teaching and Learning History,* Ed. Jere Brophy (Greenwich, Conn.: JAI Press, 1996), 105–09; VanSledright, "Fifth Graders Investigating History," 132, 142–49.

20. Rosalyn Ashby and Peter J. Lee, "Information, Opinion, and Beyond," paper presented at the annual meeting of the American Educational Research Association, 13–17 April, 1998. In another portion of this research, when students were asked to evaluate the comparative reliability of two sources of evidence, many based their judgments on the amount of information provided by the sources (rather than their status as evidence), while others made decisions based on the plausibility of that evidence, similar to those students in the United States who reached conclusions based on what they thought must have happened. See also Peter Lee and Rosalyn Ashby, "Progression in Historical Understanding among Students Ages 7–14," in *Knowing, Teaching, and Learning History: National and International Perspectives,* Eds. Peter N. Stearns, Peter Seixas, and Sam Wineburg (New York: New York University Press, 2000), 199–222, "Empathy, Perspective Taking, and Rational Understanding," in *History Empathy and Perspective Taking in the Social Studies,* Eds. O. L. Davis, Jr., Elizabeth Anne Yeager, and Stuart J. Foster (Lanham, Md.: Rowman and Littlefield, 2001), 21–50; and "History in an Information Culture: Project Chata," *International Journal of Historical Learning, Teaching and Research* 1 (June 2001), 75–98.

21. Dewey, *How We Think,* 11.

22. The College Entrance Examination Board, "The Document-Based Question (DBQ)," available from http://www.collegeboard.com/ap/history/html/dbq001. html, accessed August 2, 2002; "1999 Free-Response Question," available from http://www.collegeboard.com/ap/history/frq99/ushist_ q1.html, accessed August 2, 2002.

23. Teacher Created Materials, "Document-Based Activities Using the Internet: World War II—Europe," available from http://www.buyteachercreated.com/ estore/product/5108, accessed September 25, 2002.

24. Keith C. Barton and Linda S. Levstik, "'It Wasn't a Good Part of History': National Identity and Ambiguity in Students' Explanations of Historical Significance," *Teachers College Record* 99 (Spring 1998): 496–99; Sam Wineburg, *Historical Thinking and Other Unnatural Acts* (Philadelphia: Temple University Press, 2001), 232–255.

25. Peter Seixas, "The Community of Inquiry as a Basis for Knowledge and Learning: The Case of History," *American Educational Research Journal* 30 (Summer 1993): 310, 314–15.

26. Jack Zevin and David Gerwin, *Teaching World History as Mystery* (Portsmouth, N.H.: Heinemann, forthcoming).

27. William B. Stanley and James A. Whitson, "Citizenship as Practical Competence: A Response to the New Reform Movement in Social Education," *International Journal of Social Education* 7 (Fall 1992): 60.

28. A number of British history educators have called attention to the problems inherent in sourcework that is divorced from the larger process of historical inquiry. See Jamie Byrom, "Working With Sources: Scepticism or Cynicism?," *Teaching History* 91 (May 1998): 32–34; Christine Counsell, *Analytical and Discursive Writing at Key Stage 3* (London: The Historical Association, 1997), 7; "Editorial," *Teaching History* 91 (May 1998), 3; "Historical Knowledge and Historical Skills: A Distracting Dichotomy," in *Issues in History Teaching,* Eds. James Arthur and Robert

Phillips (London: Routledge, 2000), 58–59; "The Forgotten Games Kit: Putting Historical Thinking First in Long-, Medium- and Short-term Planning," in *History, ICT and Learning in the Secondary School,* Eds. Terry Haydn and Christine Counsell (London: Routledge Falmer, 2003), 105; Chris Husbands, Alison Kitson, and Anna Pendry, *Understanding History Teaching: Teaching and Learning About the Past in Secondary Schools* (Philadelphia: Open University Press, 2003), 70; and Alison Kitson, "Reading and Enquiring in Years 12 and 13: A Case Study on Women in the Third Reich," *Teaching History* 111 (June 2003): 13–19.

29. Tom Holt, *Thinking Historically: Narrative, Imagination, and Understanding* (New York: College Entrance Examination Board, 1995), 23; emphasis in original.

Historical Empathy
as Perspective Recognition

O wad some Power the giftie gie us

To see oursels as ithers see us!

It wad frae mony a blunder free us,

An' foolish notion:

What airs in dress an' gait wad lea'e us,

An' ev'n devotion!

—Robert Burns[1]

Perhaps no feature of history education has inspired as much discussion, debate, criticism, and avoidance as the concept of empathy. Yet many U.S. readers may be unfamiliar with the term, at least as it applies to the study of the past. It derives from the Greek *empatheia*, denoting affection or passion, and everyday connotations equate it with the willingness and ability to "feel with" others. This creates considerable confusion between empathy and sympathy, but the *International Encyclopedia of the Social Sciences* distinguishes between the two as follows: Empathy involves imagining the thoughts and feelings of other people from their own perspectives, whereas sympathy involves imagining them as if those thoughts and feelings were our own. Unlike empathy, sympathy suggests that all human beings are basically the same across time, cultural boundaries, and individual preferences, and that a single frame of reference—one's own—represents an acceptable standard with which to measure the world.[2]

Although the assumption of similarity—we are all one under the skin—may be comforting, it wreaks havoc with historical understanding, not to mention democratic participation. To begin with, sympathetic understanding is, at the very least, inaccurate. Time, culture, and individual preferences and experiences produce fundamentally different worldviews. Failure to take this basic fact of human experience into account renders the past incomprehensible, largely because it severs the connection between action and purpose. As Peter Lee and Rosalyn Ashby note

> If history is to be possible, historians must understand past meanings, whether of documents or artifacts. (Is this find a cup or a cult object? Is this document a minute or a report? Does it make a threat or a promise?) If they cannot do this, then there can be no historical evidence. Historians must also be able to give sense to actions and to social practices and institutions in terms of people's reasons for doing or believing what they did.[3]

Treating people in the past as though they were similar (or identical) to ourselves, with the same goals, intentions, beliefs, and attitudes, makes such understanding impossible. Only by recognizing how the perspectives of people in the past may have differed from our own will we be able to make sense of their practices. Also, as we argued in chapter 2, democratic deliberation depends on recognizing the potential logic and coherence of other people's perspectives; it does us no good to know that others view the world differently if we automatically dismiss their views as deluded or immoral.

This recognition has little to do with sympathy, though, and might even be considered its opposite; indeed, given the common conflation of empathy with sympathy, some scholars have abandoned the term altogether, often substituting *perspective-taking*, *rational understanding*, or simply *understanding people in the past* in its stead. (We prefer *perspective recognition* because we think the term *perspective* accords well with intuitive notions about the complex elements of individual viewpoints, and because the phrase avoids the implication that we can "take on" the perspectives of others.) Sometimes, history educators completely separate empathy from any feelings that we ourselves bring to the past: Crafting empathy into a purely analytical tool, they definite it as an intellectual achievement resting on evidential reconstruction of other people's beliefs, values, goals, and circumstances.

In summing up this approach, Stuart Foster maintains that historical inquiry "remains primarily a cognitive, not an affective, act and one that is chiefly dependent upon knowledge, not feeling or imagination." We view historical empathy somewhat differently. We agree that it must be separated from sympathy, in which we imagine another's experience as if it were our own. However, limiting empathy to a purely cognitive endeavor limits its contribution to pluralist democracy. To engage in meaningful deliberation with those whose ideas differ from our own, we must do more than understand them—we must care about them and about their perspectives. Joan Skolnick, Nancy Dulberg, and Thea Maestra conceptualize empathy as involving both affective engagement and the primarily cognitive task of perspective taking. This requires imaginative intellectual and emotional participation and suggests that empathy might best be thought of as two distinct cultural tools: One invites us to care with and about people in the past, to be concerned with what happened to them and how they experienced their lives; this kind of empathy is the topic of chapter 12. The focus of the current chapter, on the other hand, is on recognizing others' perspectives—the intellectual exercise described by most scholars who have written on the topic. In reviewing research on this topic, we use a somewhat different lens to examine how students go about reconstructing historical perspectives, because we are less interested in historical empathy as an end in itself than as a means to democratic participation. This requires more than seeing others as they saw themselves. It requires that we see ourselves as others see us—an achievement that Robert Burns long ago suggested might bring certain social advantages.[4]

THE COMPONENTS OF HISTORICAL EMPATHY

Although empathy has been a contested topic among educators for some time, in the past few years consensus has arisen in Britain and North America over the concept's core meaning: Empathy involves using the perspectives of people in the past to explain their actions. To understand why people acted as they did, we need to focus on what they were trying to accomplish, the nature of their beliefs, attitudes, and knowledge, and the culturally and historically situated assumptions that guided their thought and action. Another way of phrasing this is to say that to understand people in the past, we must contextualize their actions—we must understand, as best we can, their world and how they saw it, no matter how greatly those experiences and perceptions differed from our own. Such recognition is necessarily grounded in evidence: We use sources that come from the past as a way of interpreting historical perspectives. As Stuart Foster suggests, we can also define empathy by detailing what it is not: According to current interpretations, empathy does not involve identification (we want students to understand Hitler's outlook but not accept it as their own), does not depend on imagining oneself in the place of others (because we can never directly relive their experiences or perceptions), and does not involve emotional response (rational understanding is the goal, not sympathy or admiration).[5]

Recognition of past perspectives, of course, is not easy. Whereas recognizing contemporary perspectives is difficult, reconstructing those of the past presents even more daunting challenges. To begin with, sources for interpreting historical beliefs and values are inevitably fragmentary. Just as people do today, individuals in the past made complex choices for complex reasons and rarely felt compelled to fully document either their choices or their reasons. Indeed, as with many of us, they probably would have struggled to explain their underlying beliefs, even to themselves. To further complicate matters, where more complete documentation does exist, changing public and social meanings make interpretation difficult. Such shifts in language are amazingly common: Slang terms fall in and out of

fashion, and regionalisms, occupation-specific jargon, and idioms challenge easy interpretation. As a result, current understandings never fully
match the meanings that language carried in its own time. Moreover, interpretations of past actions are inevitably filtered through the lens of the present—shaped by the questions we ask, the values we hold, the worldviews we
maintain. This does not mean that our interpretations are worthless, only
that they inevitably represent translations of the past—with all the limitations inherent in that process. At best, then, careful historical interpretation
develops an informed but tentative appreciation of the predicaments and
viewpoints of people in the past.[6]

A number of researchers have investigated students' attempts to make
sense of historical perspectives—to use the tool of perspective recognition, as
we would put it—and several have developed hierarchies or typologies of students' thinking in this area. The most comprehensive is that of Ashby and
Lee, who describe five levels of empathetic understanding. Students at the
lowest level see the past as unintelligible and consider people in the past
mentally defective for not having adopted obviously better courses of action;
for these students, the past is essentially a catalog of absurd behavior. At a
somewhat higher level, students understand people's action with reference
to generalized stereotypes; they explain actions in terms of what they think a
very religious person would have done, for example, but without any attempt
to place actions in a specific historical context or to differentiate the knowledge and beliefs of people now from those in the past. At the third level, that
of "everyday empathy," students understand actions with reference to the
specific situation in which people find themselves but still fail to distinguish
between how we would see the situation in the present and how contemporaries saw it; they thus try to imagine how they themselves would have reacted in
a given situation rather than how people at the time would have. At the fourth
level, students understand the specific situations in which people found
themselves and recognize that they would not necessarily have characterized
those situations in the same terms we would, because their beliefs, goals, and
values were different than ours; however, these students tend to focus narrowly on specific situations. Only at the fifth and highest level do students
place actions within the broader context of other differences in beliefs, values, and material conditions within historical societies.[7]

This typology provides important guidance for examining how students
make sense of people in the past, but it also leaves out key components of the
process, some of which may be critical for developing the ability to take part in
democratic deliberation. Rather than taking perspective recognition to be a
single cognitive process that students may demonstrate at a variety of levels, we
prefer to think of it as a tool with numerous elements (or "subcompetencies,"
as Peter Knight has put it), which may or may not develop in a linear sequence.[8]
In our view, there are five such elements that teachers must be aware of and develop in the classroom—a sense of "otherness," shared "normalcy," historical
contextualization, differentiation of perspectives, and contextualization of the

present. In the following sections, we discuss research on these elements and describe how each might contribute to citizenship.

A Sense of "Otherness"

At bottom, empathetic understanding requires the obvious: recognizing the fundamental otherness of people beyond oneself. Without some sense of how other people think and feel, there is little chance of making sense of their actions. From the mundane occurrences of our daily lives all the way to the grand events of international affairs, we depend on our ability to recognize that not everyone shares our viewpoints. Adults regularly call on children to practice these interpretive skills: "How would you feel if …," they begin, asking their young charges to empathize with a peer's distress; "If you keep talking to people in that tone of voice, no one's going to listen to you," they say, reminding children to anticipate peer responses. Given time and experience, many of us acquire sufficient facility with this ability to negotiate these interactions at an everyday level; as social and cultural distances increase, however, the opportunities for misinterpreting the actions of others multiply. Not only do we misjudge how others might interpret our actions, but we misunderstand their feelings, values, and goals.

Barbara Kingsolver provides a number of vivid examples of such misunderstanding in her novel *The Poisonwood Bible*. At one point, a missionary new to a Congolese village decides to conduct baptisms in a nearby river. He cannot understand why the villagers resist; the villagers cannot understand why he insists. He interprets their resistance theologically; they interpret his insistence as flagrant disregard for their safety. Finally, an old woman explains the impasse to the obstinate missionary: Immersion may be, from his perspective, theologically sound, but from the villagers' perspective it is insane. Hasn't he noticed the crocodiles in the river? Similar failures to account for differing perspectives appear repeatedly in the diplomatic realm. When a U.S. submarine sank a Japanese fishing vessel in 2001, for example, the two countries struggled to come to grips not just with the loss of life but with each nation's expectations in regard to the incident. The Japanese expected an apology: An honorable person responsible for the loss of nine lives would surely have done so. The initial U.S. response was silence—no apology, no admission of wrongdoing—at least in part because the government did not want to accept the liability an apology might imply. The U.S. legal system made an apology almost impossible, whereas Japanese culture made it a necessity. The diplomatic dance that ensued created tensions on both sides.[9]

Recognizing that other people's values, attitudes, beliefs, and intentions may be different than one's own, then, is the starting point for mutual understanding, as well as the basis for meaningful communication. That might seem almost too obvious to mention, but Piagetian scholarship long hypothesized that young children were unable to differentiate their own perspectives from those of others. They were unable to "de-center," it was claimed, and up to a certain age could not even imagine how physical objects—such as lumps of clay—might appear to someone standing on the other side of a table. Imagining the social perspectives of people far removed in time and place appeared even more problematic, even for students at the secondary level, and for a time it was suggested that students' formal exposure to history be delayed until late adolescence. This idea continues to linger among history educators; sometimes we still hear them argue that history is inappropriate in the elementary grades because children have difficulty understanding that people in the past were different than people today.[10]

Like much Piagetian research, these findings resulted more from disembedded tasks than limitations in children's cognitive abilities. Recent studies indicate that as early as preschool, most children spontaneously role-play, differentiate points of view, talk about their own and others' mental states, and distinguish their own and others' perspectives on a variety of simple tasks. Indeed, beginning in infancy, they not only differentiate themselves from others but begin to recognize how others might be feeling. Somewhere between the ages of 2 and 3, children start to recognize that others' experiences are different from their own, comment on and ask about the causes of others' actions and feelings, and are aware that rules apply differently to different people. By age 4, they can adjust their conduct and comments to accommodate the wishes and needs of other children. Judy Dunn argues that "these developments in the ability to conceive of other minds in the second half of the third year have such profound consequences for children's understanding of their social world and their communication that a reasonable case can be made for designating this a new 'stage' in children's social understanding." The foundation for empathy, then, seems to be well in place by age 4![11]

Shared Normalcy

To take part in democratic deliberations, it is not enough to know that other people have different perspectives; we must be willing to entertain the possibility that those perspectives make sense and that they are not the result of ignorance, stupidity, or delusion. This, of course, is a much greater challenge. A young child may understand that a peer doesn't know what's in the box or that Mommy can read better than the child herself, but these are correctable deficiencies: The peer can be told what object is inside, and the child will learn to read some day. However, matters are different in the grown-up world of participatory democracy; although it is tempting to conclude that anyone who disagrees with us is mentally underdeveloped (or the victim of mindless indoctrination), such views will do little to enable communication; in fact, they are likely to destroy any such attempts. As we argued in chapter 2, we must be willing to listen to others and take their ideas seriously, at least for the moment. This requires that we recognize that others value their ideas just as we do ours, as imminently reasonable outlooks on the world. People who differ from us are not simply a reflection of ourselves who are waiting to be enlightened; they are our peers—and they may have a better sense than we do of where the crocodiles are. History provides fertile ground for developing this kind of recognition, because we have to come to grips with why people in the past did things that no longer make sense to us.

There are two obstacles to this recognition. The first is one that appeared in our classroom study of fourth and fifth graders but that we have not seen reported in other studies: the belief that people in the past knew they were being old-fashioned. Some students explained that people long ago knew that the way they went about their lives was not the smartest or easiest and that one day people would start doing things more sensibly. Their teachers continually asked them to reflect on this belief, though, and as students were exposed to a variety of historical changes, many of them began to realize that people in the past did not think they were being old–fashioned, and that people always consider themselves as "normal" or "in style." One girl, for example, commented on the fact that modern cars were prettier than older ones but quickly added, "Well, I don't know, back then they might have thought that those cars are like better than now, because they're used to their cars, and they were into that style." Similarly, in discussing a picture of a girl bathing in a sink in an early 20th-century tenement, several students were shocked by how dirty it seemed; one, though, pointed out that it would have seemed clean to them even though it doesn't to us. She also noted that if they walked into one of our houses, they might think it was "weird."[12]

Within a few weeks of the beginning of the school year, whenever a student referred to something as old–fashioned or otherwise deficient, other students automatically pointed out that it would not have seemed so at the time. As one girl wrote in a composition about the way people dressed in the past, "If they came in [here] we would think that they dress strangely because we now wear jeans, hat and a shirt. But they would think we were strange as well." This recognition that perspectives are reversible—we may think they're strange, but they'd think the same about us—is required for both historical understanding and contemporary dialogue. Although students came to this recognition rapidly, they did so only as a result of their teachers' prompting and the modeling of their peers. Educators cannot take this component of historical empathy for granted but must consciously address it as they design instruction.[13]

The second obstacle to recognizing the normalcy of other people's perspectives is one that has often been noted in research on empathy—the tendency to believe that other people's outlooks, although genuinely held, are the result of their lack of intelligence. Among these fourth and fifth graders, the recognition that people in the past considered themselves normal coexisted with the belief that they were not as intelligent as we are today. In trying to explain why some names popular today were unknown when their grandparents were born, for example, one girl suggested that "they didn't know how to pronounce that many names"; similarly, another thought that because people long ago had not gone to school, they were unable to pronounce all the letters and thus could not use certain names. Also, one student argued that a picture of a building with the world "Lexington" on it must be of recent origin because a long time ago "they probably didn't know how to spell *Lexington* that well" and that they might not even have been able to pronounce the name.[14]

Sometimes these perceptions were startling. Once, a group of students was discussing why the girl in the tenement photo mentioned earlier would have bathed in a sink; one girl suggested that they didn't have a washing machine, and that was how they washed their clothes, but a classmate asserted that they had washing machines, they just weren't smart enough to use them. Similarly, during a discussion of food in Colonial times, a student noted that they wouldn't have had burritos because "they weren't smart enough to make them." Although such observations were most common at the beginning of the year, they continued to occur periodically. Much later, for example, in trying to make sense of why people in the 17th century believed in witches, one student suggested, "They don't like, list the possibilities, and just think about it. I mean, say, 'Is this really smart?'" Thus, although many students quickly came to understand that people always perceive themselves as being normal or in style, some continued to fall back on assumptions of ignorance or stupidity to explain differing perspectives.[15]

Interestingly, Lee and Ashby suggest that certain teaching practices, especially "then and now" comparisons, lead children into just these sorts of assumptions. Rather than ground historical descriptions in the values and technologies of historical times, such comparisons may point out what the past lacked relative to the present—washing machines, enlightened policies regarding women, mass production, and the like. Thus, students learn that women in the 1920s used washboards, not as an improvement over such previous practices as crouching by a stream and pounding the laundry with rocks, but because there were no washing machines. Based on such lessons, students conclude that people were ignorant rather than innovative. Helping them move beyond this kind of reaction constitutes a major task of history education.[16]

Historical Contextualization

Most scholarship on empathy has focused on students' explanations of actions and events in terms of historical values, attitudes, and beliefs. In our study of fourth and fifth graders, two topics in particular prompted examination of such factors—the role of women in society and the Salem witch trials. In both cases, despite students' youth and their relative lack of experience with formal historical study, they consistently engaged in meaningful and accurate reconstruction of past perspectives and explained how such perspectives affected behavior. The topic of women's roles in society came up several times throughout the year, and the teachers in these classrooms often explained how attitudes toward gender differed in the past; students, in turn, appropriated this way of explaining past behavior. In describing what he had learned from a guest speaker portraying a woman from the 19th century, for example, one boy noted, "She said what she wore, it was improper to not have a hat on, or have a long dress on, because it would be like—now ladies wear short skirts, up past the knee—and if you saw a lady's ankle, it was like [making a gasping noise], 'I saw her ankle!'" Another student, during class discussion, made a similar comment about restrictions on women's clothing, and her teacher asked whether she thought a woman might have been punished for wearing trousers; the student explained that it didn't have anything to do with punishment, that it just wouldn't have happened. Both students recognized that it was the expectation of appropriate behavior for women that had changed over time, not simply fashions or patterns of behavior.[17]

Several students also pointed to the importance of attitudes in determining the kind of work expected of women in the past. One boy, for example, noted that "the men thought that the women were supposed to sit home, take care of the children, cook, clean," while another explained that "men, they thought women weren't important back then, they sorta just thought women were a lot of dumbos, and alls they could do is wash clothes at home, and men thought that was all they were good for." A girl also pointed out that "men just didn't like women and they didn't think that women were allowed to do things, and they thought that women had to do everything at home like working, like cooking, and laundry, and everything, and cleaning; they thought that they just couldn't do anything, 'cause they were just not manly enough."[18] In chapter 8, we noted the limitations of focusing exclusively on individual attitudes at the expense of larger institutional and cultural contexts, but what is notable in these examples is that students were beginning to appropriate historical contextualization as a way of explaining behavior that would make little sense if seen only from the perspective of the present. (Students in these examples also were overgeneralizing in their descriptions of past perspectives, and we will discuss this issue in a later section.)

These students' most extensive opportunity to explore differences in beliefs arose in their study of the Salem witch trials. Both teachers emphasized that people in Salem believed strongly in witches, and they discussed the kinds of evidence (moles, laziness, lack of religion) they considered evidence of witchcraft. Both also explained that it was part of their general outlook on life to blame witches for disease, mishaps, or other things that went wrong, and that people who violated other aspects of their beliefs were particularly likely to be accused of witchcraft. Students also learned about these attitudes through their independent reading of primary and secondary sources, and many of them clearly and accurately explained people's actions in terms of their beliefs. In developing a list of evidence to listen for during a simulated trial, for example, one group of jurors identified items such as marks on the body, not being able to say the Ten Commandments, and being able to float; in discussing the verdict after the evidence had been presented, many students based their decision on the same kinds of evidence. These students did not look for evidence that they themselves considered convincing but identified those items that would have been convincing to people at the time. Similarly, during an exercise in which they wrote letters to a magistrate protesting the innocence of a relative, most students pointed to exactly the kinds of evidence used in the witch trials. One boy explained in his composition,

> I know Sarah is not guilty of witchcraft because she goes to church every Sunday. That means she isn't a witch because witches believe in bad stuff and church is good. Also she doesn't float. Witches float because the people of Massachusetts believe the spirits hold them up. The next thing is that Sarah reads the Bible every night. The Bible is like going to Church. It is good to read the Bible because God's name is in it. Witches don't like God.[19]

Some educators suggest that students find it difficult to use historical perspectives rather than contemporary ones to explain the actions and events of the past; Sam Wineburg cleverly refers to it as an "unnatural act." Unnatural it may be, but our work with elementary and middle school students suggests that they are quite capable of using this tool and that they find it a powerful and intuitively sound way of making sense of why people behaved as they did. It may even be within the grasp of younger students; Lee and Ashby report research in which children as young as 7 and 8 years old recognized that those in the past would not necessarily see the world as people do today. Rather than lamenting the difficulty of the process or dismissing students' willingness or ability to engage in it, we might have a more positive impact on their historical thinking by working with teachers to implement classroom practices sensitive to students' developing facility with perspective recognition. We might find that with careful scaffolding, this tool is not so unnatural after all.[20]

Multiplicity of Historical Perspectives

Scholars interested in historical empathy usually stop at the kind of contextualization we have described, although they may break it down into finer categories than we do. However, there are at least two other components of this tool that are crucial both for making sense of history and for participating in democratic deliberation. The first involves the recognition that at any given time in history, people and groups have held a variety of values, attitudes, and beliefs, and that they often have come into conflict because of them. If students are going to take part in meaningful public discussion, they need to understand that differing perspectives are a normal part of social interaction, not an aberration to be suppressed or overcome. If they believe that all members of a community should share the same attitudes or values, they will not be ready for citizenship in a pluralist democracy such as ours. The difficult task of deliberation and participation is to agree on actions that can be taken despite differing values, not to come to agreement on "what everyone believes," and history provides abundant terrain for examining such differences.

Unfortunately, consideration of multiple perspectives is not often a part of history education; very often, the complexity of the past is simplified to such an extent that students are presented with an utterly false portrait of history, usually one of happy consensus. U.S. students, for example, rarely learn that a large portion of the colonial population opposed the American Revolution, much less that issues of representation were the subject of a great deal of disagreement within Britain at the time. Instead, they're presented with a picture in which all colonists were on one side, and all British on the other. They're even less likely to learn that many Americans opposed the First and Second World Wars. If students think everyone in a given country or community agreed on such issues, they will have few resources for understanding why people disagree today, and they will have little reason to take others' ideas seriously. Learning about differing perspectives in history doesn't guarantee students will accept such differences today, but it helps to create the conditions under which such acceptance might seem reasonable.

We often encounter this lack of experience with multiple perspectives among students in our university courses. When confronted with episodes that provoke a moral response—Columbus' treatment of Native Americans, slavery, Japanese American relocation, and the like—students often respond by pointing out that we can't apply our standards to such episodes, and that we can judge other people's behavior only by the standards of their own day. As we pointed out in chapter 5, this leads to an inability to make any judgments at all, because it exonerates people from responsibility for their actions. Yet it also demonstrates a lack of experience with this component of historical empathy, because there was no single set of standards at the time of Columbus, or in the colonial and antebellum periods, or during World War II. Some people were opposed to relocation, and some were for it; some people supported slavery, and some opposed it. If students—whether as children or as adults—think that actions can be explained solely by reference to "the attitudes of the day," then they will have an impoverished view of history. More complete use of this tool requires that they be able to identify differences both within and between groups at any given time in the past as well as to explain why—out of the range of possible beliefs—people held the particular ones that they did.

In addition, from a humanistic perspective, the assumption of uniformity limits our access to the full range of human possibility and leads to what K. Anthony Appiah and Amy Gutman call a "tyranny of ... expectations" in which only some ways of being are acceptable. Intolerance increases where dichotomous "us versus them" thinking persists, and this intolerance, in turn, leads to a greater willingness to abridge human rights.[21] In the United States in recent years, we have seen all too many examples of hatred and violence against those who are perceived as a threat to "our society" or "our country": Mexican migrants are branded as a drain on the economy, Muslims and people of Middle Eastern heritage as enemies of the state, and gays and lesbians as deviant and immoral. Even within schools, we frequently hear that "these kids" aren't motivated or capable or that "the parents around here" aren't interested in their children's education. Portrayals of men and women as being from different planets, meanwhile, are a staple of popular culture. In each of these cases, a single perspective—and set of personal characteristics—is ascribed to an entire class of people. Such generalizations are deeply embedded in our social, cultural, political, and linguistic landscapes, and they render informed discourse among diverse people close to impossible. No viable "common good" ensues when groups and individuals rely on broadbrush generalizations to determine either what they have in common or what divides them. History, on the other hand, should be able to play a role in helping students overcome this tendency by illustrating the enormous variation within any society. Through their study of history, students should get into the habit of immediately looking for a range of variation in any group. This is a difficult but by no means insurmountable task.

Research that one of us conducted together with Jeanette Groth provides some insight into students' capacity to recognize and deal with multiple, within-group perspectives. In Jeanette's classroom, eighth graders were taking part in a unit of study on the antebellum United States; the unit incorporated three themes—culture contact and conflict on the frontier, industrialization, and reform movements—and began with the perspectives of women. In the early stages of the unit, students worked in small groups to discuss a series of quotes representing different perspectives on each theme. Quotes on reform, for example, ranged from comments by Susan B. Anthony to excerpts from a popular book on the proper conduct of wives.[22]

At first, students were amazed by opponents of women's rights. How could they hold such opinions? These students first began to talk as though all women in the 19th century were "treated like slaves," and all men regarded women as inherently inferior. As they studied a wider array of sources representing within-group differences, though, their comments changed. As students developed questions to guide their inquiry in the remainder of the unit, they began asking whether "women inside the reform movement all had the same opinions ... wanted the same rights" and whether some were "moderate or right wing within the reform." Other questions included, "How did women in the movement feel about those who were not?"; "What percent of the population of women were involved in reform?"; and "Were there places where reform wasn't even discussed?" They asked about "sacrifices made in order to achieve reform," the degree of ostracism suffered by reformers, and "at the end, did [women in reform movements] lose or gain support" from other citizens?[23]

Students gathered data to answer these questions and began to develop exhibits to display at a local university. As each group's presentation developed, it became clear that they recognized that experiences and perspectives differed depending on individual beliefs and values, as well as their group's social, cultural, and political positions. Sometimes students piled sets of sources together, tentatively deciding that they represented a particular perspective. Sometimes they argued over relatively subtle differences: What motivated women to go West? Did they see the trip differently than men did? Did attitudes differ among races or economic classes? Which made more of a difference in perspective—race, class, or gender? Their displays demonstrated similar recognition of multiple perspectives. Students working on industrialization, for instance, used the image of hands—those of a millworker, an economically privileged woman, and an enslaved woman—to describe differences in condition and perspective among those involved in or benefiting from various aspects of textile production. One member of this group explained that these experiences meant that each woman would view textile production and working conditions differently—"a millworker and the mill owner's wife probably didn't see the world the same."[24]

In sum, these eighth graders understood that "women" did not exist as a single category but as a multiplicity of perspectives, and they pointed to this as one of the most important aspects of the unit; in particular, they said that they enjoyed learning about women in different social conditions. Their responses suggest that this kind of perspective recognition is attainable at least by middle school and probably sooner. Studies with elementary-age children indicate that they too recognize some within-group differences when they have access to appropriate primary sources and when their teachers provide them with sufficient time to study contrasting perspectives, discuss those perspectives, and explore different ways of making sense of them.[25]

Contextualization of the Present

Everything up to this point has been a cakewalk. Research shows that students—sometimes very young ones—can recognize that others have different perspectives from their own; that people in the past considered their own perspectives normal; that their actions depended on values, attitudes, and beliefs different from those today; and that social groups have been characterized by a diversity of perspectives. The last element of historical empathy, however, is both the trickiest and, arguably, the most crucial for deliberation in a pluralist society. This is the recognition that our own perspectives depend on historical context: They are not necessarily the result of logical and dispassionate reason but reflect the beliefs we have been socialized into as members of cultural groups. It's one thing to recognize that others' perspectives are influenced by social, cultural, religious, political, and economic forces; it's quite another to recognize that our own are just as much the result of context. This is the historical equivalent of the problem that bedevils so much intercultural communication: We can easily recognize and accept that the behavior of others is influenced by their culture—they stand closer to each other when they talk than we do, they eat from a common dining plate, they wear those funny things on their head—but we have more difficulty thinking of our behavior as culturally and historically situated; we just do things the normal way. Yet if we cannot remove ourselves from our beliefs long enough to recognize that these too have been influenced by societal factors, then we will never be able fully to entertain the possibility that they are as mutable as anyone else's. History education might be able to play a role in developing students' facility with this component of empathy by alerting them to the origins of contemporary beliefs, just as it familiarizes them with the worldviews of Viking traders, medieval peasants, or colonial farmers.[26]

However, history educators have not devoted much attention, either theoretical or empirical, to this element of perspective recognition, and we know of few, if any, teachers who emphasize the origins of present-day values, attitudes, and beliefs. There are at least two reasons for the absence of such contextualization. First, so few history classes deal with the recent past that the origins of contemporary perspectives are just as invisible as the origins of present-day economic structures or political patterns. The use of history to illuminate the origins of current institutions—one of the versions of the analytic stance we discussed in chapter 4—is not a common approach to history in schools, and this makes it improbable that students will have the chance to consider the historical origins of their own outlooks. Second, the suggestion that our own view of the world is historically situated would be highly controversial in most schools; parents, administrators, and other community members might not want students to know that the beliefs they take for granted are not timeless truths but result from a long line of historical change and development. Some elementary teachers in our part of the country are afraid to use Peter Spier's book *People* because it mentions religions other than Christianity, and they are convinced parents would complain about children being exposed to such information; they would no doubt consider it just as threatening to discuss the historical origins of current religious beliefs.

Our work with students also suggests they lack experience contextualizing their own perspectives. In our classroom study of fourth and fifth graders, for instance, students were asked, near the end of the year, if people in the future might think that some of today's ideas no longer make sense. Nearly every student agreed that they would, yet they had trouble coming up with examples. Most pointed to the impact of changing technology, particularly on transportation. One student, for example, suggested, "Maybe they'll have something where they just have to push a button and they'll be wherever they want to be, and they'll be, 'Gosh, why would they take all the energy to walk up to a store or something, or ride a bike or something, instead of just pushing a button and be in there?'" Others suggested that people in the future will probably have flying cars and won't be able to understand why we used the kind we have now. None of these actually represents a perspective that will change in the future; they're simply examples of technological changes, and students were projecting onto others the same limited ability to recognize historical perspectives that they had demonstrated earlier in the year: Just as they initially could not understand why people would have done such manifestly old-fashioned things in the past, they thought people in the future wouldn't understand why people in the 1990s used cars. Because they expected that difficulties of recognizing the shared normalcy of people in the past would continue, this is actually an example of continuity of perspectives rather than the reverse.[27]

When pushed to think of beliefs or attitudes, rather than technology, that might not make sense in the future, students had more difficulty. A few did give clear examples of potential changes in contemporary perspectives; two suggested people in the future might not understand our belief in God, and two others thought those in the future might not see why racial and gender equality is taken for granted today. More often, though, students could not identify any examples, and those who did venture suggestions usually pointed to opinions that they themselves did not share—such as the belief that ghosts or UFOs exist or that Elvis is still alive. They indicated that people in the future might consider these beliefs "stupid," but they too believed they were stupid, or at least highly questionable. Similarly, in our research with eighth graders who were studying women's roles in the 19th century, several pointed to the constraining influence of gender roles today, but they were contextualizing other people's contemporary beliefs, not their own—they knew that such current day perspectives were not inevitable, but they did not go so far as to question their own beliefs about gender.

Research with adolescents in New Zealand further demonstrates students' difficulty in removing themselves from contemporary perspectives. These students contextualized the actions of those who were distant in time and place, such as Nazis during the Holocaust or the U.S. government during a confrontation over nuclear-powered vessels in New Zealand waters. Some students of European heritage even criticized their ancestors for mistreating and "ripping off" Maori in the past, and they recognized not only that agreements between the two groups were based on differing views of the meaning of land and property but that Europeans used such differences to their advantage. However, in discussing contemporary land issues, students of European ancestry did not attempt to contextualize their own perspectives; one student, as we noted in chapter 5, even suggested that all Maori should move to Auckland! He knew other perspectives were possible, but questioning his own viewpoint would have required a degree of detachment for which he was unprepared. He had a personal stake in believing that the Maori somehow gave the land away—they could have said, "No," he declared—and he thought they shouldn't complain now about the choices they made in the past. He thus appeared unwilling to distance himself enough from a European perspective to consider any other. The history he had studied in school, meanwhile, had done nothing to encourage him to recognize the situatedness of his own perspective. If schools fail to address this element of perspective recognition or to provide the scaffolding necessary to engage with such complicated topics, we can hardly be surprised that students have difficulty with it. Unlike Robert Burns, though, we doubt the ability to see ourselves in cultural and historical context depends on a supernatural gift; it can probably come about from well-designed educational experiences.[28]

THE CONSTRAINT OF EMPATHY
AS PERSPECTIVE RECOGNITION

In each of the preceding sections, we noted the potential contribution of perspective recognition to participation in a pluralist democracy. However, all cultural tools have affordances and constraints: They allow us to do some things while preventing us from doing others; they call our attention to some issues and distract our attention from others. This observation does not render any particular tool useless; it simply acknowledges that having access to a variety of tools is more useful than being restricted to any single one. We can more effectively build furniture, cook dinner, or design a scientific experiment if we have a number of technical and conceptual tools available. Imagine cooking dinner with nothing but a potato peeler—it's a handy little tool, but it won't get the water boiled. Yet discussions of perspective recognition often treat it as though it were synonymous with historical understanding, or at least the central task of historical explanation. Peter Knight, for example, argues that "mature study of history" involves trying to reconstruct the practical inferences of people in the past and that this "is a (perhaps *the*) central feature of the discipline." Although few would dismiss other elements of history outright, the overwhelming focus of contemporary scholarship makes it clear that many regard empathy—conceived of as perspective recognition—as the key component of historical understanding and a critical element of history education.[29]

However, when history revolves so centrally around understanding the perspectives of people in the past, it manifests a constraint largely ignored in the literature on history education: It focuses on the causes of historical actions and ignores their consequences. Or, put more precisely in the language of sociocultural theory and mediated action, the tool of historical empathy can be used more effectively to explain the actions of people in the past than to evaluate what happened to them. Issues of justice, fairness, and the common good are ruled off the table, as we are encouraged to try to understand why people took the actions they did rather than focusing on the outcomes of those actions. Instead of studying how the relocation of Japanese Americans during the Second World War violated their constitutional rights, we turn our attention to examining how wartime anxiety and racism led many Whites to support such measures; instead of studying the effect of the Indian Removal Act on people of the Cherokee, Creek, Choctow, Chickasaw, and Seminole nations, we focus on the attitudes and beliefs that led Andrew Jackson to promote and enforce the act.

Perspective recognition is not irrelevant to studying the consequences of historical events, of course. It helps us understand, for example, how Japanese Americans, Native Americans, or others perceived and reacted to their circumstances. Even more fundamentally, we have to recognize the goals, intentions, and perceptions of people at the time to know "what happened" at the most basic factual level: We need to know how people categorized each other as belonging to one ethnic group or another, how they conceptualized government authority, and how they saw their relationship to land and property. Without being able to reconstruct such perspectives, we quite literally won't be able to make sense of the causes or consequences of historical events; perspective recognition is indispensable for whatever else we hope to do with the past.

Yet making this the primary emphasis of historical study leads to subtle—and sometimes not so subtle—biases that detract from our ability to deliberate over issues of the common good. To take just one example, if we see empathy as the primary tool of historical thinking, then our analysis of the end of World War II in the Pacific is likely to focus on factors influencing the decision to drop atomic bombs on Hiroshima and Nagasaki. Curricular units, replete with a variety of primary sources, have been developed around this issue, and research has been conducted on how children and adults use such sources to explain Truman's decision.[30] However, if our goal is to prepare students for democracy, this may not be the most significant way of understanding the topic. Students might be better served by using evidence to consider the feasibility of other options and their likely consequences—and not just what Truman thought about the alternatives and consequences. The importance of the president's decision-making process pales in comparison to the significance of the lives lost in the bombings or of those that might have been lost had they not taken place. "Why did the United States bomb Hiroshima and Nagasaki?" may be the question closest to the work of (some) historians, but "How could the greatest number of lives have been saved?" is closer to the work of citizens.

Causes of historical events are important, as are the intentions and motivations of those who take part in them. However, from the standpoint of participatory democracy, they may not be the most important issues. When we deliberate with others about what should be done, we will sometimes fail to agree with their motivations, because we often start with differing values. Yet this vision of democracy is not about motivation; it is about pragmatic action, about what we can agree to do despite our differing values. Although we bring our own perspectives to the table, and although we all must engage with these multiple viewpoints, the goal of deliberation is to reach agreement on the future, and that requires consideration of the likely consequences of our actions. Students who have evaluated the causes of historical events but not their outcomes may be unprepared for this task. Focusing too exclusively on the recognition of historical perspectives, in other words, may help us learn how to talk with others, but it gives us precious little to talk about. The substance of our conversations depend not on the tool of perspective recognition but on a different kind of empathy—empathy as care. We turn to this topic in the next chapter.

CONCLUSIONS

We have argued that empathy is a term that encompasses two separate cultural tools. The more familiar one involves explaining historical actions in terms of the attitudes, beliefs, and intentions of people in the past. Although there is widespread consensus that this is a critical element of history, there is less agreement over its designation. Empathy sounds too much like sympathy (and, from our point of view, fails to distinguish between cognitive and emotional elements); although perspective-taking currently enjoys some popularity, we dislike its implication that anyone can actually take the perspective of another. As a result, we have referred to this kind of empathy as perspective recognition, and we have suggested that it involves at least five different components. Two of these are rarely discussed in the literature on the subject—the recognition that any given time in history was characterized by multiple perspectives (just as the world is today) and the recognition that our own attitudes, beliefs, and intentions are historically and culturally situated, just as those of people in the past were. Our work with elementary and middle school students suggests that they are entirely capable of engaging in perspective recognition, although they have little experience with this final component. Of course, achieving the kind of contextualized historical empathy in which students not only recognize that their standards are different than those in the past but in which they attempt to understand how differing perspectives fit in a wider historical picture is a lengthy process. This is not an intellectual tool developed in a single class session or a single year. Rather, it develops with practice and careful mentoring, grounded in an ever-deepening historical knowledge base. With consistent attention and scaffolding, we suspect that students could develop greater facility even with conceptualization of their own perspectives.

We have pointed out that perspective recognition is not only a requirement for meaningful engagement with the past but may help prepare students for citizenship, because recognizing our own and others' perspectives is indispensable for public deliberation in a pluralist democracy. History, with its infinitely complex source material, should provide students practice moving beyond their own perspectives and taking seriously those of others, no matter how foreign they seem at first. However, focusing too exclusively on perspective recognition may draw attention away from an area that is just as important as understanding the causes of historical actions, if not more so—namely, the consequences of those actions. Focusing on the effects of the events of the past also requires a form of empathy, but one that revolves less around intellectual analysis and more around care.

ENDNOTES

1. Robert Burns, "To a Louse," in *The Complete Poetical Works of Burns* (Boston: Houghton Mifflin, 1897), 42–43.
2. Cited in Milton J. Bennett, *Basic Concepts of Intercultural Communication* (Yarmouth, Me.: Intercultural Press, 1998), 197. Within the discipline of history, the use of the term *empathy* derives more directly from translation of the German *einfühlung*, as used by William Dilthey, but this usage has also been characterized by confusion with *sympathy*; Peter Knight, "Empathy: Concept, Confusion and Consequences in a National Curriculum," *Oxford Review of Education* 15, No. 1 (1989): 42–43; Christopher Portal, "Empathy as an Objective for History Teaching," in *The History Curriculum for Teachers*, Ed. Christopher Portal (London: Heinemann, 1987), 89.
3. Peter Lee and Rosalyn Ashby, "Empathy, Perspective Taking, and Rational Understanding," in *Historical Empathy and Perspective Taking in the Social Studies*, Eds. O. L. Davis, Jr., Elizabeth Anne Yeager, and Stuart J. Foster (Lanham, Md.: Rowman and Littlefield, 2001), 23.
4. Stuart J. Foster, "Historical Empathy in Theory and Practice: Some Final Thoughts," in *Historical Empathy and Perspective Taking in the Social Studies*, Eds. O. L. Davis, Jr., Elizabeth Anne Yeager, and Stuart J. Foster (Lanham, Md.: Rowman and Littlefield, 2001), 170. See also Peter Knight, "A Study of Children's Understanding of People in the Past," *Educational Review* 41, No. 3 (1989): 207–08, and Lee and Ashby, "Empathy, Perspective Taking, and Rational Understanding," 22–23. Joan Skonick, Nancy Dulberg, and Thea Maestre, *Through Other Eyes: Developing Empathy and Multicultural Perspectives in the Social Studies* (Toronto, Ontario, Canada: Pippin Publishing, 1999), 9–19; Nancy R. Dulberg, "Perspective-Taking and Empathy in History and Social Studies: A Study of Fifth Grade Students' Thinking" (Ed.D. diss., University of California, Berkeley, 1998), 24.
5. Lee and Ashby, "Empathy, Perspective Taking, and Rational Understanding," 21–25; Rosalyn Ashby and Peter Lee, "Children's Concepts of Empathy and Understanding in History," in *The History Curriculum for Teachers*, Ed. Christopher Por-

tal (London: Heinemann, 1987), 62–65; Peter J. Lee, "Explanation and Understanding in History," in *History Teaching and Historical Understanding*, Eds. Alaric K. Dickinson and Peter J. Lee (London: Heinemann, 1978), 72–93; Dennis Shemilt, "Beauty and the Philosopher: Empathy in History and Classroom," in *Learning History*, Eds. Alaric K. Dickinson, Peter J. Lee, and Peter J. Rogers (London: Heinemann, 1984), 40–49; O. L. Davis, Jr., "In Pursuit of Historical Empathy," in *Historical Empathy and Perspective Taking in the Social Studies*, Eds. O. L. Davis, Jr., Elizabeth Anne Yeager, and Stuart J. Foster (Lanham, Md.: Rowman and Littlefield, 2001), 1–12; Foster, "Historical Empathy," 167–181.

6. Portal, "Empathy as an Objective," 89–90, and "Empathy," 42–43; Knight, "Children's Understanding of People in the Past," 208; Elizabeth A. Yeager and Stuart J. Foster, "The Role of Empathy in the Development of Historical Understanding," in *Historical Empathy and Perspective Taking in the Social Studies*, Eds. O. L. Davis, Jr., Elizabeth Anne Yeager, and Stuart J. Foster (Lanham, Md.: Rowman and Littlefield, 2001), 14–17; Bruce A. VanSledright, "From Empathic Regard to Self-Understanding: Im/Positionality, Empathy, and Historical Contextualization," in *Historical Empathy and Perspective Taking in the Social Studies*, Eds. O. L. Davis, Jr., Elizabeth Anne Yeager, and Stuart J. Foster (Lanham, Md.: Rowman and Littlefield, 2001), 51–68. For a more extreme view—that historical empathy is not only difficult to achieve but fundamentally impossible—see Keith Jenkins and Peter Brickley, "Reflections on the Empathy Debate," *Teaching History* 55 (April 1989): 18–23, and the counterargument in Lee and Ashby, "Empathy, Perspective Taking, and Rational Understanding," 23–25.

7. Ashby and Lee, "Children's Concepts of Empathy," 62–88; see also Alaric K. Dickinson and Peter J. Lee, "Making Sense of History," in *Learning History*, Eds. Alaric K. Dickinson, Peter J. Lee and Peter J. Rogers (London: Heinemann, 1984), 117–153, and "Understanding and Research," in *History Teaching and Historical Understanding*, Eds. Alaric K. Dickinson and Peter J. Lee (London: Heinemann, 1978), 94–120; Demis Shemilt, "Beauty and the Philosopher, 39–83, and *Evaluation Study: Schools Council History 13–16 Project* (Edinburgh: Holmes McDougall, 1980); Dulberg, "Perspective-Taking and Empathy," 73–146.

8. Knight, "Children's Understanding of People in the Past," 207–08; "Empathy," 46–47.

9. Barbara Kingsolver, *The Poisonwood Bible* (New York: HarperPerennial, 1998), 81; Suvendrini Kakuchi, "Apologies Do Little to Ease Grief Over Sea Tragedy," *Asia Times Online*, 7 March, 2001, available online at http://www.atimes.com/japan-econ/CC07Dh01.html, accessed 27 April, 2003.

10. Piagetian research on perspective is critically analyzed in Margaret Donaldson, *Children's Minds* (New York: W. W. Norton, 1978), 9–25; and in Rochel Gelman and Renee Baillargeon, "A Review of Some Piagetian Concepts," in *Handbook of Child Psychology*, Vol. 3: *Cognitive Development*, Eds. John H. Flavell and Ellen M. Markman (New York: Wiley, 1983), 167–230. Piagetian research in history is reviewed in Chistian Laville and Linda W. Rosenzweig, "Teaching and Learning History," in *Developmental Perspectives on the Social Studies*, National Council for the Social Studies Bulletin No. 66, Ed. Linda W. Rosenzweig (Washington, D.C.: National Council for the Social Studies, 1982), 54–66; and Linda S. Levstik, "Teaching History: A Definitional and Developmental Dilemma," in *Elementary*

School Social Studies: Research as a Guide to Practice, National Council for the Social Studies Bulletin No. 79, Ed. Virginia Atwood (Washington, D.C.: National Council for the Social Studies, 1986), 69–73.

11. Judy Dunn, *The Beginnings of Social Understanding* (Cambridge, Mass.: Harvard University Press, 1988), 173–74; Carolyn Zahn-Waxler, Marian Radke-Yarrow, and Judy Brady-Smith, "Perspective-Taking and Prosocial Behavior," *Developmental Psychology* 13 (January 1977): 87–88; Norma Haan, "Moral Development and Action from a Social Constructivist Perspective," in *Handbook of Moral Behavior and Development,* Vol. 1: *Theory,* Eds. William M. Kurtines and Jacob L. Gewirtz (Hillsdale, N.J.: Lawrence Erlbaum Associates, Inc., 1991), 251–273; Martin L. Hoffman, "Empathy, Social Cognition, and Moral Action," in *Handbook of Moral Behavior and Development,* Vol. 1: *Theory,* Eds. William M. Kurtines and Jacob L. Gewirtz (Hillsdale, N.J.: Lawrence Erlbaum Associates, Inc., 1991), 275–302; Paul Light, "Taking Roles," in *Making Sense: The Child's Construction of the World,* Eds. Jerome Bruner and Helen Haste (New York: Methuen, 1987), 41–61.

12. Keith C. Barton, "Historical Understanding among Elementary Children" (Ed.D. diss., University of Kentucky, Lexington, 1994), 202.

13. Barton, "Historical Understanding Among Elementary Children," 202–04.

14. Barton, "Historical Understanding Among Elementary Children," 204–05.

15. Barton, "Historical Understanding Among Elementary Children," 205–07. British studies consistently have identified similar assumptions among students there; as Lee and Ashby put it, for many students, "History is a story of feeble-minded people blundering from one self-evidently mistaken course of action to another"; "Empathy, Perspective Taking, and Rational Understanding," 27, 29–43. See also Lee, "Explanation and Understanding in History," 72; Dickinson and Lee, "Making Sense of History," 119–25; Ashby and Lee, "Children's Concepts of Empathy," 68–71; and Shemilt, "Beauty and the Philosopher," 50–51.

16. Ashby and Lee, "Empathy, Perspective Taking, and Rational Understanding," 46–47.

17. Barton, "Historical Understanding Among Elementary Children," 207–08.

18. Barton, "Historical Understanding Among Elementary Children," 208–09.

19. Barton, "Historical Understanding Among Elementary Children," 209–10; in the interest of readability, this composition has been edited for spelling and punctuation.

20. Sam Wineburg, "Historical Thinking and Other Unnatural Acts," in *Historical Thinking and Other Unnatural Acts: Charting the Future of Teaching the Past* (Philadelphia: Temple University Press, 2001), 3–27; Lee and Ashby, "Empathy, Perspective Taking, and Rational Understanding," 37.

21. K. Anthony Appiah and Amy Gutmann, *Color Conscious: The Political Morality of Race* (Princeton, N.J.: Princeton University Press, 1996), 7.; Patricia G. Avery, "Political Socialization, Tolerance, and Sexual Identity," *Theory and Research in Social Education* 30 (Spring 2002): 190–97.

22. Linda S. Levstik and Jeanette Groth, "'Scary Thing, Being an Eighth Grader': Exploring Gender and Sexuality in a Middle School U.S. History Unit," *Theory and Research in Social Education* 30 (Spring 2002): 233–54.

23. Levstik and Groth, "Exploring Gender and Sexuality," 243.

24. Levstik and Groth, "Exploring Gender and Sexuality," 242–43. This analysis is based on both published and unpublished portions of the data collected in the study.

25. Linda S. Levstik and Keith C. Barton, *Doing History: Investigating With Children in Elementary and Middle Schools*, 2nd ed. (Mahwah, N.J.: Lawrence Erlbaum Associates, Inc., 2001), 153–70.

26. Bruce VanSledright has made in a similar point in noting that even our way of understanding the perspectives of people in the past is historically situated and that in the process of trying to understand their worldview, we necessarily impose something of our own; "From Empathic Regard to Self-Understanding," 64–66. See also Jenkins and Brickley, "Reflections on the Empathy Debate," 23–25.

27. Barton, "Historical Understanding among Elementary Children," 211–13.

28. Linda S. Levstik, "Crossing the Empty Spaces: Perspective Taking in New Zealand Adolescents' Understanding of National History," in *Historical Empathy and Perspective Taking in the Social Studies*, Eds. O.L. Davis, Jr., Elizabeth Anne Yeager, and Stuart J. Foster (Lanham, Md.: Rowman and Littlefield, 2001), 69–96.

29. Knight, "Children's Understanding of People in the Past," 207, and "Empathy," 42; emphasis in original. The centrality of empathy in current theory and research is especially clear in several recent collections of essays, including Sam Wineburg, *Historical Thinking and Other Unnatural Acts*; O.L. Davis, Jr., Elizabeth Anne Yeager, and Stuart J. Foster, Eds., *Historical Empathy and Perspective Taking in the Social Studies* (Lanham, Md.: Rowman and Littlefield, 2001); and the Spring/Summer 1998 edition of *International Journal of Social Education*. Its influence can also be seen in the recommendations of the Bradley Commission on History in Schools, *Building a History Curriculum: Guidelines for Teaching History in Schools* (Washington, D.C.: Educational Excellence Network, 1988).

30. Jonathan Harris, *Hiroshima: A Study in Science, Politics and the Ethics of War* (Menlo Park, Calif.: Addison-Wesley, 1970); Elizabeth Anne Yeager and Frans H. Doppen, "Teaching and Learning Multiple Perspectives on the Use of the Atomic Bomb: Historical Empathy in the Secondary Classroom," in *Historical Empathy and Perspective Taking in the Social Studies*, Eds. O. L. Davis, Jr., Elizabeth Anne Yeager, and Stuart J. Foster (Lanham, Md.: Rowman and Littlefield, 2001), 97–114; Chara H. Bohan and O. L. Davis, Jr., "Historical Constructions: How Social Studies Student Teachers' Historical Thinking is Reflected in Their Writing of History," *Theory and Research in Social Education* 21 (Spring 1998): 173–197.

Empathy as Caring

The women wept and I wept. I too cried for the lost people, their ancestors and mine. But I was also weeping with a curious joy. Despite the murders, rapes and suicides, we had survived. The middle passage and the auction block had not erased us. Not humiliations nor lynchings, individual cruelties nor collective oppression had been able to eradicate us from the earth. We had come through despite our own ignorance and gullibility, and the ignorance and rapacious greed of our assailants.

—Maya Angelou[1]

The kind of empathy we discussed in the last chapter is often referred to as a "cognitive" or "intellectual" tool, one that has little to do with feelings or affect, except to the extent that we rationally consider the emotions of people in the past when trying to explain their actions. Usually, the analysis of empathy stops there: Our own feelings—whether as historians, teachers, or students—are not supposed to be part of the process of historical inquiry. In fact, scholars often warn us—sternly and authoritatively—that allowing contemporary cares and concerns to creep into history is a disastrous and unforgivable sin. "Presentism!" they cry, as they warn that seeing history through our own eyes rather than those of people in the past is an immature and unacademic endeavor. Real history, we are told, does not prompt indignation over the Trail of Tears; real history involves a dispassionate analysis of Andrew Jackson's motivations in forcing Native Americans from their land. In this view, authentic history education must avoid the shoals of care, lest rational understanding be drowned out by emotion.

That really makes us sore. Empathy without care sounds like an oxymoron. Why would anyone expend energy trying to understand historical perspectives if they had no care or concern for the lives and experiences of people in the past? Care is the motivating force behind nearly all historical research, and it shapes our interest in its products; we attend to books, articles, movies, documentaries, museums, and historic sites only because we care about what we find there. Care-less history strikes us as a soulless enterprise, a constraint on motivation that warrants reconsideration of the subject's place in the curriculum. We cannot interest students in the study of history—something they enjoy outside school but often despise within it—if we reject their cares and concerns or if we dismiss their feeling

228

and emotions. Moreover, without care, we could not possibly engage them in humanistic study: Students will not bother making reasoned judgments, expanding their views of humanity, or deliberating over the common good if they don't care about those things. All our concerns—whether as historians, teachers, or students—must originate in the present, because that's all we have; anything we know or believe about history derives from the questions we ask in our own lives today. If this kind of presentism is immature, then we don't want to grow up. We care a lot more about the victims of the Trail of Tears than about Andrew Jackson's thought processes.

VARIETIES OF CARE IN HISTORY EDUCATION

As applied to history education, *care* is a term that covers a variety of related meanings, but each involves some relationship between learners and the object of study, and these relationships often include emotional commitments or feelings or personal relevance. We might say that care is a tool people use to establish their connection to the past; they use it in determining how they feel about history rather than what they think about it—although in practice, the two cannot be so easily separated. In the following section, we explore four of the most common types of caring in history. Each of these is linked to a different preposition: We can care *about* the people and events of the past when we select some as more interesting or personally meaningful than others, we can care *that* particular events took place when we react to the triumphs or tragedies of the past, we can care *for* people in history when we want to respond to suffering by the victims of injustice or oppression, and we can care *to* change our beliefs or behaviors in the present based on what we have learned from our study of the past.

Caring About

We begin with the tale of two seminars. The first was a graduate course in historiography at a large university in the upper South. Most participants were doctoral students in history, but one was a high school teacher in the region's largest city. One day the discussion turned to representations of slavery in precollegiate education. Many class members had grown up in the South, and several remembered being taught that it was a benign institution. They wondered if this approach persisted, but none had recent experience in schools, and so they turned to the history teacher (who otherwise rarely spoke up) to find out how she and her colleagues approached the subject. Her answer was disturbing, to say the least. She taught at a school whose student population was predominantly African American, and she said students often wanted to discuss the relevance of slavery for present-day race relations, but that teachers always put a stop to it, because such connections had nothing to do with the history curriculum, and discussing them just made the students agitated. She was proud that she and her colleagues refused to let students get them off the prescribed curriculum and onto "all these things that aren't really relevant"—like race relations.

The second seminar was a Paidea discussion at an urban middle school in the Midwest. About a dozen eighth graders, most of them African American, were examining a short story—set on another planet sometime in the future—that centered on the theme of racial prejudice. Conversation turned to contemporary race relations, as well as to the role of slavery in U.S. history. During a lull in students' contributions, the "guest discussant" from a nearby university mentioned that his student teachers sometimes resisted teaching about slavery or other aspects of race relations in history. He explained that these teachers argued that such subjects have no relevance to the present—they're over and done with, and there's little point in bringing them up. The eighth graders were at first incredulous, and then indignant. They had trouble accepting that anyone—certainly not teachers!—could think these topics should be ignored. The guest asked what he could tell his students, and not surprisingly, the eighth graders didn't express their answers in terms of either disciplinary history or participatory democracy. In essence, their responses came down to this: We care about these things, and they should too.

We take for granted that students will derive greater benefits from history if they care about what they're studying than if they don't. When students care about the topic of study, they are more motivated to attend to instruction, to seek out information on their own, and to reflect on what they're learning; when they don't care, they have little reason to engage in the hard intellectual work of trying to make sense of distant people and institutions.[2] We also believe educators have a moral and ethical responsibility to address topics students care about; how can we call ourselves teachers if we ignore what students want to learn? In addition, we have a responsibility to extend the range and variety of students' concerns so that they have a fuller and more complete foundation for democratic deliberation: Not only do we respond to their cares, we expect them to respond to ours, and if we don't care about the topics we subject them to, they are unlikely to do so either.

Unfortunately, little systematic research has been conducted into students' concerns about history; whether based on classroom observations or open-ended interviews, most studies have examined responses to a predetermined curriculum or set of research tasks, and as a result, students have had few opportunities to identify the topics they care about. In two of our studies, however, students enjoyed some flexibility in pursuing their own interests, and research in these classrooms provided some insight into the topics they found interesting and motivating. The first was the study of sixth graders introduced in chapter 8; those students took part in an individualized reading program in which they selected, read, and responded to a variety of works of history, historical fiction, and historical biography. Most of these students clearly cared about learning history: They were inspired, moved, and sometimes angered by what they read, and they talked about their "need to know" about the people and events of the past. Many were willing to take on more difficult reading if they thought it would result in learning something they cared about.[3]

For most students in that study, motivation to learn about the past centered on exploration of the "border areas" of human experience—times when people were forced to respond to fear, discrimination, or tragedy, or when they displayed extraordinary bravery or outrageous inhumanity. A key element of students' interest was the emotional relevance of these topics to their own lives: They imagined themselves in the circumstances they read about, speculated about their own abilities to handle such dilemmas, and compared their imagined responses to those of people in history. Even students who read works involving less extreme circumstances often focused on their personal relevance, as they talked about the careers of people in history as models for their own roles as adults.[4]

Fourth and fifth graders in our other classroom study also were interested in topics with personal connections to themselves or people they knew. At the beginning of the year, for example, they were fascinated by their teachers' "personal timelines" and eagerly volunteered to read items from them aloud. They also enjoyed creating their own personal history projects, and as they worked on them, they frequently talked about events from their lives. Students also were interested in family relations, even when the families were not their own. During a field trip to a nearby cemetery, for example, students were particularly interested in the graves of infants, as well as headstones with words like *mother* or *daughter* on them; they spent a great deal of time trying to determine the relationships among people buried near each other and often used dates to help them reconstruct the connections. Later in the year, when studying immigration, one of the issues students found most fascinating was the separation of families; they talked at length about why some people came to North America without their families, how they sent for them, and what happened to families separated on arrival.[5]

The importance of personally relevant topics was also evident in these students' interest in aspects of daily life. They enjoyed developing projects on the history of everyday life and often expressed a desire to know more about how people in the past dressed, went to school, made a living, or went about routine aspects of their lives. (Other topics they focused on while studying immigration were how ship passengers got their meals and went to the bathroom.) Also, like the sixth graders mentioned earlier, these students were interested in how people experienced dramatic events such as wars, violence, and criminal punishments. Also like the sixth graders, they continually drew comparisons with their own experiences—projecting themselves into past times and imagining how they would have felt about their circumstances.[6]

We still need a great deal more insight into the range of topics that students care about, and into how those may vary according to grade level, gender, ethnicity, previous study, or other elements of students' backgrounds. (Several of the sixth graders, for example, were not especially interested in reading about people in extreme circumstances, nor did they focus on personal responses to history.) We also need to know how teachers can build on and extend students' prior interests. However, note that in these two studies at least, most students cared about precisely the areas of history ruled out of bounds by those who characterize empathy as a purely cognitive exercise—namely, personal and emotional connections between past and present. Students cared about topics that allowed them to explore the feelings and experiences of people in the past and relate them to their own. If we hope to motivate students to study history, then surely we must begin with the topics they care about, even when those topics focus on personal and emotional issues rather than more intellectual or cognitive concerns.

Nor is the process any different among professional historians. No matter how much historians or educators wrap themselves in the trappings of disciplinary practice—weighing evidence, recognizing perspectives, building supportable interpretations, and the like—they cannot escape the fact that these practices are never entirely disinterested. No matter how fragmentary its remains, the past presents us with staggering possibilities for historical investigation, and existing historical work encompasses only a tiny fraction of the possibilities; educators, of necessity, carve out an even smaller sample for use in classrooms. Their choices inevitably represent commitments, interests, and purposes beyond practicing the skills of a historian; given the limitless range of possible topics, historians study what intrigues them, what resonates with the present, and what they consider significant—what they care about. Increased attention in recent decades to dispossessed, oppressed, silent, and silenced groups and individuals provides clear evidence that care and commitment provide the foundation for a great deal of historical research. Jacquelyn Dowd Hall, for example, imagines writing for "readers who stretch far beyond the academy; for our ancestors; for our children; and for the women's movement that makes our work possible and necessary."[7] Historians do not abandon their own cares to do history; rather, their investigations depend on what they care about, and the meanings they assign to the past are shaped at least as much by personal affinities as by disciplinary practices. If practicing historians care about what they study, why would we expect students to do less? Why would we deny them access to the motivating power of care?

Caring That

As we mentioned in chapters 2 and 5, students often have strong moral responses when learning about history. Not only do they care about certain topics, they care that certain things happened—they care that slaves were mistreated, that women were discriminated against, that millions of people were killed in the Holocaust; they also care that slavery was ended, that women won the right to vote, and that some people resisted Nazi oppression. They consider historical events and patterns that revolve around issues of justice or fairness to be particularly important, and in the United States at least, they consider the progressive expansion of rights and opportunities—greater fairness, that is—to be the central theme of the national past. However, they do not approach topics of fairness in a purely cognitive fashion; they respond differently to instances of justice and injustice than they do to technological innovations, even though they also consider such inventions historically significant. Fairness matters to them in a way other historical issues do not.

As we described in chapter 5, students in our study of fourth and fifth graders responded strongly whenever they learned of injustice in the past. They were fascinated to find that English settlers in North America either intentionally deceived Native Americans or disregarded the treaties they made with them, and they were vocal about the injustice of such practices. Similarly, when studying immigration to the United States in the 19th and early 20th century, students were shocked to find that Jews were systematically discriminated against, and this led to an animated discussion of other examples of discrimination with which they were familiar, such as violence against African Americans and gays. Throughout the year, the treatment of both women and African Americans in U.S. history repeatedly provoked strong reactions among students, who were indignant that such unfair practices took place.[8]

What was particularly notable in these responses, though, was that students' indignity at such historical practices was unaffected by their recognition that perspectives were different in the past. As we discussed in the last chapter, they came to understand that historical attitudes were different from those today, but they still rejected those attitudes—and the behaviors that stemmed from them—as unfair. This was especially clear during their study of the Salem witch trials. Although students were able to identify evidence that people considered indicative of witchcraft, and even though some understood such ideas within the wider context of religious beliefs at the time, most nonetheless made it clear that this kind of evidence was unfair. During one class period, the teacher said she simply wanted to review some key points and that students should save their opinions about fairness for later; students, though, were unwilling to do so, and they repeatedly interrupted her explanation. After it was mentioned that moles were regarded as evidence of witchcraft, for example, one student exclaimed, "But anybody could have had those!" Similarly, in discussing the floating test, a student said, "They did the stupidest thing!" The issue of using floating to determine guilt or innocence, in fact, was a major topic of interest for students throughout the unit, and they spent a great deal of time trying to figure out how it was used and explaining why it was unfair.[9]

Students often demonstrated their recognition of the perspectives of people in Salem at the same time they were rejecting those perspectives. One student, for example, said that she couldn't understand how a woman could have been convicted when "they just had all that flimsy stuff, like [not being able to say] the Ten Commandments." During simulations, as students were arguing for the innocence of family members accused of witchcraft, some took issue with the reasonableness of the evidence rather than its existence, as when one wrote, "My wife is not a witch. Maybe she is different from you, but it's not her fault.... We don't deserve to be treated like pigs, just because we don't have money." Another explained that "there are no such things as witches. Maybe he or she sinks or floats or maybe he or she escapes from [illegible] hanging. What does that prove? Nothing! You float no matter what anyway because you have air in your body." Students in these classes knew that attitudes were different in the past; they had little trouble with the cognitive version of empathy. However, they nonetheless regarded those attitudes as unjust, and they cared that people were treated unfairly as a result; this was clear not only in the unit on the Salem witch trials but during their study of women's roles in the past, discrimination against immigrants, and the Civil Rights movement.[10]

This is a good thing; in fact, it is a more admirable approach to history than one that relies solely on perspective recognition. Deliberation over the common good is synonymous with making decisions about what should be done, and history can provide practice discussing and evaluating such issues. History that seeks solely to explain rather than judge—in which there is no room for caring that—provides no such preparation; it helps students understand what happened and why, but it gives them no chance to establish responses of their own. As we discussed in the last chapter, the danger of viewing empathy solely in terms of perspective recognition is that it focuses students' attention on causes and diverts it from consequences. As Betty Bardige notes, the ability to see both sides can "allow a concern for the rights or welfare of the victimizer to obscure the experience of the victim and the reality that the two sides are not equal" and can "be used to rationalize inaction, evade decisions, or shrewdly manipulate others into complacency in the face of evil."[11] Inaction, evasion, and complacency—these are the opposites of caring that, and we believe they have no place in the history classrooms of a democracy. We cannot accept that students should examine Andrew Jackson's reasons for slaughtering Native Americans without caring that it happened. Such analysis not only flies in the face of what students want to do with history, it does little to prepare them for consideration of the common good.

Caring For

When students care about a topic in history and when they care that people were mistreated, they often wish they could react in some concrete and meaningful way; in a sense, they want somehow to care for the victims of injustice by providing support or assistance, even though they know that such time travel is impossible. In a study of eighth graders who were studying the Holocaust, for example, Betty Bardige found that students sometimes became so angry at the injustices they learned about that they "wanted to stop them immediately (even violently) or take revenge." Similarly, in our study of sixth graders, students reported that they "wanted to do something" after reading about the Holocaust and other times in history, as if the events were current or they could somehow extract retrospective justice. One student wanted to "be there to see what was happening and put a stop to it all," and another hoped to "walk right up and punch Hitler in the face."[12]

Fourth and fifth graders had similar reactions to injustice. When asked what time in history she would go back to if she could, one girl said that she would return to the time of the women's suffrage movement because "it's not fair to them, and it would be neat to try to be able to stop them [from not being able to vote] and have it like all over again." A boy chose the same time period so that he could "help the women get their rights, 'cause if they didn't do this, the women would probably still not be voting." Other students chose the time of slavery. One boy explained, "I would just really be mad at the White people, and I would try to overtake the White people and then let the Black people go." A pair of students justified their choice of the same time period in the following way:

Jenny:	I'd probably go back to—this seems really weird—but where they had slaves, but I'd like to be how I am now and not be prejudiced.
Nichole:	And help them.
Jenny:	And help these people.
Nichole:	And be with the North side, and say, "Well, we don't want you to have slaves, that's wrong, they're real people."[13]

Responses like this reflect attitudes we often associate with care in everyday life. Nel Noddings describes such caring relations as involving open, nonselective receptivity to others combined with a desire to help them or address their needs.[14] Students who imagine returning in time to correct injustices display just this kind of caring: They want to help others achieve their aims or make their lives better in the same way they might help someone in the present. Moreover, they phrase their desires in highly personal terms; although they often refer to issues of justice or fairness, such abstractions are closely tied to their desire to "help" others who after all are "real people."

It is tempting to dismiss such responses, at least as a tool for historical understanding, even as we understand and appreciate their motivation. Children and adolescents, perhaps encountering examples of outrageous inhumanity for the first time, may use such fantasies to cope with feelings of helplessness. Even as adults, many of us probably wish we could do something to correct injustices in the past (or present), and we may lament our lack of the superhuman powers needed to do so. However, we can't go back in time, and so there seems to be little point in imagining ourselves caring for people in the past; such fantasies even fail to qualify as caring relations, in Nodding's definition, because the objects of care cannot respond as part of any actual relationship. At best, these responses seem like a simulation of care, not the real thing. Indeed, this kind of empathy is often criticized because of its association with simulations in which students are asked to imagine themselves in the place of people in history—imprisoned on a slave ship, for example, or involved in trench warfare. Students cannot really share these people's feelings, and pretending to do so seems superficial, even voyeuristic. The care that results from such simulations also appears shallow and self-serving: Students may comfort themselves by caring for people they neither know nor understand and toward whom they have no real obligations. Given the drawbacks of such simulated care, many educators have advised limiting or avoiding these activities.[15]

Although we share some of these concerns, we are not ready to abandon this kind of care. Certainly, simulations do not allow students directly to experience emotions of people in history. Neither they nor we can know what someone in a World War I trench felt like, because we know the simulation will be over in a few minutes, whereas a soldier at the time had no idea if he would live or die. A simulation that purports to give direct access to the feelings (or thoughts) of people in the past is simply mistaken; it's like asking students to diagram a sentence to improve their writing—there's no connection between means and ends. However, students' desire to care for people in the past may help them achieve a different kind of goal. Current scholarship on cognition recognizes the inseparable relationship of thought and feeling in cognitive development.[16] Although there is relatively little research on this aspect of history education, research in other areas of the social studies suggests that affective engagement leads to "rational" or cognitive payoffs.

In reviewing studies aimed at altering biased beliefs, for example, Nancye McCrary notes that providing accurate information without attention to affect rarely leads to changes in stereotypical perceptions; learned preferences for homogeneity make it unlikely that decontextualized information will change emotionally charged and entrenched ideas. When educational experiences are geared toward developing specific performances or skills—without attention to affective dimensions of the subject matter—they often fail either to change attitudes or behaviors or to support transfer of skills to other settings. On the other hand, aesthetically and affectively mediated information appears to increase the likelihood that learners will consider alternative perspectives. In her own research, McCrary presented adults with a computer simulation in which they imagined their behavior, as parents, in response to events in the life of a gay teenager. Each response choice was linked to relevant information, including statements by gay teens, parents, and professionals, as well as statistical information; other links within the program included resources (books, Internet sites, and organizations), historical accounts, and contemporary news articles.[17]

Participants in McCrary's study reacted to the simulation in strongly emotional ways, and to understand the characters' experiences, they often sought personal connections with their own experiences. Notably, they transferred feelings of caring for others in their lives to the events of the simulation—not a surprising reaction, given their position as parents within the simulation. In follow-up interviews, though, the changes they identified in themselves as a result of the experience were not primarily emotional ones; instead, they considered themselves to be better informed about issues facing gay youth, including homophobia, depression, and suicide; they also considered themselves to have developed a greater sense of agency or the ability to "speak up" in situations in which they had previously remained silent. McCrary concludes that participants' learning was motivated by their attempts to make personal connections with the story's protagonist.[18]

This is different than asking participants to pretend to be a character in the way some simulations ask students to pretend to be slaves or soldiers. Note that the purpose of the simulation was not to provide access to anyone else's feelings. The realism of the story, though, led participants to engage in emotional responses of their own. Because they imagined their own caring reactions to the character's plight, they felt a need to learn about issues facing gay teens. Of course, we don't know if they actually were any better informed (or able to speak up) as a result of the simulation, but it seems clear they were more willing to attend to the information presented—to care about the issues—because of their need to care for another person. The imagined caring relation, then, was neither the purpose nor the end of instruction; rather, it was a tool for making a set of social experiences more salient. Having students huddle under a classroom desk (or read historical literature) so that they will experience feelings that lead them to care for people in history seems entirely defensible if it is used in a similar way—to develop a level of motivation that inspires them to become more engaged with the subject matter. Unfortunately, such experiences too often become ends in themselves, and students' feelings of care for people in history result in nothing more than complacency (because they feel good about themselves for caring) or frustration (because they are unable to act on what they feel). Only if we recognize that this element of empathy truly is a tool, not a self-contained purpose, will it play a meaningful role in history education.[19]

Caring To

The ultimate purpose of history education, in our view, is to enable students to take action in the present, and if they are going to take action, they must care to do so—that is, they must be willing, based on what they have learned, to make changes in their own values, attitudes, beliefs, or behavior. As we emphasized in chapter 2, this does not mean leading them to any particular set of conclusions about what should (or should not) have taken place in the past or to any specific positions on contemporary affairs. The only outcomes we can legitimately aim toward are those associated with participatory democracy. As a result of their study of history, that is, students should be willing to take part in deliberations over the common good, and they should be willing to make reasoned judgments and to draw on an expanded view of humanity in doing so. This, in a sense, is the ultimate test of humanistic history education: If students learn about the past in the ways we have suggested but decline to put their learning into practice, then all is for naught. If they do not care to use history in the present, then we should put away our packets of primary sources and allow students to double up on their study of French or chemistry. As a colleague of ours says, there's no point in teaching students how to dial 911 if they're not going to do it when there's an emergency.

Our image of humanistic history education is this: Students deliberate with others over their mutual concerns about improving society. In doing so, they systematically evaluate evidence, and they examine the historical roots of contemporary issues. They demonstrate a commitment to the multiple communities of which they are a part. They work together to develop criteria for more and less defensible courses of action. They share information freely. They pay attention both to individual agency and institutional constraints. They are inspired by a belief in freedom and progress, but they are careful to consider how this belief might blind them to alternative experiences and unintended consequences. They listen to each other, taking seriously ideas that are different than their own. They care what happens to others. That's our vision, and we wish we could describe the many studies that illustrate students' willingness to take part in such deliberations, as evidence that they really care to do such things.

We wish we could, but we can't. We've described studies suggesting that students can engage in many kinds of historical study, but we can point to few that demonstrate their willingness to apply that learning to the present. In interviews, we have sometimes heard students say they are willing to do this. For example, when Kathy and Curtis, two students in our study of fourth and fifth graders, were asked why they thought it would be important to know about history, they brought up the Civil Rights movement, which they said was one of the most important events in history. Kathy explained that it was important to know about the treatment of African Americans in the past "because we don't want to treat Black people like that today," and she suggested that if she didn't know about the Civil Rights movement, "maybe I would be really mean to Black people." Curtis agreed and added that if people didn't know about immigration in the past, they "would probably treat the immigrants mean and stuff because they were from another country and talk another language." Similarly, ReeJane and Eugenie, two eighth graders who had been studying women's roles in the 19th century and said they would be interested in the history of other cultures, pointed to the value of understanding multiple perspectives. ReeJane explained, "Like if you're ever having a discussion with anybody about women and how they're *aren't* treated fairly or about how they *are* treated fairly, then having more knowledge about other cultures you bring that into play, not just American women." Eugenie agreed:

> You don't have to have specifically your own perspective; you can step back and see a big picture so that other people's ideas, you may not always agree with them, and you can have an intelligent discussion with them while disagreeing, but you can understand what they're talking about and have a good discussion that involves all sorts of things besides your view and their view and just like this *versus* thing.[20]

These comments are encouraging; they suggest not only that students are willing to apply what they have learned from history but that they have consciously reflected on the need to do so. We fear, though, that when discussion of the common good turns to more difficult or controversial topics—particularly those that threaten students' deeply held beliefs or the interests of their community—they may be less willing to act on these good intentions. One telling example of the difficulty in asking students to apply history to controversial issues in the present comes from Northern Ireland. Alan McCully relates his observation of a secondary classroom, in a school in a predominantly Unionist town, in which the teacher used a variety of materials to help students understand the causes of the 1916 Easter Rising, as well as the decision by British authorities to execute rebel leaders. In their class discussion, it was evident that students understood not only the reasoning of the British but the reaction of the Irish at the time; the actions of the British military fueled the Irish sense of injustice and swelled support for Sinn Fein. These students understood the perspective of Irish Republicans, that is, even though it was contrary to the political outlook of their own present-day community.[21]

The teacher, however, took the lesson one step further; he asked whether the events of 1916 might be analogous with those of the 1980s, when support for the Provisional Irish Republican Army increased in the wake of the Hunger Strikes. He didn't tell students the two events necessarily were analogous; in fact, he suggested that such a comparison was contentious and open for challenge. Many students, however, completely refused to engage with the issue. Those who spoke up rejected any similarities in the two situations, but more important, a significant number of students—even those who had enthusiastically taken part in the prior discussion—were unwilling to recognize the exercise as a legitimate one. As McCully puts it, "It was as if mention of contemporary events had caused an emotional wall to ascend. This wall appeared impervious to the critical thinking that had been nurtured earlier."[22]

Although the issues would be different, students (and teachers) in the United States are likely to have similar difficulty using what they have learned in history to examine controversial current issues. Not everyone wants to engage in reasoned judgment, develop an expanded view of humanity, or deliberate over the common good; many would rather stick to their own unexamined opinions, personal prejudices, and private desires. Asking them to do otherwise will not be easy, but we hope teachers will be willing to accept the challenge. Perhaps someday we will have studies showing that learning about medieval heretics makes students more willing to listen to dissenters today, that drawing conclusions from primary sources makes them better able to evaluate government policies, and that outrage over the Trail of Tears prompts outrage over contemporary racial oppression. The fact that we do not yet have such evidence is no reason to turn our backs on the hope that students will care to act on what they learn. Without such hope, history can only be studied "for its own sake," which is no sake at all.

THE PLACE OF CARE IN THE TOOL KIT OF HISTORY EDUCATION

The fact that care is so frequently dismissed as a legitimate component of historical study suggests that it must have serious constraints as a tool for making sense of the past. Such perceptions, however, seem to arise primarily from fears that care will be used in isolation, with no attention to other tools of historical understanding. Some educators, for example, worry that students will be so overwhelmed by feelings of sympathy for those they study that they will be unable to engage in rational analysis of historical actions—in other words, care will be not be accompanied by perspective recognition, which requires that we look at others from their own viewpoint, not ours. Others are convinced that using the past to make sense of the present will simply reinforce contemporary beliefs and practices—in other words, care will not be accompanied by inquiry, which requires that conclusions be grounded in evidence.

Perhaps these are dangers of using care as a tool for history education, but they are by no means insurmountable ones, as long as educators recognize that care is intimately bound up with tools such as perspective recognition, inquiry, or various kinds of narrative. Although care can be separated out for analytical purposes, in practice we can hardly imagine it functioning as a independent tool. Stories are the context for care; inquiry is its outcome; and perspective recognition is, perhaps, its object. Trying to develop care without these others tools would be folly, and we have rarely encountered teachers who tried to do so. The greater danger—and the more common one—is that the other tools will be used without care: Students will be asked to learn stories they don't care about, to inquire into events without caring that they occurred, to examine the perspectives of people without caring for them—and to study history without caring to use it in the present. In fact, this is a concise description of most history education in the United States—study without care. For teachers, it's a safe approach: Students won't get agitated, parents won't complain, and no one will question the teacher's competence.

However, just as ignoring perspective leaves historical inquirers open to misplaced sympathy, ignoring care leaves them vulnerable to indifference. Without some sense of care—of attaching personal significance to the human consequences of the events of the past—one perspective is very like another. If we only want to explain in rational terms what happened, then each event is the same, because all can be understood in terms of the perspectives of those involved. What would motivate a student to engage in perspective recognition if, in the end, there is no difference between Gandhi and Hitler, slave owner and abolitionist, Pol Pot and Nelson Mandela? Imagine (or remember) the tedium of investigating topics about which no one cared—topics that seemed to mean nothing in the present. No decent historians would squander their time so recklessly. Even if they did so, the results would likely be dreary, dull, and pointless. Just as important, they would contribute little to democracy. Care is the tool that makes it all worthwhile, the mechanism for rendering history meaningful. It should be an indispensable part of the subject's tool kit.

CONCLUSIONS

We have argued that *empathy* is a term that traditionally has referred to two separate skills—perspective recognition and care—and that much of the debate over the term's applicability to history education has resulted from a failure to separate the two meanings. Perceptions have become so hopelessly muddled that we are in agreement with those who prefer to drop the term altogether and replace it with something more focused. Unlike many history educators, though, our desire is not accompanied by a rejection of empathy's emotional component. Rather, we consider emotional connection, in the form of care, a critical tool for making sense of the past, one that should be part of all history education—although preferably under its own name rather than subsumed within the confusing label of empathy. Professional historians care, genealogists care, people reflecting on their own lives care; it makes no sense that students should not also care.

Care is the tool by which students—or any of us—make personal connections to history, and it has at least four components. *Caring about* refers to our historical interests, the topics about which we want (and feel we need) to learn. *Caring that* is the basis for moral judgments about the past, our reactions to the consequences of historical events. *Caring for* is perhaps the most emotionally laden component of this tool; it refers to the desire to help people in the past, even though such assistance is impossible, and it can be a powerful incentive to engage in the other aspects of historical study. Finally, *caring to* refers to the willingness to apply what has been learned in history to problems in the present; this kind of caring should be the endpoint of historical study in a democracy, as students deliberate over the common good, listen carefully to people with varied perspectives and backgrounds, and engage in reasoned judgments.

Some educators might prefer abandoning issues of care and reconstituting history as a purely academic, cognitive, or intellectual discipline, one focusing solely on perspective recognition, particularly if they fear that care will overwhelm more dispassionate analysis of the past. However, in our view, the task is not to define history in such a way that either perspective recognition or care is abandoned, but rather to maintain a productive tension between the two. Students are more likely to find historical study interesting and challenging if they have access to both these tools than if they try to employ either in isolation. Moreover, although we can attempt to study history without caring, we are unsure why anyone would want to; each of the varieties of care in this chapter is necessary if we hope for history education to make a difference in the lives of students or in society.[23]

ENDNOTES

1. Maya Angelou, *All God's Children Need Traveling Shoes* (New York: Vintage Books, 1991), 207.
2. On the importance of such motivation for conceptual learning generally, see Giyoo Hatano and Kayoko Inagaki, "Desituating Cognition Through the Construction of Conceptual Knowledge," in *Context and Cognition: Ways of Learning and Knowing*, Eds. Paul Light and George Butterworth (Hillsdale, N.J.: Lawrence Erlbaum Associates, Inc., 1993), 115–133.
3. Linda S. Levstik, "The Relationship between Historical Response and Narrative in a Sixth-Grade Classroom," *Theory and Research in Social Education* 19 (Winter 1986): 1–19.
4. Levstik, "The Relationship between Historical Response and Narrative," 9–13.
5. Keith C. Barton, "Historical Understanding Among Elementary Children" (Ed.D. diss., University of Kentucky, Lexington, 1994), 178–79.
6. Barton, "Historical Understanding Among Elementary Children," 180–84.
7. James R. Green, *Taking History to Heart: The Power of the Past in Building Social Movements* (Amherst, Mass.: University of Massachusetts Press, 2000), 9.
8. Barton, "Historical Understanding Among Elementary Children," 184–88.
9. Barton, "Historical Understanding Among Elementary Children," 186.
10. Barton, "Historical Understanding Among Elementary Children," 210–11.
11. Betty Bardige, "Things So Finely Human: Moral Sensibilities at Risk in Adolescence," in *Mapping the Moral Domain*, Eds. Carol Gilligan, Janie Victoria Ward, and Jill McLean Taylor (Cambridge, Mass.: Harvard University Press, 1988), 108.
12. Bardige, "Things So Finely Human," 95; Levstik, "The Relationship Between Historical Response and Narrative," 8.
13. Barton, "Historical Understanding Among Elementary Children," 187–88.
14. Nel Noddings, *The Challenge to Care in Schools: An Alternative Approach to Education* (New York: Teachers College Press, 1992), 15–16.

15. For example, Stuart J. Foster, "Historical Empathy in Theory and Practice," in *Historical Empathy and Perspective Taking in the Social Studies*, Eds. O. L. Davis, Jr., Elizabeth Anne Yeager, and Stuart J. Foster (Lanham, Md.: Rowman and Littlefield, 2001), 170. On the voyeuristic qualities of learning about others, see Bardige, "Things So Finely Human," 103, and Richard Beach, "Students' Resistance to Engagement with Multicultural Literature," in *Reading across Cultures: Teaching Literature in a Diverse Society*, Eds. Theresa Rogers and Anna O. Soter (New York: Teachers College Press, 1997), 79–80. For a review of criticisms of simulations in teaching about the Holocaust, see Simone A. Schweber, *Making Sense of the Holocaust: Lessons from Classroom Practice* (New York: Teachers College Press, 2004).

16. Jerome S. Bruner, *Acts of Meaning* (Cambridge, Mass.: Harvard University Press, 1990); Elliot W. Eisner, *Cognition and Curriculum Reconsidered* (New York: Teachers College Press, 1994); Walter R. Fisher, "Narration, Knowledge, and the Possibility of Wisdom," in *Rethinking Knowledge: Reflections across the Disciplines*, Eds. Robert F. Goodman and Walter R. Fisher (Albany: State University of New York Press, 1995), 169–192; Barbara L. Martin and Charles M. Reigeluth, "Affective Education and the Affective Domain: Implications for Instructional-Design Theories and Models," in *Instructional-Design Theories and Models*, Vol. 2: *A New Paradigm of Instructional Theory*, Ed. Charles M. Reigeluth (Mahwah, N.J.: Lawrence Erlbaum Associates, Inc., 1999), 485–509.

17. Nancye McCrary, "Narrative Simulation as Instruction to Affect Bias and Discrimination" (Ed.D. diss., University of Kentucky, 2001), 219–221; "Investigating the Use of Narrative in Affective Learning on Issues of Social Justice," *Theory and Research in Social Education* 30 (Spring 2002): 255–273.

18. McCrary, "Investigating the Use of Narrative," 263, 267–68, 270–71.

19. Simone Schweber's research in secondary history classrooms also suggests that the emotional salience of simulations can motivate students to learn about the Holocaust and consider complex moral dilemmas, but she cautions that such simulations often fail to live up to their potential; Schweber, *Making Sense of the Holocaust*.

20. Keith C. Barton, "'You'd Be Wanting to Know about the Past': Social Contexts of Children's Historical Understanding in Northern Ireland and the USA," *Comparative Education* 37 (February 2001): 96; Linda S. Levstik and Jeanette Groth, "'Scary Thing, Being an Eighth Grader': Exploring Gender and Sexuality in a Middle School U.S. History Unit," *Theory and Research in Social Education* 30 (Spring 2002): 246.

21. Alan McCully, Nigel Pilgrim, Alaeric Sutherland, and Tara McNinn, "'Don't Worry, Mr. Trimble. We Can Handle It': Balancing the Rational and the Emotional in the Teaching of Contentious Topics," *Teaching History* 106 (March 2002): 6–12.

22. McCully et al., "Balancing the Rational and the Emotional," 7.

23. On the complexity of teachers' ideas about the components of empathy—including their embrace of both intellectual and affective dimensions of the concept—see Deborah L. Cunningham, "Teaching Historical Empathy: British Teachers' Practices and Perspectives on the 'Invisible Skill,'" paper presented at the annual meeting of the American Educational Research Association, 21–25 April 2003; "Professional Practice and Perspectives in the Teaching of Historical Empathy" (D.Phil. diss., Oxford University, Oxford, England, 2003).

Teacher Education
and the Purposes of History

To produce a mighty book, you must choose a mighty theme. No great and enduring volume can ever be written on the flea, though many there be that have tried it.

—*Herman Melville*[1]

The two of us spend much of our professional time preparing history and social studies teachers. We have taught thousands of students in our methods courses, along with hundreds more in workshops or graduate classes. We know this includes a great many success stories—teachers who provide exciting instruction for their students in ways consistent with what we have taught them. Others have adopted our suggestions less wholeheartedly but with selective enthusiasm for practices we consider important—good literature, or inquiry, or conflicting viewpoints, or open-ended writing. Yet we fear these success stories may pale in comparison with the number of teachers who have ignored our ideas completely. As we look around, we have to admit that many classrooms (the majority? the vast majority?) show little evidence of the curricular and instructional perspectives we have tried to promote. Around the country, we have hundreds of colleagues who prepare teachers much as we do (many with greater ability and enthusiasm, no doubt), yet we fear their experiences may be the same as ours—plenty of individual success stories but no widespread or systematic changes in teaching.

Why is this? How can our efforts at developing teachers' understanding of instructional methods leave so little imprint on classroom practice? Why aren't all children using a variety of sources to develop interpretations of history? Surely teachers who have taken courses from us or our colleagues know that history is an interpretive, inquiry-oriented subject involving multiple perspectives, and they must know how to implement the practice in the classroom, at least in an introductory way. Yet maybe knowing isn't enough. From a sociocultural perspective, after all, what people know—conceived of as individual cognition—is less important than how they act purposefully (and how they use cultural tools to do so). To understand why teachers engage in the practices they do, perhaps we need to turn to the socially situated purposes that guide their actions. While we are at it,

maybe we should ask ourselves, as teacher educators, whether we are helping them explore themes "mighty" enough to lead to the kinds of instruction we hope for.

TEACHER KNOWLEDGE AND EDUCATION REFORM

Marilyn Cochran-Smith and Susan Lytle note that over the last two decades, teacher learning has been at the forefront of efforts at improving
education and that "it has been more or less assumed that teachers who
know more teach better." This has not always been so: Perspectives on the
teacher's role in improving instruction have undergone a number of
changes over the past half century. Behaviorists of the 1950s, for example,
emphasized the transformative potential of teaching machines and programmed instruction; from their viewpoint, the teacher was little more
than a manager of the classroom who needed little specialized knowledge.
Similarly, in the 1960s, a variety of national organizations created and
field tested new reading materials, artifact kits, and classroom activities
that focused on the concepts and procedures of the academic disciplines.
Although rarely dismissing teacher knowledge directly, these movements
clearly hoped to promote instructional reform by improving curricular
materials rather than by addressing teachers' ideas; teachers were responsible primarily for implementing the innovations developed by others. By
the mid-1970s, reform efforts (and much academic research) focused less
on curricular innovation and more on "teaching behaviors"—the set of
generic skills that were believed to result in higher levels of student
achievement (such as pacing, wait time, feedback, and so on). Although
this approach put teachers at the center of instructional improvement, it
deemphasized their role as knowledgeable professionals and centered instead on changing observable behavior through structured systems of
feedback.[2]
  Over the last 20 years, though, most theory and research on teachers' education and professional development has focused on precisely the area neglected in previous work—their active role in designing and implementing
instruction. This work has been grounded in the assumption that teachers
are ultimately responsible for what goes in their classrooms; they serve as
"brokers" or "gatekeepers" who select from and transform the array of possible curricula, resources, and instructional strategies to provide concrete
learning activities for students. As Stephen Thornton puts it, "As gatekeepers, teachers make the day-to-day decisions concerning both the subject
matter and the experiences to which students have access and the nature of
that subject matter and those experiences." If teachers' decisions shape
their students' curricular and instructional experiences, then it seems logical to assume that we need to understand the thinking behind those decisions, and a large body of research has been devoted to this topic. Although
this research has employed a number of different theoretical frameworks

and conceptual terms—including *personal theories, practical knowledge, interactive decision making, frames of reference, pedagogical reasoning,* and others—all have shared a concern with getting "inside teachers' heads" to explain how they make the decisions that determine classroom practice.[3]

One of the most influential frameworks for understanding what teachers know and believe (the distinction between the two is elusive) has been that of Lee Shulman. Shulman argues that that a critical component of teachers' expertise is their pedagogical content knowledge. Whereas some reformers insist that teachers need greater content preparation in their subject (usually conceived of as more coursework in a specific academic discipline), and others argue for greater exposure to educational theories and methods, Shulman maintains that the distinctive body of knowledge for teaching lies at the intersection of content and pedagogy. Teachers must understand the structures and principles of their disciplines, and they must also know how to transform disciplinary ideas in ways that will make sense to students. Much of the recent research on the thought and practice of history teachers has been consistent with this conception of teacher's thinking, particularly in its emphasis on teachers' understanding of the underlying conceptual structures of the history and their implications for classroom practice. As Bruce VanSledright succinctly notes, most research in the field has assumed that "history teachers need to possess deep *knowledge of their discipline* and robust understandings of *how to teach it.*" From this viewpoint, if teachers know that history involves the interpretation of evidence among members of a community of inquiry, and if they learn to apply that knowledge in the classroom, then presumably they will engage students in inquiry-based historical interpretation. Indeed, the two of us have written an entire book based precisely on that assumption: In *Doing History: Investigating With Children in Elementary and Middle School*s, we set out to help teachers understand history as an interpretive and inquiry-oriented endeavor, and we described classroom practices consistent with that ideal. However, the question remains: Is it true? Does this knowledge and understanding affect classroom practice?[4]

THE PEDAGOGICAL CONTENT KNOWLEDGE OF HISTORY TEACHERS

Several studies have investigated the extent to which teachers' understanding of the interpretive nature of history is consistent with that of historians, and each of these studies has found that teachers typically have little acquaintance with such disciplinary concerns as the context, authorship, and perspective of historical documents. Chara Bohan and O. L. Davis, Jr., for example, gave three secondary student teachers a set of primary source accounts of the bombing of Hiroshima; they asked teachers to read the documents, think aloud as they did so, and use the documents to write a narrative account of the event. On the basis of responses to this task, Bohan and Davis concluded that all three were unfamiliar with the process of creating historical interpretations: Participants failed to consider the source of the documents, they saw each as a simple statement of fact, and they failed to cite sources in writing their accounts. In a related study, Melanie Gillaspie and Davis gave a similar task to three elementary student teachers. They found that only one of the three compared the source accounts to each other or referred to them in the written narrative; one participant made no reference to the sources at all, and the third failed to explain the accounts in detail or to question their perspectives.[5]

Elizabeth Yeager and Davis also found varied levels of disciplinary understanding among both elementary and secondary teachers. They asked three secondary and three elementary student teachers to read and compare conflicting accounts of the battle at Lexington Green, just as Sam Wineburg had done with historians and high school students in an earlier study. Only one of the secondary participants noted previous experience with issues of historical interpretation (he considered history his hobby), and he read the documents much as the historians in Wineburg's study had done—he looked for the authors' assumptions, compared the audiences to which the documents were addressed, and considered the contexts and circumstances of their production. Another secondary participant more closely resembled Wineburg's high school students: He simply gathered and summarized information from the documents and saw little subtext. The third was just beginning to see problems of bias as she worked through the exercise; although she merely summarized the documents initially, she eventually began to compare them and to speculate about their authorship and potential bias. Although the three elementary teachers had more limited backgrounds in academic history, they demonstrated patterns of historical understanding nearly identical to those of the secondary teachers: One summarized the documents with little comparison or attention to context or subtext; one explored the authors' assumptions, purposes, and audiences; and a third began by summarizing but developed a more critical and interpretive perspective as she worked through the set of documents.[6]

When Yeager and Davis gave the same task to 15 practicing secondary teachers, they found three distinct profiles among participants. Some read the documents for evidence of each author's purpose and perspective; some were concerned primarily with determining on which "side" each document fell and hoped to be able to uncover accurate information about "what actually happened"; and still others, again like the high school students in Wineburg's study, simply gathered information with little attention to comparison or subtext. One of the teachers in this third category even equated credibility with interest and readability—she considered a passage form Howard Fast's *April Morning* more credible than other sources "because it was the 'most fun.... It has vivid details, and it's full of emotion.'"[7]

Although these studies do not indicate that teachers have a uniformly impoverished understanding of history (and the small sample sizes limit generalizability), they do suggest that attending to teachers' disciplinary understanding may be a critical task for teacher educators, as implied in the perspective of Shulman and others. If teachers do not understand the nature of historical knowledge, then they cannot design meaningful learning experiences for students, because they will not know what it is that students need to learn (much less how to help them learn it). A teacher who thinks sources can be evaluated on how "fun" they are surely is not qualified to teach history, and as teacher educators (whether in history departments or colleges of education), we must help our students develop more sophisticated and accurate understandings of what history is all about. A "deep knowledge of their discipline" would seem to be a prerequisite for history teachers, and its development a major task for those of us who educate them. Encouragingly, though, the study of student teachers by Yeager and Davis suggests this task may not be as difficult as it seems: Two of their six participants developed more sophisticated understandings of historical evidence and interpretation simply through participating in one research exercise! Perhaps extended exposure to historical content is less important to the growth of pedagogical content knowledge than intensive engagement in a few well-chosen tasks that allow teachers to reflect on the epistemological basis of historical knowledge.

PEDAGOGICAL CONTENT KNOWLEDGE AND CLASSROOM PRACTICE

Although the studies described in the previous section suggest teachers need greater understanding of the interpretive nature of history, there is some reason to question whether sophisticated disciplinary understanding, even when combined with pedagogical knowledge, will have an impact on instruction. Bruce VanSledright, for example, conducted a case study of an experienced secondary history teacher (a 16-year veteran of the classroom) who had just completed a doctorate in history. In her graduate studies—and particularly in her dissertation research—she had come to understand the complicated nature of historical facts and evidence, and she recognized the central role of interpretation in the creation of historical knowledge. In addition, this teacher's apprenticeship into the historical profession centered on "the new sociocultural history," or "history from the bottom up," a perspective that reflects one of the discipline's central concerns in recent decades. Although one might question whether her understanding of the discipline was as thorough as that of someone immersed in the profession for a longer period of time, her level of disciplinary content knowledge was certainly all that could be asked for in a teacher (few are going to complete a doctorate in history, after all), and her extensive classroom experience suggests that she should have had no problem putting her sophisticated knowledge into practice in the classroom.[8]

In fact, her teaching reflected little of this disciplinary understanding, and her students had few opportunities to engage with historical knowledge as she had done. Her instruction focused primarily on enabling students to reproduce a single, consensus-oriented account of the U.S. past, one that was outlined in the district curriculum and assessed, primarily through multiple-choice items, on a required district test at the end of the year. Students spent much of their time learning the content of long review lists that centered on factual information about people, places, and events. Although she addressed multiple perspectives in the past, and although she reminded students of the difference between fact and interpretation (frequently beginning sentences with phrases such as, "Some historians believe …"), she nonetheless treated the textbook as though it were an authoritative and unproblematic source of factual information. Students did not learn that the text itself was an interpretation, nor were they asked to evaluate the historical claims found in that or any other source. There were no questions about where the evidence for historical accounts came from, and there was little work with primary sources. Even the teacher's concern with history from the bottom up was limited to a single day spent lecturing about women and minorities during the Federal Period. Students' exposure to the teachers' "fact/interpretation" distinction, then, was spent primarily on the factual side of the dichotomy. VanSledright concludes that "by itself, the possession of deep *and* current subject-matter knowledge arrayed with rich pedagogical experience provides no promise of an unproblematic translation to the high school classroom."[9]

VanSledright's study is not alone in questioning the connection between disciplinary knowledge and classroom practice. G. Williamson McDiarmid interviewed 14 students (8 of whom planned to teach high school history) enrolled in an undergraduate historiography course. At the beginning of the course, students recognized that bias in historical accounts existed, but they thought such bias was simply the result of the personal beliefs or agendas of authors and that all historical texts were equally unreliable. After taking the course, about half the students had developed more complex notions of the interpretive nature of history—recognizing, for example, that historical knowledge is always tentative and that history is invariably seen through the preoccupations of the present. However, although students' disciplinary knowledge increased, their beliefs about teaching and learning history remained unchanged: They thought that lecture was the most appropriate method for teaching history and that a good history teacher was one who told "good stories" and wrote lecture notes on the board. They did not think that high school students would be motivated to engage in the kind of interpretive work they had done in their historiography class or be capable of doing so; they thought learners simply needed to be told what happened and why.[10]

The research by VanSledright and by McDiarmid points to the lack of a straightforward connection between disciplinary knowledge and pedagogy, but still more shocking is a pattern consistently found in research on history and social studies education: Even teachers' conceptions of pedagogy have little connection to their teaching. In study after study, teachers articulate a view of instruction that emphasizes active student learning, multiple viewpoints, and construction of knowledge. However, a different picture emerges when they are observed teaching or when they describe their classroom practices. What teachers actually do is cover the content of textbooks or curriculum guides through teacher-directed instruction and careful control of classroom activity and discourse. Even when teachers' ideas about the subject differ from each other, or when they have vastly difference levels of background or expertise, they wind up teaching in remarkably similar ways, and these often have little connection to their espoused beliefs.[11]

Stephanie van Hover and Elizabeth Yeager, for example, conducted a case study of a 2nd-year, high school history teacher who had graduated from an intensive certification program emphasizing historical interpretation, inquiry, and the use of a variety of historical sources and perspectives. This teacher was considered one of the program's strongest students, and she also held an undergraduate degree in history. In interviews, she demonstrated a clear understanding of historical thinking and inquiry: She saw history as an interpretive discipline that involved contextualization of actions and motivations, believed that history should be analyzed from multiple perspectives, and thought the subject should be taught through inquiry exercises, problem-solving activities, debate, discussion, and cooperative learning.[12]

In all respects, this teacher's pedagogical content knowledge seemed exemplary. Her instruction, however, bore almost no resemblance to that knowledge. She did not encourage perspective-taking, interpretation, or open-ended historical thinking or inquiry. Instead, classroom activities were heavily teacher centered. She lectured frequently—recounting a single, univocal narrative of major events in U.S. history—and students took notes from the outline of textbook chapters. When she included simulations or other group activities, she told students what conclusions they should draw, and she contradicted those who disagreed with her. Although she credited her social studies methods course with influencing her knowledge of how to teach history, she applied almost none of what she learned in that course to actual practice.[13]

As teacher educators, our commonsense explanation for this failure to influence instructional practices is to point to our own limited impact on prospective teachers. We have only a brief time to help them develop the pedagogical content knowledge they will need, typically during a social studies methods course, supplemented by other education courses that may also be relevant to instructional practices in history. (At the secondary level, teachers may also take one or more courses in historical methods as part of a history major or area of concentration; other history courses may also address the interpretive nature of history, although not usually methods for teaching it at the precollegiate level.) This brief set of experiences seems too thin to overcome the "apprenticeship of observation"—the 12 or more years students have spent watching teachers perform their daily tasks, a time during which they have developed an image of teaching that revolves around teacher control and the coverage of textbook-based information. The content of students' university courses, particularly in education, seems to have little effect on their ideas about teaching, particularly when the practices they observe in field settings contradict that content. Within history and social studies education, the view that university courses have a limited impact on teachers is supported by numerous studies showing that their ideas about education derive from a wide variety of sources, including not only their own experiences as students but their personalities, experiences with pupils, institutional factors, and the perspectives of family members, colleagues, and cooperating teachers.[14]

This can be a fairly pessimistic viewpoint, because it implies that what we do in teacher education programs has little impact on the development of teachers. When this perspective does not descend into despair, its implication seems to be that we need to redouble our efforts to develop students' pedagogical content knowledge: We have to design better history courses, with a greater emphasis on the nature of the discipline, we have to do a better job challenging students' ideas in our methods courses and helping them construct new understandings of how to teach, and we have to select field placements carefully so that students see good models of the kinds of instruction we hope to promote. Only such thorough and intensive efforts seem to provide hope of developing a clear and consistent body of pedagogical content knowledge in our students.

However, we believe this approach may be misguided, or at least insufficient. As the studies by VanSledright, McDiarmand, and van Hover and Yeager show, understanding the interpretive nature of history has little impact on teachers' instructional ideas or practices. Moreover, as we noted previously, studies consistently show that teachers who have learned a variety of pedagogical practices still fail to implement them in the classroom. There simply does not seem to be any evidence that teacher knowledge is the variable that predicts classroom practice. That is not to say such knowledge is unimportant; recognizing history's interpretive nature and knowing how to represent the subject to students is undoubtedly a necessary condition for teaching history interpretively. If teachers do not understand the underlying premises of the subject, and if they do not know how to go about implementing inquiry, or discussing historical controversies, or locating primary sources, then it is inconceivable that they will actually do so. However, this knowledge, by itself, does not appear to be a sufficient condition for transforming educational practices in history. Teachers can understand history as a discipline and know how to teach it in the ways recommended by reformers and still not do so.

THE PRACTICE OF HISTORY TEACHING

The emphasis on pedagogical content knowledge—whether conceptualized in Shulman's terms or through alternative frameworks such as personal theories, practical knowledge, or pedagogical reasoning—may be an unproductive way of thinking about instructional practice, because it assumes that teachers' behavior is primarily the result of individual cognition. From a sociocultural perspective, attention should be directed not just toward the private ideas teachers are believed to "possess" as individuals but toward the actions they engage in as members of social groups, as well as the socially situated purposes that guide those actions. Pamela Grossman, Peter Smagorinsky, and Sheila Valencia, for example, have argued that the individualistic focus of research on teaching should give way to a concern with the "predominant value systems and social practices that characterize the settings in which learning to teach occurs." These values and practices provide direction for beginners who hope to become part of the system of schooling, and they necessarily constrain the choices available to them. From this perspective, learning to teach is not a matter of applying individually constructed knowledge—whether developed in university coursework or through a lifetime of experiences—but a process of appropriating the historically and culturally situated tools and practices of school settings.[15] To this point in the book, we have emphasized how the historical actions demanded of students are situated in broader contexts; we now turn to cultural expectations for teachers' actions.

What are the predominant social practices in classrooms? The empirical evidence on this question, particularly in the fields of history and social studies, is clear: Teachers are expected to (a) cover the curriculum and (b) maintain control. In explaining the nature of their classroom practices, teachers repeatedly return to the centrality of these two activities. The need to cover a prescribed curriculum is the most common way of explaining instruction, both in published research and our own experience: A curriculum exists (whether in textbooks, district curriculum guides, or state standards), and the teacher's primary job is to ensure that students are exposed to that curriculum—principals expect it, parents support it, and teachers themselves accept coverage as their chief duty. Improving students' comprehension, developing their motivation, and enhancing their ability to work together may be important, but as instructional activities, they are distinctly secondary to delivering a prescribed curriculum (even though teachers may be mistaken about the actual content of that curriculum). If teachers perceive that primary sources, multiple perspectives, or student interpretation will interfere with that goal, coverage will win out, because covering the curriculum is what teachers do.[16]

Equally important is maintaining classroom control. Again, both research evidence and our own experience suggest that most teachers devote a great deal of effort to making sure that classroom procedures are orderly, students are quiet and still, and instructional objectives, materials, and practices are consistent and predictable. Teachers are particularly concerned about other teachers' (and administrators') perceptions of their ability to maintain control; nothing is more likely to inspire condescension from colleagues or a negative evaluation from a principal or mentor than a classroom in which students talk too much, move around too often, or pursue unstructured activities. Teachers know that the open-ended, group projects associated with historical inquiry lead to precisely those behaviors associated with a "lack of control." In Bruce Fehn's and Kim Koeppen's study of preservice teachers who had engaged in an intensive, document-based social studies methods course, for example, they found that students said they were likely to increase their use of primary sources only if they had been shown how to do it in a highly structured way, to overcome classroom control problems.[17]

This focus on coverage and control is especially clear in Linda McNeil's influential book, *Contradictions of Control: School Structure and School Knowledge*. In her study of social studies teachers at four high schools, McNeil found that despite differences in their political and philosophical views, teachers' classroom actions were remarkably similar. Although many of them professed high academic expectations for students and were themselves very knowledgeable about history, political events, and economics, their teaching reflected little of this. Instead, as they recognized, their actions revolved around controlling the method of presentation while covering the content of their courses. McNeil identifies four strategies teachers used to accomplish this goal: *fragmentation*, in which topics were presented as disjointed pieces of information; *mystification*, in which teachers made topics seem important yet unknowable, thus closing down discussion; *omission*, in which teachers left out consideration of political and economic issues that were either contemporary or controversial; and *defensive simplification*, in which complex topics were accorded only superficial attention. By using these strategies, teachers were able to cover the curriculum efficiently and limit the opportunities for potentially disruptive student discussion.[18]

McNeil's findings are consistent with much of the research on classroom practice in history and social studies. Seen from a sociocultural vantage point, the principal social acts of history teaching are coverage and control. The tools teachers use include the four approaches identified by McNeil, along with other strategies, such as limiting information to a single source (such as the textbook), requiring all students to learn the same body of information, and testing students on their restatement of predetermined facts and analysis. The purpose of coverage and control, though, is somewhat murkier. When asked for their ideas about the purpose of history education, teachers typically respond with abstract rationales that have little connection to their practices. We are less concerned with teachers' explanations than with the purposes that actually guide their practices of coverage and control. Why are they so concerned with these?

THE ROLE OF PURPOSE IN HISTORY TEACHING

Identifying the purposes that guide teachers' actions necessarily involves an element of speculation. People cannot always be counted on to give valid explanations of their actions, and it would be offensive even to ask a question like, "Why do you spend all your time controlling students?" Yet two possibilities immediately suggest themselves, and both have found support in the literature on teacher education. The first is that teachers hope to fit in: They want to be accepted as competent professionals by fellow teachers, administrators, and parents. Doing so means acting in ways similar to those around them; if everyone else covers the curriculum and maintains quiet, orderly classrooms, devoid of controversy, then new teachers will be highly motivated to do the same, regardless of what they may have learned about the nature of history or methods of teaching the subject. Out of all the potential teaching practices they have encountered—through their own experience, in readings, in teacher education courses, and elsewhere—they will understandably chose those that allow them to achieve the goal of acceptance.[19]

A second purpose guiding teachers' actions is practicality: Content coverage is an "efficient" practice, one unlikely to require unreasonable expenditures of time and energy. Teaching is hard enough without placing unreasonable demands on oneself, particularly if the additional work may not lead to meaningful results, and teachers take these energy demands into account as they develop classroom practices.[20] Notions of efficiency and practicality are relative, though, because schools differ dramatically in prevailing norms regarding appropriate expenditure of effort; in many schools, teachers continue to work in their classrooms until well after dark, and in others, the parking lot is empty 15 minutes after school is dismissed. As teachers make decisions about how to expend their energy, then, they look to those around them for cues about what constitutes reasonable and unreasonable work.

When teachers aim for group acceptance and practicality, practices like coverage and control make perfect sense. If a teacher's purpose is to fit in, then at most schools it would be nonsense to engage students in developing their own interpretations of controversial historical issues. Similarly, if a teacher hopes to make it through the day (or the year) without potentially wasted effort, there is little point in developing group projects based on original research; these require an incredible amount of work by the teacher, and they may result in learning that has little connection to the required curriculum. Whether teachers have the pedagogical content knowledge to carry out such practices is irrelevant if these endeavors do not help them achieve their goals.

Again, this kind of explanation for teachers' actions seem fatalistic, because it suggests that what we do as teacher educators has little influence on classroom practice. We can help teachers construct an understanding of history as an interpretive subject, but they may never apply that perspective, because it fails to contribute to their goal of fitting in. We can help them discover tools for engaging students in interpreting primary sources, but these will never be used if interpretation does not occur in the first place. However, this recognition—that factors beyond pedagogical content knowledge influence classroom actions—is not tantamount to consigning teachers to history's dustbin, nor does it doom teacher educators to irrelevance. Studies consistently have shown that some teachers do apply what they have learned about historical evidence and interpretation. There are thousands of such teachers around the country, and they do far more than cover the curriculum or control students. We have seen them teach, we have written about them, we have read their books and articles. Why are they so different? Because their purposes are different.

At the most basic level, this means that some teachers are not interested in conformity. Many of the best history and social studies teachers we know are unconcerned with the opinions of people at their school, particularly those of other teachers. They go about their jobs in the best way they know how and pay no attention to whether their colleagues snub their noses at them for having classrooms that are loud and messy, or students who move around on their own initiative. In fact, some of these teachers pride themselves on their nonconformity and actively challenge school norms. Other good teachers, meanwhile, seem to have little interest in practicality: They take on multiple projects, track down a mountain of resources, provide detailed feedback on every piece of student work, and win "Teacher of the Year" honors. They give the impression that efficiency is unimportant to them because they have a limitless supply of time and energy. For mavericks and dynamos like these, coverage and control have little relevance, and they are free to pursue other activities with their students.

However, as inspiring as such teachers may be, they provide only a limited model for others. First, most teachers are not mavericks, and no amount of exhortation is likely to convince them to become such; even fewer have unlimited energy, and teacher education programs can do little to change their students' metabolisms. More important, though, it is not enough that some teachers do not share the purposes that lead many of their colleagues to emphasize coverage and control, for this says nothing about what their purposes are or what practices they will adopt themselves. Without a sense of purpose that is clearly thought out and articulated, teachers may fall prey to each new fad or harebrained instructional program, or they may find themselves adopting the practices of their peers by default.

Yet on this score, the research evidence is encouraging. Teachers who have a clear sense of purpose can resist the temptation of conformity, and they can implement practices consistent with their aims. Letitia Fickel, for example, has described a secondary teacher with strongly felt and consciously articulated goals that included preparing students to become active and critically thoughtful citizens and helping them learn from the "multiple truths and knowledge inherent in a diverse, democratic society." His instruction was consistent with these goals, as he engaged students in working with primary sources, manipulating and interpreting data, and considering persistent and locally relevant social issues. Similarly, in Ronald Evans' study of five secondary history teachers, he found that the two with the clearest sense of purpose also engaged in classroom practices that most closely matched their aims; those whose goals were less deeply held (or less clearly articulated) often taught in ways inconsistent with their expressed beliefs. Jesse Goodman and Susan Adler, in their study of elementary social studies teachers, also found that in classrooms in which teachers had a clear sense of the subject's purpose, the enacted curriculum more closely matched their aims; those with less commitment to the subject were more likely to teach in inconsistent or contradictory ways. Meanwhile, comparative case studies both by Bruce VanSledright and Jere Brophy and by Suzanne Wilson and Sam Wineburg portray history teachers whose practices vary significantly but whose differences arise less from their pedagogical content knowledge than from the distinct goals they have for their students.[21]

The impact of purpose on classroom practice is particularly clear in S. G. Grant's detailed portrait of two high school history teachers. These teachers worked in the same setting—teaching the same course, to the same level of students, at the same school—and both had extensive preparation in historical content and instructional methods. Both were committed to history's importance and considered it necessary for understanding the present. Seen in terms of "teacher knowledge," the two appeared virtually identical. Yet their classroom practices differed dramatically: Mr. Blair lectured from the front of the room, displayed outlines of textbook content on an overhead, and required students to copy notes silently; Mrs. Strait not only lectured but engaged students in simulations, role playing, and small-group discussions, and she exposed them to a variety of texts and other media. Neither was a "better" teacher than the other, for Blair's lectures were not boring record of dates and facts but masterful narratives with complex characters and interesting plots; he was as accomplished at delivering lectures as Strait was at facilitating small groups and class discussion. Grant's comparison of Blair and Strait is instructive, then, because it enables us to consider the factors that influence teachers' practices without being led astray by the confounding variable of "effectiveness": Both were effective at what they were doing, but that doing differed greatly.[22]

Why were their practices so dissimilar? It was not because of differing content knowledge, for both had bachelors and masters degrees in history, and both described the subject in terms compatible with the views of contemporary historians, although they emphasized different aspects of the subject. Nor did their practices arise from differing knowledge of pedagogy, for Blair was as familiar as Strait with a variety of instructional methods—he simply chose not to use them. Rather, differences between the two derived from their differing purposes. Blair wanted students to learn the master narrative of U.S. history from the Colonial Era to the present day—a complex narrative, one that included both progress and problems. Combined with his belief that students had little or no background in the subject, Blair's goal rendered the use of overhead notes and lectures a seemingly obvious choice for classroom practice, for it allowed him to cover that narrative efficiently; as Grant notes, "Stories demand a storyteller and an audience, and there is no role confusion in Blair's classroom." Blair resembled other history teachers in attempting to cover material efficiently, but he differed from many of his colleagues in that he aimed to cover the material he considered important rather than that mandated by external authorities. (He refused to reduce his coverage of the Federal Period, for example, despite its de-emphasis in recent curriculum guidelines.) Like most teachers, Blair was motivated by practicality—hence his use of lecture—but his focus on coverage was motivated not by the desire to do what everyone else did but by his own goal of exposing students to the grand narrative of U.S. history. In this case, coverage was not a means to the end of fitting in but a clearly articulated end of its own.[23]

Strait had a different purpose. She wanted students to understand history not only intellectually but emotionally, and in particular, to become familiar with the perspectives of a diverse set of actors who were involved in historical events, with the ultimate goal of becoming more tolerant of those who differed from themselves. This goal drove Strait's classroom practice in several ways. First, she engaged students in simulations and role plays, so they were forced to consider events from the perspectives of people at the time; such activities were more effective than lectures as a way of getting students to understand multiple points of view. Second, Strait emphasized social history in addition to the political narratives that dominated Blair's narrative; because politics has traditionally been the preserve of elite White males, social history had greater potential to help students understand the diverse set of perspectives that Strait valued. Finally, Strait emphasized historical topics and periods she considered particularly effective at conveying the inner experiences of a range of participants; she devoted more attention to the Civil Rights movement, for example, than other topics that commanded as much space in the official curriculum. Like Blair, she made her own decisions about how to implement that curriculum, but whereas his decisions were most apparent when he included periods he thought necessary to understand the overall narrative of U.S. history (such as the Federal Period), Strait's were most obvious in her emphasis on topics that helped achieve her goal of developing students' understanding of diverse experiences. Strait worried that students might not be exposed to enough content for their required examinations, but like Blair, her purposes guided her instruction.[24]

Based on the studies we have described in this chapter, teachers' goals appear to have more impact on practice than their pedagogical content knowledge. Unless they have a clear sense of purpose, teachers' primary actions continue to be coverage of the curriculum and control of students, no matter how much they know about history, teaching, or the intersection of the two. Deriving from the common, and understandable, goals of fitting in and working efficiently, such practices appear to be the "default" means of teaching, and they quickly override principles based on the content of university coursework—even when teachers ostensibly understand and accept those principles. However, many teachers, including Strait and even Blair, resist the temptation to conformity. Their practices do not necessarily emphasize coverage (at least of the required curriculum) or control of students. They have alternative purposes—strongly held and clearly articulated—and they make decisions consistent with these goals. If we hope to change the nature of history teaching, then, we may have a greater impact by focusing on teachers' purposes than on their pedagogical content knowledge.

CHANGING THE PRACTICE OF HISTORY TEACHING

Most educators interested in reforming history education, despite a variety of individual backgrounds and perspectives, share a concern with changing instructional practice: They want the act of history teaching to change so that students interpret historical evidence and consider multiple perspectives. Unfortunately, reformers have long been bedeviled by the fact that the act of history teaching, like that of most subjects, is highly resistant to change. In recent years, programs of teacher education and professional development have focused on teacher knowledge as the key to reform: If teachers know more—about content, pedagogy, and the intersection of the two—then surely their instruction will be better. Our review of the available evidence, however, suggests that this is not true. Neither teachers' knowledge of history—including its interpretative nature—nor their knowledge of how to represent content to learners has a decisive impact on classroom practice. Although such knowledge is probably necessary for engaging students in historical interpretation, it is by no means sufficient.

If we want to change teachers' practices, we must change the purposes that guide those practices. To engage students in activities that involve interpreting evidence, teachers must have a purpose that can only be accomplished by such activities. This kind of purpose must be more than a slogan, and it must be more than lip service; it must be a goal to which teachers are deeply and genuinely committed, a goal that will inspire efforts to make actions consistent with beliefs. Only this kind of commitment will overcome the temptation to conform and, ultimately, to replicate existing practice.

The first task, then, is to identify an instructional purpose that requires students to take part in interpreting historical evidence and considering multiple perspectives. There are two obvious candidates for this honor. The first has dominated scholarship on history education over the past two decades: Students should learn about the past in ways consistent with the academic discipline of history. Because that discipline involves interpretation of evidence and consideration of multiple perspectives, instruction in school should do so as well. This does not necessarily mean that students will become "little historians," but it does mean they will learn how historians develop interpretations, and this necessarily involves taking part in such activities themselves. Research into student's work with primary sources and historical perspective, and corresponding recommendations for emphasizing these practices in school have generally been situated in this framework. If teachers accept the premise that school history should familiarize students with disciplinary history, and if research demonstrates that students are capable of understanding and taking part in disciplinary activities, then the implications for practice are clear: Students should work with evidence, develop interpretations, and consider multiple perspectives.

This is the educational equivalent of trying to write a great book about the flea. The goal of teaching in ways consistent with academic disciplines is an inadequate and unconvincing rationale for history or, we suspect, any other subject. Far from constituting the crowning achievements of civilization that some scholars like to claim, academic disciplines are simply institutionalized outgrowths of the professional specialization that took place during the late 19th century. Moreover, their methods and objects of study are profoundly shaped by the limited and particularistic viewpoints of those involved in creating and perpetuating them.[25] As a rationale for teaching, the focus on disciplinary history seems unlikely to inspire the intellectual and emotional commitment necessary to reform practice. It has not done so yet, and we see no reason to think it will in the future. When teachers must decide between practices that help them fit into their school communities and those that adhere to disciplinary standards, most will choose conformity.

However, the other candidate for the purpose of history education has far greater potential to inspire the conviction necessary to resist temptations to conformity: Students should learn history to contribute to a participatory, pluralistic democracy. This is the argument we have made throughout the book, and there is no need to repeat it in detail. What we want to emphasize here is not just that we believe history should be taught this way, but that this goal can provide teachers with the intellectual purpose necessary to break out of the mold of coverage and control. If teachers are committed to the humanistic goals necessary for democracy, then they literally cannot focus on covering curriculum and controlling students because those practices will not enable them to reach their goals. Preparing students to make reasoned judgments cannot be accomplished by telling them what to think; preparing them to move beyond their own perspective cannot be accomplished by demanding reproduction of a consensual narrative of the national past; and preparing them to take part in collaborative discourse about the common good cannot be accomplished by tightly controlled, teacher-centered instruction. These goals can only be achieved when students take part in meaningful and relevant historical inquiries, examine a variety of evidence, consider multiple viewpoints, and develop conclusions that are defended and negotiated with others. If preparation for democracy is the goal, then teachers will need to engage in these practices, regardless of what anyone else tells them; and if they need to engage in these practices, they will also need the tools teacher educators can provide, such as methods for finding and using primary sources, developing inquiry projects, managing discussion, and so on—the knowledge and skills usually thought of as "pedagogical content knowledge." Teachers will use this knowledge when it helps them achieve their goals.

We have no magic formula for developing such purposes among teachers. On one hand, preparation for citizenship forms the underlying rationale for all public schooling in the United States, and teachers are likely to accept that broad goal as well as their own responsibility for achieving it. Yet on the other hand, research indicates that beginning and experienced teachers alike often hold narrow or unelaborated notions of democracy and of citizenship education.[26] Thus, although it may be easy to convince teachers that history should serve the goals of democracy, it will be more difficult to help them see how that goal can be achieved by the humanistic purposes we have described throughout this book. If teachers believe history should promote citizenship but do not think in terms of the participatory and pluralist elements of democracy, then coverage and control are likely to continue as the principal actions of the history classroom.

For teachers to emphasize reasoned judgment, an expanded view of humanity, and collaborative discourse about the common good, they will have to believe—deeply and clearly—that these contribute to democracy. Of course, these beliefs cannot simply be transmitted; teachers have to reach such conclusions themselves. To create the conditions that make such conclusions possible, teacher education programs may have to become less concerned with covering technical issues related to the discipline's content and pedagogy and more with helping teachers evaluate the relevance of history education, consider alternative perspectives on the subject, and become initiated into a community that takes these questions seriously. This does not guarantee that teachers will accept the humanistic goals of history education, and we are willing to accept that they may construct differ-ent—or even better—perspectives of their own. However, we believe that given the chance, they will develop a deep and enduring commitment to de-mocracy, because democracy is a mighty theme.

ENDNOTES

1. Herman Melville, *Moby Dick; or The White Whale* (New York: Dodd, Mead, and Company, 1922), 421.
2. Marilyn Cochran-Smith and Susan L. Lytle, "Relationships of Knowledge and Prac-tice: Teacher Learning in Communities," in *Review of Research in Education*, Vol. 24, Eds. Asghar Iran-Nejad and P. David Pearson (Washington, D.C.: American Educa-tional Research Association, 1999), 249; emphasis in original. On behaviorism and programmed instruction, see especially B. F. Skinner, "The Science of Learning and the Art of Teaching," *Harvard Educational Review* 24 (Spring 1954): 86–97; on disci-pline-based educational reform in the 1960s, see John L. Rudolph, *Scientists in the Classroom: The Cold War Reconstruction of American Science Education* (New York: Palgrave Macmillan, 2002); and on teacher effectiveness research and its relation-ship to teacher evaluation in the 1970s, see Linda Darling-Hammond, Arthur E. Wise, and Sara R. Pease, "Teacher Evaluation in the Organizational Context: A Re-view of the Literature," *Review of Educational Research* 53 (Fall 1983): 285–328.
3. Jane J. White, "The Teacher as Broker of Scholarly Knowledge," *Journal of Teacher Education* 38 (July/August 1987): 19–24; Stephen J. Thornton, "Teacher as Cur-ricular-Instructional Gatekeeper in Social Studies," in *Handbook of Research on So-cial Studies Teaching and Learning,* Ed. James P. Shaver (New York: MacMillan, 1991), 237; Hugh Munby, Tom Russell, and Andrea K. Martin, "Teachers' Knowledge and How It Develops," in *Handbook of Research on Teaching*, 4th ed., Ed. Virginia Richardson (Washington, D.C.: American Educational Research As-sociation, 2001), 877–904; Christopher M. Clark and Penelope L. Peterson, "Teachers' Thought Processes," in *Handbook of Research on Teaching*, 3rd ed., Ed. Merlin C. Wittrock (New York: MacMillan, 1986), 255–296.
4. Lee J. Shulman, "Knowledge and Teaching: Foundations of the New Reform," *Harvard Educational Review* 57 (February 1987): 1–22; Bruce VanSledright, "Closing the Gap Between School and Disciplinary History? Historian as High School History Teacher," in *Advances in Research on Teaching*, Vol. 6, *Teaching and Learning History*, Ed. Jere Brophy (Greenwich, Conn.: JAI Press, 1996), 257, em-phasis in original; Linda S. Levstik and Keith C. Barton, *Doing History: Investi-gating with Children in Elementary and Middle Schools*, 2nd ed. (Mahwah, N.J.: Lawrence Erlbaum Associates, Inc., 2001).
5. Chara H. Bohan and O. L. Davis, Jr., "Historical Constructions: How Social Studies Student Teachers' Historical Thinking is Reflected in Their Writing of History," *Theory and Research in Social Education* 26 (Spring 1998): 173–197; Melanie K. Gillaspie and O. L. Davis, Jr., "Historical Constructions: How Elemen-tary Student Teachers' Historical Thinking is Reflected in their Writing of His-tory," *International Journal of Social Education* 12 (Fall/Winter 1997/1998): 35–45.
6. Elizabeth A. Yeager and O. L. Davis, Jr., "Between Campus and Classroom: Sec-ondary Student-teachers' Thinking about Historical Texts," *Journal of Research*

and Development in Education 29 (Fall 1995): 1–8; "Understanding the Knowing How of History: Elementary Student Teachers' Thinking About Historical Texts," *Journal of Social Studies Research* 18 (Fall 1994): 2–9; Samuel S. Wineburg, "On the Reading of Historical Texts: Notes on the Breach Between School and Academy," *American Educational Research Journal* 28 (Fall 1991): 495–519. The wide range of students' understanding of the interpretive nature of history is also apparent in Peter Seixas' study of secondary student teachers, "Student Teachers Thinking Historically," *Theory and Research in Social Education* 26 (Summer 1998): 310–341.

7. Elizabeth A. Yeager and O. L. Davis, Jr., "Classroom Teachers' Thinking about Historical Texts: An Exploratory Study," *Theory and Research in Social Education* 24 (Spring 1996): 146–166; quote from p. 157.

8. VanSledright, "Closing the Gap."

9. VanSledright, "Closing the Gap," 286. For another example of a teacher who understands history as a multi-perspectival, evidence-based, interpretive discipline but who does not design his instruction around these principles, see Suzanne M. Wilson and Sam Wineburg, "Wrinkles in Time and Place: Using Performance Assessments to Understand the Knowledge of History Teachers," *American Educational Research Journal* 30 (Winter 1993): 729–69.

10. G. Williamson McDiarmid, "Understanding History for Teaching: A Study of the Historical Understanding of Prospective Teachers," in *Cognitive and Instructional Processes in History and the Social Sciences*, Eds. James F. Voss and Mario Carretero (Hillsdale, N.J.: Lawrence Erlbaum Associates, Inc., 1994), 159–186.

11. Susan Adler, "A Field Study of Selected Student Teacher Perspectives Toward Social Studies," *Theory and Research in Social Education* 12 (Spring 1984): 13–30; Ronald W. Evans, "Teacher Conceptions of History Revisited: Ideology, Curriculum, and Student Belief," *Theory and Research in Social Education* 28 (Spring 1990): 101–138; Bruce Fehn and Kim E. Koeppen, "Intensive Document-Based Instruction in a Social Studies Methods Course," *Theory and Research in Social Education* 4 (Fall 1998): 461–484; Sigrun Gudmundsdottir, "Curriculum Stories: Four Case Studies of Social Studies Teaching," in *Insights Into Teachers Thinking and Practice*, Eds. Christopher W. Day, Maureen Pope, and Pam Denicolo (London: Falmer, 1990), 107–118; John T. Hyland, "Teaching About the Constitution: Relationships Between Teachers' Subject Matter Knowledge, Pedagogic Beliefs and Instructional Decision Making Regarding Selection of Content, Materials, and Activities; Summary of Research Findings," 2–7, Eric Document Reproduction Service, ED 273557; Marilyn Johnston, "Teachers' Backgrounds and Beliefs: Influences on Learning to Teach in the Social Studies," *Theory and Research in Social Education* 28 (Summer 1990): 207–232; Joseph J. Onosko, "Barriers to the Promotion of Higher-order Thinking in Social Studies," *Theory and Research in Social Education* 19 (Fall 1991): 341–366; Timothy D. Slekar, "Epistemological Entanglements: Preservice Elementary School Teachers' 'Apprenticeship of Observation' and the Teaching of History," *Theory and Research in Social Education* 26 (Fall 1998): 485–507; Stephen J. Thornton, "Curriculum Consonance in United States History Classrooms," *Journal of Curriculum and Supervision* 3 (Summer 1998): 308–20; Stephen J. Thronton and R. Neill Wenger, "Geography Curriculum and Instruction in Three Fourth-Grade Classrooms," *Elementary School Journal* 90 (May 1990): 513–31.

12. Stephanie D. van Hover and Elizabeth A. Yeager, """Making" Students Better People?' A Case Study of a Beginning History Teacher," *International Social Studies Forum*, 3, No. 1 (2003): 219–232.

13. van Hover and Yeager, "Making Students Better People?", 224–28.

14. The concept of the apprenticeship of observation comes from Dan C. Lortie, *Schoolteacher: A Sociological Study* (Chicago: University of Chicago Press, 1977). On the limited effect of teacher education programs, see Justine Z. X. Su, "Sources of Influence in Preservice Teacher Socialization," *Journal of Education for Teaching* 18, No. 3 (1992): 239–258, and Kenneth M. Zeichner and Jennifer M. Gore, "Teacher Socialization," *Handbook of Research on Teaching*, 3d ed., Ed. Merlin C. Wittrock (New York: MacMillan, 1986), 329–348. On the multiple influences on history and social studies teachers' ideas, see Jeffrey W. Cornett, "Teacher Thinking about Curriculum and Instruction; A Case Study of a Secondary Social Studies Teacher," *Theory and Research in Social Education* 18 (Summer 1990): 248–273; Jesse Goodman and Susan Adler, "Becoming an Elementary Social Studies Teacher: A Study of Perspectives," *Theory and Research in Social Education* 13 (Summer 1985): 1–20; S. G. Grant, "Locating Authority Over Content and Pedagogy: Cross-Current Influences on Teachers' Thinking and Practice," *Theory and Research in Social Education* 24 (Summer 1996): 237–72; Cynthia Hartzler-Miller, "Teaching for Social Change: The Interplay of Social Knowledge, Content Knowledge, and Personal Biography" *International Social Studies Forum* 2, No. 2 (2002): 141–55.; Melissa J. Marks, "From Coursework to Classroom: A Qualitative Study on the Influences of Preservice Teacher Socialization" (Ed.D. diss., University of Cincinnati, 2002); Marilyn Johnston, "Teachers' Backgrounds and Beliefs: Influences on Learning to Teach in the Social Studies," *Theory and Research in Social Education* 28 (Summer 1990): 207–232; E. Wayne Ross, "Teacher Perspective Development: A Study of Preservice Social Studies Teachers," *Theory and Research in Social Education* 15 (Fall 1987): 225–243; Elizabeth G. Sturtevant, "Lifetime Influences on the Literacy-related Instructional Beliefs of Experienced High School History Teachers: Two Comparative Case Studies," *Journal of Literacy Research* 28 (June 1996): 227–257.

15. Pamela L. Grossman, Peter Smagorinsky, and Sheila Valencia, "Appropriating Tools for Teaching English: A Theoretical Framework for Research on Learning to Teach," *American Journal of Education* 108 (November 1999): 1–29; quote from pp. 4–5. Similarly, Robert Yinger and Martha Hendricks-Lee propose the notion of "ecological intelligence" as a way of explaining how knowledge is jointly constructed by participants and systems in the activity of teaching; "Working Knowledge in Teaching," in *Research on Teacher Thinking: Understanding Professional Development*, Eds. Christopher Day, James Calderhead, and Pam Denicolo (London: Falmer Press, 1993), 100–123.

16. Goodman and Adler, "Becoming an Elementary Social Studies Teacher," 10–11; Fehn and Koeppen, "Intensive Document-Based Instruction," 480; David Hicks, "Examining Preservice Teachers' Conceptions and Approaches to the Teaching of History in England and America," paper presented at the International Assembly of the Annual Conference of the National Council for the Social Studies, November 2001; Hyland, "Teaching about the Constitution," 2–7; Johnston, "Teachers' Backgrounds and Beliefs," 218; Onosko, "Barriers to the Promotion of Higher-Order Thinking," 347–351; Slekar, "Epistemological Entangle-

ments," 500; Sturtevant, "Lifetime Influences," 240–241; Thornton, "Curriculum Consonance," 311–315; Bruce VanSledright, "The Teaching-Learning Interaction in American History: A Study of Two Teachers and Their Fifth Graders," *Journal of Social Studies Research* 19 (Spring 1995): 16; van Hover and Yeager, "Making Students Better People."

17. Fehn and Koeppen, "Intensive Document-Based Instruction," 480; see also Hyland, *Teaching About the Constitution*, 7; Johnston, "Teachers' Backgrounds and Beliefs," 212–214; Onosko, "Barriers to the Promotion of Higher-Order Thinking," 355; Thornton, "Curriculum Consonance," 309; VanSledright, "Teaching-Learning Interaction," 6.

18. Linda M. McNeil, *Contradictions of Control: School Structure and School Knowledge* (New York: Routledge, 1988), 157–190.

19. Linda S. Levstik, "Articulating the Silences: Teachers' and Adolescents' Conceptions of Historical Signficance," in *Knowing, Teaching, and Learning History: National and International Perspectives*, Eds. Peter N. Stearns, Peter Seixas, and Sam Wineburg (New York: New York University Press, 2000), 299; E. Michael H. Romanowski, "Issues and Influences that Shape the Teaching of U.S. History," in *Advances in Research on Teaching*, Vol. 6, *Teaching and Learning History*, Ed. Jere Brophy (Greenwich, Conn.: JAI Press, 1996), 296–299; Wayne Ross, "Teacher Perspective Development: A Study of Preservice Social Studies Teachers," *Theory and Research in Social Education* 15 (Fall 1987): 225–243.

20. Gerald Ponder and Walter Doyle, "Teacher Practicality and Curriculum Change: An Ecological Analysis," paper presented at the annual meeting of the American Educational Research Association, 4–8 April 1977, Eric Document Reproduction Service, ED 136390; O. L. Davis, Jr., "In Pursuit of Historical Empathy," in *Historical Empathy and Perspective Taking in the Social Studies*, Ed. O. L. Davis, Jr., Elizabeth Anne Yeager, and Stuart J. Foster (Lanham, Md.: Rowman and Littlefield, 2001), 10; McNeil, *Contradictions of Control*, 176; John Allen Rossi and Christopher M. Pace, "Issues-Centered Instruction with Low Achieving High School Students: The Dilemmas of Two Teachers," *Theory and Research in Social Education* 26 (Summer 1998), 401; Yeager and Davis, "Between Campus and Classroom," 5; Elizabeth Anne Yeager and Elizabeth K. Wilson, "Teaching Historical Thinking in the Social Studies Methods Course: A Case Study," *The Social Studies* 88 (May/June 1997): 121–126; Thornton, "Teacher as Curricular-Instructional Gatekeeper," 242–43.

21. Letitia H. Fickel, "Democracy is Messy: Exploring the Personal Theories of a High School Social Studies Teacher," *Theory and Research in Social Education* 28 (Summer 2000): 359–390; Evans, "Teacher Conceptions of History Revisited," 122–125; Goodman and Adler, "Becoming an Elementary Social Studies Teacher," 11–13; Bruce A. VanSledright and Jere Brophy, "'Storytellers,' 'Scientists,' and 'Reformers' in the Teaching of U.S. History to Fifth Graders: Three Teachers, Three Approaches," in *Advances in Research on Teaching*, Vol. 5, *Learning and Teaching Elementary Subjects*, Ed. Jere Brophy (Greenwich, Conn.: JAI Press, 1995), 195–243; Wilson and Wineburg, "Wrinkles in Time and Place," 729–769.

22. S. G. Grant, *History Lessons: Teaching, Learning, and Testing in U.S. High School Classrooms* (Mahwah, N.J.: Lawrence Erlbaum Associates, Inc., 2003), 3–28.

23. Grant, *History Lessons*, 8–15.

24. Grant, *History Lessons*, 15–28.

25. The assumption that academic disciplines are "the most powerful ways human beings have devised for making sense of our world" can be found in Howard Gardner, *The Disciplined Mind: What All Students Should Understand* (New York: Simon and Schuster, 1999), 157. Critical and historical perspectives on the rise of disciplines and their approach to knowledge can be found in Burton Bledstein, *The Culture of Professionalism: The Middle Class and the Development of Higher Education in America* (New York: W. W. Norton, 1978); Julie A. Reuben, *The Making of the Modern University: Intellectual Transformation and the Marginalization of Morality* (Chicago: University of Chicago Press, 1996); Laurence R. Veysey, *The Emergence of the American University* (Chicago: University of Chicago Press, 1965); John Willinsky, *Learning to Divide the World: Education at Empire's End* (Minneapolis, Minn.: University of Minnesota Press, 1998); and Bruce Wilshire, *The Moral Collapse of the University: Professionalism, Purity, and Alienation* (Albany, N.Y.: State University of New York Press, 1990). On the emergence of history as a discipline in the United States, see Peter Novick, *That Noble Dream: The "Objectivity Question" and the American Historical Profession* (New York: Cambridge University Press, 1988).
26. Christopher Anderson, Patricia G. Avery, Patricia V. Pederson, Elizabeth S. Smith, and John L. Sullivan, "Divergent Perspectives on Citizenship Education: A Q-Method Study and Survey of Social Studies Teachers," *American Educational Research Journal* 34 (Summer 1997): 333–365; Dorene Doerre Ross and Elizabeth Yeager, "What Does Democracy Mean to Prospective Elementary Teachers?" *Journal of Teacher Education* 50 (September/October 1999): 255–266.

Author Index

Subject Index

A

Academic discipline of history
  analysis and, 70, 71
  assessing historical change in,
    181–182
  historical generalizations and, 78
  history education and, x, 27
  history teachers' familiarity with con-
    cerns of, 246–248
  as purpose for history teaching, 259
Account, defined, 130
Accountability, exhibition as, 113–118
Achievement, individual, 11
  focus on in U.S., 160–161
  narrative and, xi, 150
  remembrance and, 94
Across Five Aprils, 154
Act, in sociocultural analysis, 6
Action
  collective, 155, 156
  history education and taking,
    237–238
  mediated, ix–x, 6
  in narrative, 130, 132
  purpose and, 207
  social, 78–79, 81–82
Activities, document-based, 198–199
Activity theory, 6
Actor, 130, 312
Admiration, moral response and, 91
Adults
  as active agents in historical learning,
    12–13
  freedom and progress narrative and,
    176–177
  heroes and, 103
  historical exhibition and, 119

  unwillingness to confront historic in-
    justice, 102
  uses of history among, 2
Advanced Placement exams, 198
African Americans
  evolving rights of, 51–52
  focus on collection action among,
    161–162
  freedom narrative and, 176
  identification with U.S. origins and
    development, 53
  national identification and, 54
  progress narrative and, 174, 176, 180
  racial differences in student historical
    perspectives, 174–176
  response to injustice in past treatment
    of, 233
  See also Ethnic groups/ethnicity
Agency, 6
Agent, 6
Amateur history/historians, 4, 12–13
American Heritage Dictionary, 130
American Revolution, 216
  importance accorded, 51–52, 53, 72,
    175
  narrative of freedom and progress
    and, 168
  narrative structure of student knowl-
    edge of, 133–134
  student identification with, 51–52, 55
  student interpretation of/focus on in-
    dividuals in, 156–157
  using inquiry in studying, 193
America's March Toward Democracy, 152
Amherst Project, 82
Amsterdam (McEwan), 167
Analogies, lessons of history and, 77–78
Analysis